D1548021

Latin and Roman Culture in Joyce

The Florida James Joyce Series

Latin and Roman Culture in Joyce

R. J. Schork

University Press of Florida
Gainesville/Tallahassee/Tampa/Boca Raton
Pensacola/Orlando/Miami/Jacksonville

02 01 00 99 98 97 6 5 4 3 2 1

Library of Congress Cataloging-in-Publication Data
Schork, R. J., 1933–
Latin and Roman culture in Joyce / R.J. Schork.
p. cm. — (The Florida James Joyce series)
Includes bibliographical references and index.
ISBN 0–8130–1472–7 (cloth: alk. paper)
1. Joyce, James, 1882–1941—Knowledge—Rome. 2. Joyce, James, 1882–1941—Knowledge—Lit-
erature. 3. English fiction—Irish authors—Roman influences. 4. Latin literature—Appreciation—
Ireland. 5. Rome—In literature. I. Title. II. Series.
PR6019.09Z7478 1997
823'.912—dc20   96-33050

The University Press of Florida is the scholarly publishing agency for the State University
System of Florida, comprised of Florida A & M University, Florida Atlantic University, Florida
International University, Florida State University, University of Central Florida, University of
Florida, University of North Florida, University of South Florida, and University of West
Florida.

University Press of Florida
15 Northwest 15th Street
Gainesville, FL 32611

Betsy
comiti concordi:
hic labor, hoc opus

Contents

Foreword

Schork's book is a tour de force explanation of the enormous body of secular classical allusion and language in Joyce's work. It parses Joyce's convoluted and heavily nuanced Latin, provides detailed background and explication justifying Schork's hundreds of translations of applicable passages, and glosses allusions to classical writers, history, mythology, and life. He discusses material that has become arcane, particularly in American universities; but, as he so amply documents, it is material that was a staple of classical Jesuit and university education well into the early twentieth century.

No Joyce reader can escape the plethora of Latinate and Roman vocabulary and allusion in Joyce's every work from *Portrait* on. Nearly every one of Schork's explications goes far beyond those provided by the existing allusion lists, and is the result not only of classical erudition, but of meticulous research in Joyce's notebooks, drafts, letters, and general compositional methodology. His painstaking reconstruction of the compositional history is augmented by a creative imagination that produces logical conclusions in the interpretations, and also by a scholarly mind that signals exactly which passages involve doubtful conjecture, for which he furnishes the case for his reading. It is a comfort when a scholar takes critical risks and admits exactly how thin or stable the ice is.

Zack Bowen
Series Editor

PREFACE

The purpose of this book is to analyze the great impact that the Latin language, Latin literature, and the history and culture of ancient Rome had on the works of James Joyce. This book is intended for several categories of readers: Joyceans whose memory of the form for the ablative plural of *agricola* or the plot of book 4 of the *Aeneid* has faded; classicists who find it hard to imagine that gender mnemonics or Cicero's *De Senectute* play notable roles in *Finnegans Wake;* normal book-loving people who might enjoy a work of contemporary criticism that focuses on textual detail and its irreverent (sometimes distinctly obscene) application instead of theoretical jargon.

Given his Jesuit education, early religious background, and lifelong fascination with the mechanics and functions of language, this influence on Joyce's work is not surprising. He was a first-class student of Latin and the standard school authors. In his letters and fiction he deploys that classical training for humorous effect: clever wordplay, covert allusions, comic distortions are everywhere. At the same time, Joyce's original composition in Latin is practically flawless and his exploitation of Roman life and historical detail is impressive. This collusion of competence and mockery is what I call the "Parser's Revenge," the ability of the prize student to turn grammar exercises or morally edifying passages topsy-turvy.

Joyce's manipulation of Latin reaches its peak in *Finnegans Wake.* Since I am well aware that that work, by itself, is a formidable text, I have attempted to supply a plot- or character-context for my discussions of passages in it and the more difficult parts of *Ulysses.* Considerable attention is also given to the pre-text material for *Ulysses* and to the *Wake* Notebooks, especially when the archival material can illuminate the genesis and evolution of a cryptic phrase.

It is not necessary to know any Latin to read this book—all citations are translated. With one exception, the English versions are my own, and are specifically designed to help the reader to see the linguistic point (or its distortion) of the Latin original. The primary authors—Vergil, Cicero, Horace, Ovid—are cited from the standard editions, usually the appropriate Oxford Classical

Text. Readers who wish to see more of the literary landscape can consult a volume of the Loeb Classical Library, with its facing Latin and English pages. For general information on all literary matters I have relied on Gian Biagio Conte, *Latin Literature: A History,* translated by Joseph B. Solodow (Baltimore and London: Johns Hopkins University Press, 1994). For a broad historical perspective, I recommend *The Oxford History of the Classical World: The Roman World,* edited by John Boardman, Jasper Griffin, and Oswyn Murray (Oxford and New York: Oxford University Press, 1988); for more detail, see Max Cary and Howard H. Scullard, *A History of Rome: Down to the Reign of Constantine,* 3rd edition (New York: St. Martin's Press, 1976). The best discussion of the evidence for and events in the earliest stages is T. J. Cornell, *The Beginnings of Rome* (London and New York: Routledge, 1995). There is an up-to-date, clearly organized, comprehensive guide to every aspect of Roman culture: Lesley Adkins and Roy A. Adkins, *Handbook to Life in Ancient Rome* (New York: Facts on File, 1994).

For basic guides to Joyce's last two books, I take for granted that most readers are aware of the following indispensable (but not infallible) works: Don Gifford with Robert J. Seidman, *"Ulysses" Annotated: Notes for James Joyce's "Ulysses,"* revised edition (Berkeley, Los Angeles, London: University of California Press, 1989) and Roland McHugh, *Annotations to "Finnegans Wake,"* revised edition (Baltimore and London: Johns Hopkins University Press, 1991). Details of Roman history or Latin phrases that are explicated in these two guides are frequently examined from different angles in my book; when nothing new can be added to their treatment, I usually do not repeat the standard interpretation.

Finally, I must emphasize that none of my interpretations of any passage from Joyce—particularly from *Finnegans Wake*—is intended to be the exclusive, much less the definitive reading. Latin and Roman culture are only two of the many tesserae in, by, and through which Joyce formed his literary mosaics. These elements gleam brightly, but they are always only part of the splendor.

Some of the background work on this book was supported by a Healey Grant (1988) from the Office of Graduate Studies and Research at the University of Massachusetts, Boston. The interlibrary loan staff, Elizabeth Mock and Kim Brookes (Special Collections), and Randy Brickell (Periodicals) at the University's Healey Library were a great help. Over and above the call of duty, Ann DiSessa produced disk after disk with many versions of this text.

Parts of this book have appeared in *Arion, Classical and Modern Literature, James Joyce Quarterly,* and *Notes and Queries.* I thank the various editors (especially Tom Staley, Bob Spoo, Mary O'Toole, and Carol Kealiher at *JJQ*) for permission to revise and reprint this material.

Over many years on this and other projects I have benefited immensely from the suggestions and corrections of numerous colleagues: Emily McDermott, Frank Nisetich, Ted Ahern, Gerry Sullivan, Jack Tobin, Bob Greene (Boston); Geert Lernout, Wim Van Mierlo (Antwerp); Vincent Deane, John O'Hanlon, Danis Rose (Dublin); Fritz Senn, Hansruedi Isler (Zurich); and the participants at various Joyce conferences. Many thanks for their interest, insights, and patience. The series editor, Zack Bowen, and the staff at the University Press of Florida, especially Walda Metcalf and Gillian Hillis, have been fun to work with and they get the job done well. My greatest debt of gratitude is acknowledged on the dedication page.

Throughout the text the works of James Joyce and several archival volumes will be cited parenthetically, using the following standard abbreviations.

CP   Joyce, James. *Collected Poems*. New York: Viking Press, 1957.

CW   Joyce, James. *The Critical Writings of James Joyce*. Edited by Ellsworth Mason and Richard Ellmann. New York: Viking Press, 1959.

D   Joyce, James. *Dubliners*. Edited by Robert Scholes in consultation with Richard Ellmann. New York: Viking Press, 1967.

E   Joyce, James. *Exiles*. New York: Penguin, 1973.

FW   Joyce, James. *Finnegans Wake*. New York: Viking Press, 1939.

GJ   Joyce, James. *Giacomo Joyce*. Edited by Richard Ellmann. New York: Viking Press, 1968.

JJII   Ellmann, Richard. *James Joyce*. New York: Oxford University Press, 1982.

JJA   *The James Joyce Archive*. Edited by Michael Groden et al. New York and London: Garland Publishing, 1978. The individual Notebooks are cited using the standard conventions: VI.B.13.172 indicates page 172 of Notebook VI.B.13 in *JJA*.

Letters Joyce, James. *Letters of James Joyce*. Vol. I. Edited by
I   Stuart Gilbert. New York: Viking Press, 1957;
II   reissued with corrections 1966. Vols. II and III. Edited by
III   Richard Ellmann. New York: Viking Press, 1966.

P   Joyce, James. *"A Portrait of the Artist as a Young Man": Text, Criticism, and Notes*. Edited by Chester G. Anderson. New York: Viking Press, 1968.

SH   Joyce, James. *Stephen Hero*. Edited by John J. Slocum and Herbert Cahoon. New York: New Directions, 1963.

SL   Joyce, James. *Selected Letters of James Joyce.* Edited by Richard
         Ellmann. New York: Viking Press, 1975.

U   Joyce, James. *Ulysses.* Edited by Hans Walter Gabler et al. New
         York: Random House, 1986.

UNBM   *Joyce's "Ulysses" Notesheets in the British Museum.* Edited by
         Phillip F. Herring. Charlottesville: University Press of Virginia,
         1972. Citations refer to page and line number, e.g., 142: 94.

Scribbledehobble
         *James Joyce's Scribbledehobble: The Ur-Workbook for "Finnegans
         Wake."* Edited by Thomas E. Connolly. Evanston: Northwestern
         University Press, 1961. Citations refer to Connolly's page, followed
         by the original workbook page in brackets, e.g., 95 [511].

In the endnotes and bibliography the titles of the following journals or
annuals are abbreviated:

AFWC   *A "Finnegans Wake" Circular*

AWN   *A Wake Newslitter*

EJS   *European Joyce Studies*

JJLS   *James Joyce Literary Supplement*

JJQ   *James Joyce Quarterly*

JSA   *Joyce Studies Annual*

Introduction
The Parser's Revenge

Haruspicate or scry.
T.S. Eliot, "Four Quartets: Dry Salvages, V"

Since the verb "to parse" is now practically obsolete, the title of this introductory section requires some comment. The word was once commonly used, most frequently in the singular imperative form, in Latin classrooms. The student commanded to "parse" was expected to explain, with the correct technical jargon, the grammar and syntax governing the targeted words. Observe a hypothetical parser at work on the first Latin sentence to appear in *Finnegans Wake:* "*Hic cubat edilis*" (FW 7.22–23). *Hic,* adverb: modifies the verb; *cubat,* third person, singular, present, active, indicative: main verb; *edilis,* masculine, singular, nominative: subject of the verb. The entire sentence, so parsed, comes out as "The aedile reclines here." For purposes of narrative continuity, I add the rest of the sentence, "*Apud libertinam parvulam*" (FW 7.23) (at the side of a smallish freed [and perhaps free-and-easy] woman). The Latin is, as usual with Joyce, entirely correct, even though the primary purpose of its composition was to produce, with a classical flourish, the first of many HCE-ALP acrostics in the *Wake.*

As a student of Latin at Clongowes Wood and Belvedere Colleges, James Joyce was certainly called upon to parse his share of Latin sentences. Drill in the minutiae of grammar and syntax was a hallmark of Jesuit pedagogy. Early in *A Portrait of the Artist as a Young Man,* there is a re-creation of a school Latin lesson. Father Arnall stumps Jack Lawton, who could go no farther than the ablative singular with his declension of the noun *mare* (P 47). *Finnegans Wake* is riddled with recognizable parodies of classroom recitation. "Hickheckhocks" (FW 130.20) is an obvious mutation of the familiar jingle created by the cross-gender nominative cases of demonstrative adjectives *hic, haec,*

1

hoc. An even more memorable—and thematically significant—passage is found near the beginning of *Ulysses: "Amor matris:* subjective and objective genitive" (*U* 2.165–66). Here syntax is at the service of psychology. As Stephen Dedalus waits for a forlorn pupil to finish copying out an exercise, he thinks of the relationship between the boy and his mother. The Latin "genitive" case, construed with *amor* (love), can express two aspects of the bond: a mother's love/ the love for mother; she loves him ("subjective"), he loves her ("objective"). This basic bit of Latin parsing is not incidental to Stephen's own feelings about the recent death of his mother.

After finishing their last exam in Caesar's *Gallic War,* the vast majority of students purge not only the word "parse" but also the concept of grammatical/syntactical analysis from their memories. They walk away from their encounter with Latin with little more than an enriched vocabulary, a respect for English grammar, and the satisfaction of having mastered something more challenging than "El burro es un animal" or the inane dialogue in which Jeanne-Marie buys *Le Figaro* at the kiosk. Only a few students move beyond basic grammar and syntax to wrestle with the texts of Ovid, Cicero, Vergil, Horace. James Joyce was one of these adepts, and an eagerly competent one. His academic encounter with the language, literature, and culture of ancient Rome left its mark on the rest of his life. Latin was Joyce's first second language.

The nicely nuanced translation of a Horatian ode, produced at Belvedere in 1898,[1] is proof that Joyce was more than just a competent gerund-grinder. (That term was once applied, especially in Jesuit schools, to a pupil who excels at parsing, but never displays a glimmer of literary insight. For the Latinless, a "gerund" is a verbal noun; its appearance in a text is fairly rare and its grammatical mechanics are introduced late in a basic course. To be concerned about the modus operandi of the gerund, then, is the mark of a truly dedicated parser.) Stanislaus Joyce reports that his brother and a friend, Francini, were put off by a performance of a vulgar Italian comedy in Trieste sometime around 1910. They "avenged themselves by reading *Canticum Canticorum Solomonis* (*Song of Solomon* in the Old Testament) in the Latin Vulgate in order to take the taste of *Il Cantico dei Cantici* off their mouths."[2] In the autumn of 1938 at Lake Montreux, Joyce quoted from memory appropriately valedictory verses from Horace. The author of the memoir in which that incident is reported also notes that Joyce "delighted in Horace, whom he preferred to Vergil because of his perfections, his diverse meters, his rarest music."[3] Each of these anecdotes is testimony to Joyce's lifelong appreciation of diverse literary texts in Latin.

There is another side to his mastery of the language of the ancient Romans and its perpetuation in the documents and liturgies of the Roman Catholic church. That expertise could, and frequently did, become both the object and the means of mockery, especially by students astutely trained in schools sponsored by the church. For example, two hallowed formulas of the Litany of the Saints, *Libera nos Domine* (Lord deliver us) and *Ora pro nobis* (Pray for us) were easily converted into "Libera, Nostalgia! Beate Laurentie O'Tuli, Euro pra nobis" (*FW* 228.25–26). Like the little figure drawn at the bottom of the page at the end of "Night Lessons" in *Finnegans Wake* (*FW* 308.L3), Joyce could also thumb his nose at—and most effectively *in*—Latin. That capacity is the "Parser's Revenge."

A parser exacts his retribution when he is able to manipulate his use of Latin so well that even those with some facility in the ancient tongue begin to suspect that the arcane grammar and syntax are being cleverly turned against them. What was, in the classroom, touted as the linguistic instrument of logic has been transformed, in the artist's forge, into a medium of subterfuge, burlesque and adroit vocabulary, or structural legerdemain. Sometimes really competent gerund-grinders will deliberately mock the entire system that initiated them into the rituals of declension and conjugation. I do not mean to imply that Joyce always used Latin as an instrument of satire or to deny that some learned references conceal a serious point. Rather, the evidence I have found in his texts leads me to conclude that Joyce's skill in the classics—and especially in Latin—was a major component of his sense of humor. It will surprise no one that his displays of Latin skill are often designedly hard to identify. That difficulty is part of the fun. In short, the satisfaction of having created a perennial literary challenge, in no small way due to its radical lexical and intertextual pedantry, is, *prima facie*, not merely the parser's vocation, it is also his ultimate reward.

When he was preparing his 1930 study of *Ulysses*, Stuart Gilbert worked closely with James Joyce. The following brief anecdote, recorded in one of Gilbert's personal notebooks, neatly captures the spirit that lies behind the classical ingenuity of an avenging parser. Someone seems to have indicated to Joyce that the epic parallels in *Ulysses* were not self-evident. The author comments:

> Allusions to Homer
> You say these are farfetched.
> Exactly![4]

This is the impulse that triggered the ploy of an elementary error in Latin grammar that silently trips up Buck Mulligan as he pontificates about his capacity as Ireland's premier *"Fertiliser and Incubator"* (*U* 14.660).

A colossal anecdote, with one leg in ancient Rome and the other in turn-of-the-century Trieste, is cited below as the major final example of the spirit I detect in many of Joyce's allusions to Latin literature. Again, it is that uncanny ability to deploy the ancient apparatus of an intensely philological education for purposes or in situations that are less than classically decorous. My discussion of the "plot" and background of the anecdote is designed to show how existing aids to capturing the gist of a Joycean text can disappoint a beginner. In fact, some important details in this incident have eluded the grasp of even the most careful commentators. My explication of the point of the passage cited below directs a narrow beam of esoteric classical light on its contents. It also illuminates an early—and literally epiphanic—statement by the young Joyce on his status as an artist.

The passage in question comes from a 1905 letter from Trieste. In it Joyce writes to his brother Stanislaus that he recently observed the liturgy at a Greek Orthodox church:

> While I was attending the Greek mass here last Sunday it seemed to me that my story *The Sisters* was rather remarkable. The Greek mass is strange. The altar is not visible but at times the priest opens the gates and shows himself. He opens and shuts them about six times. For the Gospel he comes out of a side gate and comes down into the chapel and reads out of a book. For the elevation he does the same. At the end when he has blessed the people he shuts the gates: a boy comes running down the side of the chapel with a large tray full of little lumps of bread. The priest comes after him and distributes the lumps to scrambling believers. Damn droll! The Greek priest has been taking a great eyeful out of me: two haruspices. (*Letters* II.86–87)

Ellmann's footnote on the final two words (one of which is Latin) misses the point. His explanation, "The priest and himself," merely specifies who the "two" mutual starers are. But what is the connection between them? Who are "haruspices," and why bother? I shall try to shed some dry "theolo-logico-philolological" (*U* 9.762) light on the mystery. Joyce links himself with the Greek celebrant because both are priests. The evidence to support that claim is primarily a matter of Greek and Latin etymology, not of Christian theology, Eastern (Greek) or Western (Roman). The Orthodox priest's right to the title is certified by his ordination to perform the liturgy for his congregation of "scrambling believers." Joyce has also consecrated his life to the celebratory enactment of literature, as an unordained "priest of eternal imagination, transmuting the daily bread of experience" (*P* 221). At the chapel in Trieste he watches, with fascination, the actions of a fellow member of a guild, one who is dedicated to transforming bread into flesh by words. Hence he and the Greek, who "has been taking a great eyeful out of" a priestly colleague, are "two" of a kind. Joyce intimates that the Greek celebrant may suspect this fraternal identity.

Joyce also notes that he and the Orthodox priest are a couple of "haruspices." Why he does so is a matter of ancient Roman religious practice, but the specific application of the term *haruspex* here depends on a remark recorded in the late first century B.C. by the Roman orator-philosopher Marcus Tullius Cicero. An early section of his dialogue *De Natura Deorum* (On the Nature of the Gods) is a criticism of an Epicurean doctrine for some inconsistent assumptions. Cicero writes that it is surprising that "You Epicureans can keep a straight face when you are all by yourselves." This jab at faulty philosophical argument comes only after Cicero has made a far more slashing attack on another sort of doctrinal hypocrisy: *Mirabile videtur quod non rideat haruspex cum haruspicem viderit* (*De N.D.* 1.71). That sentence—the key to Joyce's allusive joke—deserves immediate translation: "It seems quite remarkable that one haruspex does not laugh when he looks at another haruspex."

That witty and withering judgment lies behind Joyce's self-deprecating comment concerning his eye-contact with the Greek priest: "two haruspices," each of whom recognizes the other as a soulmate, and a participant in conspiratorial fraud. But to appreciate the full force of the identification one must know a little bit about what a *haruspex* did in ancient Rome. Haruspices were members of a venerable priestly college whose job it was to examine and interpret animal intestines, strange natural events, and lightning strikes. Observation of these phenomena—and especially the intricacies of birds' flight patterns— were an important component of Roman life. Religious ceremonies, military campaigns, political decisions could be conducted only after such omens were declared favorable by a priest. There are numerous tales in Roman history of prohibitions being violated or manipulated, especially by ambitious generals and unscrupulous politicians.[5] Stanislaus Joyce, who had a modestly competent education in the classics, could be expected to catch the point of his brother's reference to droll haruspical complicity—and to appreciate its fraternal application.

There is more here. Joyce began his letter by referring to an incident that complements his story "The Sisters." That piece was first published in the *Irish Homestead* in August 1904. It would be slightly revised in October 1905, almost six months after the letter to Stanislaus; the final, thoroughly rewritten version would not be produced until the summer of 1906.[6] A significant aspect of the revisions of this story is an increasing emphasis on religious ritual. A flaw in his performance of the eucharistic liturgy (the dropping of a chalice) is the ostensible cause of Father Flynn's fall from grace. The narrator in this story is a young boy, to whom the invalided priest used to explain the meaning of "the different ceremonies of the Mass and the different vestments worn by the priest . . . the duties of the priest towards the Eucharist" (*D* 13). These are details that were *added to* the first version in the course of Joyce's Triestine revisions. There seems to me to be an implicit and typical "identity glide" between a Dublin boy whom a priest instructed in the proper form of the ceremony of the mass and a Trieste boy who assisted a priest at the end of the Greek liturgy.[7] Of course, it would be rash to argue *post hoc, propter hoc* here, but Joyce's impulse to expand the eucharistic dimension of his story and the boy's instruction in priestly lore had to come from somewhere. The coincidence of situation and agents is certainly worth pointing out, as Joyce does, in what otherwise might seem to be an unconnected leap from the mention of his first published story to the "Greek mass," in the first paragraph of his letter.

James Joyce plays a different but equally important role in both of these rituals. As the author and reviser of "The Sisters," he creates, then re-creates both priest and boy. As a witness to the Orthodox ceremony in Trieste, he recognizes that he and the Greek celebrant are part of a silent conspiracy of "priests." Like the Roman haruspices, they belong to a college of observers, interpreters, and transformers; both have been consecrated to metamorphose the profane into the sacred, and vice versa. In theological terms, an Orthodox priest performs the central act of the eucharistic liturgy by *epiklēsis:* he "calls upon" the Holy Spirit to transform bread and wine into Christ's body and blood. In one of Joyce's earliest statements about his work, a summer 1904 letter, he uses what was for a long time thought to be a Latinate version of the same term: "I am writing a series of epicleti—ten—for a [news]paper. I have written one. I call the series *Dubliners*" (*Letters* I.55). A recent article has convincingly demonstrated that Joyce's actual phrase was "a series of *epiclets*" (my emphasis). That latter term is his coinage for his short stories—they were mini-epics. The suffix "-let" is an English diminutive, not a Latinization of a Greek liturgical term.[8]

Joyce did, in fact, use an authentically Greek semiliturgical term to describe the series of genetic literary impulses that are of great importance to his early fiction: epiphany. The Greek verb *epiphainō* means "to display," "to appear," as in the feast of the Epiphany, which commemorates Christ's first public manifestation to the gift-bearing Magi. In the report of his visit to the Greek church, Joyce specifically notes that "[t]he altar is not *visible* but at times the priest opens the gate and *shows himself*" (my emphasis). The priest's appearance is a genuinely liturgical application of "epiphany."

Now, back to Joyce's 1905 letter to Stanislaus, and to additional classical notation. The Greek priest and Joyce look each other up and down—not in an intransitive epiphany, but as part of an active inspection. To Joyce, this mutual attention suggests the conspiratorial smile of the two haruspices in Cicero's anecdote. By "conspiratorial" I do not mean that the priest's completed ritual or the author's contemplated composition are nothing but frauds perpetrated on unwilling victims. Far from it, the congregation to whom the priest "comes out of a side gate . . . and reads out of a book" and the congregation of readers who clamor to enter the gates of Joyce's esoteric fiction—both—are eager participants in their analogous and communal transformations of the word. Conspirators literally "breathe-together." In this instance, each celebrant breathes new life into the mystery of re-creation, the one on the table of the altar, the other on the page of the book. At the same time, the Orthodox priest's post-liturgical glance is seen by Joyce as a likely acknowledgment of complicity in some sort of scam. And Joyce's unacknowledged citation from one of Cicero's theological works is certainly a damn droll intimation of his own priestly ambivalence.

To go any farther with these etymological and metaphorical—and they are just metaphorical—flights is to invite a monitory bolt of lightning from the appropriate god of one or the other of the various haruspices identified in the last few pages. What the postmodern world most definitely does not need is another pre-Raphaelite tract on Joyce's putative priesthood.[9] My purpose in this excursus on the Trieste letter has been not theological distinction, but philological explication of a text, based on an awareness of the language used and the customs described. In an analysis of Joyce's methods and works, from *Dubliners* to *Finnegans Wake*, there is considerable material for a continued application of this type of inspection. It is probable that none of the collegial ministrants alluded to above—Greek, Roman, or Irish—would be terribly put off by my intention to go about the task with conscientious irreverence. Writers of fiction and self-aware haruspices have always known that their vocation is a "hoax redeemed by awe."[10]

So much for the general angle from which I propose to examine Joyce's Latinity. What is necessary next is a preview of the various topical components of the project. This summary of contents of the book's ten chapters is followed by a brief attempt to situate the entire enterprise within a tradition more of humanistic literary criticism than of professional classical philology. At the same time, each of my chapters is based on the premise that, especially in case of *Ulysses* and *Finnegans Wake*, the initial—and sometimes essential—foray in the direction of meaningful discussion of a text can be taken only after one has carefully scouted its linguistic foreground.

For a novel set at schools and a university, there is relatively little really crude humor in *A Portrait of the Artist as a Young Man*. One example, however, is couched in the pedantic language of grammar: "He is a ballocks. . . . That word is a most interesting word. That's the only English dual number" (*P* 231–32). For those who are grammar-shy, "dual" is a technical term that intersects the "singular" and the "plural." In classical languages it is primarily used for natural pairs: chariot horses, eyes, oxen, testicles. The impact of Latin grammar, per se, on Joyce's works is the topic of chapter 1. The next chapter demonstrates how a perennial rival, Gogarty/Mulligan, is beautifully skewered by Joyce, where it would hurt most. The plumply smug Greek-flaunter is brought on stage late in *Ulysses* to conclude his moment of Latin glory with a howling error in basic, schoolboy syntax.

Chapter 3 covers the range of Roman history as it appears in Joyce's fiction: from the Trojan refugees led by Aeneas to the rival twins, Romulus and Remus, who found the city; through the challenges of the Sabine Women and Hannibal to the bloody fall of the Republic (*"Dear Brotus, land me arrears"* [*FW* 278.L3]). The survey then swiftly sweeps across the Empire to the barbarian conquest of the Eternal City. Included in this material are substantial references to the major historians (Livy, Caesar, Sallust, and Tacitus). These events and these textual memorializations—as well as other hallowed instances of grandeur and decadence—were no small part of Joyce's formal education in history. He remembered them and recycled them, sometimes with a Vichian twist, in his works.

The gods of any ancient city were intimately connected with the life—and particularly the military success—of its citizens. Chapter 4 explores the intervention of the members of the Roman pantheon in the secular and sometimes sordid episodes of Joyce's fiction. Jupiter, Juno, and Venus are everywhere; some of the other Olympians less so, but their appearances are certainly worthy of notice, especially those of the sinisterly ambivalent Mercury and the "guffawably eruptious" Vulcan (*FW* 79.18). The detailed ceremonies of Roman ritual also receive due attention. Augurs lean on their rods and scan the proper quarter of the sky for favorable omens in *Portrait*, *Ulysses*, and the *Wake*.

The four major authors of what is called the "Golden Age" of Latin literature (first century B.C.) are Cicero (oratory and philosophy), Vergil (pastoral and epic poetry), Horace (lyric poetry, satire, verse epistles), and Ovid (mythological and amatory poetry). Each of these writers had a significant enough impact on Joyce's work to merit an individual chapter. This section of my book naturally contains the highest level of purely literary attention and allusion. The Joycean practice of intertextual citation, echo, and/or parody, however, defies generalization—and often frustrates detection. Thus, the presentation of the evidence in the following chapters is designed to promote clarity of exposition, and the discussion of the material is not necessarily organized in parallel categories, nor does it lead to the creation of a universal theory of allusion. After the extended discussion of these four major literary figures, chapter 9 is devoted to several other classical authors (Catullus, Hadrian, the *Priapea*, Petronius, Martial, Plautus) and brief notation of the contributions of a number of minor figures.

Chapter 10 scrutinizes the original Latin in Joyce's works, primarily through the translation of and commentary on the two extended passages in *Finnegans Wake*. Each has its own purpose and tone. The first (*FW* 185.14–26) is Shem's graphic recipe for concocting the ink that was used to inscribe the famous "Letter." The other passage (*FW* 287.20–28) is situated in the "Night Lessons" episode. It appears to be an attempt to display—in a single, supercomplex sentence—Shem the Pen's skill in Latin prose composition and his grasp of the cyclic ebb and flow of human history. The rest of this chapter involves examples of the incidental Latin preserved in the published text of the *Wake* and the frequent use of Latin in the Notebooks. My favorite example is a pretext synopsis of the scene from "Ithaca" in which Stephen and Bloom relieve themselves in the latter's backyard. Years before, Bloom had apparently triumphed in a urinating contest at his school (*U* 17.1186–98). The following is the pertinent crossed entry in a *Ulysses* Notebook: "ᵇLB & SD pissjets / (LB palmarius)" (*UNBM* 473, line 45); the last word in this note is the Latin adjective, more correctly *palmaris*, that means "deserving the palm of victory," "winning first prize."

Several years ago, one of the industry's publications sported a banner headline announcing "A Joyce Poem—in Latin—Published for the First Time." That attribution of authorship was incorrect. The poem, which I entitled "Balia," was in fact composed in 1803 by the Reverend George H. Glasse. Despite a congenial source and tantalizing internal evidence of Joyce the master linguist at work here, the twenty-four lines of "monkish" Latin were, ineluctably, only copied, not composed by him.[11] Thus, there is no chapter on "Balia," only this brief *renuntiatito*.

Following these ten chapters are two appendices. The first is a summary-outline of the major topics and texts assigned for Latin examinations during Joyce's years at Belvedere and University Colleges. The second appendix is a demonstration of genetic criticism, involving several Notebook indices on the names of the Roman months and on roads and vehicles. There are also several tables of citations from ancient works and from Joyce's fiction. These have been arranged to facilitate identification of sources, allusions, and so forth, and to promote ready cross-reference. The bibliography is limited to those items, books, and articles, from the vast list of Joycean studies, that are directly concerned with the classical dimension of his education, compositional practices, and works.

Having stated my critical perspective and previewed the topics of each chapter, it behooves me to offer a compact justification of the entire enterprise. The geography of Dublin, popular song, eccentric theories about the genesis of *Hamlet,* Vico and Aquinas, pantomimes, *Les Phéniciens et l'Odyssée,* Celtic legend, geomaters and gnomons—no one would deny the essential relevance of these matters to a serious study of the works of James Joyce. But a book on Joyce's use of the languages and literature of ancient Rome? Stuart Gilbert's guide and the schemata would seem to have revealed all anyone needs to know about epic analogues for *Ulysses.* Existing commentaries and annotations, and the 653-page *Classical Lexicon* compiled by O Hehir and Dillon in 1977 could be considered to have pretty well covered the hoary linguistic territory, especially for *Finnegans Wake.* What insight, beyond superficial platitudes and praise *temporis acti* (of the good old days), can a teacher of Greek and Latin bring to bear on the works of a modernist author, especially one who delighted in creating a character who boasted to "had have only had some little laughings and some less of cheeks" (*FW* 125.15)?

There are several ways of responding to the rhetorical queries posed in the previous paragraph. Initially, the standard annotations to *Ulysses* and *Finnegans Wake* are, in fact, fairly weak with regard to classical and, specifically, Latin-language material. The entries are frequently incomplete, contextual information is minimal, and translations are too often brutally literal or simply wrong. The *Lexicon* appears to be marvelously detailed; but many of its Latin (and Greek) glosses merely address roots or cognates, and there are relatively few direct identifications of actual quotations from ancient authors. The subtitle of O Hehir and Dillon's work is *A Glossary;* as such it cannot (and does not) deal, except in passing, with literary, historical, cultural, or grammatical matters. Yet these factors naturally and consistently matter most in the interpretation of a work of literature.

A 1944 issue of *Horizon* contains a twelve-page essay by Stuart Gilbert, "The Latin Background of James Joyce's Art."[12] The qualifications of the author would seem to guarantee informed insight: Gilbert "read Greats" (that is, studied classics) at Oxford; Joyce worked closely with him on his booklength study of *Ulysses;* during the "*Wake*-in-progress" years Gilbert was often involved in collaborative "research" on esoteric topics that struck Joyce's fancy. Yet the essay is a vapid hodge-podge of generalities, including an extension of the "Latin" in the title to embrace "affinity with the French genius" and breathing freely of the sparkling atmosphere of Paris. To be sure, Gilbert approaches Joyce's work with all the Vergilian *pietas* that he ascribes to Joyce's feelings for Dublin, but this is about as close as his essay gets to real Latin or actual Roman writers.

Secondly, just as a considerable number of Joyce's allusions to Latin literature are entrenched well beneath the surface of the text, so too are most of the references to Roman history and religion definitely "far fetched." Initial detection of their presence—not to mention a discussion of their significance—is not easy. This primary problem is acute even for someone who has spent years teaching the same basic selections that Joyce studied in school and to which he returned—sometimes in his memory, sometimes from the texts—throughout his life. For example, I seriously doubt that anyone would have guessed a classical source for the adjectives that modify the "Unseen brazen highland laddies" at the end of the "Wandering Rocks" chapter of *Ulysses* (*U* 10.1249). These words come from, in order, an erroneous etymology of Hades and two references to Aeneas' wandering in the first book of Vergil's *Aeneid.* That claim can be supported by direct (but hardly self-evident) documentary evidence: Joyce's 1918 handwritten notes for *Ulysses.*[13] A noteworthy number of other echoes from Roman culture, especially in *Finnegans Wake,* either stem from or are backed up by similar archival references. The twofold perspective that I bring to this project—considerable experience with both Latin and Joyce's Notebooks—should generate new insights, from new angles.

At this point it is necessary to call attention to an archival enigma. Although there are significant direct citations in the *Wake* from the original Latin texts of Vergil, Cicero, Horace, Ovid, and a series of other Roman authors, there are *no* Notebooks crammed with quotable snippets from Roman epic, lyric, history, or oratory. In fact, direct quotation from any ancient text is extraordinarily rare in the Notebooks.[14] One presumes, then, that Joyce might have referred to the texts themselves, especially since school assignments would have introduced him to the "classic" portions of major authors. Editions of Vergil's works, a heavily annotated copy of Cicero's *Tusculan Disputations,* and the poems of Pope Leo XIII were part of Joyce's Trieste library.[15] In his Paris library (essential for the *Wake*) there are only two books that have any connection with Latin: M-M. Matharan, *Casus de matrimonio fere quingenti quibus applicat et per quos explicat sua asserta moralia circa eamdem materiam* (Almost five hundred matrimonial cases, to which [the author] applies and through which he explains his ethical statements about this material) (Paris, 1893) is balanced by a largely uncut Librairie Hachette translation of Sallust.[16] Certainly no classical treasures lie buried in either of these two volumes. There are likewise no lists of Latin quotations in the archival material of Stuart Gilbert or Paul Léon. Scattered throughout Gilbert's records are a number of explicit notes for his "study" of *Ulysses* which indicate that he (and presumably Joyce) had Latin texts at hand. I conclude, therefore, that a basic collection of Roman authors, standard dictionaries of classical antiquities, and any Notebooks from Joyce's Paris years that might contain references to such texts have been lost. They would not have been taken to Switzerland in 1940.

Acknowledgment of minor frustration at the absence of primary archival data for the major Latin encourages a frank declaration of critical parameters. The results of my research have not revealed a new key to *Ulysses* or the cabalistic secret of the *Wake*. In most instances, for example, Vergilian or Horatian references are fully in keeping with the personality of the character with whom they are associated, or the tone of the episode in which they are placed. In other cases, however, the classical items—along with snatches from operatic arias, titles of the *suras* of the *Koran*, repeated occurrences of certain dates, miniquotations from Shakespeare—are just there. Even if these allusions or phrases fully participate in the wordplay or onomatopoeia of a passage, they only rarely permit absolutely secure application to a wider narrative, much less psychological field. At the present state of *Wake*-research, then, a number of these classical items seem to be essentially of ornamental significance: virtuoso displays of Joyce's quirky mastery and authorial mixture of a mass of high- and low-culture trivia.[17] Finally, the detection of a covert Latin phrase or an allusion to Roman history is rarely the only, never the exclusive critical insight that can be made about a Joycean passage. In the expanding universe of the *Wake* there are no definitive comments.

People who do not like this sort of challenge, ambivalence, or verbal one-upmanship in their reading will already have set aside most of *Ulysses* and all of *Finnegans Wake* long before they have a chance to be disturbed by cryptic allusions to the *Aeneid* or the sacrificial functions of a *flamen*. On the other hand, readers who are fascinated by a 628-page polylingual puzzle may experience momentary flashbacks to a high-school Latin class, or an impulse to consult McHugh's multicultural glosses to see what is going on, and in what language. For those curious adepts my identification of and comment on the patent and latent Latin will be part of the fun. Their conspiratorial glances—and perhaps an appreciative laugh—are the ultimate justification of the book.

Hactenus causae excitantur. Ad Latinitatem pergamus.
(Enough of this special pleading. Let's get down to the parsing.)

1

Grammar and Syntax

In the spring of 1938 James Joyce reported a paternal enterprise that, on first hearing, sounds as bizarre as some of the academic exercises in the "Night Lessons" episode of *Finnegans Wake*. On April 20 of that year he wrote to his daughter-in-law, Helen Joyce, that he had spent "all Easter with Lucia, teaching her some Latin" (*Letters* III.420). At that time Joyce's daughter had been a resident in a *maison de santé* in Ivry for two years. Her mental problems, intermittently serious for quite a while, had become acute enough to preclude home care. The thirty-year-old Lucia, in short, would seem to be a highly improbable candidate for drill in perfect passive subjunctives or ablative absolutes. Perhaps, however, Joyce found that the regularities of declension and conjugation intrigued his daughter and enabled her to produce simple but consistent results in elementary sentences that were grammatically correct. These Latin lessons, then, might have served as a challenging diversion for Lucia, and for Joyce as a way to engage both of them in an activity in which he could regard even minimal success as a real accomplishment and reason for praise. Whatever the motive or outcome, the project is a moving, ultimately pathetic example of the love of a father, *amor patris* (objective and subjective genitive). An authentic comparison of a Latin adjective from the *Wake* seems to offer the most appropriate comment on this endeavor: "Tristis Tristior Tristissimus" (sad, sadder, saddest) (*FW* 158.1).

However strange the use of language drill might seem as a factor in emotionally charged family relationships, Latin grammar was an important aspect in James Joyce's personal and professional life. In the schools at which he consistently demonstrated high levels of academic achievement, mastery of the intricacies of the classical languages was a primary means of attracting local and extramural attention and reward. Letters, notebooks, and the published recollections of his friends also testify to Joyce's lifelong interest in the grammar and syntax of the first foreign language that he studied. My purpose in this chapter is to review the many instances in which Joyce's fiction evokes scenes and displays metaphors that could come only from the pen of a dedicated parser. A number of these references appear in scenes that re-create the setting or techniques of schoolboy instruction in the language or history of ancient Rome. In other contexts, the mechanics of Latin act as counterpoint to the plot or tone of the episode in which the reference appears. From first to last, Joyce's fiction is evidence of his fascination with all parts of "upset latten tintacks" (*FW* 183.20).

In Joyce's first published story, the young narrator of "Sisters" reports that Father Flynn "had studied in the Irish college in Rome and he had taught me to pronounce Latin properly" (*D* 13).[1] Early in *Portrait,* two of Stephen Dedalus' classmates at Clongowes are stymied by the declension of a Latin noun. When faced by *mare* (sea, ocean), Jack Lawton "stopped at the ablative singular and could not go on with the plural." Father Arnall then "asked Fleming and Fleming said that that word had no plural." A few minutes later the prefect of studies enters the classroom, pandybat in hand. He is informed that Fleming not only "wrote a bad Latin theme" but also "missed all the questions in grammar." The punishment is swift: "The pandybat came down on [Fleming's hand] with a loud smacking sound: one, two, three, four, five, six. —Other hand!" (*P* 47–49).[2]

A bit later in *Portrait,* Stephen himself is asked to demonstrate his classical competence. During the trip to Cork with his father, the boy underwent one humiliation after another. Some of Simon's friends in Newcombe's coffeehouse decided

> to put his [Stephen's] Latin to the proof [and] made him translate short passages from Dilectus and asked him whether it was correct to say: *Tempora mutantur nos et mutamur in illis* or *Tempora mutantur et nos mutamur in illis.* (*P* 94)

First of all, the maxim means "Times change and we change with them." Next, the only grammatical crux in the two versions has been created by the examiner, who presumably knows that "*nos*" is the nominative subject of the second verb not the accusative object of the first (which is passive and therefore cannot be construed with a direct object). The two positions of *nos*—before and after *et*—are meant to cause confusion. Finally, the humor in this episode is directed, not at an embarrassed Stephen, but at one of his father's oafish cronies. This self-styled expert seems to think that "Dilectus" is a Roman author. The word means "Selection," and undoubtedly refers to some compendium of morally edifying adages—which was probably as far in the study of Latin literature as the examiner had progressed.

In *Ulysses,* Cyril Sargent must stay after class to work out some math problems in his copybook. Stephen inspects the student: "Ugly and futile: lean neck and tangled hair. . . . Yet someone had loved him." These thoughts—and a recollection of his own mother—trigger a response that is phrased in terms of Latin syntax: "*Amor matris* [love of mother]: subjective and objective genitive" (*U* 2.165–66; compare 9.842–43). The distinction between the two grammatical constructions referred to in that Latin phrase (and in my paternal variation on it in the opening paragraph of this chapter) depends on the relationship between "love" and "mother." If one intends a love for someone *by* a mother, then the genitive is "subjective," since the mother is the agent of the action. If, on the other hand, one intends a love by someone *for* a mother, the genitive is "objective," since the mother is the recipient of the action. This phrase is probably the most memorable occasion in his fiction on which Joyce couched a statement about a deep and fundamental human emotion in terms that derive from Latin grammar, but it is scarcely the unique case.

Even in the midst of the catechetical format of "Ithaca," for example, the act of sexual intercourse is examined from every angle using the highly technical vocabulary of language-analysis:

> the fallaciously inferred debility of the female: the muscularity of the male. . . . the natural grammatical transition by inversion involving no alteration of sense of an aorist preterite proposition (parsed as masculine subject, monosyllabic onomatopoeic transitive verb with direct feminine object) from the active voice into its correlative aorist preterite proposition (parsed as feminine subject, auxiliary verb and quasimonosyllabic onomatopoeic past participle with a complementary masculine agent) in the passive voice. (*U* 17.2215–23)

All of this yields, in plain English, "He fucked her. She was fucked by him."

In the same chapter, when Bloom shaves in the dark, this feat—and his primary quality as a husband—is described in terms literally meant to be associated with the parsing of Latin nouns and verbs: "Because of the surety of the sense of touch in his firm full masculine feminine passive active hand" (*U* 17.289–90). Allusive vituperation from the same general source recurs in the *Wake.* Shaun accuses Shem of avoiding work, "like a *thoroughpaste prosodite, masculine monosyllables of the same numerical mus*" (*FW* 190.34–36; my emphases). The items that I have italicized can be at least partially explained in grammatical terms. "Thoroughpaste" is another way of describing the subtle distinctions in verbal tense. When an action is so thoroughly finished in the past that its impact is still felt in the present, it is "perfect": *I was dying* (incomplete past act) is "imperfect"; *I died* (simple past act) is "aorist"; *I have died—and therefore am dead*—(completed past action) is "perfect." The second emphasized word in the passage cited above, "prosodite," sounds something like "prosody," which is the technical term for the process of versification: word-quantity, accent, rhythm, line-length, stanzaic structure, and so on. (In Italian, the phrase *prosa dite* means "speak prose"; perhaps this is an additional comment by Shaun on his brother's highfalutin literary pretensions.) In Latin, the word *mus* is indeed a "masculine monosyllable," meaning "rodent," "mouse." Maybe Shaun is hinting that Shem is a fraternal rat. Maybe the reader is being invited to become poetically recherché here and to detect in the volatile action of Shem's pen an allusion to the Horatian *mus,* which was born from the mountains' labor (see page 146). And maybe the reader is subtly being reminded that *mus* is an exception to the general principle of gender according to which nouns ending in *-us, -ris* are usually neuter; indeed, *mus* is most correctly designated "common" in gender, since it is used for both male and female rodents.

Acoustically, the most memorable and absurdly reverberative of all Latin exercises is the following declension, in the masculine, feminine, and neuter; nominative, genitive, and dative singular of a familiar demonstrative: *hic, haec, hoc; huius, huius, huius; huic, huic, huic* (this man, this woman, this thing; of this man, of this woman, of this thing; to or for this man, etc.).[3] There is a fairly close representation of these case-gender-jingles in *Finnegans Wake:* "hicky hecky hock, huges huges huges, hughy hughy hughy" (*FW* 454.15–16). An abbreviated version appears in "hicks hyssop! Hock!" (*FW* 423.10; compare *FW* 33.27, *FW* 358.21; VI.B.6.93: "hoc, hic, huck/er"). In *Ulysses* a Circean parody of these demonstrative adjectives is put on the lips of "Panther, the Roman Centurion."[4] There the hallowed declension sounds like "*gibbering baboon's cries* ... Hik! Hek! Hak! Hok! Huk! Kok! Kuk!" (*U* 15.2599–603).

A short burst of interrogative pronouns is worked into the start of the "Questions and Answers" section of the *Wake,* "quisquiquock" (*FW* 126.6). A much longer string of similar Latin adverbs is found in a later chapter: "*Cur, quicquid, ubi, quando, quomodo, quoties, quibus auxilis?*" (Why, what, where, when, how, how often, by what means?) (*FW* 188.8–9). A briefer, vernacular version (but with a pseudo-Latin introduction) is used by Bello in his interrogation of the terrified Bloom in one of the hallucinations in "Circe": "quick, quick, quick! Where? How? What time? With how many?" (*U* 15.3054).

In Latin there are three elements that are used to signal the different responses that interrogators expect to get to the questions they pose. The suffix *-ne* is used to indicate a question that may generate either a positive or a negative reply ("Is it raining?"). The adverb *num* expects a negative reply ("It isn't raining, is it?"). The adverb *nonne* expects a positive reply ("It's raining, isn't it?"). Joyce plays around with both the forms and the functions of these three interrogative elements:

> Can you *nei* do her, *numb?* asks Dolph, suspecting the answer know. Oikkont, ken you, *ninny?* asks Kev, expecting the answer guess. (*FW* 286.25–28; my emphases)

The most impressive original display of this sort of Latin vocabulary is found in the following two sentences (also note the author's concern for correct tense):

> If there is a future in every past that is present *Quis est qui non novit quinnigan* and *Qui quae quot at Quinnigan's Quake!* (*FW* 496.35–497.1)

> (Who is there who does not know quinnigan . . . What man, what woman, how many at Quinnigan's Quake!)

Tense (the time-value of an action) is the most obvious way of manipulating a verb to bring it into conformity with a variety of situations. Narrative and causal clarity depend, to a large measure, on a precise delineation of time relationships. The comic consequences of tense are acknowledged in the *Wake:* "But the world, mind, *is, was and will be* writing its own wrunes for ever" (*FW* 19.35–36; my emphasis). This basic formulation of the present, past, and future of the verb "to be" is repeated over and over in the *Wake*, sometimes in Latin: "fuit, isst and herit" (*FW* 128.1–2); "*Erat Est Erit*" (*FW* 140.4–5).[5] Some of the expressions of these permutations of verbal tense are fairly elaborate. In the neologism "anteprDopreviousday" (*FW* 407.29), each of the compounding prepositions (*ante, pro, prae*) means, in terms of time, "before." An adjacent phrase extends the perspective: "with the memories of the *past* the hicnuncs [Latin for "here and now"] of the *present* embelliching the musics of the *futures*" (*FW* 407.31–33; my emphases). Other temporal statements reflect the fundamental confusion of the Four Old Men: "the past and present (Johnny MacDougall speaking, give me trunks [long-distance] miss!) and present and absent and past and present and perfect" (*FW* 389.17–19). Occasionally another grammatical point will be introduced into the statement, as in "There's a split in the infinitive from to have to have been to will be" (*FW* 271.21–22).

Another passage calls attention to Joyce's concern with tense-usage involving two languages. McHugh glosses "in the ersebest idiom I have done it equals I so shall do" (*FW* 253.1–2) with the following: "[I]rish ta se deanta agam: I

have it done = I promise you." Clear enough, and a nice example of the idiomatic value of tense, in which an Erse (Irish) perfect is the equivalent of an
English future. For Joyce, however, I suspect that a third language was meant
to be part of the comparative paradigm: the final element in the Irish phrase,
"agam," is also the Latin verb for "I shall do," *agam*.[6]

An error in the use of a verb's principal part can also, it seems, assume a
theological dimension. Shem was once expelled from school "for the sin against
the past participle" (*FW* 467.25). To put a verb through its temporal paces in
English one must know how variants of the word's present tense are used
to form the past tense and past participle. These verbal variations are the
principal parts, as in the vernacular example "swimswamswum" (*FW* 7.1).
Joyce occasionally plays around with the principal parts for English strong
verbs: "wrath wrackt wroth" (*FW* 58.31); "bedeed and bedood and bedang
and bedung" (*FW* 185.31–32). The prize example is Kevin's description of his
glimpse of Issy's underpants:

> —Peequeen ourselves, the prettiest pickles of unmatchemable mute an-
> tes [*mutande* means "drawers" in Italian] I ever bopeeped at, *seesaw
> shallshee*, since the town *go went gonning* on Pranksome Quaine.
> (*FW* 508.26–28; my emphasis)

Joyce also displays his firm grasp of more elaborate Latin principal parts:
"*Mingo, minxi, mictum, mingere*" (*U* 9.762). This quartet of model tense-
forms comes from a genuine Latin verb (but one not likely to appear in the
normal high-school vocabulary list). The forms mean "I piss, I have pissed, it
has been pissed, to piss."[7] By far the most ingenious display of this sort of
verbal dexterity occurs in a short passage, the full import of which I never
would have detected without the prodding of McHugh's annotation: "Pharoah,
with fairy, two lie, let them!" (*FW* 580.12–13). Neatly sounded out in these
four phrases are the common, but highly irregular (and therefore matter for
constant drill) principal parts *fero, ferre, tuli, latum* (I bear, to bear, I have
borne, it has been borne). In my judgment as an experienced parser, if one
were searching for a grammatical "*Superlative absolute*" (*FW* 276.L5), that is
it.

In the aftermath of the *Wake*'s convoluted canon-law case in various marriage problems, there apparently follows a civil-law procedure involving "a
foreign firm, since disseized, registered as Tangos, Limited" (*FW* 574.4). The
other party in the case is the "holders of Pango stock, a rival concern" (*FW*
574.28). Why the litigants have names that mean "I touch" (*tango*) and "I
pound" (*pango*) is not immediately—or even after considerable rumination—

clear. At any rate, the verb-names also appear in the passage in "perfect" forms: "wellknown tetigists" (*tetigi*, "I have touched") (*FW* 575.19); "Monsignore Pepigi" (*pepigi*, "I have pounded") (*FW* 575.29). In fact, the play on the word's principal parts becomes more blatant in two other phrases: "Pepigi's pact" (*FW* 576.5) and "pango with Pepigi" (*FW* 576.8). The last pair puts the Latin verb through three of its four tense-paces: *pango, pangere, pepigi, pactum* (I pound, to pound, I have pounded, it has been pounded). One does not wish to beat a lexical *equum mortuum* (a having died horse) here, but I venture to guess that Joyce selected these two names not because their meanings (touch-pound) had any significance; rather, they appear because the two Latin verbs from which they derive are usually memorized together as the prime examples of reduplicated perfects, *tetigi, pepigi*. For Joyce, especially in *Finnegans Wake*, eccentricity in the choice of characters' names based purely on grammatical terms can be as significant a factor as thematic onomatopoeia might have been for Dickens, Trollope, or Henry James.

To back up the suggestion offered in the previous paragraph, I cite below a number of examples in which Joyce displays his lifelong fixation on verbs, primarily in their thinly disguised Latin configurations. The paradigm comes, fittingly enough, from a footnote in "Night Lessons" that pivots around the familiar *amo, amare, amavi, amatum* (I love, to love, I have loved, it has been loved):

> When we will conjugate together toloseher tomaster tomiss while morrow fans amare hour, verbe de vie and verve to vie, with love ay love have I. (*FW* 279.F1.8–10)

The verb "conjugate" used in the first line of the previous quotation comes from the Latin root *iugo* (to yoke together [as, for example, oxen]). Thus, when students conjugate a verb, they link its lexical base with functional endings, as in the following examples: *am-o* (I love); *am-as* (you love); *am-at* (he, she loves).

The full conjugation of a Latin verb is extraordinarily complex. It involves literally scores of different forms (additions to the word's base) that distinguish between two *numbers*, three *persons*, six *tenses*, two *voices*, two *moods*, and assorted other procedures such as the *imperative, infinitive, participle, gerund, gerundive,* and *supine*. Thanks to his instruction and drill in these necessary minutiae at the hands of the Jesuits at Clongowes Wood and Belvedere Colleges, Joyce would have been able to run any Latin verb through these extended formal loops. A glance at the virtuoso at work is given in "*mutatis mutandis* . . . mute antes" (*FW* 508.23, 27; Joyce's emphasis). These are three participles (perfect passive, future passive, present active, respectively) of the verb *muto, mutare* (to change). Joyce would also not have hesitated, if called upon, to assign, in the prescribed order, the appropriate technical term to identify each step of this process. As has been indicated before, this type of grammatical analysis is called "parsing." In *Finnegans Wake* there are several passages, each too extensive to be cited in more than illustrative summary or paraphrase, in which Joyce displays his skill in the arcane details and jargon of Latin grammar and syntax.

The most important of the extended passages that confirm Joyce's parsing ability is found in the midst of "Night Lessons." There Issy cites several actual dictionaries and handbooks of grammar in French, English, and Latin, and reviews the essential terms and operations for a number of languages. In four pages the diligent daughter of the family covers not merely verbs, but also nouns (*FW* 268.16–272.8).[8] Several shorter but equally impressive compact exercises are those by "JUSTIUS" (*FW* 187.28–32) and by Shaun (*FW* 468.5–19 and *FW* 523.5–13). Joyce makes certain that one does not miss his pedantic intention and high seriousness of these displays by having the studious Issy start a section of her discourse with some obvious technical terms: "Yoking apart and oblique orations parsed to one side" (*FW* 270.3–4).

The last quotation is meant by Joyce, in my opinion, to sound something like not real English, but some sort of language-classroom approximation thereof. The grammatical term for both constructions used in that passage is "ablative absolute." It is comprised of a noun and participle (here a partially understood "[set] apart" and "parsed") that are not syntactically linked to the rest of the sentence (hence "absolute"); in Latin both components of this construction would be placed in the ablative case. In other words, Joyce's "yoking" (conjugating) and his "oblique orations" (reported speech) are Latin terms that have been expressed in English by Latinate constructions. On the off chance that this is not clear the first time through, the following is another example, also from "Night Lessons": "these things being so or ere those things having done" (*FW* 275.3–4). Though the language is ostensibly English in this citation, there can be no doubt that Joyce is imitating a typical classroom rendition of a quintessential ablative absolute, *his/illis factis,* in the second unit in this quotation ("those things having done"). The first phrase is also probably meant to be the accepted academic translation of *Quae cum ita sint* (Since those things just mentioned are so). Both of the aforementioned constructions are frequently heard in classrooms as suitable renditions of Latin transition formulas.

Rapid-fire recital of principal parts, guttural demonstrative pronouns, pedantically awkward ablative absolutes, and the conjugation of verb may be the most frequently recalled—or quickly forgotten—aspects of the study of Latin, but there are other dimensions to the linguistic enterprise.

Included in the encyclopedic scope of *Finnegans Wake* is more than one excursus into areas of language study that are far more exotic than the basic matters of grammar and syntax that have been discussed above. An exercise in *phonetics*, for example, is involved when Shaun indicates that "I will pack my comb and mirror to praxis oval owes and artless awes" (*FW* 458.35–36). The twin seems to be attempting to smoothe out his harsh Dublin pronunciation of the vowels "o" and "a." More technical matters of speech production are brought out into the open in "allvoyous, demivoyelles, languoaths, lesbiels, dentelles, gutterhowls and furtz" (*FW* 116.28–29); "vellicar frictions" (*FW* 385.12); "vealar penultimatum" (*FW* 424.26); "semiological agglutinative" (*FW* 465.12); "uval lavguage" (*FW* 466.32). This aspect of linguistic study also has a pronounced erotic aspect: kissing a woman all over is recommended, because "It's good for her bilabials" (*FW* 465.26). Joyce sums everything with a parodic precis of "Gramm's laws! . . . In the buginning is the woid, in the muddle is the sounddance" (*FW* 378.28–30). The allusions here are to a secular-sacred contamination of Grimm's law (which governs certain sound shifts in Germanic languages) and the opening verse of St. John's *Gospel* ("In the beginning was the word").

The highly technical topic of *metrics*, the rhythmic basis of classical poetry, is mentioned in several of Joyce's works. Mr. Kernan's reformers in *Grace* remind their fallen colleague that Pope Leo XIII "was a great scholar" and that the Supreme Pontiff "wrote Latin poetry" (*D* 167).[9] The repentant (and cloyingly modest) Dedalus also learned "what little he knew of the laws of Latin verse from a ragged book written by a Portuguese priest" (*P* 179).[10] Stephen's later comment on "A catalectic[11] tetrameter of iambs" (*U* 3.23) and its erotic perversion in the *Wake*, "A cataleptic mithyphallic!" (*FW* 481.4), are evidence of a mastery of metrical jargon. Joyce left an early record of his interest in these matters. In a 1902 essay on the poetry of James Clarence Mangan, he commented on the metrics of "Kathaleen-Ny-Houlahan," in which "the refrain changes the trochaic scheme abruptly for a line of firm, marching iambs" (*CW* 80). In *Ulysses*, Professor MacHugh notes—and his observation probably was not fully appreciated in the office of the *Evening Telegraph*—that "Ohio" is "A perfect cretic! . . . Long, short and long" (*U* 7.369).

Many aspects of metrics, its basis, application, and terminology, are a challenge even to advanced students of the classics. One fundamental fact is neatly summarized in the midst of the extended grammatical passage mentioned above: "Quantity counts though accents falter" (*FW* 270.2–3). Exactly, since the primary determinant of rhythm in Greek and Latin verse is not word accent, but the pronounced length (quantity) of syllables. One example will be sufficient. On the same page of the *Wake* as the general metrical principle just cited, the readers are instructed to "volve the virgil page and view"; then they are informed that "the O of woman is long" (*FW* 270.25–26). In Latin verse the "o" of the adjective *Rōmanus, -a, -um* is indeed long, as can be demonstrated by reference to a famous and highly spondaic line in Vergil's *Aeneid*—which would appear on the second ("volved," or turned) page of a school-text: *tantae molis erat Romanam condere gentem* (what an epic task it was to found the Roman race)(*A* 1.33). It is best to leave this topic, which is capable of immeasurable refinement, at that.

There are two other areas, both situated at the margin of basic grammar and syntax, that are too specialized to be more than mentioned in this chapter. The first topic is that of *language* itself, its origins, categories, and so on. Joyce was interested in this question, but, as usual, he allowed other matters to impinge on his coldly scientific analysis. Language, it seems, is that human activity which

> is told in sounds in utter that, in signs so adds to, in universal, in polygluttural, in each auxiliary neutral idiom, sordomutics, florilingua, sheltafocal, flayflutter, a con's cubane, a pro's tutute, strassarab, ereperse and anythongue athall. (*FW* 117.12–16)

(Those interested in the linguistic import and relevance of each of the items in that sentence can begin their enlightenment by glancing at McHugh's annotation to the passage.)

Another massive topic to which Joyce turns his attention time after time is that of the various forms of *scripts* which have been used to memorialize spoken language. In the "Telemachus" chapter of *Ulysses*, it is revealed that Molly Bloom used to occupy herself by covering "a sheet of paper with signs and hieroglyphics which she stated were Greek and Irish and Hebrew characters" (*U* 17.676–78). During "their mutual reflections" Bloom and Stephen take this topic to absurd levels of hypothetical comparison and cataloguing (*U* 17.724–75). In the midst of their discussion each makes "a glyphic comparison of the phonic symbols" of Hebrew and Irish on "the penultimate blank page of . . . *Sweets of Sin.*" Stephen wrote the characters for "gee, eh, dee, em, simple and modified"; Bloom wrote "ghimel, aleph, daleth and (in the absence of mem) a substituted goph" (*U* 17.733–39). There is more than meets the eye in this exercise of comparative orthography.[12] But, as far as grammar is concerned, the essential point is this: Bloom's and Stephen's competence in their two ancestral languages did not extend far beyond a command of the respective alphabets; any other knowledge was "[t]heoretical, being confined to certain grammatical rules of accidence and syntax and practically excluding vocabulary" (*U* 17.743–44).

After the completion of *Ulysses* and during the years of the progressive composition of *Finnegans Wake*, James Joyce himself obviously strove to extend—some would say beyond the limits of intelligibility—his own polyglottal vocabulary. Shem summarizes this state of affairs nicely: "Mynfadher was a boer constructor and Hoy was a lexical student, parole. . . . Letter purfect!" (*FW* 180.35–181.2). Throughout this chapter I have tried to demonstrate that, in addition to his obsession with words, Joyce never lost his curiosity about various basic "grammatical rules of accidence and syntax." This is especially true when the material involved Latin, the language in which he personally experienced his first, longest, and most intense academic drill. At the same time, there are scores of passages in the *Wake* which indicate that purely graphic exercises in alphabets and more exotic forms of writing also continued to fascinate Joyce. The following citation of several of these "script-ural" texts is designed to illustrate that paralinguistic aspect of his final work.

The wedge-shaped (*cuneus* in Latin) writing system of early Mesopotamian civilizations is referred to several times in the *Wake*. Once the graphic, fishbone appearance of the messages impressed on clay tablets is highlighted: "a cunifarm school of herring" (*FW* 524.20). Another phrase manages to squeeze an obscene note into the script: "cunniform letters" (*FW* 198.25). *Cunnus* is Latin for what the school dictionaries define as the "female pudenda." (The latter word is a directly transferred Latin gerundive; it means "something feminine which ought to be a source of modesty or shame.")

The origin of the system of signs that we call the alphabet is encapsulated in the following sentence: "When a *part* so *ptee* does duty for the *holos* we soon grow to use of an *allforabit*" (*FW* 18.36–19.2; my emphases). The second italicized word is phonetic French for "small" (*petit*); the third emphasized word is the Greek adjective *holos*, meaning whole, complete. An alphabetic element is a conventional sign for a sound; strings of these components "spell" out whole words, sentences, and so on. The actual shape of an alphabetic sign can also be conceived of as an example of the process of a "part for the whole." The original form of a Semitic "aleph" (ox) was an 𐤀; a "beth" (house) was a ﻮ, and so on. (For a better visual representation of the evolution of our alphabet from Phoenician to Greek to Latin to English, consult an encyclopedia or the initial entry for each letter in a comprehensive dictionary.) When they are strung together in a system of "signs for sounds," these graphic (and phonetic) synecdoches make up an "alpha-bet," or, as Joyce puts it, an "allforabit."

The details of the formation and evolution of the alphabet outlined above may seem ridiculously remote and academic, but Joyce was certainly aware of this basic information—and he did not think his readers would miss the allusion in "(it's as semper as oxhousehumper!)" (FW 107.34). The "-humper" in the final word refers to the "camel," which is a *gimel* in Phoenician. That animal gave its name to the third letter in the Semitic alphabet; and its "hump" served as the graphic model for the third sound sign in that system, a $\wedge$.[13] Another passage connects the Semitic origins of the English alphabet with the Irish ogham system in which the signs were named after trees: "in alphabeater cameltemper, from alderbirk to tannenyou" (FW 553.2–3). Finally, there is a cross-cultural, Celto-Semitic version of these initial three letters in "Mac Auliffe . . . MacBeth . . . and MacGhimley" (FW 290.6–7).

There are a number of more straightforward alphabetic lists in the *Wake*. A complete run begins with "apple, bacchante, custard" and ends with "xray, yesplease, zaza." The entries follow the order used in the English alphabet, with the exception of "feldgrau" which does double duty for "f" and "g";[14] "philomel" and "theerose" are appended to accommodate the Greek "phi" and "theta" (FW 247.35–248.2). Issy's twenty-eight Rainbow Girls appear in English alphabetical order: "There's Ada, Bett, Celia . . . Xenia, Yva, Zulma"; this string yields twenty-six female names, plus "Phoebe, Thelma. And Mee!" (FW 147.11–15). Other, less fully developed strings of letters can be found in the feminine diminutives "alpilla, beltilla, ciltilla, deltilla" (FW 194.22–23); an abbreviated Highland version, "ach beth cac duff" (FW 250.34); two eclectic versions, "aiden bay," and so on (FW 327.34) and "alfi byrni gamman dealter etcera zezera," and so on (FW 568.32–33).

In *Ulysses* five letters of the Hebrew alphabet helped Leopold Bloom to remember the value of π, 3.14. The evidence to support that claim involves the arithmetical functions assigned to "ghimel, aleph, daleth, and . . . a substituted qoph" (U 17.738–39). Those letters were Bloom's mnemotechnic, a hallowed pedagogical gimmick to aid one's memory.[15] Several times in the novel Bloom uses the acronym list "Roygbiv" to help him recall the colors in the spectrum: *red, orange, yellow, green, blue, indigo, violet* (U 13.1075–76, 15.1604–5). However popular mnemotechnics might have been in turn-of-the-century science classrooms in Dublin, their most pervasive and intensive deployment was in the elementary stages of Latin grammar.

In the language of the ancient Romans, the gender of nouns was not natural but conventional. Almost all males were "masculine," females "feminine," but "things" were not necessarily "neuter." Rather, the names of places, things, abstractions, processes, and so on were assigned, with little apparent reason, to any one of these three gender-categories. Latin grammar-texts and the experienced instructors who taught from them traditionally offered a ready store of mnemotechnics to make the task of vocabulary drill a bit less daunting. Here is a personal example. Almost all the third-declension Latin nouns that end in "-er" and "-or" are masculine. The very few words that do not conform to this principle were permanently implanted into my adolescent memory by the following pair of jingles:

> Linter ("skiff") and arbor ("tree")
> FEMININE will always be.
> NEUTER always are these four:
> iter, ver, cavader, cor.

There are many other hokey but useful rhymes of this ilk. Joyce, of course, had been memorably drilled in these matters of monumental linguistic importance. For example, in the Wake the following comments refer to the word "mens" (mens in Latin means mind, intelligence): "The form masculine. The gender feminine" (FW 505.24–25).[16] What Joyce is doing here is contrasting the meaning of the doubly pluralized English word "mens," which is resolutely masculine, with nominative singular form of the Latin noun mens, which is unexceptionably feminine in gender.

As a matter of fact, the gender of most third-declension nouns that end in "-s" is feminine, as for mens above. There are, however, numerous exceptions, and to assist in the recognition of this important grammatical factor, there are numerous mnemotechnics. In a Wake passage that has other indicators of its grammatical concerns (including "parsenaps"), there occur the following four words, "Amnist anguished axes Collis" (FW 256.24–25). The capitalized "A" and "C" are a hint that the words are meant to be understood as a unit. Indeed, since in Latin each is a third-declension noun, ending in "-s," all happen to be exceptions to the rule. They are masculine in gender: amnis (stream), anguis (snake), axis (axle), collis (hill). These words once formed part of a longer gender-mnemotechnic, as is shown in a parallel passage (also embedded in a highly grammatical context): "Hammisandivis axes colles waxes warmas like sodullas" (FW 468.10–11). Here McHugh cites the official source and the original form of a rhymed memory-aid, "Kennedy's Latin Primer":

> "Many nouns in -s we find
> to the Masculine assigned:
> amnis, axis, caulis, collis, etc."

I welcome McHugh's precise information and the exact order of the nouns, especially since this published version of the mnemotechnic includes *caulis* (stalk) as well as *collis*. Naturally I emphasize *caulis*, because that word most definitely has an obscene application in Latin as a slang for *penis*. I suggest, then, that Joyce has, with consummate ingenuity, introduced an erotic element into a classroom gender jingle: someone's stalk is waxing warm here.[17]

As a testament to the high seriousness in Victorian England with which both students and masters approached their task of parsing there is the immensely popular *Comic Latin Grammar* by Percival Leigh (1840).[18] It thoroughly (and with scrupulous attention to the most minute detail) covers the ground; but its mode of presentation is relentlessly facetious. This irreverently illustrated work is capped by 191 lines of ingeniously rhymed doggerel that exemplify the quantity of final syllables in Latin words. The following is a typical excerpt:

> Some [nouns] terminate in *b, d, t;*
> All these are short; but those in *c*
> Form toes—I mean, form ends of feet
> As long, as long as Oxford Street.
> Though *nec* and *donec* every bard
> Hath written short as Hanway Yard.
> *Fac, hic,* and *hoc* are common though
> Th' ablative *hoc* is long you know.

There is no evidence that Joyce (who would have enjoyed it immensely) ever read or used this grammar.

Finally, in the same paragraph of the *Wake* from which the *caulis* example is taken, there is another, heavily camouflaged grammatical mnemotechnic. The Latin noun *nemo* (nobody, no one) has an extraordinarily odd declension in its singular cases; after *nemo* (nominative) the following are the preferred forms: *nullius* (genitive), not *neminis; nemini* (dative); *neminem* (accusative); *nullo* (ablative), not *nemine*. The genitive and ablative are thus based on a stem borrowed from another word, *nullus* (which also means no one). In his re-creation of the memory aid for this word, Joyce tried to hide almost every detail about its exceptional declension, except the fact that he clearly remembered how *nemo* works: "Fond namer, let me never see thee blame a kiss for shame a knee" (*FW* 468.18–19). In plain English the jingle goes:

> For *nemo* let me never say
> *neminis* or *nemine*.

If that claim for grammatical allusion seems too improbable even for Joyce and *Finnegans Wake,* try this doublet from "Night Lessons": "from Nebob see you never stray who'll nimm you nice and nehm the day" (*FW* 270.27–28). In both versions there is also a decidedly amorous, even nuptial cast: "Fond namer," "never . . . blame a kiss," "for shame a knee"; "nimm ['take' in German] you nice," "nehm the day."

Here, in those last four examples of classroom gender-mnemotechnics, each with a deft sexual slant, is positive proof that an important aspect of the *Wake's* humor is the opportunity it provided for Joyce to revel in the role of an avenging parser.

2

Buck Mulligan as a "Grammaticus Gloriosus"

The personal enmity and literary rivalry between James Joyce and Oliver St. John Gogarty were often expressed in terms of the classics. By this I do not mean that the two were caught up in some sort of *odium philologicum,* or even that they traded insults laced with Juvenalian indignation or Housmanic venom. Rather—and this is as much a matter of class as of classics—Gogarty, B.A. (T.C.D.), was the consummate Hellenosnob, an affectation that his academic affiliations do much to explain. Although he was resolutely Irish and Catholic, his education was essentially English. His secondary studies were at a Jesuit boarding school of "tone," Stonyhurst in Lancashire. After taking his degree at Trinity College, Dublin's Palladian keep of the Anglo-Irish ascendancy, he spent Hilary (spring) and Trinity (summer) terms 1904 at Worcester College, Oxford.[1]

Although only a tiny minority of Victorian and Edwardian students could read the work of classical Hellas in the original, the pride of the elite English public schools and the two ancient universities was the fact that they alone, of all European institutions, placed special emphasis on Greek language and literature. Oxford undergraduate jargon for the *literae humaniores* (which also includes Latin) is to the point here: the major section of this classical curriculum is called "Greats," and its final series of examinations is the "great go." Victorian literature is punctuated with references to bright young men on "long vac" reading parties, preparing for the special papers that would crown their careers with the "double first" in the classics, leading to a fellowship or entry into the corridors of power. This attitude is illustrated in Shaw's roughly contemporary *Major Barbara* (1907). The on-the-make fiancé of the Major speaks to Lord Andrew Undershaft: "Greek scholars are privileged men. . . . Other languages are the qualifications of waiters and commercial travellers: Greek is to a man of position what the hallmark is to silver."[2]

In Ireland and on the Continent, mastery of Latin was the sign of the cultivated person—although even here, except for Germany, its status as the working tongue of the Roman church dulled some of the liberal sheen and antique gloss on what was, from an insular perspective, a lesser accomplishment.[3] In England, on the other hand, every educated gentleman was expected to endorse, if not practice, "keeping the Greek up."[4]

The thinly disguised embodiment of Gogarty in *Ulysses,* "[s]tately, plump Buck Mulligan" (*U* 1.1), is clearly meant to sound just like a caricature of a blustering Hellenizer when he offers to instruct Stephen Dedalus:

> Isn't the sea what Algy calls it: a great sweet mother? The snotgreen sea.
> The scrotumtightening sea. *Epi oinopa ponton.* Ah, Dedalus, the Greeks.
> I must teach you. You must read them in the original. *Thalatta! Thalatta!*
> She is our great sweet mother.(*U* 1.77–81)

The condescension cannot be read as anything other than a slur, from "Trinity's surly front" (*U* 8.476), on Stephen's linguistic parochialism.

Greek, although available, was not touted as the acme of the curriculum in the Jesuit schools and university that Stephen Dedalus—and his creator—attended. National competition lists show Joyce attaining very high results in the yearly Latin examinations, and throughout his life he was quick to demonstrate that Latin was his first second language. At the same time, Joyce was, and remained, in the fullest sense of the term, an amateur in ancient Greek.[5] He never studied it formally, although he did learn some modern Greek and his command of Latin grammar and syntax certainly enabled him to follow the gist of notes in a commentary on a text. Taking full advantage of the word entries and etymologies in a Greek dictionary, such as the standard Oxford edition of Liddell and Scott, would have caused him no difficulty; throughout *Finnegans Wake* there is ample evidence that he used some sort of lexical compendium.[6]

Joyce read widely in the translations of Greek literature and in works on them and general Greek culture. In the *Wake* Notebook VI.B.20.33 there is an entry on "Wolf's Theory of Homer." At the time, that theory would be familiar only to specialists interested in the possibility that the Homeric epics were the oral productions of an unlettered poet. His fascination with Victor Bérard's books on the Semitic dimensions of Homer's *Odyssey* is too well known to require further comment. It should, however, be pointed out that in the midst of Joyce's Notebook entries from this source, which include a number of phrases in Greek, there are also several specific citations of Latin words from the Odyssean first half of Vergil's Roman epic, the *Aeneid.*[7] In general, however, a fair assessment of Joyce's competence with the *ipsissima verba* of ancient Greek can be illustrated by a glance at his rendition of the Greek alphabet on the back cover of a 1926 *Wake* notebook (VI.B.21); it is incomplete and slightly out of order, the hesitant script of an enthusiastic tyro.

On the other hand, Gogarty's command of Greek and Latin is a reflection not only of his native intelligence but also of his early and thorough training in the most demanding English traditions of the classics. Some biographical detail is a necessary preface to a further discussion of the shape and function of the "Hellenization" motif in *Ulysses*. While not Eton or Harrow, Stonyhurst was the type of school whose top sixth-formers paraded their skill in verse composition before university scholarship committees. In fact, Gogarty reminisces about his frequent recourse to the *Gradus ad Parnassum*, a thesaurus of Latin phrases in a number of metrical patterns that schoolboys consulted to bolster flagging inspiration as they patched together imitations of Horace or Ovid. Even this recollection, however, is meant to damn Jesuit pedagogy and discipline by comparison with "any 'public school'": "Protestant schools as a rule were better."[8]

At a later stage of his education, the two professors at Trinity whom Gogarty singles out for special comment are both classicists: Mahaffy, "the greatest don I ever met," and Tyrrell, the "man I loved most."[9] Robert Yelverton Tyrrell, frequently called *graius homo* ("the Greek") urged Gogarty to go to Oxford, not to take a second degree, but to compete for the Newdigate Prize in English verse. Thirty years before Gogarty arrived at Worcester, Mahaffy had sent Oscar Wilde, fresh from success at Trinity, to Magdalen College for the same purpose. Wilde not only took a double first in his classical examinations, but also won the 1878 Newdigate with his poem on "Ravenna." Gogarty was less fortunate; his effort was judged *proxime accesit* (it came close) to George K. A. Bell's "Delphi." A series of letters from Gogarty to Bell are full of graceful acknowledgments that the better man's "lank eagle" had won.[10] In his "unpremeditated autobiography," published exactly a half-century later, Gogarty tells how he downed a five-pint, silver tankard of bitters in the Worcester refectory, "a feat unprecedented in the history of the college." He caps the tale of his bibulous triumph with the comment, "On the whole, I'd rather have drunk the sconce than won the Newdigate."[11] One rather doubts that.

In a letter to Bell, Gogarty re-creates a literary interview with Yeats, including their discussion of Moschus's "Lament for Bion" and its influence on Shelley's "Adonais." This level of competence is quite impressive: critical insights on and exact quotation of a late Hellenistic pastoral poem by an obscure *grammaticus* (teacher of basic language and literature) to which even encyclopedic histories of Greek literature devote only a short paragraph. Gogarty's terminal reference, "I think it's line 196, but it doesn't matter,"[12] confirms one's suspicions that the entire exercise (and the gossip about Yeats) is meant to be just that, impressive.

A far more mature Gogarty was capable of similar gestures. A poem in a collection published in the United States in 1944 contains the following couplet:

> Or that gowned man who loved to foster
> My waking wits, *Tyrrellus noster.*[13]

The reference is to Professor Tyrrell of T.C.D., the cultural docent of generations of its brightest and most privileged undergraduates. (As an aside, I also wonder if "waking wits" might not be Gogarty's alliterative claim to have, while still in college, anticipated *Finnegans Wake.*)[14] In the same slim volume is an elegy to a dead American military aviator. It begins with what can charitably be called false humility:

> Had I the proud Pindaric tongue
> To praise men who strove well when young.[15]

Dropping the name of the poet of the fifth-century B.C. victory odes that celebrated triumphs in the ancient games in the first line of a lament for a pilot killed in a training crash is pompous and bathetic. It bears the mark of a grandly self-deprecating stage Oxonian, who repeatedly relishes his Heliconic success— and even his near miss, the *proxime accessit* in the 1904 Newdigate.

I adopt this hostile tone not because I think it a fair assessment of Gogarty's personality or distinguished lifelong medical and literary achievement. Rather, for this chapter in my review of Joyce's use of the classics, I have appropriated the critical equivalent of what some commentators call the "Uncle Charles" principle: Joyce's adaptation of a character's typical diction or structural idiosyncracies even in the presumably "neutral" narrative contexts that frame his or her direct speech.[16] Thus, Joyce reports that "Uncle Charles repaired to his outhouse" (*P* 60). My portrait of Gogarty's status as a hendecasyllabic-flaunting poseur and a nabob-wit about Dublin and Oxford is, by design and exaggeration, partisanly and acerbically Joycean.[17]

The hostility between Joyce and Gogarty was frequently articulated in terms of the latter's genuine dedication to and swaggering advertisement of his expertise in Greek and Latin. Yet there is much more than classics at work here. Their rivalry and the later bitter enmity were fundamentally a matter of class. Joyce, of course, could not have read Gogarty's 1954 autobiography; but he must have been aware, for a long time, of its author's feeling:

> His father was an alcoholic, an old alcoholic wag. His mother was a naked nerve; and Joyce himself was torn between a miserable background

and a sumptuous education. . . . He had the formal and diffident manners of a lay brother in one of the lower orders of the Church. . . . He was not out of the top drawer: not out of any drawer for that matter.[18]

These scurrilous *ad hominem* comments make Mulligan's "*O, it's only Dedalus whose mother is beastly dead*" (*U* 1.198–99; compare *U* 15.4178–80) seem almost sensitive and consolatory. And surely Joyce knew that those were the views which Gogarty held about his background and behavior. Their mutual animosity festered in the awareness by each of the other's perception.

In contrast to Gogarty's sort of suavely brutal assault, Joyce, by far the greater artist, created the character of Malachi Mulligan, and allowed the pinguid double dactyl to speak for himself in *Ulysses*. At the center of Joyce's counterattack is Gogarty's vaunted success in his classical studies at elite English and Anglo-Irish schools and its perpetuation in his highly popular vernacular verse. By this I mean that, over and above his studied role as a "medical," Mulligan establishes himself in the novel as the ultimate authority on the classics—and it is precisely on this field that Joyce has him bite the dust. In *Ulysses,* Mulligan is the *grammaticus gloriosus* (blustering language-teacher). As such he shares his comic model's fate and is destined to be hoist with his own linguistic petard.

First, in the passage from the book's initial episode quoted above, Mulligan caps his pseudo-Homeric, noun-adjective epithets for the sea with an accurate quotation of one of Homer's favorite formulas "*Epi oinopa ponton*" (over the wine-faced sea) (*U* 1.78); this is followed by "*Thalatta! Thalatta!*" (the sea! the sea!) (*U* 1.80), the cry of what was left of Xenophon's ten thousand fugitive Greek soldiers when they breasted a barren hill, then saw the Black Sea and safety. The first citation is found primarily in the *Odyssey,* the second is from the *Anabasis.* To the Greekless, these ancient works (and their strange alphabet) may appear to be—and they are ostensibly meant to be—incredibly difficult academic challenges. They are, in fact, among the first texts a beginning student encounters; to a new classicist they are about as exotic as the basic theorems in geometry are to a budding mathematician.

Mulligan's offer to instruct Dedalus in Greek, then, includes two appropriate and authentic, but decidedly elementary, flourishes. The Greek was chosen to underscore the potential pupil's marginal status. Perhaps, however, Joyce is actually mocking his Moschus-quoting Oxonian by putting a pair of fairly leaden examples into his golden mouth. At any rate, Gogarty would not have been overly impressed by Joyce's re-creation of Mulligan's first Ulyssean display of classical acumen. These phrases hardly soar with Pindaric wings.

Gogarty/Mulligan's final noteworthy foray into ancient languages, in "Oxen of the Sun," is a different story. The passage is extensive and is meant to be ornately Ciceronian. The evidence for my suggestion that these lines constitute Joyce's philological revenge on his rival is complex and subtle; but the impact of an error in basic Latin grammar by Mulligan is intended, if my insight is valid, to skewer both the character and its model.[19]

The scene is the National Maternity Hospital in the evening of June 16, 1904; the progressively "woozy wobblers" (*U* 14.1562) are awaiting news of the accouchement of Mrs. Mina Purefoy. Buck Mulligan arrives and makes "court to the scholarly by apt quotation from the classics":

> *Talis ac tanta depravatio hujus seculi, O quirites, ut matresfamiliarum nostrae lascivas cujuslibet semiviri libici titillationes testibus ponderosis atque excelsis erectionibus centurionum Romanorum magnopere anteponunt.* (*U* 14.705–10)

This nicely balanced sentence is, in fact, not a "quotation," but a more or less original composition by Joyce. Its diction and periodic structure, however, have fooled more than one commentator to take Joyce at his word and to attribute the passage to Cicero, whose prose it is clearly meant to imitate—or parody.[20] Putting the "quotation . . . , as it dwelt upon his memory," into the mouth of Buck Mulligan would seem, then, to be in keeping with his established position as the premier classicist in the group of carousers. Before I challenge that interpretation, the Latin sentence itself deserves some comment. First, a literal translation:

> Such and so great is the depravity of this age, O fellow citizens, that our mothers of families greatly prefer the wanton titillations of some one or another half-male barbarian to the massive testicles and sky-high erections of Roman centurions.

There is evidence that Buck Mulligan had previously toyed around with similar thoughts, albeit in the vernacular. Near the end of "Scylla and Charybdis," Mulligan sings two lines of an obscene song:

> Then outspoke medical Dick
> To his comrade medical Davy . . . (*U* 9.908–9; Joyce's ellipsis)

Later in the same episode, he adopts the pen name "Ballocky Mulligan" (*U* 9.1176) and informs the prospective audience for his onanistic play that the pair of "MEDICALS" mentioned above are "two birds with one stone" (*U*

9.1184). The source of Mulligan's couplet—and, by extension, for the main point of his later Ciceronian sentence—is in a letter sent to Joyce, sometime around 1902–1904, by Oliver St. John Gogarty.

Readers of *Ulysses* are familiar with Gogarty/Mulligan's "Ballad of Joking Jesus" (*U* 1.584–99).[21] James F. Carens discovered and published the complete text of another ballad, also by Gogarty, the "superbly obscene 'Song of Medical Dick and Medical Davy'."[22] This work, now in the Cornell University collection of Joyceana, is the original version from which the Ulyssean lines are taken. The gist of the four-stanza piece is Davy's claim that his rival's "Bloody Big Prick" would not, by the women of their choice, be rated above his own "Buckets of Gravy." (Those excerpts from the opening stanza permit the astute student of poetic form to deduce not only the level and tone of the ballad's discourse, but also its ABAB + refrain rhyme scheme.) The song concludes with the following stanza:

> Every bullock were a bull
> But for the little matter of ballocks
> If your prick can keep the women full
> You'll find they'll never grumble at its small looks
> To show [—to show—to show what Medicals are].

The similarity of theme between Gogarty's song and Mulligan's pompous Latin sentence is obvious. Moreover, bulls are everywhere in "Oxen of the Sun," the chapter in which the pseudo-Ciceronian passage occurs. In the last paragraph of that episode a definitive allusion to the song appears: "*Ut implerentur scripturae.* Strike up a ballad. Then outspake medical Dick to his comrade medical Davy" (*U* 14.1577–78). The "scriptures" that are to be "fulfilled" here—and the verb is certainly meant to be interpreted on various levels—are Gogarty/Mulligan's own lines from the song.

What is of primary significance, however, for my argument in this article is not the content, but the context of this obscene song. The opening section of the four-column missive reads:

To
James Augustine Joyce
this work is
Dedicated
as I wish to have before my work
the holder of the highest of
contemporary names and the
hugest of contemporary tools.

Flanking this dedication are two flying phalluses, both with appended tes-ticles. It would be foolish to attempt to parley this dedication into either an assignment of the song's rival roles ("Dick" and "Davy") to Gogarty and Joyce or to engage in any psychosexual speculation about their relationship: a dirty song is a dirty song. But there is more. Immediately after this "dedication," Gogarty adds an involved sentence of proleptic apology for failure "to sustain that passion and lyric ardour which breaks into music" and asks to be "cred-ited with good intention and accredited with a place among those mighty minds who have unsparingly endeavoured before the world to show what medicals are." Having given this preview of his topic and a hint of its refrain, Gogarty inscribes the four stanzas of the "Song."

Then comes a final page-and-a-quarter of "Notes," from which I quote the following excerpts:

No details diminish the naked and
sublime conception of the protagonists.

. . . in the mannerism of the opening of Stanza 11 'out spoke'
compare Homer:—

τὸν δὲ ἀμειβομενος προσέφη
πòδας ὦκυς Ἀχιλλευς
[some accent marks are neglected or incorrect; rhythm also askew]

line iii [of Stanza II] Carefully observe the deprecatory past
subjunctive tense in the "I'd swap" for "I would swap."

The name too is symbolical,
Did not the stones of David [cf. *U* 9.1185]
overcome the ponderous Goliath?

Stanza III notice the catalepsis

Stanza IV Idyllic
Vergilian or Theocritian influence [—]
returns to nature the brave Davy [—]
overwhelming scorn and satire.

Maybe this is the sort of thing one did to impress one's tutors at T.C.D.—or to flummox the *viva*-board when trying for a First in the "great go." More likely, this parody of a learned commentary on an ancient text is Gogarty's way of reminding the benighted Joyce of the critical necessity of maintaining a high-level classical knowledge. Hence the presence of "catalepsis,"[23] a Homeric verse ("then in answering him swift-footed Achilles spoke out") in the original, and "Vergilian and Theocritian influences." In short, the antique patina of these notes—of which the showy Greek script is emblematic—is typical of Gogarty.

Now, I assume that Gogarty sent this song to Joyce sometime during their preexilic friendship, and that Joyce undoubtedly enjoyed its unabashed ribaldry. Later, however, after their friendship soured, I suggest that Joyce went back to the song and saw an opportunity to use it in *Ulysses* in two related, but distinct, ways. First, the direct quotation at *U* 9.908–9 and very close paraphrase at *U* 14.1577–78 are clear evidence that he had the text at hand. Moreover, there is a superscription (in what looks like Joyce's handwriting) across the opening of Gogarty's dedication, just beneath his [Joyce's] own name: "Scorner of Mediocrity & Scourger of the Rabblement." In these two epithets, I detect disdain, not so much for the crude, medical-student, "kips" humor in Gogarty's song, but for the self-aggrandizing manner of its presentation. The author of *Ulysses* has passed beyond this sort of creation, and its creator. Second, just as Joyce transmuted the real Gogarty into the fictional Mulligan, he also saw an opportunity retrospectively to mock the pretension of "literary medicals" by returning to Gogarty's "Song" and its contention that penis length is not the crucial factor in a woman's sexual preference.

Joyce's literary "reprise" of this ballad by Gogarty is, of course, Mulligan's periodic Latin sentence at the maternity hospital: Roman matrons reject centurions' sky-high erections for the titillations of barbarian half-men. Why they do so is not, in this passage, directly tied to Gogarty's thesis that the amount of sperm ejaculated is the most significantly pleasing factor.[24] Rather, it seems to me that Joyce is here—as elsewhere in the chapter—inverting the "fertility" motif of "Oxen of the Sun" by suggesting that women want (and will get) sexual satisfaction without danger of constant and repetitive conception: "Copulation without population!" (*U* 14.1422). Thus, women resort to potent but infertile "eunuchs." Joyce's contraceptive bias is well known;[25] there is also archival evidence that he had a Latin source—particularly appropriate in this context—for the preferences of his Roman matrons. In his preliminary notes for *Ulysses* Joyce wrote, "Roman wives prefer eunuchs."[26] This claim appears to be a synopsis of a slightly garbled couplet from the Roman epigrammatist Martial, which Joyce cited in *Scribbledehobble*.[27] The correct lines (and translation) are:

Cur tantum eunuchos habeat tua Caelia, quaeris,
Pannyche? vult futui Caelia nec parere. (Martial 6.57)

(Pannychus, do you ask why your Caelia has only eunuchs?
Caelia wants to get fucked, not to get pregnant.)

A brief summary: one of Mulligan's primary characteristics in *Ulysses* is his advertisement of his mastery of the classics, especially Greek; this fictional emphasis is consistent with the status of his model, Gogarty, as a man of "tone"[28] from T.C.D. and two terms at Oxford; Joyce uses Mulligan's portentous citation of Greek as a mild means of deflating both the fictional character and the model; the Latin language (in real life and in *A Portrait of the Artist as a Young Man* and *Ulysses*) is the forte of James Joyce/Stephen Dedalus; thus, when the longest and most impressive Latin quotation in the entire novel is put into Mulligan's mouth, Joyce must be up to something. I suggest that Joyce is using Gogarty's "Song of Medical Dick and Medical Davy"[29] as a pretext for the phallocentric topic of Mulligan's Ciceronian sentence, and that Gogarty's mock-classical commentary also contributed to the fun.

To support my last contention, note a pair of lexical parallels between Mulligan's Latin and Gogarty's English: "*sublime* conception": "sublimis[30] *erectionibus*"; "*ponderous* Goliath": "*testibus* ponderosis" (my emphases).[31] I admit that these two similarities may be due to a common theme and are not, of themselves, proof that Joyce was selecting some material from Gogarty's "Notes." There are several other vocabulary items in the Latin passage that need comment. Joyce's manuscripts and typescripts show several stages in the composition of these lines.[32] None of the changes in vocabulary (for example, "*ponderosis*" for "*pergravibus*," "*matresfamiliarum*" [note "ᵀmatres familiarum" {*UNBM* 209: 64}] for "*matronae*") is significant. The substitution of "*semiviri*" for "*spadonis*"[33] is typical and probably indicates that Joyce's purpose in revision was to select genuine Latin synonyms the meanings of which would be more apparent to a lay reader.[34]

In the first draft, the word *libici* appears as *Libycci* (or *Libyeci*) (V.A.12.18); in all subsequent versions, it is *libici*, as in the text of *Ulysses*. The uppercase version with a *y* (*Libyci*) means a North African, a Libyan;[35] the spelling with an uppercase L and an *i* (*Libici*) is found only once in Latin (Pliny, *Natural History* 3.17.124) for the inhabitants of Gallia Transpadena; the lowercase form as it appears in *Ulysses* (*libici*) is not a Latin word. (Joyce is, however, careless in his capitalization of proper words.) The rhetorical function of the adjective is obviously to set up a cultural contrast with *Romanorum*; hence I translate *libici* as "barbarian," without specifying his geographic locus.

Before I leave the word *libici*, however, I want to try my hand at what a nineteenth-century Oxonian classicist would surely regard as the highest calling of a philologist: a stab at textual emendation—second-guessing the generations of manuscript scribes, and perhaps the author himself. In Gogarty's

"Song" the "protagonists" are distinguished by, on the one hand, "a Bloody Big Prick," and, on the other, "Buckets of Gravy." A Latin adjective for "wet," "slippery," "doused with 'gravy'," is *lubricus, -a, -um*. If one were to modify Mulligan's *semiviri* with an emended *lubrici* instead of the received *Libycci* or *libici*, then one would create an exact parallel between song and sentence: "gravy" would not merely endure, but prevail.

In the abstract, the vocabulary variants of Mulligan's sentence are of interest only to the most specialized critic of the evolution of Joycean texts and/or Latin lexicography. This does not mean that the "history" of this text is not significant. Joyce is recalling Gogarty's obscene song and the attendant commentary not to honor, but to mock, its author. The essential evidence for that motive lies in a basic point of Latin grammar, the mood of the final verb in the sentence, *anteponunt*. This word emphatically terminates the result/consecutive clause that is introduced by *ut* and signaled by the prominent *Talis ac tanta*. In Latin of any age, all such clauses take the subjunctive mood; Mulligan's sentence, from Joyce's first draft through all typed versions and printed editions, has *anteponunt*, in the undeviatingly indicative mood.

As I see it, there are two possible explanations for this basic error in elementary Latin grammar:

1. James Joyce, whose command of Latin was superb, made this error as he composed the sentence, and did not correct it through several handwritten and typed revisions, even though he made other adjustments of format and diction of the sentence.[36]

2. That same James Joyce *intended* the basic mistake in Latin grammar, and *intended* it to reflect on Gogarty/Mulligan's competence in that ancient language. He designed a pratfall right at the end of the major performance by his *grammaticus gloriosus.*

Joyce must have relished the fact that the mistake was not detected by Gogarty (who probably would have found a way to impute the error to Joyce, and never admit that the author of *Ulysses* carefully planned the characterizing gaffe) or any other critic. There may even be some cryptic indication that Joyce wanted to direct attention to the passage:

Latin me that, my trinity scholard, out of eure sanscreed into oure eryan! Hircus Civis Eblanensis! He had buckgoat paps on him. (*FW* 215.26–27)

This is a challenge to a scholar of Trinity to translate something into Latin. The "-lard" at the end of "scholard" and his "paps" seem to suggest that the translator was plump. Gogarty himself, by the way, testifies to his gain in weight: when he sends a photograph to his Worcester College comrade (and rival for the Newdigate), he remarks that the picture was taken "before I became mentally and physically 'pinguis' in Oxford."[37] The Latin adjective is a typical touch in Gogarty's firsthand admission of his increased girth at just the time he and Joyce were in the Martello tower—and a coy reminder that he was not, after all, mentally lean and hungry when he composed his *proxime accessit* verses. Be that as it may, *Hircus* in the citation above is Latin for "he-goat," "buck"; Joyce's "buck-goat of the city of Dublin" has flabby pectorals. In short, this intertestamental (*Ulysses-Wake*) parallel involves T.C.D., Latin scholarship and translation, and a plump he-goat. The concatenation of motifs cannot be coincidence, although I grant that, in its *Wake* context, the passage (like everything else in that text) is more than just another jab at Gogarty. But a jab at Gogarty/Mulligan it is, and Joyce lands the blow on a pugnacious and—at least since the indicative in *anteponunt*—exposed classical chin.[38]

This minor exercise in linguistic snobbery and grammatical Gogarty-bashing is presented as offering additional insight into how—and why—Joyce transformed his autobiography and diverse source material into art in *Ulysses*. The classics, Joyce's Latin and Gogarty's Greek and Latin, are important participants in that process, a process that was directed by a design more subtle and fundamental than allusion to ancient authors or Homeric schemata. There is something cosmically ironic, then, in the two books that were on Joyce's desk the day he died: Oliver St. John Gogarty's *I Follow St. Patrick* and a Greek Lexicon, perhaps to help decipher the learned quotations (*JJII* 742).

3

Roman History and Culture

"The Apache Chief! Is this what you read instead of studying your Roman History?" The outraged speaker is Father Butler, history master at Belvedere College. He has just apprehended Leo Dillion devoting his attention to "the glory of the Wild West" rather than to the grandeur that was Rome (*D* 20). Although the young James Joyce was not immune to the thrill of adventure tales, it is improbable that so conscientious a young scholar as he could have been found guilty of the same offense. At Belvedere prescribed texts and periods of Roman history were part of the national-examination curriculum, and that part in which Joyce usually did particularly well. The studious Stephen Dedalus early in *Portrait* is a more likely true-to-life reflection of the author than "clumsy" Dillion cited above. Early in his stay at Clongowes Wood College, Stephen is confident that the rector would exonerate him, because "the senate and the Roman people" always backed those who had been wrongly punished. He has read "all about those men and what they did and that was what Peter Parley's Tales about Greece and Rome were all about" (*P* 53).[1]

My purpose in this chapter is to discuss Joyce's use of the history of ancient Rome in his later works, especially in *Finnegans Wake*. The most frequently cited ancient author is Livy, but there are scattered references to such major figures as Caesar, Sallust, and Tacitus. Joyce read selections from all of these writers in the original Latin. There is also archival evidence that he was aware of the special emphases of several of his foremost sources for historical detail: "Hist. Suetonius (his) / Livy (speeches) / Caesar (military)" (VI.C.5.59). Moreover, despite a quirky disclaimer, Joyce was well read in the standard modern treatments of Roman civilization, from the basic *The Student's Rome* to Momsen's authoritative *Provinces of the Roman Empire* and Ferrero's five-volume *Grandezza e decadenza di Roma.*[2] For example, the following is the topic assigned for the essay portion of Joyce's Second University Examination (Summer 1901) at University College:

Show the relative positions held by the armies of Otho and Vitellius on the day before the battle of Bedriacum [A.D. 69], and discuss the plans and movements entered upon by the Othonianists on the day of battle.[3]

Joyce's grade for his treatment of this topic does not survive; but even to know where to begin a discussion of the tactics of the Othonianists would be, today, a feat beyond the historical horizons of all but a very few specialists.

For clarity of presentation and precision in reference, this chapter is divided into two sections. In the first part, allusions to the major Latin historical authors are gathered. The second part is a review of general cultural material assigned to several basic periods of Roman history: Monarchy and Early Republic, Late Republic, Empire.

LIVY

There is ample evidence that Joyce wished Titus Livy (mid-first century B.C.– early first century A.D.) to participate in the composition of his own "history of world." The Roman author's massive chronicles were arranged in roughly year-by-year accounts of his nation's history; hence, they are frequently referred to in English as "annals." In *Finnegans Wake* Livy appears as "our herodotary Mammon Lujius in his grand old historiorum . . . bluest book in baile's annals" (*FW* 13.20–22); "the tome of *Liber Lividus*" (*FW* 14.29–30); "Whose annal livves the hoiest" (*FW* 340.21–22); and "through all the annals of our . . . efferfreshpainted livy" (*FW* 452.18–19).

Well before these allusions in the *Wake*, Livy's text made a contribution to one of the fantasies in *Ulysses*. In the midst of the celebration of the coronation of "Leopold the First" in "Circe," the stage directions indicate that *"Bloom with his sceptre strikes down poppies. The instantaneous deaths of many powerful enemies . . . are reported"* (*U* 15.1565–68). Gifford and Seidman annotate this as an allusion to the last king of Rome, the Etruscan interloper Tarquinius Superbus, who was expelled from the city by Brutus and the outraged family of Lucretia. The arrogance of Tarquin's reign was prefigured (so legends claim) by his childhood sport of beheading poppies with the toy scepter.[4] This information is only partially correct. There is no known ancient tale of the king's boyish floral sadism. But Livy's history of Rome tells of an odd response by King Tarquin to his son's request for instructions about how to deal with enemies of the throne. The king did not speak in reply to the messenger; rather, he walked through the palace garden, silently lopping off the heads of tall poppies with his scepter. When the messenger reported the king's behavior, his son understood its implication and executed their enemies.[5]

In his last year at Belvedere College Joyce's Latin course included Livy, book 5. There is no external evidence that he read the Latin text of book 1, in which the Tarquin-poppy message occurs. On the other hand, in the 1894 Boys Preparatory Examinations, given by the Intermediate Education Board for Ireland, Joyce won a £20 prize-exhibition. His highest mark (700 out of 1200) was in Latin. In addition to the standard exercises in grammar, composition, and translation, he was required to write an essay about "early Republican history." The primary original source for this period of Rome's development is Livy's annals, and it is quite likely that Joyce read about Tarquin's cryptic response while preparing for the exam. Stories about Tarquin, especially about the tacit eloquence of his scepter, are also just the sort of anecdotal diversions used by skillful teachers to resuscitate a Latin class after a deadly session of grinding gerunds. There is, however, an equally likely literary source, for which we have Joyce's own testimony of familiarity with the text.

Well before James Joyce (or Stephen Dedalus) would have been assigned readings in the Latin text or an English version of Livy's *Ab Urbe Condita*, the author (and his fictional counterpart) pored over "a ragged translation of *The Count of Monte Cristo*" (*P* 62). Stephen's boyhood fantasies about Mercedes and the "sadly proud gesture of refusal . . . —Madam, I never eat muscatel grapes" are as memorable as the "wonderful island cave" made out of paper "on the parlour table" (*P* 62–63). In one of the later chapters of Dumas' novel, M. de Villefort decides to exact full punishment from his wife for her crimes: "and in a gloomy mood, similar to that in which Tarquin lopped off the tallest poppies, he [Villefort] began knocking off with his cane the long and dying branches of the rose-trees."[6]

Since Joyce knew the works of Livy and Dumas, it would normally be impossible to decide which (or both?) he had in mind when referring to the "sceptre" and the "poppies" at Bloom's coronation. There is, however, a decisive internal clue in the next sentence of the *Ulysses* passage: "The instantaneous deaths of many powerful enemies" (*U* 15.1566–67). In Dumas' novel the punishment of a *single* woman is contemplated by her husband, "le juge"; in Livy, *many* leaders of the state (of the Gabii) are reported to have been treacherously slain (*primores civitatis. . . . Multi . . . interfecti* [1.54.8–9]) after the poppy-message has been decoded by Tarquin's son. This bit of textual specificity, as well as the omission of Tarquin's scepter in the translation from Dumas, argues in favor of Livy as Joyce's primary source for this allusion.

Early in "Telemachus" on the parapet of the tower, Buck Mulligan waxes poetic about the sea. He cites several appropriately classical epithets and then resorts to a brief prose quotation to exhort Stephen that "you must read them in the original. *Thalatta! Thalatta!*" (*U* 1.80; compare *U* 7.254–55). The standard commentaries correctly identify the cry raised by the Greek mercenaries in Xenophon's *Anabasis* (4.7.24) when they breasted the hill and first saw the sea, the source of safety in their desperate retreat from Persia.

There is, however, another, seemingly similar Joycean passage for which a quite different classical source is clearly intended: "and raptist bride is aptist breed (tha lassy! tha lassy!)" (*FW* 328.28–29). Here Joyce is alluding to the rape of the Sabine women, as narrated by Roman historian Livy in the first book of his annals. Romulus and his comrades suffered from a shortage of brides, since Rome's neighbors scorned the city's humble origins and feared her potential power. The first Romans therefore invited people from nearby communities to celebrate the solemn festival of the Consualia inside their walls:

> At a given signal all the able-bodied men burst through the crowd and seized the young [Sabine] women. Most of the girls were the prize of whoever got hold of them first, but a few conspicuously handsome ones had been previously marked down for leading senators, and these were brought to their houses by special gangs. There was one young woman of much greater beauty than the rest; and the story goes that she was seized by a party of men belonging to the household of someone called Thalassius [*Thalassi*], and in reply to the many questions about whose house they were taking her to, they, to prevent anyone else laying hands upon her, kept shouting, "Thalassius, Thalassius!" [*Thalassio*] This was the origin of the use of the word at weddings.[7]

Despite initial resentment by the victims of the outrage and their families, the children born from these inauspiciously inaugurated unions tied the Sabine women to their Roman men. Thus, in Livy's strange mixture of early Roman sexual barbarism and an etymological explanation of the origins of an ancient Latin wedding chant, Joyce found an analogue to the shenanigans taking place in this section of the *Wake*.[8]

Just before that Livian echo Joyce mentions what seems to be the title of a book, *The Steeplepoy's Revanger* (*FW* 328.27). I suggest a probable allusion to Romulus who worked on a farm and tended flocks until he and a band of herdsmen were able to free Remus from captivity and depose their grand-uncle, Numitor. He was the usurper who had ordered the infant twins to be exposed on the banks of the Tiber. In another passage, there may also be a series of muted references to the Latin text of Livy's version of the Romulus and Remus legend. It begins with their "flock" of comrades and ends with

Remus' insult to Romulus' rising city walls, an act of defiance for which the rampart-leaping brother died at his twin's hand:

gregarious (*FW* 99.21) : *et cum his crescente in dies grege iuvenum* (1.4.9) (and with these men a flock of young men which was growing day by day).

fortitudo fraught or prudentiaproven (*FW* 99.23) : *hinc robore corporibus animisque sumpto* (1.4.9) (from this source strength was added to their bodies and minds).

place of inauguration on the hill (*FW* 99.26) : *Palatium Romulus, Remus Aventinum ad inaugurandum templa capiunt* (1.6.4) (for taking their auguries, Romulus marked out a sacred space on the Palatine Hill, while Remus occupied the Aventine).

real [that is, "royal"] murder (*FW* 99.27) : *ita regem obtruncant* (1.5.7) (thus they slew the king).

rampart combatants (*FW* 99.29) : *Remum novos transiluisse muros* (1.7.2) (Remus had leapt over the new walls of the city).

According to Roman tradition Romulus did not die. Rather, from the Campus Martius (Livy 1.16.1) or from a grove on the Palatine Hill (Ovid *Metamorphoses* 14.816–25) he was assumed into the heavens in a thick cloud. There he was vested in the robes and form of the god Quirinus. Thus, in an extraordinarily rare change of status—Hercules is an example from the Greek world—Romulus earned posthumous immortality. Joyce links this miraculous final stage of the earthly life of Romulus with his equally blessed rescue as an infant by the nurturing she-wolf: "Hillcloud encompass us! You mean you lived as milky at their lyceum, couard, while you learned, volp volp, to howl yourself wolfwise" (*FW* 480.26–28). The Greco-Latin adjective *lyceus* is associated with wolves; "couard" may also be meant to recall the period when Romulus served as a stableman or *cowherd* (also note "you lived as a milky") while waiting to reclaim his royal heritage.

A short index in an early Notebook also strongly suggests that Joyce jotted down the following entries while referring to a text of Livy—or, perhaps, to a source that was extensively quoting from the Latin author: "[b]gaulish moustaches / pulls senators beard / [b]Brennanus Vae Victis / falsed balance" (VI.B.4.141). Livy concludes the first book of his annals with a detailed account of the disaster that struck Rome as the result of the Gauls' capture of the city after the Battle of Allia (390 B.C.). A small cohort of Roman soldiers withdrew to a final redoubt on the Capitoline Hill, but the city itself lay open to the victorious barbarians. A group of older magistrates and senators vowed to await death in their stately mansions near the Forum. When the barbarians saw these dignitaries in their purple-trimmed togas, seated majestically on the inlaid chairs of office, they were dumbfounded. Some thought they were almost in the presence of the gods. Finally, one barbarian dared to tug the beard of a Senator, and was struck over the head by the outraged official's ivory baton. A slaughter of the defenseless citizens ensued and the city was burned (Livy 5.41).

That episode is the source of Joyce's first Notebook entry cited above. In fact, Livy explicitly states that "long beards were grown by all [the Senators] at that time" (Livy 5.41.9), perhaps to heighten the contrast between this Roman tonsorial flourish and the more modest Gallic moustaches. The Notebook entry that refers to the latter feature is also crossed out and reappears, untouched, in the text of "Night Lessons" as "gaulish moustaches" (FW 291.23–24).

The commander of the marauding Gauls was named Brennanus. He negotiated with the Romans for the surrender of the besieged and starving Capitoline garrison, and demanded a thousand pounds of gold for its ransom. Livy reports that "An ultimate insult was added to this most disgraceful affair: the weights brought by the Gauls were heavier than standard." When the Roman officer protested, Brennanus tossed his iron sword into the balance and spoke "those words which are intolerable to any Roman, Vae victis" (Woe to those who have been conquered) (Livy 5.48.9). The third Notebook entry gives the barbarian leader's name and his retort. It is used in the text four lines after the previous crossed entry, in a slightly different Latin form: "Vae Vinctis" (FW 292.1). The addition of "n" to the second word significantly changes its meaning. It is no longer a perfect passive participle from vinco, vincere, but now must be derived from an entirely different Latin verb, vincio, vincire. Hence, the altered spelling yields "Woe to those who have been tied up." It may seem rash to suggest that there is a leap from early Roman history to sexual bondage here, but three nearby phrases support a suspicion that malice aforethought lies behind Joyce's kinky switch in Latin conjugation: "that batch of grim rushes" (FW 292.3), which suggests birching; "heaven help his hindermost" (FW 292.3–4), which reinforces that suggestion; and a salacious periodical that reports the perversion, "Spice and Westend Woman" (FW 292.6).

The last entry in the Notebook index ("falsed balance") certainly refers to Livy's report that Brennanus and the Gauls used false weights to increase the value of their gold ransom. That insult, however, is not the end of the affair. The besieged warriors on the Capitoline did not, in fact, have to surrender in disgrace. A rescue column of Roman legionnaires entered the city at the last minute. In a metallic figure of speech that reverses the mockery of the Gallic sword flung on top of the ransom, Camillus, the Roman general of the deliverers, exhorted his troops "to recover their fatherland by cold steel not gold" (Livy 5.49.3). They did so, and the Gauls fled.

Before I leave the sack of Rome by the Gauls, it is possible to point out another Wakean echo of Livy's vivid narrative. Only a few Roman troops had survived the slaughter in the pitched battle against the invading Gauls at Allia. As mentioned above, they retreated to the Capitoline Hill, the religious citadel of the city. There they could defend what was left of gods, men, and the reputation of Rome (Livy 5.39.10). One night during the siege, Gallic commandos tried to scale the steep sides of the Capitoline. They escaped the notice of the sentries and their guard dogs, but they did not slip by the sacred geese of Juno. The goddess's hallowed fowls were being fed even during the utmost scarcity of provisions for the troops themselves. Warned by the honking and wing-beating of the geese, the Romans threw the Gauls off the capital city's most holy hill (Livy 5.47). I detect the slurred presence of these sacred geese in a pseudoliturgical passage at the end of Jaun's sermon: "Sacred ease there!" (FW 454.34). A formal civic Roman context for this phrase is established by the next line in the text: "The seanad and the pobbel queue's remainder" (The Senate and the Roman People, S.P.Q.R.) (FW 454.35). Later in the Wake the divine patroness of the geese is commemorated in an oath, "by Juno Moneta" (FW 538.1). The goddess's epithet here (from moneo, "to remind," "to advise") is more probably a function of her role as mother of the Muses than the "warning" that her geese gave. At any rate, the temple of Juno Moneta, near Jupiter's on the Capitoline, was the place where money was traditionally coined. Hence the English adjective "monetary," which has lost all connection with the events of the Gallic commando raid.

Finally, there is an archival reference to Livy that seems to have influenced the final text of "Oxen of the Sun." The crossed entry is "ʳWoman 9 yrs island conceives (Livy)" (UNBM 213: 50). Nowhere in Livy's annals is there anything like an anecdote about a miraculous conception by a woman on a [deserted?] island for a long period. Joyce's note appears in the midst of a combination of Latin phrases and obstetrical references. There may be some undetected source for this data—and the incorrect attribution to Livy. At any rate, there appears to be an indistinct echo of the note at the beginning of the "embryonic development" chapter of Ulysses. A man arrives at the National Maternity Hospital who "ere was living with dear wife and lovesome daughter that then over land and seafloor nine years had long outwandered. . . . Her to forgive now he craved" (*U* 14.87–88; compare 120–22). One must presume that the offense that the returning husband craves to forgive is the sinful occasion (during his considerable absence at sea) that brought his dear wife to the hospital.

CAESAR

The triumvir and historian Gaius Julius Caesar (100–44 B.C.) is clearly referred to in the margin of the biographical essay-topics section of "Night Lessons": "*Julius Caesar*" (*FW* 306.L). The suggested theme is "Is the Pen Mightier than the Sword?" (*FW* 306.18–19). The famous general-author crops up all over the *Wake*. As strange as it may sound, the single word "seesaw" (*FW* 4.33) has just as valid claim to be a direct allusion to the Roman triumvir as the apparently obvious title, "Sire Jeallyous Seizer" (*FW* 271.3). The latter is surrounded by "Cliopatria" (271.L1) and the members of the Second Triumvirate, "Oxtheivious, Lapidous and Malthouse Anthemy" (Octavian Augustus, Lepidus, Mark Antony) (*FW* 271.5–6). Thus, there is no doubt of a primary allusion to the Roman dictator. But there was also a real-life, true-born Englishman, Sir Julius Caesar. This sixteenth/seventeenth century jurist earned a knighthood for his legal service to the Crown and his legendary generosity.[9] The noun "seesaw" (*FW* 4.33), on the other hand, needs explication. It is closely associated with HCE in context, and there is another Caesarian name nearby, "Caligulate" (*FW* 4.32). These factors must be viewed in the light of a Notebook entry "Seesaw (Caesar)" (VI.B.8.107 and VI.C.13.81). Archival evidence, then, marks the apparently frivolous "seesaw" as a bit of Joycean wordplay on the cognomen—and perhaps a comment on the volatile political career—of Julius Caesar. As will be discussed on pages 69–70 below, this Notebook item might also be connected with a bizarre event in the life of the third Roman emperor, Gaius Caesar (Caligula).

In Latin the title of Caesar's most famous work is *Libri VII De Bello Gallico* (Seven Books about the War in Gaul). For generations selections from these war commentaries have been the first real Latin texts that students read. Hackneyed passages are assigned in most classes after an initial year devoted to the fundamentals of the language. The title of this work has naturally been the object of repeated schoolboy parody and derision. Stephen Dedalus reports that a fellow student at Clongowes Wood College inscribed, "in backhand in beautiful writing," the following graffito on the wall of a toilet closet: "Julius Caesar wrote The Calico Belly" (*P* 43).

Probably the most famous of all statements in Latin literature is Caesar's three-word summary of the speedy completion of the Pontic campaign: *veni, vidi, vici* (I came, I saw, I conquered) (Suetonius, *Julius Caesar* 37). Joyce reproduced two, nearly adjacent, semi-Latin versions of the motto: "Velivision victor" (*FW* 610.35) and "Winny Willy Widger" (*FW* 610.36); the latter is articulated according to the "restored" pronunciation in which the Latin "v" sounds like the English "w." A fully English rendition (with an amorously lisped appropriation of the central verb) also appears during the interrogation of Yawn: "he came, he kished, he conquered" (*FW* 512.8). Another distorted translation is "ulvy came, envy saw, ivy conquered" (*FW* 58.5–6).

Several commentators have also pointed out that the same Leo Dillion who was caught red-handed reading *The Apache Chief* was also tripped up by a reference to Caesar's *Gallic War*. During Roman history class Father Dillon demands "This page? Now, Dillon, up! *Hardly had the day* . . . Go on!" (*D* 20; Joyce's ellipsis). The italicized phrase most likely represents a partial translation of *prima luce* (at the crack of dawn), a formulaic phrase for daybreak that occurs frequently in Caesar's account of his wars in Gaul.

In those campaigns the foremost Roman opponent was the chieftain Vercingetorix, who led the great revolt of the Gallic tribes against the Romans in 52 B.C. After a devastating siege at the fortress of Alesia, he and what was left of his army surrendered (*Bellum Gallicum* 7.1–90). The captive war-leader was led through Rome in Caesar's triumph and then executed. Vercingetorix, at the crack of dawn and on other occasions, makes several appearances in the *Wake*, usually with appropriately barbaric variations of his name: "Farseeingetherich" (*FW* 54.3–4), "Fierceendgiddyex" (*FW* 66.12), "Vercingetorix" (*FW* 88.22), "Valsinggiddyrex" (*FW* 281.F1), "versingrhetorish" (*FW* 346.19), "Farcing gutterish" (*FW* 518.25), "Force in giddersh" (*FW* 617.12). Although Joyce obviously liked to ring all sorts of phonetic changes on this memorable name, I have been able to discover no common thematic or narrative element in the placement of these machinominations. The title of another barbarian chieftain, the annual leader of the Aedui, was Vergobretus (*Bellum Gallicum* 1.16.5). Joyce appropriates his name in "Vergobretas" (*FW* 48.7). The commander of the combined enemy forces during Caesar's second expedition to Britain in 54 B.C. (*Bellum Gallicum* 5.11–22), Cassivellanus, also appears in the *Wake* as "Castlevillainous" (*FW* 77.3).

On the same page of *Portrait* as the graffito cited a few paragraphs ago is the record of some schoolboy art:

And behind the door of one of the closets there was a drawing in red pencil of a bearded man in a Roman dress with a brick in each hand and underneath was the name of the drawing: *Balbus was building a wall.* (*P* 43)

A possible source of inspiration for this minimural is an exercise-sentence in an elementary textbook: "Translate *Balbus murum faciebat.*" On the other hand, there was a fairly prominent Lucius Cornelius Balbus who served for several years in Spain and Gaul as Caesar's *praefectus fabrum* (superintendent of engineers) and was an important political supporter of the triumvir.[10] His lower-case name also appears in the midst of an archival list of references to ancient Roman roads (VI.B.8.106).

Balbus' capability to undertake major construction projects (including the Woolworth building in New York) is clearly signaled and hallowed in his initial appearance in the *Wake:*

> Oft while balbulous, mithre ahead, with goodly trowel in grasp and ivoroiled overalls . . . to raise in undress maisonry upstanded (joygrantit!), a waalworth of a skyerscape. (*FW* 4.30–36; my ellipsis)

Three other appearances emphasize—the first two with distinct liturgical rings to them—his reputation as a master stonemason: "Tower of Balbus" (467.16); "Handwalled amokst us. Thanksbeer to Balbus!" (*FW* 518.33–34); "that was why Balbus was razing his wall" (*FW* 552.19–20).

SALLUST AND TACITUS

These two Roman historians—the one of the late Republic, Sallust (86–53 B.C.); the other of the early Empire, Tacitus (A.D. c56–c115)—are treated together because they were significantly linked by James Joyce. In a March 20, 1920, letter from Trieste to Frank Budgen, Joyce wrote:

> Am working hard at *Oxen of the Sun.* . . . Technique: a nineparted episode without divisions introduced by a Sallustian—Tacitean prelude (the unfertilized ovum). (*Letters* I.139; my ellipsis)

The author's declaration of his classical models for the style of the better part of two pages at the start of the most self-consciously literary chapter of *Ulysses* (*U* 14.7–70) deserves respect. It has, for instance, been taken as gospel by the author of the most influential guide to *Ulysses.*[11] On the other hand, in his 1950 revision of his *Study* of *Ulysses,* Stuart Gilbert, whose Latin prose was polished at Oxford, offered a modest, but definitive, rebuttal to Joyce's "work-in-progress" claim. In a footnote that directly quotes the revelation of "a Sallustian-Tacitean prelude" cited above, Gilbert wrote:

But no style could be further than this [the paragraphs in *Ulysses*] from the concision of Sallust and the epigrammatic brilliancy of Tacitus. A comparison of this letter, written while Joyce was working on the episode, with the printed version shows that he made some changes in his programme, and this is one of them.[12]

Since Joyce cooperated with Gilbert in the preparation of the latter's study of *Ulysses*, one feels that this "revised" version of the literary influences on the opening of "Oxen of the Sun" is authentic. That surmise is backed up by lexicographical data.

The opening paragraphs of "Oxen of the Sun" contain a number of extraordinarily exotic words and phrases. Moreover, the bizarre word-order of this section seems meant to reinforce the illusion that it is some sort of literal translation, perhaps from an ancient language. In the face of normal classroom teaching techniques, a secondary-school Latin lesson might seem to invite just such a parodic treatment. If the style of this section were designed to reflect a specific Latin original, then some of the distinctly foreign vocabulary should be able to be identified as characteristically Sallustian or Tacitean.

The following phrases are certainly grotesque: "the tribute of its solicitude for that proliferant continuance" (*U* 14.14–15); "omnipollent nature's incorrupted benefaction" (*U* 14.16–17); "with prophecy of abundance or with diminution's menace" (*U* 14.30–31); and "parturient in vehicle thereward carrying desire immense" (*U* 14.53). They are, in my judgment, purposefully meant to sound like a typical, but totally botched, translation. The orotundity of the vocabulary has definitely been selected to heave with emanations of thematically appropriate fertility. But a thorough check of the comprehensive lexicon, *Thesaurus Linguae Latinae* (Treasurehouse of the Latin Language), shows that these words—especially the pseudoparticipial "proliferent," "omnipollent," and "parturient"—were never used by Sallust or Tacitus. What's more, they do not occur, in *any* Latin author, in the absurd collocations into which they have been contorted by Joyce. The extremely rare adjective "lutulent" (*U* 14.19) could be a faint echo of a phrase from a text that Joyce knew, *lutulenta . . . sus* (a mud-spattered sow) (Horace *Epistle* 2.2.75). And I will argue for a parody of Cicero's disgust with Mark Antony's public vomiting after a night of carousing in another passage (see page 120). What is certain, however, is that nothing in these intentionally superfecund pages can be shown to be derived *from* the works of Sallust or Tacitus or intended to be an English imitation *of* Sallustian-Tacitean style.

Although Sallust's name must be expunged from the list of writers whose style is parodied in "Oxen of the Sun," the Roman historian does in fact momentarily walk on to the stage of *Ulysses*. Bernard Benstock's recent work on

Ulysses has repeatedly demonstrated that there are few phrases—let alone motifs—that are not significantly connected to other sections of the work.[13] In "Aeolus" Professor MacHugh, a disgruntled teacher of Latin, praises the Greeks as the spiritual lords of Western civilization. He singles out Pyrrhus for his "last attempt to retrieve the fortunes of Greece. Loyal to a lost cause" (*U* 7.567–70). Lenehen sniggers at MacHugh's pedantic sentimentality, then whispers a mildly mocking limerick in Stephen Dedalus' ear. In the passage there is another comment on the situation: "In mourning for Sallust, Mulligan says. Whose mother is beastly dead" (*U* 7.583–84).

Why Mulligan thinks that MacHugh should be in mourning for the Roman historian is not explained, nor does there appear to be any logical connection between Sallust, MacHugh, and the dead Mrs. Dedalus. That line of critical inquiry, however, follows a false clue. In fact, Buck Mulligan is not present in the office of the *Telegraph* during this episode. The last comment cited above, then, is meant to be understood as Stephen's *recollection* of some previous remark by Mulligan, a remark that has some bearing on the present situation. The case for this brief introspective intrusion into the newspaper-office dialogue is supported by the present tense of the contextual verb "says"; the words of the other speakers are reported in the past tense. The direct-address dash used throughout the episode is also omitted. Earlier in the novel Mulligan has been quoted as speaking insensitively about Stephen's dead mother: "— You said, Stephen answered, *O, it's only Dedalus whose mother is beastly dead*" (*U* 1.198–99; Joyce's emphasis). But there is nothing to suggest a Sallustian allusion here, or in the reprise of this motif in "Circe" (*U* 15.4170–80).

Back to "Aeolus," then, and to another statement by MacHugh that Stephen has just overheard:

—We were always loyal to lost causes, the professor said. Success for us is the death of the intellect and of the imagination. We were never loyal to the successful. We serve them. I teach the blatant Latin language. . . . Where is the spirituality? . . . But the Greek. (*U* 7.553–59; my ellipses)

Not long afterward MacHugh continues in the same vein:

They [the Greeks] went under. Pyrrhus, misled by an oracle, made a last attempt to retrieve the fortunes of Greece. Loyal to a lost cause. (*U* 7.568–70)

These two pronouncements establish Professor MacHugh as a frustrated booster for the glory that was Greece. They also provide a plausible context for explaining the connections between the several (apparently unrelated) motifs introduced by Stephen's recollection of Mulligan's comment. In a previous chapter, I demonstrated that Buck Mulligan (and Oliver St. John Gogarty) shared MacHugh's conviction of the superiority of Greek culture. They are Hellenosnobs. That attitude is one of the contextual links between MacHugh's lament and Stephen's recollection of Mulligan's comment. The following are two other elements involved in the allusive enthymeme.

Pyrrhus' military confidence in an oracle and his own academic position as a teacher of "blatant Latin" are MacHugh's two examples of lost causes. Mulligan's attempt to excuse his offensive remark about Stephen's mother must be introduced as a factor in explaining the "logic" of that recollection. Mulligan had defended himself with a medical student's paraprofessional dismissal of death: "It's a beastly thing and nothing else. It simply doesn't matter" (*U* 1.206–7). He continues by deriding Stephen's refusal to kneel and pray at his mother's deathbed: "Why? Because you have the cursed jesuit strain in you, only it's injected the wrong way. To me it's all a mockery and beastly" (*U* 1.208–10). Both Mrs. Dedalus' appeal to her son's filial piety and Stephen's rejection of his mother's dying wish are, to Mulligan, equally *lost causes.* In the newspaper office, Stephen associates these two conscience-gnawing events with the group's underhand mockery of Professor MacHugh's classical pedantry and academic frustration.

The final link in this long chain of evidence, which began several pages ago as an attempt to explain the presence of Sallust in "Aeolus," is that Roman historian's reputation as a frustrated politician. After loyal service to the cause of Julius Caesar in the final years of the Republic, Sallust retired from public life and devoted himself as an embittered private citizen to writing history, rather than making history. The Ides of March, 44 B.C., would have brought home to Sallust the conclusive fact that his long dedication to Caesar's faction was a lost cause. All the motifs of futility that I have been discussing are brought together in a scene set in Mr. Deasy's school. Stephen Dedalus reflects on a botched lesson in Roman history:

—End of Pyrrhus, Sir? . . . Had Pyrrhus not fallen by a beldam's hand in Argos or Julius Caesar not been knifed to death . . . to Caesar what is Caesar's, to God what is God's. . . . Ugly and futile. . . . Yet someone had loved him, borne him in her arms and in her heart. . . . *Amor matris:* subjective and objective genitive. (*U* 2.19–166; my ellipses)

The reference to "Pyrrhus' end" at "a beldam's hand" needs a final—and maternal—comment. The famous Greek general was killed, according to tradition, when the mother of a soldier whom he had just slain in a battle on a city street hit him on the head with a roofing tile.[14] In short, MacHugh's thwarted academic ambition, Mrs. Dedalus' pious petitions to her son, the density of Stephen's pupils, Pyrrhus' ignominious death, *and* Sallust's dashed political career are all "lost causes," tenuously linked in the newspaper office.

As for Sallust himself, only two of his works survive; one deals with the conspiracy of Catiline, the other is an account of the war that the Romans waged in North Africa against Jugurtha.[15] The only other reference to Sallust that I have detected is an invocation of the conniving and bellicose king of Numidia at the beginning of Book III.1 of the *Wake,* "Gugurtha! Gugurtha!" (*FW* 403.12–13).

Having said just about all that can be said about Sallust and lost causes, I now turn to the presence of a far more important Roman historian in the works of Joyce. Tacitus is best known for his two larger works on the development of the early Empire. The *Annals* cover the period (though some sections are lost) from the principate of Augustus to the turmoil after the assassination of Nero (A.D. 69). The *Histories* (again incomplete) deal with events up to the murder of the Emperor Domitian (A.D. 96). Two shorter works of Tacitus are also frequently read in schools, especially in England and Germany. *Agricola* is a record of the early stages of Roman imperial rule in Britain by a general who was also Tacitus' father-in-law. *Germania* is a description of the customs of the barbarian tribes who settled east of the Rhine and north of the Danube.

There is an apparent reference to the historian's name and occupation in "Taciturn pretells" (*FW* 17.3). McHugh suggests that the next phrase in the *Wake's* text, "our wrongstory shortener" (*FW* 17.3–4) alludes to the fact that Tacitus, whose style is notoriously concise, mentions Irish ("our") prehistory in his *Agricola.* Indeed, in section 24 of that work Tacitus compactly reports that General Agricola pacified that portion of Britain which looks across the sea to Hibernia. Tacitus estimates that one legion and modest support troops would be enough to pacify the adjacent island. He goes on to speculate that, if Roman arms and the "freedom" they ensure were to be taken away from Britain, Ireland would challenge its larger neighbor. The Citizen-barkeep in "Cyclops," usually regarded as an ignorant jingoist, is aware of this classical source for early Irish history. In the midst of a paragraph of fairly exotic details and sources, he advises his claque: "Read Tacitus and Ptolemy (*U* 12.1250–51).[16]

Using that uncharacteristic display of historical erudition as support, I suggest another echo from *Agricola* in "Cyclops." Its source is the memorable epigram which is put into the mouth of a British war-leader who is exhorting his people to oppose the Romans. He claims that the invaders' "imperial domination is a false name for looting, butchery, and rape. Where they make a desert, they call it peace" (*Agricola* 30.7). When the Citizen and his cronies are harassing Bloom, the "Arranger" reports that they mill "round him like a leprechaun trying to peacify him. —Let me alone, says he" (*U* 12.1786–88). Tacitus' text reads *ubi solitudinem faciunt, pacem appellant*. A claim for direct Latin allusion here may seem stretched to the outer limits. The assailants' verb "peacify" is odd-sounding, whereas the victim's plea for self-protective solitude is natural. There can, however, be no doubt that Joyce had Tacitus' original phrase in mind while he was composing "Cyclops." In his Notesheets for that chapter of *Ulysses,* he jotted down the following entry: "Solitudinem faciunt et pacem appellant" (*UNBM* 101: 62).

Tacitus also records that General Agricola received an Irish prince who had been exiled by a domestic revolt, and offered him shelter. The kindness was done "under the pretense of friendship," but for possible tactical benefit (*Agricola* 24.3). This incident (only one sentence in Tacitus) is also the topic of an archival entry in one of the *Finnegans Wake* Notebooks: "Agricola received I[rish] chief" (VI.B.6.143). This note, which appears at the beginning of an index of entries on early Irish history, may have left a faint trace in the text: "chief celtich chappy . . . . Outcaste thou are not" (*FW* 237.19–21). But there are far too many contenders for the title "Chief" in Irish history to support a claim for direct Tacitean allusion here.

The *Wake* camouflages several other brief allusions to *Agricola*. The first involves two generic Welsh geographical features and a pair of specific ethological terms: "the craogs and bryns of the Silurian Ordovices" (*FW* 51.28–29). The proper names of the two ancient Welsh tribes are mentioned in a brief Notebook index headed "Wales & Monmouth," followed by four entries: "⁸Silures / Decaigi / ᵇOrdovicus / Demitae" (VI.B.32.112). I do not know the documentary source for this index—indeed, it could come from any general description and history of Wales. On the other hand, whatever the *direct* source of Joyce's information, the *ultimate* authority for the names and dispositions of the Welsh tribes who faced the Roman invaders is certainly Tacitus.

The Roman historian mentions the fierce and swarthy Silures at *Agricola* 17.3. Just a few lines later (18.2) he records the presence of the Ordovici, a wild Welsh tribe whom Tacitus' father-in-law subdued during his first campaign in Britain in A.D. 78. Both of these Cambrian foes of the Romans also appear in another of Tacitus' works. As recorded in the *Annals* 12.32–39, they were stirred into action against the Romans in A.D. 50. I suggest that this latter passage from Tacitus may have influenced Joyce's compound mention of the two Welsh tribes ("the Silurian Ordovices") on the following grounds:

1. Just a few lines before the primary passage in the *Wake*, there appears a weird Joycean town, "Battlecock Shettledore-Juxta-Mare" ("near the sea" in

Latin) (*FW* 51.22–23). This parodic name includes an element that is suspiciously like Tacitus' description of the coast of Wales: *haud procul mari quod Hiberniam insulam aspectat* (not very far from the sea which overlooks the Hibernian island). This bit of geographical specificity is recorded at the start of Tacitus' description of the Roman campaign in Wales (*Annals* 12.32.3). And Ireland is, of course, the "sisterisle" that is mentioned two lines later in Joyce's text (*FW* 51.25).

2. The native war-leader who has roused the Silurians and Ordovicians into action is the redoubtable Caractacus. His name appears throughout the section of Tacitus' *Annals* that I have just cited. It also appears several times in the *Wake*. Once not far from the names of his Welsh allies, in a catalogue of some of Rome's Celtic foes, "the crowd of Caraculacticors" (*FW* 48.7); a second time, "Charachthercuss" (*FW* 54.4), which is adjacent to a corruption of Vercingetorix.

Complicating the matter of which—or whether—Tacitean influence is at work here is another *Wake* passage in which Caractacus appears. The immediate context is a series of post-war "sham bottles . . . as betwinst Picturshirts and Scutticules, like their *caractacurs* in an Irish Ruman" (*FW* 518.21–22; my emphasis). Here Celtic local color in Wales is moved north to where gaudily garbed Picts and wee Scots are going at each other, as fiercely as Caractacus once led his tribes against the Romans in the far west of Britain. What is not immediately evident here is the Latinate word-formation of the Joycean "Scutticules." The suffix "-iculus" is a diminutive; hence the aforementioned Scots are small. The Latin word *scutula* (literally "little shield") has various contextual meanings, such as "small platter," "lozenge-shaped figure or object." It is used by Tacitus to describe the shape of Britain up to Scotland: *formam totius Britanniae . . . oblongae scutulae adsimulavere* (*Agricola* 10.3) (they [previous Roman historians] have compared the outline of all Britain to an oblong, small shield).

The emperor Claudius appointed Aulus Plautius to command a renewed Roman expedition into Britain (*Agricola* 14.1). In Joycean translation, the general becomes "awlus plawshus"; this name appears directly beside that of "happyass cloudius" (Appius Claudius) (*FW* 581.22–23), in a context that is filled with terms associated with roads. Appius Claudius built the famous Via Appia, the primary road from Rome to the south of Italy. It would require radical philological pleading of the first order to point to a Tacitean passage linking these two men. Rather, the source for the first name is biographical: in May 1924 Phyllis Moss (Stein) visited the Joyces and revealed that "during her childhood in Ireland, she had a donkey named Aulus Plautius" (*JJII* 565). A Notebook index supplies the basic information for the road-building career of "8Happyass Cloudius" (VI.B.8.106).[17] Finally, these distorted names were juxtaposed by Joyce not to suggest a classical source, but to create (phonetically if not graphically) both an ALP ("*awlus* *p*lawshaus") and an HCE ("*h*appyass *c*loud*i*ous") acrostic.

The focus of this chapter now shifts from literary historians to a Joycean review of three fundamental periods in Roman history.

MONARCHY AND EARLY REPUBLIC

According to Roman legend, the foundation (and the name) of the city can be traced to Trojan Aeneas' distant descendants, Romulus and Remus. The site of Rome is at a ford over the Tiber River where the twins had been abandoned by their usurping granduncle. After they have reclaimed their royal position and avenged their mistreatment, Romulus and Remus become rivals, not collaborators in the actual foundation of the city. Each seeks a divine sign to certify his primacy. Then they argue over which augury is the more authentic. Finally Remus mocks his brother's ramparts by leaping over their growing courses. For this ultimate personal—and civic—insult, Romulus kills his twin. No one can violate Rome's ramparts with impunity. Throughout its history, Rome's leaders seem fated to repeat that original sin of fratricide. This ill-omened inauguration of the city inspired a Joycean distortion of several aspects of this inauspicious Roman foundation legend: "Seven ills . . . are your hill prospect" (*FW* 541.1–2).

In my earlier discussion of the possible references to the Latin text of Livy, those elements in Rome's foundation-legend were examined in some detail. There are, in addition, several more general references to the heroic twins in the *Wake*: "O'Remus pro Romulo" (*FW* 122.9), in which we are exhorted to pray (*oremus* in Latin) for Romulus; "reconciled Romas and Reims" (*FW* 209.25), in which the twins—one Italian, one French—are civically rejoined. "Roamaloose and Rehmoose" (*FW* 236.19); "rheasilvar ormolus" (*FW* 467.35), in which the twin's priestess-mother, Rhea Silvia, appears with one of her sons; "Romunclus Remus" (*FW* 525.33–34), in which the fictional narrator of nineteenth-century American, black-dialect folktales makes a compounded appearance.

One of the phrases cited just above appears within a list of all seven kings of Rome:

"prisckly" (*FW* 467.32): Tarquinius Priscus, fifth king
"numan" (*FW* 467.33): Numa Pompilius, second king
"ancomartins" (*FW* 467.33): Ancus Martius, fourth king
"ormolus" (*FW* 467.35): Romulus, first king

"torquinions superbers" (*FW* 467.35): Tarquinius Superbus, seventh king
"serving my tallyhos" (*FW* 467.36): Servius Tullius, sixth king
"tullying my hostilious" (*FW* 467.36–468.1): Tullus Hostilius, third king

In a Notebook index of the numbered names of these traditional monarchs, the Sabine king Titus Tatius is listed on the same line as Romulus (VI.B.8.123). According to some legends these two were corulers of Rome after the Sabine women reconciled both peoples. Tarquinius Superbus, who was discussed as a "decapitator of poppies" earlier in this chapter, briefly re-appears in another section. There, however, his Latin cognomen ("the Arrogant") has been converted into English: "Strutting as proud as a great turquin" (*FW* 278.F7).

The Tarquinian Dynasty—and the monarchy as a political institution at Rome—was brought down by a sexual crime committed by the king's son. Sextus Tarquinius grossly violated the chastity of the young Roman matron Lucretia, a fellow officer's wife, in her own bedroom. Although totally innocent of any complicity in the outrage, she committed suicide to prevent any stain from darkening family honor. Lucretia's father, her husband, and her husband's comrade, Brutus, avenged these crimes and expelled the Tarquins, thus ending their dynasty and making the very term *rex* (king) thereafter taboo in Rome. Sextus was subsequently assassinated. All of these lurid events have been retold by writers from Livy to Shakespeare, but Macaulay does not include the episode in his *Lays of Ancient Rome*. That work's general title and the related topic of Lucretia's rape, however, are commemorated in a nearly adjacent footnote in the "Night Lessons" chapter of the *Wake:* "a ripping rude rape in his lucreasious togery" (*FW* 277.F2) and "the lays of ancient homes" (*FW* 277.F4).

On another, quite obscure item of the earliest phase of Roman history, Joyce appears to make a minor error. In a December 3, 1906, letter, written to Stanislaus from Rome itself, the following sentence occurs: "O.G., I understand, writes in Sinn Fein under the name of 'Mettus Curtius', the gent who leaped into the chasm in the forum, I think" (*Letters* II.198).

There was a Sabine war-leader named Mettius (less correctly "Mettus") Curtius. During the reign of Romulus he commanded the attack to free the Sabine women who were being detained as brides by the Romans. In the confusion of battle his frightened horse carried him into a swampy portion of the flat land between the seven hills. The enemy commander had to be rescued by his troops. Some say that this story accounts for the origin of the name "Lake Curtius" for a small water-filled depression in the Forum. Others claim that the hallowed site was named for a fourth-century B.C. Roman hero, *Marcus* Curtius. At that time, when a mysterious cavity suddenly opened on the Forum, the priests declared that it could be closed only by putting into it that which was most valuable to Rome. Realizing that military courage was the city's greatest asset, Marcus Curtius, in full armor, mounted his horse and galloped into the chasm. It closed over him, and observers decided that the human sacrifice had been accepted. The later version is, from a Roman perspective, far more patriotic and, therefore, far more "probable" as an edifying model of conduct and, at least, as a revised tribute to Roman—and presumably to Irish—civic pride.

The article mentioned above, which Joyce attributed to Gogarty, appeared in *Sinn Fein* on November 10, 1906. It refers mockingly to "our" glorious army. In context, the "our" in Gogarty's tirade refers to the Irish volunteers who have flocked to the British army. These are the troops—nearby in Ireland, or afar in India—who brutally enforce commerce-driven imperialism:

> A British soldier, when he is not a disease, is a shopwalker. The "army" is composed of Irish dupes and English diseases. . . . Our glorious army! If you want to battle with England *Don't Buy.*

That is the message directed at the readers of *Sinn Fein* by Gogarty's editorial *persona*, "Mettus Curtius before plunging into the Gulf."[18] There can be no irony intended here by the author of this piece. Mettus Curtius is clearly meant to be the archetype of a heroic warrior, willing to sacrifice himself for his people; he is held up in contrast to the Irish mercenaries in their Britannic overlord's service. Thus, either Gogarty (and following him, Joyce) has mixed up the two praenomina "Mettus" and "Marcus," or their history-book sources have failed to make clear the distinction between a Sabine in the swamp and a Roman in the chasm.

After the last king, Tarquin the Arrogant, had been expelled, a Republic was established at Rome (509 B.C.). The deposed Tarquin clan, however, appealed to a fellow Etruscan monarch, Lars Porsena of Clusium, to help them win back their throne. In a series of encounters with the Romans, Porsena displayed the highest level of honorable conduct in his dealings with the enemy. The *Lays of Ancient Rome* by Macaulay attest to the sanctity of the enemy king's word: "Lars Porsena of Clusium / By the nine gods he swore." This fidelity is why, in *Finnegans Wake*, HCE is inspired to select the Etruscan hero (and his bevy of personal gods) as a guarantor of an oath of innocence in the face of the Cad's charges: "[he] forthright sware by all his lards porsenal" (*FW* 83.7–8).[19]

Two Roman opponents whose courage greatly impressed Porsena may also cast a fleeting shadow across this same scene in the *Wake*. After he had been captured by the Etruscans, the Roman warrior Gaius Mucius thrust forth his right hand deep into a brazier of glowing coals. This defiant act was meant to demonstrate his dedication to the mission of killing the enemy commander. Porsena was astounded at the display of courage and ordered the maimed soldier released. The Romans received Mucius back with honor, and from that day on he was known by the heroic cognomen *Scaevola* (Lefty). I detect a flicker of this ardent patriotism in a multilingual analysis of "forthright sware" (*FW* 83.7): a truncated *fortis* ("brave" in Latin); a compounded "-right"; a phonetic *es war* ("it was" in German). The dubious link in my verbal chain might appear to be *fortis.* Three lines below the original phrase, Joyce inserts "marx my word fort" (*FW* 83.10) to support his bold foray into comparative philology. In short, the *Wake* confirms that when the right Roman hand was called for, Scaevola proved to be as brave as they come.

That suggestion is admittedly far-fetched. The presence of a second Roman hero in the same passage is quite a bit more forthright. Even before Mucius displayed his courage to Porsena, the Etruscan king had witnessed the valor of Horatius at the bridge. The latter Roman fought to cover his comrades' retreat across the Tiber River; then, to prevent the enemy from crossing into the city, he ordered them to demolish the bridge on which he stood. After this incredible show of individual ferocity in the face of the Etruscans, both Horatius and the bridge he was defending crashed into the river. Even though he was wearing full armor, the battered warrior swam safely to his fellow Romans. The defiantly stubborn Horatius (along with a battle in the American Civil War and a Russian "Thank You") has been detected in the *Wake* in "hurooshoos . . . at a bull's run over the assback bridge" (*FW* 84.2–3). There is also archival evidence that Joyce had this Roman hero in mind as one of the countless avatars of HCE. Perhaps the link between the two was their mulish refusal to turn tail in the face of their enemies' assaults. At any rate, the following entry not only marks Horatius with the HCE siglum, but also includes the Roman hero's Latin cognomen (he was "one-eyed"): "Horatio Cocles ᗰ" (VI.B. 18.264; VI.C.8.201).

It is safe to say, then, that at the time of his siege of the city, King Porsena of Clusium may not have appreciated all the elements in a "nobiloroman review of the hugely sitisfactuary conclusium of their negotiations" (*FW* 84.15–16), but he certainly did witness two extraordinary examples of Roman courage in his encounters with Mucius Scaevola at the brazier and Horatius at the bridge.

A witty article by Marion Cumpiano contains anything anyone ever wanted to know—and then some—about the role of Cincinnatus in the *Wake.*[20] This poor but aristocratic farmer-warrior was twice appointed "Dictator" by the

Senate to avert disaster from the city. On both occasions he left his fields, donned his toga, and assumed command. After each emergency, Quinticus Cincinnatus retired to his modest farm. An initial Wakean passage contains a double reference to the hero's status as a dirt farmer: "like cabbaging Cincinnatus the grand old gardener" (FW 30.12–13). His refusal of civic honors or permanent office is alluded to in "turned his back like Cincinnatus" (FW 139.5). In "Finnfinnotus of Cincinnati" (FW 285.L1) and "Here endeth chinchinatibus" (FW 367.4) distortions of his cognomen (it means "curly" in Latin) are paramount, once in combination with Finn, the second time in a slightly askew HCE phrase.

The terms for the early political divisions of the Roman people lie behind parts of "hands his secession to the new patricius but plumps plebmatically for the bloody old centuries" (FW 129.18–19). The patricians were the patriarchal aristocrats, from whose exclusive hold on the city's power the plebeians frequently threatened to secede. The enmity of these two groups created the basic components of ancient Roman class struggle. Matters came to a head in 494 B.C. when a segment of the plebeians who had been enrolled in the army left the city and camped on the Sacred Mount. The senatorial party (all patricians at that time) dispatched Menenius Agrippa to convince the commoners to settle their differences. His speech was the parable of the "Revolt of the Parts of the Body": Once upon a time the various parts resented supplying everything for the belly, so the hands stopped carrying food to the mouth, the teeth refused to chew, and so on. Soon, just as the belly was deprived, so too was the whole body wasting away, since the veins had no nourishment to return to the members through the blood supply. Menenius' rhetoric convinced the deserters to negotiate, and special magistrates were appointed to protect the interests of the people. Thus, the "Secession of the Plebs" came to a happy conclusion. Joyce's choice of "hands," "plumps," "plebmatically" (phlebs is Greek for "vein"), and "blood" in the sentence cited above is certainly intended to echo the anatomy of the political parable. His source of information might be the original in Livy 2.32.9–12 or its close imitation in Shakespeare's Coriolanus 1.1.90–150.

A less obvious element in the Wake passage just cited is the "centuries," the assemblies in which citizens were divided by "hundreds" to elect higher magistrates. There is a Notebook entry specifying this context: "centuries (Rome)" (VI.B.20.108). From Livy to Shakespeare to Brecht the ramrod aristocrat Marcius Coriolanus has been depicted as both villain and victim of the division between the patricians and the plebeians. Joyce has two, apparently nonthematic, references to this tragic hero-exile: "coriolano" (FW 228.11) and "corollanes" (FW 354.33). Finally, the basic sociopolitical division of ancient Rome was, archivally at least, superimposed on the *Wake's* primary rivals, Shem and Shaun: "patrician/plebeian," followed by the siglum λ (VI.B.18.266).[21]

The earliest Roman laws were those inscribed on twelve wooden tables, publicly displayed for the citizens to read. In 451–450 B.C. two special panels of ten men (the *decemviri*) were appointed to prepare this code of statutes and procedures designed to avert the perpetuation of conflict between patricians and plebeians. The Law of the Twelve Tables was the result of their deliberations (note "around their twelve tables" [*FW* 389.3]). Joyce includes some slightly ungrammatical "decemvers" (*FW* 282.26) in a paragraph that also mentions a "rota" (*FW* 282.25), which is the Latin term for an ecclesiastical panel of ten Roman Catholic prelates who serve as an appeals court for canon law cases. Several lines later the word "*caius*counting" (*FW* 282.29; my emphasis) appears. Its first part has a strong link with the law of Rome: Caius was the foremost ancient jurist; his extensive second-century A.D. works include a commentary on the Law of the Twelve Tables.

The earliest law code itself is alluded to twice in the *Wake*. In the first instance the Roman legislation is linked with Solon, the famous reformer of early Greek society: "around their old traditional tables of the law like Somany Solans" (*FW* 94.26–27). In fact, in the last two words cited, it might also be possible to hear a garbled version of Solomon, the wise Hebrew judge. The other appearance of the primitive Roman code of laws involves an awkward verb derived from *edictum*, the Latin legal term for the public pronouncement of magisterial procedures: "Twelve tabular times till now have I edicted it" (*FW* 167.23).

About ten lines down the page from that last reference to the Law of the Twelve Tables, Joyce re-creates the actual words of this traditional code, in its original archaic Latin: "Ubi lingua nuncupassit, ibi fas! Adversus hostem semper sac!" (*FW* 167.33–34). A literal translation is "Where someone has formally made a declaration by his tongue, there exists a legal right! Against the alien let it always be accursed!" Both formulations approximate the actual texts of provisions in the law that deal with a contract and with rights of a citizen as opposed to those of an alien. The Latin formulas that Joyce has imitated here are prominently cited in Vico's *Scienza Nuova*, which is likely to be the actual source of the references.[22]

The probability of an intermediate step between the details of ancient Roman law and the *Wake* is increased by Joyce's reference to "acta legitima plebeia" (*FW* 85.13). The phrase, which means "legislative actions of the people," is not, in fact, an official term for any sort of formal Roman legal enactment or procedure. I suggest that Joyce has coined this phrase on the basis of Vico's use of *"actus legitimi* of the Romans."[23] This phrase occurs in his discussion of the "figurative knot in the Law of the Twelve Tables" that held Roman society together. Joyce's adaptation involves a switch in genders from masculine to feminine and creates a phrase that can be translated as a "stirred up, lawful woman of the people." That description neatly fits HCE's frequently hard-pressed wife, ALP. Indeed, a primary motive for Joyce's adaptation of Vico's phrase (if my source-suggestion has any merit) is its ready conversion into an ALP formula.

On the same *Wake* page as the first reference to the Law of the Twelve Tables is an odd protest: "No! Topsman to your Tarpeia! This thing, Mister Abby, is nefand" (*FW* 167.18–19). This passage occurs very near the end of the "Eleventh Question" in Book I.6. In this section of the *Wake*, a large part of the rhetorical energy is derived from the fierce theological debates in which factions in the early Christian church argued over the correct description of Christ's nature. Shaun is emphatically summarizing his negative response to Shem's inquiry as to whether he would save the soul of a wandering Irish poet. "No!" he says, "Let your traitor hang!" "Topsman" is slang for a hangman; the Rock of Tarpeia is the crag from which Romans convicted of treason were flung. Shaun then accuses his brother of being a Christological waffler. I construct this accusation by reducing the text's "Abby" to an elemental "A" and "B"; then I have Shaun claim that Shem holds that "A" is equal to "B," where "A" and "B" are the human and divine natures of the son of God.[24] Or, perhaps Shem is merely a rigid ecclesiastic (*Abbé*) of French ultramontane persuasion. Whatever the apparent vocative means, it is clear that Shaun excoriates Shem's suggestion. His proposition is literally "ineffable," *nefandum* in Latin!

Before leaving the passage cited at the start of the last paragraph, it is worth pointing out that the most memorable figure in Roman history to be executed by being cast from the Tarpeian Rock was Marcus Manlius. He was the commander of the warriors who defended the temples of Jupiter and Juno on the Capitoline from capture by the Gauls in 390 B.C. As mentioned above, the sacred geese alerted him that the enemy was climbing to the citadel via the Tarpeian Rock. The barbarians were repulsed just in time, and Manlius won the city's greatest gratitude. But there is a terrifying postscript to this tale of heroism. Several years later Marcus Manlius himself was convicted of treason and was executed in the traditional way. As Livy reports, "The monument to Manlius' glory and his shameful punishment was one and the same, [the Tarpeian Rock]" (6.20.12).[25] One of the consequences of Manlius' disgrace was the fact that thereafter no member of the Manlian family was ever named "Marcus" (Livy 6.20.14).[26] This extraordinary nominal—and literal—anathema does not pass unnoticed in the *Wake:* "and, arrah, sure there was never a marcus at all at all among the manlies" (*FW* 96.5–6).

Etruscan incursions, Gallic invasions, and Pyrrhus' futile victories in southern Italy were severe tests of early Roman military discipline. But nothing in the history of the Republic posed a threat that was as potentially disastrous as the campaigns of Hannibal. In no uncertain terms Joyce records his awareness of the trans-Mediterranean threat to Rome: "a hunnibal in exhaustive conflict" (*FW* 132.6). The genealogy and the race of the most famous of Carthaginian generals are duly recorded in the *Wake:* "Hannibal mac Hamiltan the Hegerite" (*FW* 274.9–10). Hamilcar was Hannibal's father. "Hegerite" seems to refer to an offspring of Hagar, the Egyptian slave woman whose son Ishmael is the founder of the Arabian people (Gen. 21, 25). The Arabic noun "hegira," which is used to designate Mohammed's flight from Mecca in A.D. 622, also contributes to this word. The Carthaginians were *not* Arabs, but they were Semites. And their North African descendants later embraced Islam as preached by the Prophet.

With his elite African troops, Spanish auxiliaries—and, of course, a troop of elephants—General Hannibal crossed the Alps into Italy in 218 B.C. His slaughter and desecration of the corpses of Roman legionnaires at Cannae (216 B.C.) is linked with another military disaster at Caudine Forks (321 B.C.) in the margin of "Night Lessons" (*FW* 273.L2). For the next dozen years the Romans avoided pitched battles in a series of strategic retreats to prevent the enemy from sacking their capital city. Vergil commemorates the Roman commander who kept the Carthaginians at bay: *unum qui nobis cunctando restitues rem* (you will be the only man in our history to restore the Republic by delaying) (*Aeneid* 6.846). For his heroic tactics of nonengagement Fabius Maximus earned the cognomen *Cunctator* (the Delayer). In "Night Lessons," the name "Fabius" is keyed to the essay topic "Circumspection, Our allies are the Hills" (*FW* 307.L and 13).

During the years of hit-and-run fighting in Italy, Hannibal's younger brother Hasdrubal was killed in action. His loss is lamented in "(O the hastroubles you lost!)" (*FW* 192.16). Two other important Carthaginian participants in the Italian campaign may also appear in "malherbal Magis" (*FW* 478.9). Maharbal was Hannibal's chief cavalry officer. Mago was the general's youngest brother, who died of wounds on his way back to Carthage after being defeated by Roman legions in 203 B.C.

The Vergilian allusion to the delaying tactics used during the Hannibalic campaign cited above can serve as an appropriately epic introduction to the wars, especially their reflection in literature. Later Roman tradition traced the origins of the bitter trans-Mediterranean rivalry between the two powers back to Aeneas' desertion of Dido. On her deathbed, the Carthaginian queen called on her citizens to pledge eternal vengeance against Aeneas' descendants in Rome-to-come. The response to her dying plea was a series of three long and enervating Punic Wars, which stretched over the course of two centuries. The impact of these wars and their heroes has been felt for centuries, and in areas far beyond Rome and Carthage.

One of Joyce's most astounding bits of cross-cultural data is his mention of the claim that some Irish peasants speak a language almost the same as that of ancient Carthage (CW 156). In a 1907 Trieste lecture, this absurd notion by an eighteenth-century scholar is cited but not endorsed. Be that as it may, long before his more mature examination of comparative world history, Joyce would have been introduced to the Carthaginians and their bellicose role in Mediterranean affairs. At Clongowes Wood College the students in the lower grades were sometimes divided into two opposing "camps" to encourage classroom competition. The "Red Roses" of Lancaster versus the "White Roses" of York (P 12, 52) and "Romans" versus "Carthaginians" are typical turn-of-the-century academic opponents in Jesuit schools.[27] One can also imagine the young Joyce being fascinated by the extraordinary range of meaning for the Latin noun *phoenix* (and, of course, its Greek cognate):

> a Phoenician or Carthaginian; a purple-red dye derived from a mollusk; the shellfish itself; the desert palm tree and its dates; a stringed guitar-like musical instrument; the fabulous Arabian bird which periodically flies out of the desert to die, then rise from its own ashes in Egypt.

Citizens of Joyce's Dublin would have recognized the Phoenix Brewery ("bottle of Phenice-Bruerie '98" [FW 38.4]) and the Phoenix Fire Insurance Co. ("by Phoenis, swore on him Lloyd's" [FW 590.5]). By far the most prominent of the reincarnations of the phoenix in Dublin, however, was the city's great park, the largest in Europe, which bears that name: "Finnish pork," "Fiendish park," "sphoenix spark," and so on (FW 39.17, 196.11, 473.18). Actually the application of this title "Phoenix" to the park is the result of a misunderstanding by Anglophones of the Irish words *fioun uisge*, the "clear water" of the spring that originally provided a name for the enclosure.[28] This etymological error has been memorialized by the erection of a pillar, topped by a monumental phoenix ("a well of Artesia into a bird of Arabia" [FW 135.14–15]), in the center of the 1,752-acre park.

In Notebook VI.B.24.40–41 there are eleven references to Phoenician or Carthaginian terms or names; seven of these are crossed out with blue or orange crayon, usually a sign that Joyce included these items in the text of the *Wake*. "[b]Phoenicia Proper" appears as "Phenitia Proper" (FW 85.20); "[o]punic" is imbedded and expanded in "(whereon punic judgeship strove with penal law)" (FW 90.36). "ᵒBaal & Astarte" and "ᵒMarkarthy" appear almost side by side as "Markarthy" and "Baalastartey" (FW 91.13–14). "ᵒTyre" is transposed into "Tyre-nan-Og" (FW 91.25–26), which is Joyce's transliteration of the Gaelic "land of the young," a legendary island in the west of Ireland. The final crossed-out Notebook item is more cryptic: " ⊓ &△ 's hair (bowstring)." Joyce developed this entry into "betterwomen with bowstrung hair of Carrotha-genuine ruddiness" (FW 87.27–28). The genetic incident is a Roman historian's report that the women of Carthage shamed the city's warriors by cutting their hair and braiding bowstrings in a vain attempt to save their city from the final siege in 146 B.C. The placement and adjustment of this note into its Wakean setting shows that Joyce was aware that one of the meanings of *phoenix* is "deep-red dye." He puns on the martial readiness of Carthage's women: "Carro-thage-" and "ruddiness." The Punic context (for someone who knows Roman Republican military history—and Joyce did) is fairly obvious; the etymological elaboration is the mark of a radically comic genius, whose range of linguistic and literary analogues was staggering. All of these items entered the work in progress when Joyce added them to the text at a comparatively late stage, sometime not long before 1936.

A second cluster of notebook references to Carthage is found at VI.B.24.188–89. Four entries on these two pages ("ᵇCarthage & Tyre," "ʳMelkart," "ʳhon-nibel," and "ʳcrudelty") have been crossed out with crayon and reappear in the *Wake's* text. There the Punic city-god has been transformed into "melk-kaart" (FW 538.8), which is Dutch for "milk card," not "cart." In the light of "hamilkcars" (FW 192.6) and "ancient cartage" (FW 538.12), however, there may also be a Romano-English "honeycart" (manure wagon) on the scene here, since *mel-* is the Latin root for "honey."[29] Both nuances are compactly contained in "to suckle in Millickmaam's honey" (FW 277.F1).

One final Carthaginian reference involves an obscure document which contains all that remains of an original report of an ancient voyage. This trip took the fifth-century B.C. navigator, Hanno, to the west coast of Africa. The surviving Greek version of the details of this feat is entitled the *Periplus* (the "sail around"). All of this is compacted into the following passage:

the littleknown periplic . . . of the wretched mariner . . . a Punic admiralty report. . . . The original document was in what is known as Hanno O'Nonhanno's unbrookable script. (FW 123.22–33; compare FW 182.20)

My search for a definite source of Joyce's Carthaginian material has not yet turned up another startling revelation of the author's dedication to outrageously exotic research. A clue to a possible source is, however, a nonfictional French language source suggested by the presence of "(eclair)" between "Hamilkar Barkars" and "Barak" on one of the Notebook pages mentioned above.

These entries are garbled spellings of the name of the famous Carthaginian family "Barka," which means "lightning" (*éclair* in French). Joyce, well versed in Vergil and the basics of ancient Mediterranean history, merely added his own twists when inserting his notes into the *Wake.*

After years of conducting his trans-Alpine campaign in Italy itself, Hannibal became frustrated with Fabius Maximus' "wild-goose-chase" tactics. He returned, unbeaten but not victorious, to North Africa. His enemies, however, were not convinced that the Carthaginian threat to their homeland and their control of the western Mediterranean was over. So the famous Roman commander and guardian of public morals, Cato the Censor, took it upon himself to add a monitory coda (involving a nice gerundive) to each of his public statements: *delenda est Karthago* (Carthage must be destroyed). Cato's long years of military and political service to Rome are commemorated in the *Wake.* In the margin of "Night Lessons" the name "Cato" suggests the essay topic "Duty, the daughter of discipline" (*FW* 306 L2, 15). The elder statesman's longevity is also acknowledged in "catoninelives" (*FW* 462.31; compare VI.B.10.17).

More than two centuries of tension between Carthage and Rome ended in 146 B.C.—despite the sacrifice of their long, red hair for bowstrings by the Carthaginian women. The North African capital was utterly razed by Roman troops after the Third Punic War. Cato's warning was finally and resolutely heeded, as Joyce reports in an approximation of the Censor's original language: "Delandy is cartager" (*FW* 64.3).[30]

LATE REPUBLIC

Many surveys of Roman history mark the period that begins the Fall of the Republic with the death of the Gracchi brothers. Although their family was part of the landholding aristocracy, both Tiberius Sempronius Gracchus and his younger brother, Gaius Sempronius, pushed hard to bring about a radical program of agrarian and political reform. For their popular opposition to the property-owning Senatorial class, Tiberius and Gaius were assassinated (133 and 121 B.C.). There may be an allusion to the brothers in the *Wake.* If so, Joyce has expanded the pair into a trio by converting their gentilic nomen into a third praenomen: "Titius, Caius and Sempronius" (*FW* 128.15; also note "Mopsus or Gracchus" [*FW* 614.1]). This identification also involves a misrecollection (and a misspelling) of "Titus" for "Tiberius." Some commentators have seen the three Roman names as recalling, not Republican history, but Shakespearean tragedy: Caius and Sempronius are two kinsmen of the titular character in *Titus Andronicus.*

At any rate, the death of the Gracchi at the mob's knives inaugurated, in fact and in popular memory, the century of political violence that finally brought down the Roman Republic. Here there can be no doubt about Joyce's awareness of and reaction to this period. When Bloom is attempting to sober Stephen up in "Eumaeus," he offers him some coffee and a stale bun: "— Liquids I can eat, Stephen said, But O, oblige me by taking away that knife. I can't look at the point of it. It reminds me of Roman history" (U 16.815–16).[31]

The most famous political assassination in all of Roman history is, of course, the assassination of Julius Caesar on the Ides of March, 44 B.C. Five years before that, the triumvir Caesar began the series of events that led to his murder by crossing the Rubicon ("Rubiconstein" [FW 211.15–16] and "°Rubicon" [VI.B.9.96]) at the command of his troops. This defiance of Roman custom and law sparked a civil war with his former ally, Pompey the Great ("Pompeius Magnus . . . The Roman Pontiffs and the Orthodox Churches" [FW 307.L1, 17–18]). Caesar defeated his rival at the battle of Pharsalus, 48 B.C. ("*Parsuralia*" [FW 353.24]). After eliminating his armed opposition, Caesar assumed the office of dictator; but a number of his fellow Romans began to worry that he would accept a royal crown. This would be an unforgivable political sin, since even the term "king" had been anathema at Rome after the Tarquins had been expelled in 509 B.C. Thus, a group of patriots assembled to prevent even the possibility of Julius Caesar's accession, as *rex*, to a new Roman throne.

Plutarch and Shakespeare have transmitted all the details leading up to the conspiracy, and its oratorical and military aftermath. The *Wake* reenacts its own zany version of these momentous events in the "Burrus-and-Caseous" interlude. These lactic names applied to the antagonists thinly disguise two of the most prominent conspirators, the "lean" Cassius and Brutus, "the noblest Roman of them all." Behind the Franco-Hispano-Germanic aliases lurk the rival twins, Shaun and Shem. The former threatens the latter, "if I don't make away with you I'm beyond Caesar outnullused" (FW 161.36).[32] He continues, "The older sisars (Tyrants, regicide is too good for you!) become unbeurrable from age" (FW 162.1–2). The actual weapons of the assassins flash at several instances in the passage: "nineknived" (FW 162.5), and "knife knickknots" (FW 162.10). An oblique comment on the role of the two conspirators is encapsulated in another pun on their names, "brutal and cautiouses" (FW 366.25–26). In the margin of "Night Lessons" the famous Shakespearian re-creation of Caesar's funeral orations is given a new twist: "*Dear Brotus, land me arrears*" (FW 278.L3).

Caesar's avengers, the victors at the battle of Philippi (42 B.C.), are also commemorated as "the tryonforit of Oxtheivious [Octavius/Octavian Augustus], Lapidous [Lepidus] and Malthouse Anthemy [Mark Antony]" (FW 271.5–6; see pages 102–4 for a discussion of the bases for these name puns). In fact, there is an odd collocation of the pro- and the anti-Caesarians in the phrase

"This Antonius-Burrus-Caseous grouptriad" (*FW* 167.3–4). Even the site of the military engagement at which the remnants of Caesar's assassins (including Cassius and Brutus) were defeated is mentioned very early in the *Wake*, appropriately enough during the guided tour of "Willingdone Museyroom," which commemorated Napoleon's downfall at Waterloo. There, in the midst of a minicatalogue of war-weapons, including "Sexcaliber hrosspower," the compound noun "phillippy" (*FW* 8.36–9.1) gallops past. The wordplay here comes from the Greek *philos* (loving/beloved) and *hippos* (horse). There is also a hint of the victors' successful siege of the conspirators' camp and their consequent deaths in the nearby "obscides" (*FW* 8.35), a Wakean verb formed from *obsideo*, Latin for "to blockade, to besiege" and *obcido*, "to strike down," "to slay."

The site of the momentous battle is also cited in Joyce's *Exiles*. Robert Hand tells Richard Rowan that they will get together later at the vice chancellor's dinner. Richard replies to his friend's "We shall meet tonight" with the cryptic "at Philippi" (*E* 45). The direct model of this allusive exchange is undoubtedly Shakespeare's *Julius Caesar*. There, near the end of the play, the Ghost of Caesar appears in Brutus' tent on the night before the fatal fight. Brutus asks, "Why, then I shall see thee again?" The Ghost replies, "Ay, at Philippi" (4.3.284–85). The theme of betrayal permeates both plays, but it is impossible to draw a specific parallel—Elizabethan or Roman—between the two situations. Nonetheless, Robert's later, repeated use of "noble" to excuse his friend is countered by Richard's more honest appraisal: "No. Not noble. Ignoble" (*E* 69). These adjectives are surely meant to remind the audience of the Shakespearean Antony's final tribute to Brutus.

The Second Triumvirate itself was soon torn apart by the dynastic ambition of those who formed it. The climactic event took place at Actium in 31 B.C. when Octavian Augustus routed the fleet of Mark Antony and Cleopatra (see page 85). After a century of recurrent domestic strife and bloodshed, Augustus then took control of the state and the military. Though he did not use the title—preferring to see his tenure as the "Principate"—Augustus functioned as an emperor.[33] Thus, after almost a half millennium, genuine republican government in Rome was finished.

EMPIRE

In "Aeolus," J. J. O'Molloy offers a comparative comment on a modern rival of the "bloody old Roman empire": "—*Imperium romanum*. . . . It sounds nobler than British or Brixton. The word reminds one somehow of fat in the fire." That judgment is almost immediately challenged by Professor MacHugh,

"We mustn't be led away by words, by sounds of words. We think of Rome, imperial, imperious, imperative" (*U* 7.478–86). Apart from that rhetorical generalization and despite the frequently spectacular excesses of the early emperors, Joyce rarely alludes to this period of Roman history, and then only in the *Wake*. A dozen or so paragraphs are enough to survey the entire period from the accession of Augustus to the deposition of the last emperor, Romulus Augustulus, at the hands of a mutinous barbarian mercenary in A.D. 476.

Augustus was succeeded by Tiberius, whose goatish sexual depravities are briefly discussed in connection with Roman comedy (pages 210–11). The next emperor was a sadistic megalomaniac, whom Joyce nicely introduces with "a brut! But a magnificent brut! 'Caligula'" (*FW* 60.26).[34] The praenomen of the third emperor was Gaius, but he is best known by the nickname *Caligula* (Little Boots), earned when he wore a miniature legionnaire's uniform as a child. Caligula's most absurdly autocratic gesture was the report that he planned to award his favorite horse, Incitatus ("Swifty"), a consulship. In one of his notes for "Circe," Joyce records both that political insult to Rome's chief magistrate and the emperor's scandalous late-night song-and-dance performances (Suetonius, *Caligula* 54–55): "Caligula dances / ᵇhorse made consul" (*UNBM* 314: 51–52). The latter entry reappears in the text when the momentarily enthroned Leopold announces, "We hereby nominate our faithful charger Copula Felix [Happy Fucking][35] hereditary Grand Vizier" (*U* 15.1504–5).

No less zany an incident of imperial insanity is also recorded by Suetonius. Caligula drew up his legions on the Gallic shore of the Channel in A.D. 40 as if he were about to launch an amphibious attack on Britain. Suddenly he gave the order, "Gather *seashells!*" He called the shells "plunder from the ocean" and made the troops fill their helmets and tunics with them. He commemorated this phantom "victory" by building an extraordinarily tall *tower* (*altissimam turrem*) like the *Pharos* whose *beacon-fire shone far out to sea* from the harbor at Alexandria. Finally Caligula promised each soldier a bounty for bravery and told them, "Go away happy, go away rich!" (Suetonius, *Caligula* 46). In an August 24, 1926, letter from the Channel port of Ostend, Joyce recounted the following anecdote to Sylvia Beach:

> A curious thing. I was sitting on a rock under the *phare* a few sunsets ago when a child, a barefoot girl of about four clambered up the slope and insisted on filling my pockets with tiny *shells* from her apron. . . . It was only after I had given her a *coin* and she had gone that I remembered the *lighthouse* of [St.] Patrick's papa and *Caligula's order to his soldiers at the tower to gather up the seashells.* (*Letters* I.243; my emphases and ellipsis)

Just as bizarre as that seaside encounter and the classical reminiscence it triggered are their mutual contributions to the opening of the *Wake*. Finnegan/ HCE is being evoked as a master mason who

> would *caligulate* by multiplicables the *alltitude* and malltitude until he *seesaw* . . . a skyerscape of most eyeful hoyth en*towerly* . . . celescalating the himals and all . . . with a *burning bush* abob off it baubletop. (*FW* 4.32–5.2; my emphases and ellipses)

In my judgment, the italicized items in the three passages cited above establish, beyond any reasonable doubt, the uncanny interplay between the monumental delusions of a Roman emperor, James Joyce on vacation at the Belgian coast, and the *Wake*'s heroic "man of hod, cement and edifices" (*FW* 4.26–27). The pivotal "seashells" are, of course, present in the *Wake*'s "seesaw," a portmanteau word that is designed to echo not only a demented "Caesar," but also the anonymous "she" who "sells sea shells by the seashore" in the nursery rhyme.

The ineffectual Claudius was raised to the purple after his nephew Gaius Caligula had been murdered by an officer in the Praetorian Guards. Joyce may allude to several of the emperor's congenital disabilities in "an occasional twinge of claudication" (*FW* 444.3). The last word in that phrase not only echoes Claudius' name, but it also is directly derived from the Latin noun *claudicatio* (limping, stuttering). This association is confirmed by Joyce's convoluted discussion of the various alphabetic signs for the sound "v/w": "those throne open doubleyous," "illvoodawpeehole," "topplefouls," "fretful fidget eff," "the hornful digamma" (*FW* 120.28–34). In the midst of these orthographic minutiae, the name "Claudian" appears, followed by an "Ⅎ" and an "Ⅎ" (*FW* 121. 1, 3, 7). The first of these signs was, in fact, proposed by the scholarly Claudius as an addition to the Latin alphabet. It would represent the sound of consonantal "u," since the Latin alphabet did not distinguish, graphically, between "u" and "v." The case for a muted imperial presence here is strengthened by a cluster of references to Claudius' limp: "paces with a frown, jerking to and fro," "with some half-halted suggestion," "dragging its shoestring" (*FW* 121.5–8).

The last Julio-Claudian emperor in the *Wake*, Nero, is appropriately associated with a "madhouse," a "monstrous marvellosity," and a "mental and moral defective" (*FW* 177.13–16). His most memorable crime against the city of Rome is commemorated in the essay topic that appears with his name in "Night Lessons": "*Nero*. . . . the Great Fire in the South City Markets" (*FW* 306.L2, 15–16). After Nero banished (and subsequently murdered) his wife

Octavia, he married his paramour, Poppea. She plays a cameo role in the *Wake* by being named as one of several women who have allegedly been "tenderly debauched" in the grotesque canon law marriage case (*FW* 572.36–573.2).

The speed with which Joyce dispatched the later Roman emperors can be illustrated by three unrelated references in a single—though extraordinarily long—sentence: "an otho to return . . . you feel he is Vespasian yet you think of him as Aurelius" (*FW* 132.6–19). The thematic connection between these three very different emperors and HCE, who is being described in this section of the *Wake*, is not at all clear. Indeed, Otho's only claim to fame is his suicide after defeat in the scramble to claim imperial power following the suicide of Nero. The general who vanquished Otho and next rose to the purple was Vitellius. His name appears as an essay topic in "Night Lessons": "Proper and Regular Diet Necessity For" (*FW* 307.L2, 26–27). Suetonius reports that Vitellius was a notorious glutton and that he frequently took emetics so he could return unburdened to the banquet table (*Vitellius* 13).

Apart from the mere mention of his name (*FW* 132.18), Vespasian does not appear in any of Joyce's fiction. There is, however, authorial evidence of his awareness of the emperor's most enduring contribution to Western civilization. On June 27, 1924, the publication of the French translation of *Ulysses* was celebrated at a "déjeuner Ulysse" at the restaurant Chez Leopold. Joyce reported on the festivities in a letter to Valery Larbaud, who did not attend. The pertinent episode took place on the return trip. Samuel Beckett, "deeply under the influence of beer, wine, spirits, liqueurs, fresh air" and so on, was abandoned when he left the chartered bus to use "one of those temporary palaces which are inseparably associated with the memory of the Emperor Vespasian" (*Selected Letters* 34, 280). Joyce is referring to a *pissoir*. The link between the emperor and a public urinal is explained by Suetonius: Vespasian established a tax, *urinae vectigal*, on the contents of the city's urinals (*Vespasian* 23). The human waste was used by fullers in the felting process. This obscure historical fact is commemorated in French vocabulary: a genteel term for a street *pissoir* is a *vespasienne*.

Vespasian's son and successor was Titus. His command of the Roman legions that razed the Temple at Jerusalem in A.D. 70 has not left its mark on the *Wake*, but another historic event that occurred during the first year of Titus' reign is certainly commemorated by Joyce: the destruction of Pompeii and Herculaneum (A.D. 79). (Pliny the Younger's report of the havoc caused by the eruption of Mount Vesuvius is discussed on pages 93–94.) There are three other brief allusions to the burial of the cities of Pompeii and Herculaneum. "Ghostown Gate," a district in Dublin, is said to be "like Pompeii up to date" (*FW* 329.25). HCE is reported to be "exceedingly herculeneous" (*FW* 570.16–

17), a comparison in which his reputed strength (like that of Hercules) is called in question by being compared to a totally devastated and long-buried site near Mount Vesuvius. One of the most frequently reproduced of the mosaics unearthed by archaeologists at Pompeii is a picture of a chained, snarling dog. Beneath it is a warning in Latin, *Cave Canem* (Beware of the dog). Joyce, who had a great fear of dogs, used this phrase several times in the *Wake:* "*caveman* ... Then two bitches ought to be leashed, *canem!*" (*FW* 60.14–15; my emphases); "Pave Pannem" (*FW* 531.3); "Cave and can em" (*FW* 579.8).

Domitian is another emperor mentioned in "Night Lessons" and paired with an essay topic: "On the Benefits of Recreation" (*FW* 306.L2, 22). In Suetonius' *Life of Domitian* there are two items that probably triggered Joyce's choice of this apparently frivolous topic. At the beginning of his reign the new emperor would spend hours catching flies and stabbing them with a needle-sharp pen (*Domitian* 3). Domitian was also famous for the many extravagant shows he put on in the Colosseum and Circus: chariot races; infantry, cavalry, and naval battles; wild-beast hunts; gladiatorial shows in which competitors of both sexes fought; oratorical, choral, and musical contests (*Domitian* 4). This sort of public spectacle sponsored by the emperor gave rise to Juvenal's biting judgment that the once indomitable Roman people had only two concerns, *panem et circenses* (cheap bread and circus-races) (*Satire* 10.81). Joyce expanded this comment: "We move in the beast circls. Grimbarb and pancercucer" (*FW* 480.24–25).

"Marcus Aurelius" (A.D. 161–180) also reappears in "Night Lessons," where the suggested topic is "What Morals, if any, can be drawn from Diarmuid and Grania?" (*FW* 306.L3, 27–28). There is a thematic link between the philosopher-emperor (he wrote the highly ethical and relentlessly stoical *Meditations*) and the pair of lovers in early Irish mythology. Marcus Aurelius' wife, Faustina, was reputed to have been scandalously promiscuous. She was implicated—sexually and politically—with a rival general, Cassius, who mounted a rebellion in the East to overthrow the emperor. Faustina was, however, never rejected; indeed, she was commemorated by Marcus Aurelius as his "docile and affectionate" wife. "Diarmuid and Grania" (Diarmaid and Gráinne) are the Irish equivalent of Tristan and Isolde. Their tale involves an eternal triangle between a young warrior, a young woman, and an aging suitor, the king. In this case, Finn pursues the couple over all of Ireland; finally, after many miraculous escapes, the young lovers are forgiven, thanks to the intercession of Oenghus, the god of love.[36]

When the "Mookse" and the "Gripes" were debating the finer points of ecclesiastical policy, Issy tried to entice the pair with her feminine wiles. They refused to be distracted, since they "were conclaved with Heliogobbleus and

Commodus and Enobarbarus" (FW 157.26–27). The first two names in this passage can be directly associated with Roman emperors. Commodus was the elder son of Marcus Aurelius; his twelve-year reign (A.D. 180–192) ended when he was strangled by a hired muscleman. [H]elagabalus was the title, honoring a Syrian sun god, that was used by Marcus Aurelius Antonius (the latter names were also assumed, to support a claim of imperial descent). Aenobarbus (or Ahenobarbus), which means "bronze-beard," was a cognomen closely associated with the members of the Domitian clan. Nero's paternal ancestors all bore this name, as did the emperor himself. More than just the cachet of imperial power, however, unites the three historical figures whose "names" are used by Joyce in the passage cited above. A standard Roman history text reports that Elagabalus was a "voluptuary of the stamp of Nero and Commodus, [and that] he allowed the administration to go to rack and ruin."[37] Taking that information into account, then, the following are the two primary and related "reasons" for Joyce's selection and collocation of these imperial names:

1. The *Wake*'s two Christian controversialists are ironically presented as meeting this trio of pagan debauchees in conclave to bolster their defense against the erotic blandishments of Issy.

2. The initial letter of each "imperial" name creates an HCE acrostic, thus associating the randy *paterfamilias* of the *Wake* with three of the more notorious sexual profligates in the annals of declining Rome.

In the late third century the Emperor Aurelian began to construct a massive ring of new walls around Rome, most of which survives to this day. Joyce commemorates the enterprise in the phrase "aurellian gape" (FW 478.14), which occurs in the midst of a cluster of terms associated with Roman roads. Thus, the "gape" most probably refers to the Porta Aurelia (Aurelian *Gate*) through which the Via Aurelia traversed the walls. There is another less likely possibility here. After Aurelian was assassinated in A.D. 275 there was a six-month interregnum before a new emperor was named—an Aurelian *gap* in succession.

The later emperors, including Diocletian, Constantine, Theodosius, play no role in the *Wake*. The Christianization of the empire and the establishment of a second capital in the East are also ignored, except for an unemphatic reference to "constantonoble's aim" (FW 548.16). The last "pagan" emperor is referred to in an uncrossed Notebook entry: "Julian [the Apostate] proconsul at Paris" (VI.B.4.127). In short, after a brush with the standard cases of autocratic excess in the early Empire, Joyce seems to have shifted his center of historical and geographical interest from the late antique world of Rome to a new frontier in the farthest western reaches of Europe, Hibernia. This ultimate island could boast of having remained untouched by the Roman legions that once conquered the known world, from Britannia to Armenia, Numidia to Germania Inferior, along the Thames, Ebro, Nile, and Tigris.

According to national legend, Roman history begins with the journey of the Trojan refugees led by Aeneas from Asia Minor to Hesperia. Centuries later, historical fact marks another east-west migration as a primary factor in the collapse of Roman power in Europe. This time the invaders were barbarian hordes who swept across the Danube and Rhine, over the Alps and the Pyrenees. In the *Wake* Joyce does not distinguish between the waves of these invaders. "Gothewishegoths" (*FW* 148.20) are mixed with "ostrovgods" (*FW* 289.16); the reasons for and results of their conquests are confused in "hope of ostrogothic and ottomanic faith converters" (*FW* 263.10–11); their languages and scripts are reduced to a "Ostrogothic kakography" (*FW* 120.22–23). The only group of barbarians to whom Joyce gives particular attention is that group which excited the most dread in the hearts of Rome's citizens, "that hun of a horde" (*FW* 362.12). They pour across once secure borders "by the wrath of Bog [Russian for 'God'], like the erst curst Hun in the bed of his treubleu Donawhu [phonetic German for 'the blue Danube']" (*FW* 76.31–32). When the *Wake's* patriarchal protagonist is described, one of his most fearsome qualities is the presence of "his suns the huns, his dartars the tartars" (*FW* 135.23–24). And there can be no doubt about the threat they pose to everyman's castle: "Attilad! Attattilad! Get up, Goth's scourge on you! There's a visitation in your impluvium. Hun! Hun!" (*FW* 251.1–3). Both Attila and Alaric, the king of the Visigoths who sacked Rome in A.D. 410, are present in "Mr A (tillalaric)" (*FW* 336.12).

In a later passage HCE's children are assigned a slightly different role to play in this confrontation of civilization and barbarism. In "Night Lessons" the twin boys are cast as a Roman and a Hun: "ere commence commencement catalaunic when Aetius check chokewill Attil's gambit" (*FW* 266.24–26).[38] This bit of cryptic history requires some interpretation. In A.D. 451 the Roman patrician Aetius and his Visigothic allies defeated Attila and his Huns at the battle of the Catalaunian Plains, near the modern town of Chalons-sur-Marne. Issy also enters the picture here; in the next line of text her aid is invoked in the moment of crisis: "lead us seek, O *june of eves* the jenniest" (*FW* 266.27; my emphasis). The italicized words are meant to be interpreted as a prayer for the intercession of St. *Genevieve*. When Attila's horde threatened to destroy Paris before moving south in 451, the visionary nun Genevieve led the city's inhabitants in a prayer-crusade. At the last minute, the barbarians turned away and left the city unharmed.

My survey of the impact of Roman history on Joyce's works began with a discussion of the ancient authors whom he cited, whose facts and legends he manipulated to suit his own narrative or thematic purposes. This chapter ends, fittingly enough, not in the Eternal City[39] at the dawn of its greatness, but at the City of Lights beside the Seine in the deep twilight of its Gallo-Roman history. It is here that Joyce completed his crepuscular *Finnegans Wake*, just at that point in history at which a new wave of barbarians was about to sweep across the Rhine. St. Genevieve is still honored as the patron saint of Paris. And the city, always secure in the face of internal and external threats (ancient and modern), justifies the optimism of its Latin motto, *Fluctuat Non Mergitur* (It is tossed to and fro, but it does not sink).[40]

4

⊰•≻

Roman Gods, Goddesses, and Ritual

It is impossible to understand Roman civilization without some attention to the elaborate system of worship accorded the vast pantheon of its gods and goddesses. These supernatural beings and forces range from the Capitoline triad who ensured the security of the city to the Lares and Penates who guarded the produce and property of each household. Thus, in addition to his appropriation of the language, history, and literature of ancient Rome, Joyce often throws a handful of literary incense on the altars of its gods. This chapter begins with a survey of the appearances of the major Olympian divinities (for example, Jupiter, Venus, Mars) in Joyce's works. Since Roman religion was far more a matter of ritual than of theological precision or moral edification, a large section is devoted to Joycean reference to festivals, priesthoods, and the arcane science of augury. A final section briefly treats the numinous appearance of minor divinities and their literary-cultural functions.[1]

JUPITER

Early in 1935, Joyce wrote to Paul Léon requesting that his friend and helper try to come up with the name of an ancient male god beginning with the letter "C." Appended to the letter is Léon's list of names from Greek and Roman mythology beginning with "B" and "C."[2] From this request (and its response) one could deduce that Joyce was planning some sort of alphabetical catalogue of classical divinities for his work in progress. Only a few traces of that project in ancient theological nomenclature remain in the final text of the *Wake*:

> Every letter is a godsend, ardent Ares, brusque Boreas and glib Ganymede like zealous Zeus, the O'Meghisthest of all. (*FW* 269.17–19)

Although the gods' names in this passage are cited in their Greek form (that is, "Ares" instead of "Mars"; "Zeus" instead of "Jupiter"), there is abundant evidence, especially from *Finnegans Wake*, that Joyce's personal lexicon of classical mythology was usually presented in Latin form.[3] For example, he uses two of Jupiter's traditional Latin epithets as guardian of the city of Rome: "Stator and Victor" (*FW* 179.11); these terms come directly from a Notebook entry: "ᵇStator / ᵇvictor" (VI.B.18.270). In another archival note the entry "Jupiter Stator" is followed by a parenthetical "Standfast" (VI.B.8.124). That English term is an accurate and literal translation of "Stator," but it imparts an ironic spin to the two definitely non-Latin epithets that appear in the text of the *Wake* immediately after the original Roman pair: "Kutt and Runn" (*FW* 179.11). Comic distortion aside, this sort of "theological" detail is typical of Joyce's attention to the depiction of Rome's gods.

There are numerous other examples of the divine intervention of Jupiter in *Finnegans Wake;* but before they are examined, it is useful to scan the principal god's appearances in the earlier works. The differences in allusive complexity that are revealed by the comparative analysis will surprise no one. In *Portrait,* for example, "By Jove," is invoked by Heron in a parody of the idiom of a stage-Englishman (*P* 17). In Joyce's only drama, the primary Roman deity plays a role in the following entrance-line (which does *not* appear to be meant facetiously): "By Jove, Archie, too, is arriving in a characteristic way" (*E* 26). The oath's highfalutin tone is confirmed as it falls from the lips of a true son of Albion, Haines (*U* 1.359). Sociolinguistic accuracy, however, requires mention that "By Jove" is twice used by the all-too-Irish Simon Dedalus, both times in markedly native contexts: first on the way to Glasnevin Cemetery (*U* 6.371) and then in the bar at the Ormond Hotel (*U* 11.219). The Hibernian propriety of an appeal to the Roman Thunderer is also illustrated by Leopold Bloom's recollections of Milly's "tomboy oaths. O jumping Jupiter" (*U* 6.87–88). A moment in Stephen Dedalus' Shakespearean ruminations in "Scylla and Charybdis" contains effective mythological paradox and metonymy: "in pairing time. Jove, a cool ruttime send them. Yea, turtledove her" (*U* 9.539–40). Finally, there are two astronomical references to the planet Jupiter (*U* 12.359 and 17.1095).

Even more exotic is the appearance, in a passage concerning the weather, of "shoepisser pluvious" (*FW* 451.36). *Juppiter Pluvius* is a title of the father of the Roman gods in his capacity as "Rainmaker" (*pluvis* is Latin for "rain"). The original of his divine appellation occurs in *Ulysses,* "Jupiter Pluvius" (*U* 16.41). The interpretation of its Wakean variant is confirmed by collateral the presence of "raining water laughing, per Nupiter Privius" (*FW* 390.22–23) and "the Rainmaker" (*FW* 87.6). (There is a more mundane archival application: "Jupiter Fluvius" [VI.B.1.30]; here the Latin adjective means "associated with flowing water," "riverine.") Moreover, Aristophanes comically attributes the cause of rain to Jupiter's pissing in a sieve, an odd meteorological fact that was also known to Joyce: "peecieve" (*FW* 609.30). This compound verb appears only a few lines after some pseudo-Latin in the debate between *Muta* (St. Patrick, whose Latin is weak by his own admission) and *Juva* (the Druid whose command of any language is obscured by hieratic profundity): "Dies is Dorminus master and commandant illy tonobrass" (*FW* 609.28–29). The first phrase can be twisted in two complementary directions: "the Lord is our God" (*deus est dominus noster*) and "the daylight (*dies*) is the master of the time of sleep (*dormitio*)."[4] The second phrase is probably meant to be understood as meaning "that person (*ille* [the Lord God]) rules over ('commands') the darkness (*tenebras*)." The last word, "tonobrass," may also contribute to the confusion of divinities: *tono* is Latin for "I resound," "I thunder"; one of Jupiter's primary epithets is *Tonans* (the Thunderer). Here, then, the god may be making a brass cymbal resound. In an earlier passage mortals are told to listen (*audite*) to their "sovereign beingstalk, Tonans Tomazeus. O dite!" (*FW* 504.19). A similar exhortation, in this case an appeal to the chief god to listen to the truth, is heard in "*Audi*, Joe Peters! *Exaudi* facts!" (*FW* 152.14; compare *FW* 159.22–23).[5]

Almost all of the references to Jupiter in the *Wake* emphasize some aspect of his Olympian status as the all-powerful father of the gods. That celestial distinction is spelled out in the Latin for Jupiter's most hallowed cult-title in his principal temple on the Capitoline Hill, "Optimus Maximus" (*FW* 153.17–18); this epithet is loosely translated in "Besterfarther Zeuts" (*FW* 414.35–36). Jupiter's natural environment, of course, is the "specious heavings" (*FW* 153.17) or, in slightly more cosmogenic terms, "joepeter's gaseytotum" (*FW* 426.21). In that expansive region of primal gases it is possible for a minor divinity to eavesdrop behind a primal space cloud and to "hear how Jove and the peers talk" (*FW* 624.10).

Jupiter's regal weapon is the lightning-bolt, accompanied by a peal of thunder. Readers are reminded of these fearsome symbols of power: "The folgor of the frightfools is olympically optimominous" (*fulgor* is "lightning" in Latin) (*FW* 613.28–29). In a July 28, 1934, letter to Miss Weaver, Joyce himself testifies to the divine cause of frightening phenomena: "I read of the usual terrible thunderstorms in England this summer. Thank Jupiter, we have escaped so far" (*SL* 369). The reference to "that ligtning lovemaker's thender apeal" (*FW* 335.11) also alludes to Jupiter's mythological reputation as the omnivorous lover of mortal women. This polymorphously erotic aspect of the king-god's personality is mirrored in a series of astronomical references to the planet Jupiter and its satellites: "juniper arx. . . . the bulloge she bears! . . . jovial. . . . io, io. . . . ganymede" (*FW* 583.2–11; compare VI.B.41.147). Europa was a Phoenician princess borne on the back of Jupiter, in the form of a bull, to Crete.

Callisto was also seduced by Jupiter, then changed into a bear, and finally taken to the sky. Io, another victim of the Olympian king, was transformed into a heifer. Ganymede was a beautiful mortal youth abducted by Jupiter to serve as his heavenly cupbearer. These four mythological figures lend their names to the major satellites of the planet Jupiter, dimly glimpsed in "jompetter from his sodalites" (FW 241.34–35). The celestial primacy of the god Jupiter and the regal dimension of his planet are associated with an *arx*, the Latin word for "citadel," "summit." On Rome's citadel hill there were temples to Jupiter Capitolinus and his divine consort Juno Moneta, whose jealous wrath was responsible for a number of the transformations of Jupiter's mortal playmates.

The remaining appearances of Jupiter need little more comment than mere listing:

"Jove" (FW 80.28); "jove's" (FW 206.3); "by Jova" (FW 351.35); "*Deo Jupto*" (pseudo-Latin for "by the god Jupiter") (FW 353.18).

"Jove Chronides" (FW 231.23); here the epic patronymic *Cronides* ("son of Cronos," or *Saturnus* in Latin) is blended with the unrelated Greek noun for "time" (*chronos*), yielding "son of time."

"joebiggar" (FW 15.30; compare 70.34–35); "*Gross Jumpiter*" (FW 342.14) (*gross* means "great" in German); "Greates Schtschuptar!" (FW 343.21).

JUNO

Juno has already been mentioned as the patroness of the Capitoline temple dedicated to "Juno Moneta" (FW 538.1). It was at this site in early Rome that the goddess's sacred geese were fed and coins were minted. Her annual feasts are mentioned in "the jiboulees of Juno" (FW 87.6). In conjunction with the day named after the goddess Venus (*vendredi* is "Friday" in French), Juno's special time of the year is commemorated in "one venersderg in junoluly" (FW 203.19–20). The primary Joycean feast, Bloomsday, is cited in suitably Homeric terms as "the sixteenth day of the month of the oxeyed goddess" (U 12.1111). Finally, at FW 207.1–11 there is a long description of ALP dressing herself for maximum effect. This passage is closely modeled on Homer's detailed re-creation of Hera's (the Greek equivalent of Juno) toilette as she prepares to seduce her husband Zeus (Jupiter) in the *Iliad* 14.161–86. While the original context is Greek, not Latin, I include this episode since it is the *Wake's* most elaborate scene, in which the characteristics of a mythological goddess are transferred to one of Joyce's epic heroines.

All of the appearances of Juno in *Ulysses* emphasize her appearance in ancient and Renaissance art as the voluptuous queen-mother of the gods. In this sexually attractive sphere of her divine activity Juno is naturally associated with Venus, as in Bloom's recollection of "Shapely goddesses, Venus, Juno. . . . Lovely forms of women sculped Junonian" (*U* 8.920–28). In a dream-episode of "Oxen of the Sun," Phyllis (who seems to have backed the wrong horse in a race) becomes "silent: her eyes were sad anemones. Juno, she cried, I am undone" (*U* 14.1133–34). Even Shakespeare shares some of the goddess's iris-eyed allure: "greyedauburn. An azured harebell like her veins. Lids of Juno's eyes, violets" (*U* 9.652–53).

VENUS

In *Finnegans Wake* Venus makes several significant appearances. Her sphere of mythological influence—and her many amorous escapades—explain the presence of her name in what appears to be a pornographic play, "the *Smirching of Venus*" (*FW* 435.2–3). Even more directly erotic is the "Vicus Veneris" (literally "Venus' Alley") (*FW* 551.34), which can be translated as "red-light district" or a Ulyssean "nighttown." Issy, on the other hand, is once called "chariton queen" (*FW* 208.33). A direct translation from Greek of the first word marks her as "queen of the Graces," the three traditional attendants of Aphrodite/Venus in classical mythology. Frivolously plural sex-goddesses are also placed seductively beside their not-overly-bright, but explosive husbands: "Venuses were gigglibly temptatrix, vulcans guffawably eruptious" (*FW* 79.18).

The traditional tale of Venus' birth from spume floating on the top of the sea is specifically alluded to in "foamborn Aphrodite" (*U* 9.610). This extremely odd birth-story is retold in the *Wake,* but its narrative and stymological details are Greek, not Latin. There are, however, several Venus-passages that have a distinctly Roman origin. Section I.5 is primarily dedicated to ALP and her letter. It is traditionally called the "Mamafesta," from a long list of titles with which it begins. Not far into this section of the work is a paragraph introduced by "Lead, kindly fowl!" (*FW* 112.9). This request is usually glossed as a parody of the title of Cardinal Newman's hymn "Lead, Kindly Light" (see *Letters* I.305). In terms of the *Wake*'s plot, a fowl (usually identified as Biddy Doran's hen) is being called upon to lead the way to uncover the letter as she scratches and pecks at the midden heap. There is, however, another literary allusion lurking in the shadows here. Lucretius' long philosophical poem, *De Rerum Natura* (On the Nature of the Universe), begins with an elaborate invocation of Venus Genetrix. The goddess is saluted as the nurturing mother of the creative process that brings peace and life to the world: *aeriae primum volucres te, diva, tuumque / significant initium* (first the fowls of the air proclaim you, goddess, and your arrival) (Lucretius 1.12–13). Venus will strike love (*amorem* [19]) into the breasts of all creatures and cause them to propagate their species (*generatim saecla propagent* [20]). A few lines after introducing his kindly fowl into the *Wake*, Joyce adverts to the bird's "volucrine automutativeness" and indicates that she was "born to lay and love eggs (trust her to propagate the species . . .)" (*FW* 112.12–14). I find it very difficult to ascribe this cluster of lexical parallels ("volucrine"/*volucres*, "lay and love"/*amorem*, and "propagate the species"/*generatim . . . propagent*) to some fortuitously mutual swerve of both Joycean and Lucretian word-choice. Rather, the goddess Venus and her escort-fowls from the introduction to the Latin poem have—by design, but covertly—been introduced into the description of the advent of the *Wake*'s epistolary hen.[6]

During Stephen's Shakespearean tour de force in the National Library, the Roman goddess is listed with two other seductive characters from the Bard's classical works: "Cleopatra, fleshpot of Egypt, and Cressid and Venus" (*U* 9.883–84).

Near the end of *Portrait* Venus also appears, tangentially, in the midst of the hero's disquisition on the static nature of tragedy. The classical goddess of sexual rapture is introduced in a bit of irreverent incidental refutation of Stephen's claim that the aesthetic emotions rise above desire. Lynch counters: "one day I wrote my name on the backside of the Venus Praxiteles in the Museum. Was that not desire?" (*P* 205; compare 208). In a January 30, 1916, letter to Joyce's literary agent, James B. Pinker, Ezra Pound made the following comment: "as for altering Joyce to suit [the publisher] Duckworth's readers—I would like trying to fit the Venus de Milo in a piss-pot" (*Letters* II.373).

NEPTUNE

Even though he is Jupiter's brother and the lord of the sea, Neptune gets little by-play in either *Ulysses* or the *Wake*. Joyce, however, fully respected the god's power. In a letter to Miss Weaver he wrote that "Neptune, hearing I had reached the seacoast, sent out a storm posthaste" (*Letters* I.185). In terms of the Homeric underpinning of *Ulysses*, this lack of emphasis is odd, since Poseidon/Neptune was the chief divine nemesis of Homer's hero. In the editorial offices of the *Telegraph*, Ned Lambert quotes a purple passage from Dan Dawson's speech: "*to the tumbling waters of Neptune's blue domain*" (*U* 7.244–45). "Neptunian" appears in a list of possible extra-terrestrial, planetary races (*U* 17.1095). A more subtle allusion is included in Stephen's "Scylla and Charybdis" catalogue of the world's "incests and bestialities": "queens with prize bulls" (*U* 9.851–54). The reference is to the myth about Pasiphae's terrible punishment—passion for a bull sent to Crete by Neptune (see pages 156–57).

In the *Wake* Neptune appears briefly in the exclamation "Posidonius

O'Fluctuary!" (FW 80.28–29). The Greek form of his name (Poseidon) is glossed with a functional Hiberno-Latin surname (*fluctus* is the word for "wave," "flood"). As the patron of a Dublin rowing club, the god teams up with another minor marine divinity, who lent his name to a Dublin seaside road. They both compete with Leander, Oxford University's prestige boat-club: "Neptune sculled and Tritonville rowed and leandros three bumped heroines two" (FW 203.12–13). These two sea-gods also reappear as "Neptune's Centinel and Tritonville Lightowler" (FW 585.2) Finally, Neptune applies the components of his stormy realm to scatological purposes: "he forgot himself, making wind and water, and made a Neptune's mess of all of himself" (FW 391.17–18). In fact, Joyce adds a specific aquatic detail to the last allusion by immediately revealing the precise location of Neptune's incontinent disgrace. It took place at the Diamond Sculls, the world-class, single-sculls race at the Henley Regatta. In the Wakean sports report of the annual competition, the details are garbled into "sculling over the giamond's courseway" (FW 391.18–19; compare " ⊥ diamond / sculls" [VI.B.9.46]).

DIANA

Diana is the virginal goddess of the deep forest and wild animals, which she hunts as well as protects. This aspect of the goddess is briefly mentioned in a description of the quartet of old men who hear Hosty's first recitation of the ballad: they have not forgotten "a deuce of dianas ridy for the hunt" (FW 43.11). In the forest, with the nymphs as her companions, Diana fiercely guarded her privacy and chastity. In his *Metamorphoses* (3.155–252), Ovid tells the gory tale of a wandering hunter, Actaeon, who accidentally came upon the goddess while she was bathing in a forest pool. His punishment was swift and brutal. Diana changed him into a stag; while he tried in vain to call them off, his own pack of hounds tore the transformed Actaeon to pieces. In the "Proteus" chapter of *Ulysses*, Stephen Dedalus is suddenly accosted by a dog as he walks along the tidal flats at Sandymont. Although his terrible fear of dogs stops him in his tracks, Stephen does not share Actaeon's fate: "The dog's bark ran towards him, stopped, ran back. Dog of my enemy. I just simply stood pale, silent, bayed about. *Terribilia meditans*" (U 3.310–11). The terminal Latin phrase (pondering fearful events) strongly suggests a literary analogue for Stephen's frightening experience, but the metrical shape of those words precludes any direct reference to Ovid.

The goddess's name also appears, for no discernable reason, in an avian-Aristophanic context in the *Wake*, "Diana" (FW 276.19). A later passage blends her with the horn-blowing Dinah of the popular song, "the bugle dianablowing" (FW 475.36–476.1). Finally, there is an acknowledgment of one of her most important cult sites, the Temple of Diana at Ephesus (see Acts 19: 23–41). That shrine is included in a jumbled list of the seven wonders of the ancient world that is part of the children's homework assignment in "Night Lessons": "delighted in her dianaphous" (*FW* 261.11).

Dis

In classical mythology the dark realm of the lord of the Underworld is far more important than its immortal master. This emphasis on infernal geography is reflected in Joyce's treatment of the god Dis, whom the Greeks called "Hades." The River Styx, for example, is well known to students of the topography of the Greco-Roman afterlife. Another Latin term for the land of darkness is *Erebus*, which is momentarily present in a pseudoarchaic passage in the "Cyclops" chapter of *Ulysses*, during the discussion of execution by hanging (*U* 12.447). The only other evocation of the "unseen" god (for this etymology see pages 126–27) of the Underworld in *Ulysses* is a formulaic "By Hades" exclaimed by the consistently classical J. J. O'Molloy (*U* 15.967). And "Hades" is mentioned as the source of "fresh horrors" in a *Wake* passage in which some of the consequences of and traditional treatment for syphilis are detailed (*FW* 183.35–36).

Dis, Jupiter's brother, is incredibly "rich" (the Latin adjective *dis* corresponds to the Greek *ploutos*), because sooner or later every mortal soul is deposited into his infernal account. Dis's consort is Proserpina, the daughter of the goddess Ceres, whom he kidnapped to become his queen and whom he forces to reside in the Underworld during the unfertile quarter of each year. The royal couple (he in the Greek form of his name) are united in an amorous context in "Night Lessons" as "plutonically pursuant on briefest glimpse from gladrags, pretty Proserpronette" (*FW* 267.9–11).

Mars

Mars is the Roman god of war and its bloody consequences, the lord of the body count. In the margin of "Night Lessons" there is a cryptic entry: "*Mars speaking*" (*FW* 263.L1). Most likely this announcement is meant to be understood as a gloss on the adjacent text, which is packed with all sorts of historical belligerents: "Egyptus," "Cyrus"; "ostrogothic and ottomanic faith converters." The cross-European carnage of the First World War also seems to be commemorated in the nearby "despair of Pandemia's post-wartem plastic surgeons" (*FW* 263.6–12).

In classical myth Mars is an offspring of Jupiter and Juno, a genealogy that Joyce commemorates in a pseudoepic epithet, "Tumult, son of Thunder" (*FW* 184.6). His bellicose tendencies are universalized and pluralized in "martiallawsey marses" (FW 64.13) and a familiar proverb is recorded, in low fidelity, in "allsfare for the loathe of Marses ambiviolent" (FW 518.2). The terminal adjective may echo the ruthless impartiality of the lord of combat; he is far more concerned with the casualty toll than the victory. And as a matter of fact, in the *Wake* as in life, love does have its superpassionate, even violent side. Perhaps it is in recognition of the ambivalent nature of sexual attraction that mythology links Mars and the goddess Venus as lovers. In his Greek manifestation, Mars is "ardent Ares" (FW 269.17) on the couch of love as well as on the field of battle. The (more-or-less) Greek and Latin names for this god appear side by side in "Ers, Mores" (FW 494.12). His martial craft also has an aesthetic aspect, as is acknowledged in "ars all bellical" (FW 122.7). In this phrase the Latin word *ars* (art, craft) suggests Ares. The noun is then modified by what is *either* a Latin adjective associated with wars (*bellica*) *or* by a common Romance-language root that means "fine," "pretty," "graceful" (*bella*). This etymological ambiguity is most emphatically spelled out in the following, adjacent questions and exclamations:

—Yet this war has meed peace? . . . Ab chaos lex, neat wehr?
—O bella! O pia! O pura! (FW 518.31–33; compare FW 178.17, 389.3–4, and 486.32)

Here the wars (*bella*, neuter plural) generated by attempts to purify religion in Vico's heroic age[7] can also be read as a Latino-Italian adjective (feminine singular) that is frequently applied to Issy, who is *pious, pure, and pretty*, as in "Pia de Purebelle" (FW 27.16). Finally, there is another translingual pun embedded in "ars all bellical." One is certainly nudged to hear the British slang "arse" in the first word. Thus, the entire phrase (but applied here to the goddess's male Olympian lover) is the Latinish equivalent of the Greek epithet *Kallipyge* (with beautiful buttocks), which was twice applied to Mars' consort, Venus, in *Ulysses* (U 9.616 and 15.1705).

Other Joycean allusions to Mars fall into four conventional categories: astronomical or zodiacal (U 12.359, 17.1095, 17.1114); Zoe's palmistry reading of Stephen's character: "Mars, that's courage" (U 15.3657); a pair of funereal Wakean references to ancient Rome's *Campus Martius* (the Field of Mars): "Champ de Mors" (FW 119.32) and "champdamors" (FW 551.10); in both instances, the Latin word *mors* (death) is substituted for the god's name. A final calendric note, "the twentysecond of Mars" (FW 134.12) is the earliest day on which Easter can occur, according to the calculations of the Western Church.

JANUS

Closely associated with Mars is Janus, the two-faced divine guardian of doors, "the doublejoynted janitor" (*FW* 27.2–3). In a heavily Roman index in one of the Notebooks, Joyce pairs Vesta (the goddess of the city's hearth flame) with Janus; he is modified by the Latin adjective "bifrons" (with two faces) (VI.B.18.270). In ancient Rome, the entrance to Janus' temple was shut in wartime, open during periods of total peace. This peculiarity of Roman political-ritualistic practice is mentioned in the *Wake:*

> figure right . . . figure left . . . shows the sinews of peace in his chest-o-wars . . . is aldays open for polemypolity's sake when he's not suntimes closed for the love of Janus. (*FW* 133.3–19)

There is archival evidence to support this interpretation: "⁸Janus ʎ " (the siglum, most appropriately, stands for the conjoined Shem-Shaun) and "ᵇopen in war" (VI.B.8.124). In the passage cited just above the "polemypolity" is composed of roots springing from the Greek words for "war" (*polemos*) and "city" (*polis*). This portmanteau word connects the open temple to belligerent civic policy. Janus' link with war is also alluded to in the exclamation, "But, holy Janus, I was forgetting the Blitzenkopfs!" (*FW* 272.16–17). *Blitz* is German for "lightning," as in *Blitzkrieg* (lightning war); *Kopf* is German for "head"—which Joyce pluralizes here, perhaps to allude to Janus' two faces. Immediately after this passage, the Jutish conquerors of England, Hengist and Horsa, are cited as the pair of *lightning-heads*, "Hengegst and Horsesause" (*FW* 272.17). Although these two Germanic war-leaders are merely brothers, not twins, they serve as stand-ins here for the fraternal combatants Shem and Shaun. And holy Janus is appropriately involved, since the two-faced god was sometimes evoked as "Geminus" (the Twin).

One of the most famous battles in Roman history is the victory of Octavian-Augustus' fleet at Actium (31 B.C.), where the ships of Mark Antony and Cleopatra were decisively defeated. This battle and its marine venue are mentioned on the same page of the *Wake* as the previous Janus-lightning quotation: "hot off Minnowaurs and naval actiums, picked engagements and banks of rowers" (*FW* 272.10–12; compare "ʳnaval actium" [VI.B.33.67]). Roman history records only three occasions on which the doors of the temple of Janus were ceremonially closed, the most significant of which is after the battle of Actium, the naval victory that ushered in the *Pax Augusta*.

Another phrase, "the first of Janus' straight" (*FW* 542.15–16) refers to the god's gift of his name to what became the first month of the year. After calendar reform in A.D. 153, January replaced March (named after Mars) as the beginning of the Roman political and religious year. (See pages 249–51 in appendix II, for more discussion of the Roman calendar in the *Wake*.) A final reference to the doorkeeper (*janitor*) god involves the origin of the traditional designation of the Janiculum, one of Rome's seven hills (*collis* is "hill" in Latin). Joyce accurately reports that this topographical name was "inhebited after his colline born janitor" (*FW* 224.11).

MERCURY

Mercury was the male messenger for Jupiter and the other Olympian gods. His worldwide travels established him as the divine protector of merchants, a function that seemed warranted by the suggestion that his name was derived from *merx, mercis,* the Latin word for "trade" and "commerce." A childhood escapade discussed below also earned the god the patronage of sharpers, thieves, and con-men. Finally, Mercury served Dis as what the Greeks termed a "psychopomp"; that is, he acted as an "escort" (*pompē*) for the "soul" (*psychē*) of a dead human on its trip into the Underworld. All of these activities require interplanetary speed, as well as supranatural levels of mental and physical agility: "swifter as mercury" (*FW* 454.20–21). There are brief references to the planet Mercury at *U* 17.1095 and *FW* 494.12.

It may seem a bit paradoxical, then, that especially in *Ulysses*, Mercury is consistently associated with "[s]tately, plump Buck Mulligan" (*U* 1.1). This process begins with Mulligan's claim to a right of contradicting himself: "Mercurial Malachi" (*U* 1.518; compare *U* 15.4171). The identification is reinforced by the description of Mulligan as he capered down the path to swim in "the fortyfoot hole, fluttering his winglike hands, leaping nimbly, Mercury's hat quivering in the fresh wind" (*U* 1.600–602). But it was not, I think, Mulligan's athletic grace or even his puckish character that lies behind his identification with Mercury. Rather, he was a medical student and, as a kips-wise physician-to-be, Mulligan would have been regarded as a potential prescriber of the state-of-the-art therapy to counteract syphilis: mercury. At the end of an inventory of the cluttered contents of Shem's quarters in the *Wake*, "fresh horrors from Hades, globules of mercury, undeleted glete" stand side by side (*FW* 183.35–36). One of the side effects of therapeutic mercury treatment was a darkening of the patient's teeth and skin. These indicators are evident in a "*sinister figure*" who accosts Bloom in Nighttown, with "*visage unknown, injected with dark mercury*" (*U* 15.212–13). This unidentified functionary, apparently from the Castle, reappears as "*A dark mercurialized face*" (*U* 15.748–49). In addition to its use in cases of venereal disease, mercury has other physicochemical applications. It was applied as backing on mirrors: "a murcery glaze of shard to mirrow" (*FW* 548.31). And it is one of the principal elements in alchemical experiments and a component in some zodiacal systems: "in his horrorscup he is mehrkurios than saltz of sulphur" (*FW* 261.24–26).[8]

One of Mercury's most ingeniously executed mythological adventures was his rustling, while still a youngster, of some of Apollo's prize cattle. The locale of this bit of divine juvenile delinquency may be obliquely represented in the *Wake* by a pun on the name Octavius, "Oxthievious" (*FW* 271.5–6). On the same page of Joyce's text, the Old Testament's primary confidence man, the Serpent in Eden, is certainly present: "Coax Cobra. . . . Hail Heva . . . ! This is the glider that gladden the girl . . . in the garden Gough gave" (*FW* 271.24–29). A faintly phallic and resolutely tricky Mercury also slithers just beneath the surface here. In Joyce's own footnote to the passage just cited, the Serpent is described as being "deadleaf brown with *quicksilver* appliques" (*FW* 271.F5; my emphasis).

On two occasions in the *Wake*, versions of a cryptic Latin proverb are reproduced: "*Nex quovis burro num fit mercaseus*" (*FW* 163.15) and "*Eggs squawfish lean yoe nun feed marecurious*" (*FW* 484.36). Allowing for specifically Joycean distortion *in situ* and regional variations in the pronunciation of Latin, the text can be restored to read *ex quovis ligno num fit Mercurius* (Mercury is not made from any piece of wood, is he?). The saying seems to be the Roman equivalent of "You cannot make a silk purse out of a sow's ear." Mercury, here, is most probably meant to refer to a *herm*. This shaft was a boundary marker, topped by a bust of Hermes/Mercury, with a representation of the god's phallus protruding from the middle of the column. Thus, the piece of wood selected to be turned into this indicator of property limits should have, in the appropriate places, natural knobs that can be shaped into the god's head and shaft.

I have no idea where Joyce picked up this version of the proverb. In Apuleius' *Apology*, a little-known work in which the second-century A.D. author of *The Golden Ass* refutes those who accuse him of magic, there appears an obviously similar statement: *non enim ex omni ligno, ut Pythagoras dicebat, debet Mercurius exculpi* (A statue of Mercury ought not to be carved from every piece of wood, as Pythagoras used to say) (*Apology* 43). The proverb is used by Apuleius to bolster his argument that magicians probably cannot enchant young boys to perform wonders. If this *does* happen, Apuleius argues, it would be entirely fitting for pure, healthy, intelligent, young boys to be the receptacle of supernatural power, since you cannot situate a seer in a sow's ear. The philosopher Pythagoras, who was vitally interested in metempsychosis, would have recognized the propriety in such a transfer and placement of energy.

Bacchus

Bacchus is the Roman equivalent of Dionysos. As the lord of everything liquid, he is the power behind sap, semen, wine, the rush of blood in frenzy or intoxication. The god's name, venue, and function are clearly present in these summons of drinkers to the pub: "So let Bacchus e'en call! Inn, inn! Inn inn! Where. The babbers ply the pen. The bibbers drang the den" (FW 262.26–28).

In the list of titles in the "Mamafesta," there is a slightly askew line from the drinking song "Anacreon in Heaven": "*When the Myrtles of Venice Played to Bloccus' Line*" (FW 104.24–105.1). The original verse was "When the myrtle of Venus joins with Bacchus' vine." In the bar of the Ormond Hotel in "Sirens," Simon Dedalus urges Ben Dollard to sing a favorite song, "*Love and War*" (U 11.459 and 553). The chorus of that song invokes several Roman gods, including Bacchus:

> Since Mars Lov'd Venus Venus Mars
> Let's blend loves wounds with battle's scars
> And call in Bacchus all divine,
> To cure both pains with rosy wine.[9]

Other evocations of the god do not appear to have any marked thematic purpose: a mathematically cerebral "baccbucuss of his mind" (FW 118.16); a gastronomic-alphabetic "apple, bacchante, custard" (FW 247.35); a malty goat able "to sate with Becchus. Zumbock! Achevre!" (FW 276.13); a smithy's "peer of bellows like Bacchulus" (FW 365.6); and a gustatorial treat "We could ate you, par Buccas, and imbabe through you" (*bucca* is "cheek" and *imbibo, imbibere* is "to drink" in Latin) (FW 378.2–3).

Because his divine grace liberates his devotees from the normal restraints of propriety and sobriety, the Romans sometimes called Bacchus *Liber* (free, freed). Joyce so invokes the god in an alliterative toast: "Lift your right to your Liber Lord. Link your left to your lass of liberty" (FW 250.20–21). Not only is Bacchus a liberator here; he is also the "dear [*lieber* in German] Lord." The same multilingual play on words—with an offhand allusion to William Ewart Gladstone—is found in "liberaloider" (FW 336.24).

Apollo

In a passage in which Jaun recalls how he and his brother ("we younkers twain") once played in bed, there is a pair of exclamations that are directed to one member each of two of mythology's most famous twins: "O Phoebus! O Pollux!" (FW 431.35–36). The first pair is gloriously divine, Phoebus Apollo and Artemis/Diana; the second pair was, in the first days of the Trojan War, tragically mortal, Pollux and Castor (note "Castor's oil" in the next line [*FW* 432.1]). This direct address to the "brilliant" (*phoibos* in Greek) lord of all that must be measured—music, archery, medicine, poetry, prophecy—is only one of numerous allusions to Apollo in the works of Joyce.

At the maternity hospital in *Ulysses,* there are many utopian educational schemes proposed by the various pseudoacademics to reverse a "fallingoff in the calibre of the race." Buck Mulligan opts for, among the other "graces of life," the dissemination of "plastercast reproductions of the classical statues such as Venus and Apollo" (*U* 14.1250–54). Another artistic reference to Apollo in *Ulysses* is a perfect example of a Bloomerism, a telling error of fact that usually involves speculation on some esoteric topic. While walking through the burial monuments ("saddened angels, crosses, broken pillars" [*U* 6.928–929]) in Glasnevin Cemetery, Bloom spots a Catholic religious statue:

> The Sacred Heart that is: showing it. Heart on his sleeve. Ought to be sideways and red it should be painted like a real heart.(*U* 6.954–55)

The statue's lack of realistic detail, perspective, and color bothers Bloom; but the basis of his criticism stems from exotically aesthetic, not sentimentally devotional matters. As he continues to ruminate about the Sacred Heart's defects, Bloom wonders:

> Would birds come then and peck like the boy with the basket of fruit but he said no because they ought to have been afraid of the boy. Apollo that was. (*U* 6.957–59)

This passage requires comment. The thrust of Gifford and Seidman's note is right on the mark, but its report of the details is not crystal clear. Joyce has Bloom remember an anecdote about a Greek painter that is recorded in Pliny's *Natural History* 35.36.66. In that Latin encyclopedia, which includes a section on art history, it is reported that Zeuxis painted some grapes so realistically that birds flew up and tried to peck at them. Pliny writes that the ancient Greek artist then created another work, *Puerum uvas ferentem* (A Boy Carrying Grapes). When the birds dove at the painted fruit, as before, Zeuxis became furious and said that, if he had made the boy as lifelike as the grapes, the birds would have been afraid to approach the painting. That anecdote is the basis of Bloom's comments about the Sacred Heart, but how does the *Apollo* fit into this picture? The same two-tiered story of the birds' reaction is sometimes attributed to the birds' reaction to the work of another great artist, the greatest painter of antiquity, Apelles. Thus, Bloom, characteristically, has confused a painter with the god, probably due to the coincidental similarity of their names.[10]

It was not likely that Bloom's error would have been noticed by the other mourners at Paddy Dignam's funeral. There is, however, another passage from Pliny the Elder embedded in the *Wake*. In the same section of his encyclopedic *Natural History* as the Zeuxis anecdote about the boy and grapes, the Roman writer records a second and distinct example of the scrupulous attention to realistic detail displayed by ancient painters. This time it is Apelles who is reported to have exhibited a portrait for public inspection. A passing cobbler detected that there were too few loops in the subject's sandal straps. The painter corrected the defect, but the cobbler then found fault with the drawing of the leg itself. Apelles retorted, *ne supra crepidam sutor iudicaret* (Let the cobbler not criticize beyond the sandal) (*N.H.* 35.36.85). The rebuke became proverbial. Joyce includes a portion of Pliny's Latin text in the *Wake*: "sopper crappidamn" (*FW* 326.32). The source of the citation is confirmed by the presence of "sutor" (cobbler) nearby in the same paragraph of the text (*FW* 326.27). This semi-Latin fragment is not, however, directly attributed to the writer Pliny or to the painter Apelles; rather, Joyce's next move in the text is to indicate that he may have thought that Horace was the author of the proverb: "as Harris himself says" (*FW* 326.32). Be that as it may, the same Joyce who created Leopold Bloom's bloopers was also easily capable of injecting a purposely misleading reference to a classical text into his work. Joyce's purpose would have been to recommend that future commentators should be sure to check the allusive measure of their philological "lasts," lest they perpetuate a scrambling of the names of Apelles and Apollo, or of Horace and Pliny.

SATURN

In the detailed answer to a cathechetical question about astronomy in "Ithaca," the rings of the planet Saturn are ponderously cited as "annular cinctures" (*U* 17.1107). This phrase is based on the conjunction of a misspelled Latin adjective *anularius* (not -*nn*- as if from *annus* [year]) meaning "ringlike" and the noun *cinctus* (belt, sash). In the *Wake*, Saturn and one of its satellite moons are named in the midst of a cluster of celestial detail: "Satyrdaysboost besets Phoebe's nearest" (*FW* 583.19). As a matter of fact, Phoebe (named after Artemis-Diana) is Saturn's most distant, ninth satellite. "Night Lessons" also records a month with "two lunar eclipses and its three saturnine settings" (*FW* 264.4–5). Later in the work, Jaun gazes at Issy with "his onsaturncast eyes in stellar attraction" (*FW* 449.2–3).

Saturn is the Father-King of the second divine dynasty. He thrust his own father from the heavenly throne by removing the patriarch's prime claim to power: Uranus was castrated with a sickle. Saturn himself was deposed in turn, and exiled to the Isles of the Blessed by Jupiter. Even though Saturn did not participate in the Revolt of the Titans, an archival note associates him with his first-dynasty siblings, and with Shaun and Shem: "Titans/Saturn ⋏" (VI.B.4.319). In later mythology, Saturn's reign is often associated with the Golden Age, fondly commemorated in nostalgic tales by mortals, as in the *Wake*: "'Tis golden sickle's hour" (*FW* 360.24). Joyce is aware of this mythic remembrance of times past; he uses an adjectival form of Saturn's Greek name (Cronos) with appropriate modifiers: "And so time wags on: but father Cronion has dealt lightly here" (*U* 14.1336).

In English, Saturn lends his name to the seventh day of the week. Joyce more or less alludes to this in "Saturnay Eve" (*FW* 366.15–16), which is when Issy was generated during her father's Uranus-like nocturnal ejaculation. Another reference to the god's name day may be intended in a vaguely Egyptian passage in which the "Games funeral at Valleytemple" are connected "Saturnights pomps" (*FW* 602.22).

Just as Saturn overthrew his progenitor Uranus to become king of Olympus, so too did Jupiter depose his heavenly father to inaugurate the third divine dynasty. According to the standard mythological tale of the coup, Saturn was worried that one of his own offspring might attempt to depose him; so he swallowed each of his children immediately after their birth. Finally his wife Rhea hid the infant Jupiter in a cave. She then presented her mate with a stone wrapped in swaddling clothes, which he devoured. After Jupiter matured, he emerged from hiding to confront his father, punched him in the stomach, and forced him to regurgitate the siblings whom he had swallowed. Saturn and Rhea were then exiled, and Jupiter and his now-liberated sister-wife, Juno, ascended to the throne. A helter-skelter version of this bizarre story of pedophagy and deliverance seems to be retold in the *Wake*:

One feared for his days. Did there yawn? 'Twas his stomick. Eruct? The libber. A gush? From his visuals. Pung? Delivver him, orelode! He had laid violend hands on himself. (*FW* 97.29–31)

The supertext deals with HCE's bodily reactions, on arising, to the effects of intemperate drinking. He yawns noxiously; his stomach erupts; his liver contributes to a gush of urine; from his vitals, he drops an acutely pungent overload of waste. In the subtext, I detect a fist (*pugnus* in Latin; *poign* in French) in the stomach, which triggers vomiting (*eructus* in Latin), which liberates the engorged children. Jupiter freed his brothers and sisters by treating Saturn as violently as he deserved.

A few lines later on the same page of the text there is a reference to "the triduum of Saturnalia" (*FW* 97.33). This ancient Roman festival in December is most famous for its ritualistic merrymaking: slaves were allowed temporary liberty, presents were exchanged, a King of Misrule was crowned. As its name suggests, this celebration may well be associated with Saturn, as the divine patron of the winter sowing (*sero, satum*) of grain.

There is another famous Roman feast, the Lupercalia. It is a mid-February ritual, at which youths would run naked (except for sashes of goatskins) through the Palatine area in the center of the city. During their revels the boys would strike women with their goatskins to induce fertility. Joyce seems to have associated this celebration with the Saturnalia, since in the very next line after the citation given above he records that during the three-day period of the Lupercalia "his goatservant had paraded hiz willingsons in the Forum" (*FW* 97.34). Although it would be rash to call HCE much of a servant of god, he certainly might have shown off his twin sons (*Zwillinge* in German). By stretching mythological allusion to its limits here, it is also possible to imagine Jupiter's proud display, to the Olympian world, of his two brothers who have just been freed from Saturn's stomach. Dis and Neptune are not twins—but they are participants in the famous tale of a divine son abrogating his father's power. In fact, later in the *Wake*'s text it is not HCE and his twin sons, but their mother ALP who is associated with the Lupercalia: "I'll homeseek you, Luperca as sure as there's a palatine in Limerick" (*FW* 444.35–36; compare VI.B.14.208 "°lupercae"). According to a late source, *Luperca* is the name applied to the deified wolf (*lupa* in Latin) who suckled Romulus and Remus beside the banks of the Tiber. She and her husband *Lupercus* may have been invented by a commentator who wanted to personify the "wolf-divinities" whom the ceremonies of the Lupercalia were meant to appease. Modern scholars disagree on the primitive origins and purposes of the ritual. At any rate, the humane she-wolf lurks, more as Latin-Quarter vamp than as a Palatine-Tiburtine wet nurse, in another passage where she is called "Lupita Lorette" and "Luperca Latouche" (*FW* 67.33, 36).

VULCAN

If there were such a subspecialty in mythology as a narrow focus on the activities of Vulcan (Hephaestus in Greek), it would be called "vulcanology" (*FW* 494.7). The Wakean environment of this term clearly relates it to volcanoes, active or "Extinct": "etnat athos? . . . for the lava of Moltens" (*FW* 494.7–8; compare *FW* 89.28). In ancient tales the massive forge of the blacksmith-god is naturally associated with the fire and rumbling of seismic disturbances, "[l]ike Heavytost's envil catacalamitumbling . . . into the Vulcuum" (*FW* 514.11–12) or "the crater of some noted volcano" (*FW* 410.10–11).

A rare glimpse into the sometimes troubled course of divine domestic relations is given at the end of the first book of the *Iliad.* There Homer tells how Jupiter once flung Vulcan off the peak of Mt. Olympus because the young god had dared to defend his mother Juno in a family argument. Vulcan plunged through the air for a full day until he landed on the volcanic island of Lemnos. It was in this epic fall that the Lord of Technology probably suffered the leg injury that left him lame. Milton imitated this Homeric incident in his description of Lucifer's plunge from heaven in *Paradise Lost.*[11] Joyce combines elements from both versions:

> comming nown from the asphalt to the concrete. . . . to this same vulganized hillsir from yours, Mr Tupling Toun of Morning de Heights, with his lavast flow and his rambling undergroands. (*FW* 481.12–15)

Another ultimately Homeric reference to Vulcan involves a Wakean synopsis of the bard's tale of the "Divine Triangle" from book 8 of the *Odyssey.* While the blacksmith-god is purportedly away on a business trip, his wife Venus arranges an assignation with her lover, Mars. Vulcan, however, has arranged for the couple to be caught, *in flagrante,* by a set of almost invisible golden chains that he has forged. Joyce comments on this comic tale of celestial infidelity: "Venuses were gigglibly temptatrix, vulcans guffawably eruptious and the whole wives' world frockful of fickles" (*FW* 79.18–19). The most famous volcanic eruption in the Roman world caused the destruction and burial of Pompeii and Heraculaneum in A.D. 79. Among those killed by the fumes, debris, and lava from Mt. Vesuvius was Pliny the Elder, who had sailed to the disaster area to investigate its effect firsthand. The primary source of information about this famous catastrophe was a detailed account requested from Pliny the Younger by the historian Tacitus. Joyce summarizes the momentous event and its personalized documentary source: "haunting hesteries round old volcanoes. We gin too gnir and thus plinary indulgence makes collemulas of us all" (*FW* 319.6–8). There is also a Wakean allusion to Bulwer-Lytton's popular historical novel, which ends with the fatal eruption: "the third last days of Pompery" (*FW* 64.14–15).[12] Just across the page from this reference to the eruption of Vesuvius is the phrase "Ethna Prettyplume" (*FW* 318.12). I see and hear the first word as an allusion to Sicily's renowned volcano, Mt. Aetna. The ornamental epithet "Prettyplume" describes the apparently harmless smoke and steam spiraling from the crater. When Pompeii was destroyed, Pliny the Younger used a far more ominous simile to describe the deadly cloud that formed over the volcano in the Bay of Naples: it was shaped like an umbrella pine (*arbor . . . pinus*) (*Letters* 6.16).[13] A reference to the effect of this cloud is encapsulated in a question about the intensity of a rainstorm: "Or did wolken hang o'er earth in umber hue his fulmenbomb?" (*FW* 588.19–20). The Latin words for "shadow" (*umbra*)—and perhaps "rain" (*imber*)—as well as "thunderbolt" (*fulmen*) are neatly blended into this inquiry. Another distinct allusion to the consequences of the eruption of Mt. Vesuvius picks up several of the motifs mentioned above:

> viceuvious pyrolyphics, a snow of dawnflakes, at darkfall . . . all assombred. Some wholetime in hot town tonight! (*FW* 570.5–8; see "ᵇassombred" [VI.B.4.190])

The primary reference to Vulcan in *Ulysses* also involves a noxious cloud. When Bloom contemplates "Agendath Netaim: planters' company" (*U* 4.191–192), he imagines Yahweh's destruction of Sodom and Gomorrah:

> A cloud began to cover the sun slowly, wholly. Grey. Far. . . . A barren land, bare waste, Vulcanic lake . . . . Brimstone they called it raining down. (*U* 4.218–22)

There is another Ulyssean reference to Vulcan, but it requires a leap from the Old Testament to early-twentieth-century rubber technology. Among the furnishings in Bloom's "Ithacan" dreamhouse is a "vulcanite automatic telephone receiver with adjacent directory" (*U* 17.1525–26; compare "vulcanite smoking" [*FW* 334.9]).

My review of Joyce's treatment of the major divinities of ancient classical myth, primarily in their Roman manifestation, is complete. The project started with an excerpt from a letter to Paul Léon, in which Joyce requested help in compiling an alphabetical list of male gods. The letter "C" seems to have stymied the master. This is understandable since, even after consulting a comprehensive handbook, only Chaos, Charon, and Cronos appear as likely candidates—and in each case the source of the name is Greek rather than Latin. At any rate, in the final version of this catalogue in the *Wake* only four gods are made manifest as the list leaps from "glib Ganymede" to "zealous Zeus" (*FW* 269.18).

Another archival document records Joyce's abiding interest in the details of ancient theogony: an early Notebook contains the entry "°30,000 gods Varro" (VI.B.12.13; compare VI.B.2.132). This statistic—surely a record-breaker, even in the face of polytheistic excess of all sorts—is attributed to Varro, the first-century A.D. Roman encyclopedist. Joyce's immediate source of this bit of classical theology is Michelet's "Discours."[14] The Notebook entry appears in the text of the *Wake* only after having been modified into "name of the multitude" (*FW* 73.4–5). This deeply buried reference is confirmed by the adjacent presence of "fishguds" (*FW* 73.6), an odd portmanteau word that echoes Michelet's example of Roman theological procedure: the deification and personification of *le mar* into *Neptune*. The lightly disguised sea lord, however, is the only one of the gods who worked his way into this section of the text—which is probably just as well, since a 30,000-item catalogue would have taxed the patience of even the *Wake*'s most fervent devotee.

ROMAN RITUAL

In ancient Rome there was a chief priest who, in effect, supervised all religious activity, public or private. He was called the *pontifex maximus*, which literally means "the most important bridge-builder."[15] Joycean comment on the archaic "civil-engineering" aspects of the chief priest's duties is found in the initial entries in the following catalogue of the various titles that have accrued, over the centuries, to HCE and his avatars:

> Prospector projector and boomooster *giant builder of all causeways woesoever*, hopping offpoint and *true terminus* of straxstraightcuts and corkscrewn perambulaups. (*FW* 576.18–20, my emphases)

The first italicized phrase in that citation is a more-or-less accurate translation of *pontifex maximus*. The second emphasized term also held special meaning for the Romans: *Terminus* was the god of boundaries. Each year on February 23 elaborate sacrifices were offered to him on the feast of the *Terminalia*. Within the temple of Jupiter on the Capitoline was the original *terminus*-stone, from which all Roman distances were calculated. It was, then, the true "hopping offpoint" for every die-straight, cross-country road or twisting walkway of the city itself. (For more information about Roman roads, see pages 251–52 in appendix II.)

Earlier in the *Wake* HCE is described as "that pontificator, and circumvallator" (*FW* 139.17–18). The occupation of the person described in the first word is obvious; the second component is also a genuine Latin term for the person who surrounds an area with ramparts, or someone who besieges a city. In addition to its military applications, the word may also be connected with the hallowed Roman practice of defining a settlement's boundaries with a plowed furrow and the ritual enclosure of the area with city walls.

The chief priest's title also appears in the *Wake* as "*potifex miximhost*" (*FW* 345.29). Here the Latin word for "drink" (*potus*) supplies the first element in the compound; the subsequent adjective blends two English words to indicate that the aforementioned "drink-maker" is a "host who can mix up a large number of potent potables." Another linguistic concoction of Latin and English elements is served up as "maximost bridgesmaker" (*FW* 126.10–11).[16]

As the person who supervised all aspects of the national cult, the pontifex maximus made appointments to the priesthoods, male and female, and wore distinguishing vestments. All of this is commemorated in a description of HCE's wardrobe: "flamen vestacoat, the fibule of broochbronze to his wintermantle of pointefox" (*FW* 242.34–35). A *flamen* was an important Roman priest; his female counterpart was a virgin caretaker of *Vesta's* fire. A *fibula* was a metal brooch that might secure the *mantellum,* a heavy cloak worn in cold weather.

In addition to overseeing the annual cycle of religious festivals, the pontifex maximus was responsible for declaring, at the start of each month, the days during that period on which it would be either legitimate (*fas*) or illegitimate (*nefas*) to conduct civic, legal, and commercial transactions. The traditional bases for determining this shifting calendar of business days and holidays were kept strictly secret, but they gave the chief priest tremendous power over every aspect of Roman society.

The intricate web of statute and tradition within which Roman civic affairs were conducted is specified in the following mélange of languages: "Live, league of lex, nex and mores! Fas est dass and foe err you" (*FW* 273.5–6). In this citation there are three genuine Latin words: *lex* (law), *nex* (murder), *mores* (custom). Just beneath the surface of *nex* one can also read and hear *nexum* (debt-security) or *nexus* (linkage, binding, restraint). Traditional Roman political intrigue, with its personal connections and not infrequent assassinations, is thus neatly tied together in this Wakean web of endorsement of the status quo. The exclamation is followed by a confirmation of the legitimacy of the proposition: *fas est* (it is legally and ritually permitted). This is sealed by a reminder of the consequences of a failure to abide by bond nexus of law and custom: if *you err,* you are an outlaw (*foe*). The second sentence, moreover, is also meant to be heard and read as two Germano-English questions: "Was ist das?" (What is that?) and "Who are you?"—or perhaps a trilingual "Where (*wo* in German) are you wandering off to (*erras* in Latin)?"

There was an archaic link between a citizen's obligation to observe what is declared *fas* and the exclusion of those who are outside the Roman socio-politico-religious nexus. That customary antinomy is expressed in Joyce's quite accurate re-creation of several of the provisions of the most ancient Roman legal code, the Law of the Twelve Tables: *Ubi linqua nuncupassit, ibi fas! Adversus hostem semper sac!* (Where the tongue has made a formal declaration, there is a legitimate act! Against the foe [let there be] an abiding curse!) (*FW* 167.33–35).[17] In another passage packed with terms referring to Roman law and custom, Joyce uses the phrase "nuncupiscent words" (*FW* 432.10) as part of Jaun's defense against the charge of sexual interest in his sister. The Latin verb *nuncupo, -are* means "to call by name"; its primary legal application is in cases in which one names an heir publicly before witnesses. As usual in the *Wake*, however, Joyce's alteration of the verbal root may serve other purposes. The first element, "nun-" could refer to a chaste member of a Catholic sisterhood, or be meant to be a negative prefix, "non-." At any rate, "-cupiscent" is certainly an active participle from another Latin verb, *cupisco, -ere* (to begin to lust for). Ancient Roman legal terminology, like so much else in the *Wake*, has its erotic aspects.

There are several other instances of the antithetical presence of these traditional Latin terms. The first involves the etymological connection between fate (*fata* "that which has been formally uttered" by Jupiter) and what may be uttered or may not be uttered: "Are those their fata which we read in sibylline between the *fas* and its *nefas*?" (*FW* 31.35–36; Joyce's emphasis). (The role of the oracular Sibyl in all of this is discussed below.) In another passage there is an elaborate concatenation—in Latin, German, English, and Greek—of the various sources of ritual legitimacy: "What words of power were made fas between them, ekenames and auchnomes, *acnomina ecnumina*?" (*FW* 98.26–27; Joyce's emphasis). What is implied here is a link between names or terms (*nomina* in Latin), laws (*nomoi* in Greek), and divine spirits (*numina* in Latin); "eke" is archaic English for "also," which is *auch* in German; the prefixed *ac-* means "and," while *ec-* means "out of." Thus, the words of the law derive their power and legitimacy from two related sources, their traditional formulation *and* supernatural aura, which guarantees their authenticity. There is also some related wordplay here between the Latin *agnomina* and the archaic English "ekenames," both of which mean "nicknames."

A final reference to basic Roman legal terminology occurs in more narrowly juridical context in which there is a question of proceedings being brought forward "before a bunch of magistrafes and twelve good and gleeful men? *Filius nullius per fas et nefas*" (*FW* 443.11–13; Joyce's emphasis). A translation of the second sentence is "A son of no one, by what is legal and what is illegitimate." Lawyers love mystifying Latin phrases to burnish their pronouncements with the pedantic patina of a dead language. In this case, the *fas et nefas* can be traced all the way back to the decisions of the pontifex maximus as to what days of the month Roman courts were ritually permitted to be in session.

When Christianity became the established religion of the Roman empire, its Latin-speaking leaders adopted a number of old-order terms. Prominent among these borrowings was *pontifex maximus* as one of the titles of the

Pope, the premier Western bishop, who resided in the city of Rome. This accommodation of cultures is commemorated in "the pontificate of Leo" (*FW* 544.23–24), a possible tribute to Pope Leo XIII, whose Latin poem on photography was praised by Mr. Cunningham in "Grace" (*P* 168). In the list of essay-topics in "Night Lessons," one of the proposed titles is "The Roman Pontiffs and the Orthodox Churches" (*FW* 307.17–18). In Joyce's earlier works the Pope is referred to several times by a title that retains its solemn origins in the ancient pagan city, "sovereign pontiff" (*P* 147; *U* 12.1883, *U* 14.280).

A priest dedicated to the sacred service of a specific god was called a *flamen* in ancient Rome. The term is derived from the verb *flo, flare,* which means "to blow," "to kindle a fire" and is naturally associated with the ritual of sacrifice. Three such priests held the highest ranks: the *flamen Dialis* (of Jupiter), *Martialis* (of Mars), and *Quirinalis* (of a Sabine god much like Mars, although later identified with the deified Romulus). These technical terms are recorded by Joyce in Notebook VI.B.8.124, but the entry is uncrossed and it does not seem to have left an impression on the *Wake.*

The etymological and ritual connection between a flamen and both wind and fire is present in two of the appearances of this Latin term in the text of the *Wake.* Indeed, the first reference manages to encompass the four primary elements (fire, water, air, and earth) with remarkable economy: "in all the flamend floody flatuous world" (*FW* 23.10). Another passage emphasizes the flamen's holy duties but does not ignore the root-meaning of the word: "torchpriest, flamenfan, the ward of the wind that lightened the fire that lay in wood that Jove bolt, at his rude word" (*FW* 80.26–28). Here the Roman house that Jack built is not only struck by Jupiter's lightning, but also lapped by a Pentecostal wind and tongues of fire.

The virgin priestesses of Vesta ministered in the goddess's temple, where they guarded the eternal flame of the city of Rome. In a Notebook entry "vesta" is linked with the Greek goddess of the hearth-fire, "hestia" (VI.B.35.41). They were selected and overseen by the pontifex maximus. If convicted of a violation of the strictest vow of chastity, a vestal virgin was dressed like a corpse and immured; the alleged paramour was scourged to death in the Forum. This emphasis on priestly purity is emphasized in "Keep cool your fresh chastity. . . . Sooner than part with that vestalite emerald of the first importance" (*FW* 440.31–33). Apart from that passage there are very few references to the primary sacred college of women in the *Wake.* "Vesta Tully" (*FW* 526.30), for example, is an allusion to a popular music-hall male impersonator, Vesta Tilley. Wooden or wax matches were often called "vestas" because of the association with the goddess's perpetual flame: "He would redden her [his cigar] with his vestas" (*FW* 536.18); "fallen lucifers, vestas which had served" (*FW* 183.16).

A final reference has already been mentioned above; it correctly links the most important representatives of male and female Roman priesthoods: "flamen vestacoat" (*FW* 242.34).

The regulations concerning the festal calendar and the offering of appropriate sacrifices were important aspects of Roman religion; another large portion of its practice was dedicated to the interpretation of various types of signs. The traditional categories into which these signs were grouped are complex, overlapping, and frequently contradictory. An act of *augurium* or an *auspicium* generally involved the ritual observation of the behavior of birds, in flight or while feeding.[18] Auspicious signs, however, were also derived from thunderclaps or lightning-strikes or from extraordinary animal activity. A *haruspex* (as mentioned in the introduction) practiced divination on the basis of information obtained from an examination of the entrails of sacrificial animals. There is evidence in several of his works that Joyce was familiar with—and fascinated by—all three types of soothsaying.

Near the end of *Portrait* Stephen spots a flight of birds around a house on Molesworth Street, and observes that they are "circling about a temple of air" (*P* 224; compare *U* 9.1206). The use of a lightly translated version of a Latin technical term is significant here. When observing the patterns or number of wild birds, a Roman augur would use his staff to draw two intersecting lines and connect them to form a rectangle, his window of observation. That consecrated space was called the *templum*. Joyce confirms the fact of Roman allusion with additional ritual detail:

And for ages men had gazed upward as he was gazing at birds in flight. The colonnade above him made him think vaguely of an ancient temple and the ashplant on which he leaned wearily of the curved stick of an augur. (*P* 225; compare *U* 3.410–11)

In "Circe," Stephen asks "Where's my augur's rod?"; then he beats *"his foot in tripudium"* (*U* 15.4013–14). The Latin noun *tripudium* refers to a solemn religious three-beat dance. It is also the technical term for a favorable omen that is obtained when the sacred chickens eat so greedily that the grain falls from their beaks to the ground.

In *Finnegans Wake* there are a number of references to the practice and purpose of Roman augury. Several of these relate to the signs that validated an ancient marriage contract and predicted happiness for the couple so united. The nuptials of the Norwegian ship's captain and the Dublin tailor's daughter, for example, are sealed by the presence of two Latin terms: "we'll pull the boath toground togutter, *testies* touchwood . . . under all the *gaauspices*" (*FW*

332.12–14; my emphases). In Latin, a *testis* is a "witness" to some legal act. (The application of this word to "testicle" indicates the high value the Romans placed on what they swore by to support the truth of their statements.) Auspices are also so intimately associated with the ancient Roman marriage ceremony that the phrase "to set out under a good auspice" became a typical metaphor for a successful marital union.[19] When ALP testifies on behalf of HCE, her wifely loyalty is certified in quasi-Latin terminology: "Hora pro Nubis" (*FW* 514.22). This pseudo-Latin phrase (derived from the formulaic *Ora pro nobis* of the Roman Catholic litany) can be twisted to mean "pray for the married couple," since *nubo, nubere, nupsi, nuptum* is the Latin verb for "to cover with a veil," "to marry (for a male)." The pair's vows had been exchanged, it would seem, "at the *Auspice* for the Living," and the ceremony was solemnized by a "*Pontifical* mess" (*FW* 514.25–27; my emphases). An earlier reference is clearer: "Birdflights confirm abbroaching nubtials" (*FW* 324.36–325.1).

In the passages cited above there is every indication of an auspicious (in the vernacular sense) beginning for both of the marriages involved. In an *ex post facto* comment on the nuptials of the tailor's daughter, however, one learns that the original report might not have been completely accurate—or, in typical *Wake* fashion, multiple versions of the same event have been included in the evolving narrative. Here I see the happy pair, under the names of "Laughing Jack" and "Kitzy Kleinsuessmein," avoiding a ritual blessing of their union. They are presented as "eloping for that holm in Finn's Hotel Fiord, Nova Norening." A Joycean autobiographical element cannot be missed here. What has not been noticed is an ancient Roman dimension to this rejection of a formal marriage ceremony; that is, the couple elopes "all augur's scorenning" (*FW* 330.22–25).

In the midst of Jaun's sermon, the ardent orator proposes to send Issy "loveliest pansiful thoughts touching me dash in-you through wee dots Hyphen, the so pretty arched godkin of beddingnights" (*FW* 446.3–5). This lightly coded message invokes the Greco-Roman god of the wedding ceremony, Hymen. Although "godkin" establishes his status as a minor divinity, Hymen's sexual venue is indicated in "beddingnights." An archival version of this sort of godplay exists in "*b*Hyphen, god / of marriage" (VI.B.20.30). The Joycean distortion of Hymen's name may also allude, typographically and verbally, to the practice in some marriages of joining the bride's maiden name to that of the groom by a hyphen.

A number of conspicuous birds, whose presence a Roman priest might well interpret as signs, can be detected, "by observation," in the text beside the marginal reference to "AUSPICIUM. AUGURIA." (*FW* 282.R2). (The Latin theological term *numen* [divine will, supranatural spirit] also appears on this same ominous page of the text [*FW* 282.21].) In another augurial passage, the Latin noun is transformed into an English imperative to request supernatural guidance in a criminal investigation. During the interrogation of Yawn, one of the Four Old Men commands two wading birds to reveal information: "Dunlin and turnstone *augur* us where, how and when best as to burial of carcass" (*FW* 479.17–18; my emphasis).

In one of his *Eclogues* Vergil writes that the appearance of a crow (*cornix*) from the left side is a favorable sign (*E* 9.15). In *Finnegans Wake* the bird apparently flies in from the right because Joyce regards the "Cornix inauspicously" (*FW* 49.13). Close relatives of crows are also associated with extreme ill-luck in another passage: "by the auspices of that raven cloud, your shade, and by the auguries of rooks in parlament, death with every disaster" (*FW* 189.33–34). Perhaps, then, Joyce was following the lead of Pliny the Elder, not Vergil, when he attached malign purport to the crow's presence. In his encyclopedia of *Natural History* (10.12.14.68), the Roman author declares that the "incessent cawing of a crow (*inauspicata garrulitas* [*cornicis*]) is a baleful omen."

The *Wake* also includes several examples of the practice of deriving favorable or unfavorable signs from the weather, "meteoromancy" (*FW* 228.20–21). Matt, another of the Four Old Men, is a sorry sight "under all the auspices, amid the rattle of hailstones" (*FW* 392.27–28; compare *FW* 555.18). Thunder, Jupiter's celestial klaxon, is the primary weather omen in the *Wake*. The ten thunder words are too well known to require commentary. At the end of the "Mime," however, just after one of the hundred letter detonations, there is a triple clap: "Upploud!" (*FW* 257.30); "Uplouderamain!" (*FW* 257.33); "Uplouderamainagain!" (*FW* 258.19). My use of the word "clap" is designed to call attention to both the applause and the heavenly noise that culminates the performance of Mick, Nick, and the Maggies. In case one misses the fact that Joyce meant these explanations to be directed at Jupiter as well as to the audience, this stage direction is added: "the Clearer of the air from on high has spoken in thumbuldum tambaldam to his tembledim tombaldoom worrild"(*FW* 258.20–21). The classical source for this type of sign is in Vergil's *Aeneid*. The Trojan refugees know that their years of wandering are over when Jupiter sends three thunderclaps (and three lightning bolts) to certify their arrival in Latium (*Aeneid* 7.141–47). Vergil specifies that this phenomenon, if it occurs when the sky is clear (*clarus*), is the *omen magnum*. A closely related source of supranatural admonitions were lightning strikes (*fulmen, fulminis* in Latin) sent to sanctify ceremonies of all sorts: "sullemn fulminance, sollemn nuptialism, sollemn sepulture and providential divining" (*FW* 599.12–13).

A less well known medium of seeking divine advice was the practice of sleeping in a temple and sifting one's dreams for significant signs. The Latin verb *incubo, incubare* literally means "to lean on," "to lie in," but it is frequently used to designate vision-inducing sleep at a sacred place. This is the source of Joyce's Notebook entry "⁸incubation / ⁸temple sleep" (VI.C.13.241; from VI.B.22.162). The passage in the text of the *Wake* is even a bit sharper. The Four Old Men, temporarily metamorphosed into the Primary Irish Chroniclers, need "further auspices . . . for to regul their reves ["dreams" in French] by incubation" (*FW* 397.29–34; compare *FW* 112.21 "sublime incubation"). The allusion continues on the next page of the text, with a Latinate HCE and ALP in bed: "for meter and peter to temple an eslaap" (*FW* 398.14).

A final type of sign that the Romans regarded as a monitory prediction of how events would turn out is purely verbal. Chance utterances that yielded unexpected messages were not regarded as accidents, but divine warnings or warrants of success. A significant example of this sort of word-alchemy is the term "Augustus." A senatorial supporter of Octavian suggested that this term was the preternaturally appropriate title for the first Roman emperor. He argued that places declared hallowed by the augurs are henceforward "august"; and he derived the origin of that word either from the verb *augeo, augere, auxi, auctum* (to increase, to magnify) or from a compaction of the phrase *avium gestus gustusve* (the behavior and the eating of birds).[20] In both cases, the man designated "Augustus" was to be regarded as emphatically consecrated by Rome's guardians of ritual purity and interpreters of the will of the gods.

Joyce, in fact, seems to have had just this sort of etymological example in mind when he placed the phrase "ORDINATION OF OMEN, ONUS AND OBIT" in the margin of "Night Lessons" (*FW* 271.R). In the adjacent text are the significantly garbled names of the three Romans who filled the power vacuum created by the assassination of "Jeallyous Seizer." They formed the Second Triumvirate, two-thirds of which eventually degenerated into deadly competitors for sole mastery of Rome: "the tryonforit of Oxthievious, Lapidous and Malthouse Anthemy" (*FW* 271.3–6). Each of these "ominous" puns on the names of Octavius Augustus, Lepidus, and Marcus Antonius—and the choice of the three four-letter words that match each man in the margin—requires extended commentary.

- "Lapidous" = Lepidus: I follow McHugh's lead here in seeing and hearing a reference to the Latin adjective *lapidosus* (full of stones). In Great Britain and Ireland, "stone" is a unit of weight (14 pounds). Thus, the overweight Lepidus is characterized as an "ONUS" (burden, load) in the marginal jingle.

- "Malthouse Anthemy" = Marcus Antonius: This triumvir, with his ally Cleopatra (see "*Cliopatria*" [FW 271.L1]), was defeated by Augustus at the battle of Actium. He was a notorious drinker.[21] His only literary publication was a public defense of his character, revealingly entitled *De Sua Ebrietate* (Concerning His Drunkenness). Hence, the distorted praenomen "Malthouse." I suggest that "Anthemy" can be traced to the same source: *anthemon* is a Greek word for "flower." When carousing, Mark Antony would ring his head with a floral garland. There is another possibility here. During his stay in Egypt, Mark Antony sometimes assumed the role of the god Dionysos/Bacchus (associated with Osiris), who is often crowned with garlands and is the patron of intoxication. Antony's ceremonial suicide in Egypt after the defeat at Actium lies behind his marginal "OBIT."

- "Oxthievious" = Octavius as he is called in Shakespeare's *Julius Caesar;* the more common form is Octavian. The similarity in sounds between the two versions of the emperor's name hardly scratches the surface of the verbal topography here. Octavian was born in his family's home in the Palatine district of Rome. The specific location, which later became a shrine in his honor, was called *ad capita bubula* (at the Oxheads). I believe that Joyce was aware of this esoteric bit of information about the earliest phase of Caesar's life and that he used the fact to form a perverse (but typical) pun. One commentator on the origin of this odd Roman place-name suggests that there was a nearby building or monument decorated with ox-head sculpture ("bucrania" is the term used by art historians). Plausible; but I think it more likely that the name represented some natural formation—a series of rocks or protuberances in the surface—which looked like the heads of oxen. When he blended the name of the birthplace with a phonetic approximation of "Octavius," Joyce turned the projecting heads upside down, and converted them into depressions. Then he translated his topographical inversion into German: *Tief* means "depression," "hollow," "low-lying area." Lastly, he added a vaguely Latinate adjectival ending, "-ious." I am aware that this explanation of the derivation of "Oxthievious" may seem outrageously convoluted. It is, however, based squarely on the sentence in the *Wake's* text that immediately follows the triple puns on the names of the Second Triumvirate: "You may fail to see the lie of that layout, Suetonia" (*FW* 271.6–7). The only work that records the name of Octavian's birthplace is *De Vita Caesarum* (The Lives of [the Twelve] Caesars) by Suetonius (*Augustus* 5). Joyce, in short, not only presumes to invert the Latin text's "heads," but he also chides its errant author, or some feminine reincarnation of Suetonius. He or she,

Joyce claims, certainly did fail to see that the *capita* constitute a lie about the true contours of that august layout. Finally, the "OMEN" in the margin is definitely relevant both to the derivation of the emperor's title ("Augustus") and to the area on the Palatine, not far from Octavian's birthplace. It was at that place, the *auguratorium*, that the augurs stood to watch for bird signs. If my trilingual leap—supported by the textual presence of the sole ancient authority, Suetonius—in the preceding paragraph is not convincing, there are several other ways and means of linking Octavian with the theft of cattle, but these are best relegated to a learned footnote.[22]

On a less erudite but quite eerie level is the following anecdote about an omen that affected James Joyce personally. Djuna Barnes reports that she was walking with the Joyces in the Bois de Boulogne on February 1, 1922. A man whom no one had ever seen before brushed by Joyce. The author of *Ulysses* immediately trembled and turned white. Then he told Ms. Barnes, "That man . . . said to me as he passed, in *Latin*, 'You are an *abominable* writer!' That is a dreadful *omen* the day before the publication of my novel" (*JJII* 524; my emphases).

The impulse to see significance in all sorts of phenomena—natural, avian, verbal—is everywhere in Roman culture. In several examples that I discussed, names and what they signify are not casually, but causally, connected. In Latin this link would be expressed by the catch-phrase *nomen omen* (the name is an omen). This notion is anagrammatically present in "Night Lessons": "omen nome" (*FW* 279.5). One of Joyce's closest friends during the "work-in-progress" years, Carola Giedion-Welcker, reports that he applied "'Nomen est omen' to his own name too . . . [it was derived] genealogically from the old French name 'de Joyeuse'."[23] That etymology is a favorable note on which to conclude this section of the review of the role of Roman ritual in Joyce's works.

Minor Roman Divinities

In the previous discussion of auguries, the presence of the Latin noun *numen* (*numina* in the plural) was briefly mentioned to highlight the ominous aura of a number of textual birds. The concept of a divine spirit present in various natural phenomena, of a divine will that manifests itself in countless ways, is expressed in that term. By extension, those places, customs, forces that were felt to be special or crucial by mortals were regarded as possessing and being able to disseminate a supranatural force, called a *numen*. Joyce demonstrates his competence in comparative theological terminology when he indicates that the pious Four Old Men "are ruled, roped, duped and driven by those numen daimons" (*FW* 142.23). The Greek *daimon* (a [beneficent or malevolent] supranatural being) is a rough equivalent for a Roman *numen*, but the latter is sometimes personified and named. In Wakean terms, any hallowed area or action that was seen in anthropomorphic terms by Joyce was given a "propper numen out of a colluction of prifixes" (*FW* 162.13). Stuart Gilbert indicates that he and Joyce were aware that names were frequently dictated by supernatural forces: "*nomina* are *numina*."[24]

The most vivid example of this process of the creation of all sorts of godlings is the Latin call to celebrate the anticipated birth of young Purefoy in "Oxen of the Sun": "*Per deam Partulam et Pertundam nunc est bibendum*" (*U* 14.1439).[25] This semi-Horatian toast means "By the goddess Birth and by the goddess Virginal-Penetration, now is the time for drinking." The *Wake*, typically, goes one step farther. In Matt's overview of HCE and ALP in the midst of intercourse, he also takes a census of the sleeping children. Issy's sweetness is saluted by invoking three Roman goddesses of childhood: "Cunina [Cradle], Statulina [First-Step] and Edulia [Baby-food]" (*FW* 561.9).[26] Reference to ancient religious practice is reinforced by the adjacent sentence, "They are numerable" (*FW* 561.7). The predicate refers to the fact that the three siblings, Issy, Shem, and Shaun, can easily be counted; it also suggests that they are watched over in their beds by the Roman divine guardians (*numina*) of early childhood. On the same page of the text, Issy is apostrophized as "O Charis! O Charissima!" (*FW* 561.22). Linguistically this is a mix of the Greek noun for "grace" or "charm" (*charis*) and the Latin adjective for "dearest" (*carissima*). Again, Joyce conspicuously displays his command of etymological byplay: "To speak well her grace it would ask of Grecian language" (*FW* 561.17–18). In Roman mythology the three *Gratiae* (Graces) are daughters of Jupiter who preside over what is lovely and charming. Joyce quite likely invokes their aid at the summary-conclusion of a highly Latinate song that is the finale of the interlude of the Ondt and the Gracehoper: "*(May the Graces I hoped for sing your Ondtship song sense!)*" (*FW* 419.6).

The best-known examples of Roman *numina* are the Lares and the Penates. The former are the guardian gods of the family home; Roman houses usually included a shrine in their honor near the domestic hearth. The Penates watched over a household's larder, and frequently are depicted on a plaque in the atrium of the family residence. The phrase "licensed pantry gods" (*FW* 179.10) reflects this specific area of their protection. There are two crossed Notebook entries that are relevant here. They occur in the midst of several pages that record ancient Roman customs and religious terms: "ᵍpantry gods" (VI.B.18.268) and "ᵍincensed god" (VI.B.18.269). The latter phrase appears in the text immediately before the reference to the Penates, as "incensed privy" (*FW* 179.10). I do not know why the original ritualistic phrase has been redirected into a scatological channel. At the same time, there was a Roman deity who presided over the production and spreading of manure. His name is "Sterculius," from *stercus* (dung, excrement, shit). Although this agricultural *numen* does *not* appear in the *Wake*, the Latin noun from which his name was derived is most definitely in Joyce's vocabulary: *stercus* (singular neuter accusative), and *stercore* (singular neuter ablative) contribute to Shem's medieval recipe for concocting organic ink (*FW* 185.19, 24).

A trio of these minor but important divinities stand behind Joyce's oath "by all the manny larries ate pignatties" (*FW* 432.14–15). Just as the "ate" in that phrase represents a Latin *et* (and), so too does the word "manny" stand for the *Manes*. These latter are the deified spirits of the dead, which were once closely associated with the Lares because Roman households had to be scrupulously purified after a death in the family. Certainty in the identification of these three closely related *numina* is provided by a crossed Notebook entry that occurs in the same cluster mentioned in the previous paragraph: "ᵍlares / manes / penates" (VI.B.18.266; compare VI.B.20.2).

The remaining "numinous" Roman gods are fairly obviously presented in the text. "Pomona," the goddess of fruits and orchards appears immediately after "Lotta Crabtree" (*FW* 62.34). Another pair of divinities, the one a general god of the natural world, the other the goddess of flowers, appear as "Faun and Flora" (*FW* 33.28; compare "Flora & Fauna —⊣ " [VI.B.21.229]). Pales is one of the oldest Roman goddesses; originally she presided over flocks and fertility. Her festival was April 21, which came to be considered the anniversary of the founding of the city. The ceremony originally involved a purification ritual and the shepherds' celebration of spring lambing; it also included rites to honor the dead and to cleanse the dwellings of the malignant presence of unappeased ghosts. Joyce seems to allude to this combination of functions in "old Pales time ere beam slewed cable" (*FW* 289.8–9). With an eye and an ear toward some silent metathesis of the first three letters of the alphabet, McHugh glosses "beam" with "Cain" and "cable" with "Abel"; they are the sons of Adam and Eve, the archetypical farmer and shepherd of Genesis. The attendant footnote on that page of the *Wake* is "They just spirits a body away" (*FW* 289.F2). I read this as a comment on the primeval fratricide of Abel by Cain—and on the Roman ritual purification of corpse pollution during the festival of Pales.

In the midst of their interrogation the Four Old Men wonder if Yawn, silent as some sleeping giant, might not "be an earthpresence" (*FW* 499.28). Then they hear the ground trembling and beg to learn what is going on, "tell us" (*FW* 499.34). The Latin proper noun *Tellus* designates the great Earth Mother, who was especially invoked during earthquakes. She is also the com-

mon grave of all mortals, and thus an appropriate source for the many resur-
rections in the *Wake*. The bilingual pun and personification that I suggest above
seem to be confirmed by another request for information, this time concerning the attributes of ALP: "Do tell us all about. . . . So tellus tellas allabouter"
(*FW* 101.2–3; my ellipses).

When the Four do not get the answers they want from Yawn, they place a
"priority call" to "Sybil!" (*FW* 501.12). In classical mythology, the most famous of the prophetic priestesses of Apollo was the Pythia at Delphi in Greece.
In the western Mediterranean the oracular honors go to the Sibyl at Cumae, a
headland in the Bay of Naples. Aeneas consulted her for information about
the fate of his Trojan refugees when they finally reached Italy. Her Irish equivalent is located in County Kerry; she answers the telephone call: "Sybil Head
this end!" (*FW* 501.13).

There was a written collection of the ecstatic utterances of various seer-
priestesses, composed in Greek hexameter verse. In the case of the Cumaean
Sibyl, the poetic prophecies were originally inscribed on palm leaves. This oc-
cult practice has left a minor mark on *Ulysses*. When Stephen Dedalus mocks
the one-letter titles for his proposed books, he also reveals that his "epipha-
nies [were] written on green oval leaves" (*U* 3.141). That curious report of
self-deprecation is very likely meant to reflect actual fact. In a June 26, 1904,
letter, Gogarty wrote the following to a friend in Oxford:

> Joyce has written two pretty songs. I am disposing of 30 of his lyrics for
> a £ a piece or 5/- for one! (Joyce's reckoning) to pay his digs' bill. He was
> lately seen perambulating this tuneful town(!) with a large Malay book
> made of palm leaves borrowed of Starkey!—it looked like a Venetian
> blind—under his arm looking for a buyer.[27]

That malicious bit of literary local color in the Irish Pale strikes a fittingly
oracular note on which to conclude this long chapter on the gods and rituals of
the Romans.

5

Cicero

When they realize that an otherwise docile class is about to mutiny against forced marches through grammar and vocabulary exercises, Latin teachers sometimes try to vary the pace with a little pedantic humor. A hallowed source of momentary relief is a discussion of the homey derivations of Roman *cognomina:* Caesar means "curly-haired," Plautus "flat-footed," and Cicero comes from *cicer,* "the chick-pea," a plant with short, hairy pods. The usual (but probably apocryphal) classroom explanation is that Cicero—or his ancestors—had warts on their noses. It was customary in ancient Rome that such names (which were inherited by family members) were based on physical peculiarities or traditional quirks of character. The following is a Joycean example: "—Sounds are impostures, Stephen said after a pause of some little time, like names. Cicero, Podmore. Napoleon, Mr. Goodbody. Jesus, Mr. Doyle" (*U* 16.362–63).[1] Roman orators, always quick to inject a personal sting into their political or judicial speeches, have left numerous examples of these nominal puns used to ridicule an opponent.[2]

Cicero, Rome's foremost statesman-orator, produced a mass of speeches, letters, philosophical, rhetorical, and political studies, even some poetry that touts his service to the Republic as *pater patriae* (father of his country). For centuries Cicero's orations have been assigned in first-level advanced classes as the models of Latin prose, structural elegance, and forensic argumentation. Jesuit schools throughout the world traditionally find an honored place for his works in their curriculum.[3] With a mixture of sublimated anguish and exaggerated accomplishment, sentimental alumni recall with pride crescendos of tricolonic structure in the *Manilian Law* or a nicely balanced past contrary-to-fact condition from *De Amicitia* (On Friendship). A number of the characters in (and many of the original readers of) *Ulysses* went to such schools; they were exposed to this type of syntactical gymnastics and rhetorical prestidigitation and could recognize its use or abuse in literature.

It is not surprising, then, that Cicero is dragged into the windblown precincts of "Aeolus." The assembled experts are engaged in reading and discussing a letter that the archbishop of Dublin has written to the newspaper. By episcopal command, it is "to be repeated in the *Telegraph*" (*U* 7.181). Among those present for the recitation is Professor MacHugh. He makes his living as a Latin teacher, but is no admirer of Cicero. Like Buck Mulligan, MacHugh worships at a Greek altar. In his judgment, the primary Roman contribution to Western civilization was their "*Cloacae:* sewers" (*U* 7.489). Simon Dedalus has just summed up the opinion of those in the newspaper office who have been listening to snippets of the prelate's purple prose: "Shite and onions!" (*U* 7.329). MacHugh concurs, and his judgment emphasizes the condescension of his earlier statement that the pastiche of clichés in the letter were from a "recently discovered fragment of Cicero" (*U* 7.270). Coming from an avowed Hellenosnob, this bit of literary criticism may not be quite as colloquial as Mr. Dedalus', but it is certainly meant to be no compliment to the archbishop's epistle or its periodic style.

There is a second explicit (but counterfeit) reference to Cicero in *Ulysses*, and a third (also false) lead that has fooled a number of commentators. But before examining either of these passages, it is necessary to make a brief excursus into the contexts of these two references and into some Joycean prose that masquerades as a literal translation not of Cicero, but of a late Republican and an early Imperial Roman historian.

The "technic" of "Oxen of the Sun" is Joyce's chapter-long parallel between the development of English prose and the gestation of a human embryo. The first stage in that dual process is a short, Irish-Latin-English fertility incantation, followed by three paragraphs of stultified and stultifying sentences in a language that pretends to be English. Joyce himself claimed that this section imitated, in what is a designedly unintelligible cascade of ridiculously Latinate English, the prose styles of the Roman historians Sallust and Tacitus (*Letters* I.139). For reasons that have already been explained in pages 49–50, I am convinced that this specific identification of classical models is probably one of Joyce's many attempts to delude academic annotators. He is not really translating actual Latin here. This entire passage—with a single exception—is Joyce's personal concoction of a mess of fake Latinesque diction and syntax. Nevertheless, the fraudulent "translation" reads enough like a genuinely botched attempt at a verbatim Englishing of Sallust or Tacitus to hoodwink those former Latin students who have tried to do just that.

The single exception to Joyce's sham rendition of Latin prose style is a deeply buried echo of a famous sentence of Ciceronian invective. Without a prod from a bit of archival material, I never would have suspected an actual model here. In the British Museum Notesheets for *Ulysses*, there is a series of pseudo-translations among the notes for "Oxen of the Sun"; one of these reads "ꞌO thing not merely in being heard foul but even in seeing" (*UNBM* 212: 23). This entry was transferred into the text of *Ulysses*, with another nearby Note-sheet phrase, as "O thing of prudent nation not merely in being seen but also even in being related worthy of being praised" (*U* 14.56–57). Joyce lifted the basic structure and thrust of this passage from Cicero's venomous *Second Philippic*, an attack on Mark Antony that was composed (but not actually delivered) in October 44 B.C., during the turmoil in Rome following the assassination of Julius Caesar.

Personal invective was a prominent part of Roman political oratory, and in his attack Cicero does not hesitate to speak "of the vilest sort of vulgarity" (*de nequissimo genere levitatis*). He reports that Antony, still hungover from a wild wedding reception, vomited at a public assembly, in sight of the Roman people gathered there to conduct the affairs of state: *O rem non modo visu foedam, sed etiam auditu* (O thing not only hideous to see, but also to hear) (*Phil.* 2.25.63). This sentence has naturally appealed to the imagination of more than one Latin student, especially those with an ear for the nuances of republican rhetoric at its finest. Joyce bootlegged this bit of Cicero into his parody of grotesquely translated Roman literature—and went out of his way to turn its original meaning topsy-turvy. Among the dozen or so similar fragments in the Notesheet, this extract is the only one for which I can pin down a literary source.

Years later when he was assembling *Finnegans Wake*, Joyce did not forget Cicero's *Philippics*. In the same section as the appearance of "Antonius-Burrus-Caseous grouptriad," which is an unfocused group portrait of the Second Triumvirate, special attention is given to "an elusive Antonius" (*FW* 167.1–4). The "elusive" may be a glancing reference to Mark Antony's notorious passion for gambling, since one of the meanings of the Latin verb *eludo, eludere, elusi, elusum* is "to win at a game." But, as indicated above, there were many more direct ways for a clever author to display "an antomine art of being rude like the boor" (*FW* 167.3). Perhaps that simile is meant to be a general jab at Antony's crudity; there is also the distinct possibility of a specifically Ciceronian insult here. One of the orator's most famous cases was the successful indictment of a high Roman official for criminal corruption during a period of provincial administration. The culprit was Verres; his name is also the Latin word for a "swine," "boar" (*verres*). That double meaning gave rise to Cicero's most memorable forensic insult. During his prosecution of Verres, Cicero accused him of dishing out *ius verrinum* (*Verres* 2.1.46.121); the phrase means *both* "Verrine [corrupt] justice" *and* "pork gravy." That magnificent example of a Latin pun and Roman invective is frequently cited. I do not doubt that Joyce knew it. Perhaps he transferred its application—pivoting around the English homonyms "boar, bore, boar"—to Mark Antony, another object of Cicero's oratorical thrusts, and one who was no slouch at corruption and boorishness.[4]

Joyce's second direct and acknowledged citation of Cicero in *Ulysses* also occurs in the parodic trek across the various contours of English prose in "Oxen of the Sun." It is "a choppy Latin gossipy bit, style of Burton-Browne" (*Letters* I.139): "Assuefaction minorates atrocities (as Tully saith of his darling Stoics)" (*U* 14.383–384). In plain English this adage means "Becoming accustomed to horrors mitigates their pain." "Tully" is the chatty seventeenth-century way of citing Marcus *Tullius* Cicero. Here, once again, the text of *Ulysses* deliberately misleads the reader. The quotation does not have anything to do with Cicero or any ancient Roman Stoic author. It is lifted (and modified) from Sir Thomas Browne's *Christian Morals:* "Forget not how assuefaction unto any thing minorates the passion from it."[5] Joyce labeled the expropriation as coming from "Tully" as part of his ongoing project to keep professors—from English, Philosophy, and Classics Departments—busy for a century.

The final Ulyssean nod to Cicero is Buck Mulligan's "apt quotation from the classics," which also appears in "Oxen of the Sun." These four lines of polished Latin are certainly Ciceronian in style, but they were never uttered in the Roman forum. The Latin sentence (*U* 14.707–10), in short, is an original composition by Joyce. That example of pseudoclassical rhetoric and its carefully poised syntactic snare have been discussed in detail in chapter 2; an endnote there reveals a highly improbable connection with an Irish "Tully."

References to Cicero in the *Wake* are more extensive and more subtle than those in *Ulysses*. In one of the *Wake* notebooks, there are two entries which indicate that Joyce continued to play around with the literal meaning of the Roman orator's name: "°a cicero of beans" (VI.B.17.94) and "ᵇʳChicero" (VI.B. 17.106). When transferred into the text, the allusion is reinforced by a Latinate verb chosen to evoke an image of Cicero grandly winding up one of his speeches: "I'd perorate a chickerow of beans" (*FW* 425.19). A similar play on the orator's name is present in the Professor's exposition of the fable of "The Mookse and the Gripes" to a group of "muddlecrass pupils" lined up in a row, "etsitaraw, etcicero" (*FW* 152.8, 10). The pedant also complains that, when he has "to sermo" (the Latin noun for "conversation") with these students, he must "give all my easyfree translation" (*FW* 152.7, 12–13). But at the same time as he indicates his willingness to communicate in the vernacular, the *Wake's* pompous Professor demands attention with two untranslated, authentically Latin imperatives, which are reinforced by an appeal to the Roman king-god: "*Audi,* Joe Peters! *Exaudi* facts" (*FW* 152.14).

A few pages ago I discussed an example of a piece of oratorical invective against Verres that might have been applied by Joyce to the boorish Mark Antony. There is another equally probable allusion to the shocking crimes of the same Roman culprit in a section of the *Wake*. The twin sons of HCE are rerecounting their father's alleged offenses. They mention a "hearse and four horses with the interprovincial crucifixioners throwing lots inside" (*FW* 377.23–24). McHugh glosses this passage with the "massacre by British troops of Irish [fans] leaving [a] football game" in Dublin in 1920, and connects the colonial perpetrators to the Four Horsemen of the Apocalypse. That bit of historical local color seems entirely reasonable. I suggest a concomitant allusion to an equally heinous crime prosecuted by Cicero in 70 B.C. The defendant was Verres; the charge stemmed from his cruelty and rapacity while he was provincial governor of Sicily. The corrupt official went so far as to scourge and crucify a Roman citizen who had opposed his malefaction. What is more, Verres was reported to have said "Spectet patriam; in conspectu legum libertatisque moriatur" (Let him look at his fatherland; let him die in sight of law and liberty). In his peroration for the prosecution, Cicero claimed that the enormity of Verres' outrage was magnified by the fact that the cross was raised in that corner of the province nearest Italy (*Verres* 2.5.66). For generations schoolboy students of Cicero have read and memorized this climax of his indictment. I suggest, in short, that Verres' crime has been transferred to Dublin and that its details have colored the choice of "interprovincial crucifixioners" to characterize the Wakean culprits. There is no way of proving that claim, but it is satisfying to contemplate, "By jurors' cruces!" (*FW* 375.5).

The following are additional textual excerpts designed to illustrate Joyce's uncanny ability to lace his narrative with appropriate flourishes, in both Latin and Wakese, from the works of Cicero. The allusions fall into two major clusters: prosecutorial phrases from the *First Oration against Catiline* and thematic snippets from the dialogue *On Old Age*. A third category includes several significant references to miscellaneous works.

"The Catilinarian Orations"

In the outline of the "triv and quad" (*FW* 306.12–13) that concludes the children's homework session in II.2, there is a catalogue of the "Master Figures and Themes" that constitute their curriculum. Among these is *"Catilina,"* linked with "The Value of Circumstantial Evidence" (*FW* 307.L1, 24). The reference here is to Lucius Sergius Catilina, a hyperambitious patrician who was the mastermind of a coup attempt in 63 B.C., the year Cicero was Rome's chief magistrate.[6] The conspiracy was detected, exposed, and smashed, thanks to the overwhelmingly convincing evidence that Cicero presented in a series of four slashingly brilliant speeches, which are still assigned in Latin classes. (A

Notebook entry seems to refer to these orations: "Catiline tales" [VI.B.8.73].)
The most famous of these works is the *First Catilinarian*. Joyce certainly read
it during his years at Belvedere College; he did not forget the experience.

Memorable (and meant to be recognizable) phrases from this speech reappear in the *Wake* in situations in which accusations of treachery are being
leveled at various guilty parties. The Four Old Men of II.4, for example, sit in
judgment as self-appointed censors of the sexual shenanigans of Tristan and
Iseult. Their discourse is peppered with Latinate vocabulary. In the midst of
their pontifications, there is a parenthetical exclamation that I interpret as an
authorial aside. It summarizes exasperation not only with the foursome's diction, but also with the extent of their senescent voyeurism: "(how long tandem!)" (*FW* 395.6). Joyce's partially translated phrase is lifted directly from
the opening words of Cicero's *First Catilinarian*: *Quo usque tandem* (How
long finally, [Catiline, are you going to abuse our patience]).

At the start of the *Wake*, HCE is accused of some sort of crime in Phoenix
Park. His detractor beats around the bush in a convoluted sentence that features a series of quasi-inquisitorial Latin terms: "interdum" (meanwhile),
"quidam" (a certain man), "quoniam" (because), "Ibid" (the same man), "ali-
cubi" (somewhere or the other). In the midst of this antique verbiage is the
central point of his indictment: "quondam (*pfuit! pfuit!*)" (once there was!
yes there was!) (*FW* 33.34). The phonetic spelling (*pf* for *f*)[7] is meant to convey the speaker's disgust at the imputed misbehavior of the alleged perpetra-
tor. In 63 B.C. Cicero felt exactly the same way about Catiline's treason, and
reminded the chief conspirator that "Once there was, yes there was [in Rome
a government brave enough to deal with scoundrels like you]": *fuit, fuit ista
quondam* (*Cat.* 1.3).

Twice in his speech, Cicero calls upon Jupiter to inspire contemporary Rome
with the same courage that the city's ancestors displayed in previous times of
peril. The special manifestation under which the supreme god is invoked is
that of *Juppiter Stator* (the Supporter, the Stabilizer) (*Cat.* 1.33). This Roman
divinity also has a walk-on role in the *Wake*. Although the narrative context
here is not an indictment of HCE, there is conflict and rivalry present, as Shem
and Shaun trade accusations. In an obviously Roman mode of prayer, Shaun
asks for information and assistance from "the incensed privy and the licensed
pantry gods and Stator and Victor" (*FW* 179.10–11).[8]

The paragraph in which those words appear begins with what is probably
the best-known expression in all of Cicero's works. Side-by-side accusatives
of exclamation sum his disgust at the fact that Catiline is still alive and dares
to sit in the Senate: *O tempora! O mores!* (O the times! O the standards!)
(*Cat.* 1.2). This phrase reappears in the *Wake*, in the ablative case, "*in omnibus moribus et temporibus*" (*FW* 251.29), to indicate the universal reach of

masculine lechery. Joyce also recreates a grammatically correct imitation of the original exclamation, but with an ethnic instead of an ethical emphasis: "(O tribes! O gentes!)" (*FW* 552.14).

At the start of the *Wake*, HCE's accuser expresses his frustration at the fact the "foenix culprit" and his wife have refused to react to the charges: "Quarry silex, Homfrie Noanswa! Undy gentian festyknees, Livia Noanswa?" (*FW* 23.19–21). A rough "translation" is "Why are you silent, Humphry Noanswer! From where in the world would you rush off, Livia Noanswer?" The interrogative adverb *quare* (why? for what reason?) is used throughout the actual oration, as Cicero fires barrages of rhetorical questions at Catiline. Joyce's English spelling "quarry" not only echoes the Latin pronunciation of *quare*, but it also specifies that HCE is a fugitive (compare "quare quandary" [*FW* 303.26]). The portmanteau verb-noun "silex" also does double duty. It phonetically hints at HCE's tight-lipped stance and, since it is the Latin word for "hard stone," "flint," suggests that the accused is unlikely to crack under pressure.

In a May 13, 1927, letter to Harriet Shaw Weaver (*SL* 322), Joyce explicated a number of the items in the original version of the passage discussed in the previous paragraph. (What Joyce did not reveal in this commentary to his patroness is his specific debt to Cicero.) He indicated that "Undy gentian festiknees" means (in Latin) "Where the dickens are you hurrying from?" The same type of shocked incredulity as is also found in Cicero's *Ubinam gentium sumus?* (Where in the world are we?) (*Cat.* 1.9). In fact, Joyce repeats most of the original sentence, in genuine Latin, a bit later in the *Wake*, in a similar context of unanswered questions: "*Quare hircum?* No answer. *Unde gentium fe. . . ?* No ah." (*FW* 89.27; Joyce's ellipses). "*[H]ircum*" is Latin for "billy goat," an animal associated in Roman comedy and invective with dirty old men.[9] It is also Wakese for "here come" and/or "come here." Thus, the two sets of parallel double queries have roughly the same meaning and are obviously intended to echo each other.

My final example of Joycean allusion to Cicero's orations against Catiline is short, pithy, and from *Ulysses*. In "Wandering Rocks," the Subsheriff, Long John Fanning, meets several strollers as they make their way to Kavanagh's winerooms. "[W]ith rich acid utterance," he then inquires, "Are the *conscript fathers* pursuing their peaceful deliberations?" (*U* 10.1004–5; my emphases). The italicized term was used in formal address to members of the Roman Senate. Subsheriff Fanning transfers its venue and venerability to the notoriously acrimonious members of the Dublin City Council. Cicero used the solemn phrase in his revelations of Catiline's conspiracy to the Senate. He asks for the attention of the members of that august body (*patres conscripti*) as he rhetorically accuses himself of possible dereliction of duty: *M. Tulli, quid agis*

(Marcus Tullius, what in the world are you doing?) (*Cat.* 1.27). Both the original context and formulation would have been immediately evident to Joyce's characters—and many of his readers. Hence, the rich acidity of its local adaptation.

Book II.3 is one of the most difficult sections in the entire *Wake.* The scene is HCE's pub where the innkeeper and customers watch two television plays, which are continually interrupted, put on fast forward, and/or rerun with a different sound track. Among the establishment's regular patrons are the Four Old Men, who put in appearances throughout the entire work, at various times, as the Evangelists, the Four Annalists of Irish history, the Northern Provinces, or a number of other likely quartets. Since they are keen critics of contemporary society, particularly the sexual mores of the younger generation, the age of these hypocritical duffers is frequently emphasized—sometimes in Latin. For example, their intensely prurient scrutiny of the embrace of Iseult and Tristan elicited the Ciceronian comment "(how long tandem!)" (*FW* 395.6) discussed above.

"On Old Age"

In the pub episode, the quartet is introduced as the "avunculusts" (*FW* 367.14), a term that combines the Latin word for "uncle" or "granduncle" (*avunculus*) and the plain old English word "lust." These gaffers are, in fact, archetypical dirty old men. Shortly thereafter in the same section of the narrative, they are also labeled "The scenictutors" (*FW* 372.12). The Four are not much to look at, even in terms of local color, nor is their function here primarily pedagogic. Thus, while admitting the presence of a compound English noun, I also hear a distinct reference to the Latin title of Cicero's well-known dialogue-essay "On Old Age," *De Senectute.* The text of that work is directly quoted several times in the "Mamalujo" section of the *Wake.*

Certainty in this claim for allusion is provided by an entry in one of the early Buffalo notebooks:

De Senect 'Cato' book /
about   'O Tite' /
'to Scipio here' (VI.B.2.148)

These disjointed notes lightly conceal the following data. The official title of Cicero's work is *Cato Maior De Senectute;* the elder Cato is the primary speaker in this dialogue on the advantages of growing old. The legendarily stern Censor shares his thoughts here with the younger Scipio, who carries the *cognomen* "Africanus" to commemorate his own military exploits and those of his ancestors against the Carthagians.[10] The opening words of Cicero's prologue to the work are "*O Tite,*" the start of a three-line verse quotation from Ennius, an early Roman epic poet. None of these entries is crossed out in the Notebook, but there can be no doubt that Joyce's "The scenictutors" (*FW* 372.12) is intended as a direct allusion to Cicero's animadversions on old age and that the original text of that work has left its imprint on the *Wake*. Moreover, *De Senectute* was on the Latin syllabus for the 1897 Intermediate Examinations in which Joyce did quite well (see appendix I). Finally, in his notes for rhetorical figures in *Ulysses,* Joyce wrote the following: "*paromoeon* / O Tite, tute, Tati tanta tyranne tulisti / OED" (VIII.A.5.24). Ennius's line (O Titus Tatius, tyrant, you took upon yourself such great misfortune) from another section of his *Annals* was in fact cited by the current *Oxford English Dictionary* as an example of "paromoeon" (alliteration).

On the next page and a half of the *Wake* Notebook, Joyce left a unified cluster of 21 lines of entries, in both Latin and English. Most of these items can be traced directly to Cicero's text. Fourteen are crossed out, but only some of these can be identified in the text of the *Wake*, where they occur in a relatively close pattern in II.4, "Mamalujo." These two Notebook pages on which the entries are written offer a rare glimpse of Joyce's methods and mind of the artist at work. Just before the initial references to "De Senect" quoted above, there are five lines of notes that have been crossed out. Three of these items are thematically very significant, since they function as both a stenographic preface to the Ciceronian material and an introduction to the dominant motif of the entire episode. These entries, which are transferred verbatim into the text, are "ᵇthe elder" (*FW* 385.3) "ᵇancient" (*FW* 396.7), and "ᵇhis old age coming on" (*FW* 392.3).

The arrangement of these entries strongly suggests that Joyce's train of thought highballed onto its Ciceronian line when he connected *De Senectute* to "his old age was coming on," the final pre-Latin phrase in this cluster of Notebook entries. Despite his perennial eye problems, a purely personal motive for jotting down a comment about imminent old age is unlikely here. Joyce himself was just over forty when he added the items in this Notebook.[11] By any reckoning—including that of the Romans—he was hardly an old man. Standard commentaries on *De Senectute* state that Cicero composed the dialogue in 44 B.C., when he was sixty-two years old; in ancient Rome, a man was not counted a *senex* until sixty.[12] It is probable, then, that the explanation for Joyce's notes on aging was literary, not autobiographical. It is also highly probable that, on its basic "plot" level, the primary narrative principle for the "Mamalujo" episode responds to Four Men's old age.[13] The three crossed-out Notebook entries cited above, then, accurately predict the more than 41 instances of the word "old" (as a separate adjective or as a part of a compound term) and the five instances of "auld" that serve as a senescent refrain in the published text of the chapter.

The details of the contribution of *De Senectute* to Joyce's process of composition can be seen below in a three-step illustration of textual interaction: (a) the decipherment of the pertinent entries in Notebook VI.B.2.148–49 (transcribed in bold); (b) the indication of their genetic source in Cicero's Latin text (printed in *italics*); (c) the citation of the parallel *Wake* passages (in quotes), followed by comment on the function of the entries that have been transferred into the text.[14]

1. (a) **pedestrian battles** (VI.B.2.148).
   (b)*pedestres . . . pugnas* (*De S* 13).
   (c) "drowning of Pharaoh and all his pedestrians" (*FW* 387.26). Here the Latin adjective for "pertaining to foot-soldiers"[15] is applied to Moses' triumphant crossing of the Red Sea. This specification is somewhat illogical, because *Exodus* emphasizes that Pharaoh's troops were cavalry. The Old Testament miracle occurs here in the *Wake* as an item in a list of notable drownings.

2. (a) **with top of voice / bonis lateribus** (VI.B.2.148).
   (b)*magna voce et bonis lateribus* (with a loud voice and good lungs) (*De S* 14).
   (c) "the top loft of the voice box" (*FW* 397.11). The two phrases in the Notebook (one English, the other Latin) have been combined by Joyce to produce both a "voice box" (the sound and the organ) and the breath or air (*Luft* [German]) from the lungs that produces the sound. These words remind the narrator of enthusiastic "community singing" by the monkish quartet of Mamalujo. Their rendition works its way "up the wet air register" (*FW* 397.11–14) in HCE's pub-residence.

3. (a) **I can't control / tribute** (VI.B.2.148).
   (b)*gubernatorem in navigando nihil agere* (the steersman can do nothing during the sailing) (*De S* 17); *tribunus* (*De S* 18).
   (c) "Don Gouverneur Buckley's in the Tara Tribune" (*FW* 375.23–24). The Latin *gubernator* supplies the etymological basis for the title of Donal Buckley, the last Governor-General of Ireland. A Roman tribune (here linked to Ireland's ancient capital, Tara) was the representative of the people in the machinery of republican politics.

4. (a) **Old Marcus Appius** (VI.B.2.149).
   (b)*ad Appi Claudi senectutem* (toward the old age of Appius Claudius) (*De S* 16).

(c) "Old Marcus" (*FW* 384.8, 11; compare "happyass cloudious!" [*FW* 581.22–23]). Appius Claudius Caecus was one of the proverbial "grand old men" of Roman history. His moral rectitude—and old-age blindness—recommend him to Joyce as a destined-to-be-perverted model for the peeping Mark, "*the rummest old rooster ever flopped out of Noah's ark*" (*FW* 383.9).[16]

5. (a) [b]Schoolboys (VI.B.2.149).
(b) *ab adulescentibus* (by young men) (*De S* 20).
(c) "the schooler" (*FW* 393.33). In this section of the *Wake* and throughout his dialogue—but with opposite intent—Joyce and Cicero contrast the moral judgment of the young and the old.

6. (a) [b]read *tombstones* you lose memory (VI.B.2.149; Joyce's emphasis).
(b) *nec sepulcra legens vereor quod aiunt ne memoriam perdam* (I don't fear that I'll lose my memory, so the saying goes, by reading tombstones) (*De S* 21).
(c) "Themistletocles, on his multilingual tombstone" (*FW* 392.24–25). In the process of transferring the note into the *Wake,* Joyce obliterates the Roman superstition about sepulchral memory-loss[17] and injects the name of Themistocles. This Athenian statesman's feat of memorizing the names of all his fellow citizens is cited by Cicero in *De Senectute* in the same paragraph (21) as the adage about tombs and amnesia. I have checked the biographies of Themistocles by Plutarch and Nepos (*FW* 389.28, *FW* 392.18); there is nothing in them about his "multilingual tomb." Since Themistocles died disgraced and in exile, there is no genuine monument to him. On the other hand, in his life of the famous Athenian, Nepos reports that Themistocles spent all his time in exile learning the Persian language, and that he is reported to have spoken to the Shah with greater fluency than the king's native-born subjects (Nepos, *Themistocles* 2.10). I suspect that that historical anecdote is the source of Joyce's "multilingual," even though in the text of the *Wake* the adjective seems to apply only to the tombstone.

7. (a) [b]multa quae non vult, videt (VI.B.2.149).
(b) *multa quae non vult videt* ([old age] sees many things which it does not like) (*De S* 25).
(c) "this unitarian lady . . . lived to a great age . . . where she was seen by many and widely liked" (*FW* 389.11–14). Joyce typically turns the meaning of the Latin, which is itself a poetic quotation by Cicero, upside-down.

There are number of additional Notebook entries from *De Senectute* that do not seem to have left any trace in the *Wake.* What about a source for these items? It is possible to venture a solid guess that Joyce read Cicero's work in an edition that included a general introduction and perhaps a commentary. Evidence for this is the Notebook entry "chi era Carneade?" (VI.B.2.149). This is Joyce's query (in Italian) about the identity and relevance of Carneades to the discussion. Carneades was a second-century B.C. Greek philosopher, whose works, reflecting the skepticism of the New Academy, had a great influence on Cicero. Joyce must have run across the unfamiliar name in a footnote to *De Senectute* and made a note to himself to look him up. If he did remember to do so, it does not seem that Carneades or any of his doctrines merited the immortality of being inserted into the *Wake*.[18]

The two clusters of references to works of Cicero that I have presented so far in this chapter each have specific thematic force. The phrases from the *First Oration against Catiline* are reused by Joyce in situations in which a prosecutor marshals the incriminating evidence against a disturber of the peace or a rival. The second set of allusions and citations, reworked into English from *De Senectute*, enter the already Latinate disquisitions of the Four (dirty-minded) Old Men in "Mamalujo." Detection of this group of Ciceronian echoes was made possible thanks to two pages of explicit excerpts from the Latin work in one of the earliest Buffalo Notebooks.[19] There is also another, tenuous link between these two works of Cicero and the *Wake*. The *First Catilinarian* was delivered to the Roman Senate. The Latin root of that word (*sen-*) indicates that it is a body of "elder" statesmen. On occasion in the text the Four Old Men are called "senators four" (*FW* 474.21) and their assembly (with a parochial Dublin qualification) is referred to as "the old trinitarian senate" (*FW* 388.36; compare *FW* 513.29–30).

Miscellaneous

My final category of material from or about Cicero is an omnium-gatherum of items that have no apparent overarching narrative or thematic purpose, but are none the less typical of Joyce's encyclopedic impulse in the *Wake*. Just before the famous geometrical diagram of the *vescia piscis* (fish's bladder), the words "some somnione sciupiones" (*FW* 293.7–8) appear. This is an allusion to Cicero's *Somnium Scipionis* (Scipio's Dream), a moralizing piece in which the illustrious Scipio Africanus appears in a dream to his grandson. The younger Scipio, who has already been mentioned in my remarks about *De Senectute*, is exhorted to lead a life of Roman patriotism and rectitude. The citation appears in one of the most complex sections of the *Wake*; and a reference to a famous dream sequence in Roman literature is not out of place. The problems being posed by Joyce's "Professor" or pondered by the three pupils in this densely dreamlike part of the text, however, are concerned with nothing that would have seemed even remotely virtuous to Scipio or his grandfather.

One of the great tragic heroes of early Roman history was Marcus Manlius. He was the military commander whom the vigilant sacred geese alerted; then he repulsed an assault by Gallic commandos against the Capitol. This incident is discussed in some detail on pages 46 and 62–63. Here it is sufficient to note that Cicero, as well as Livy, recorded Manlius' later fall from glory. In one of his *Philippics* aimed at Mark Antony's squalid conduct, Cicero succinctly cited a Roman precedent for the consequences of familial disgrace: *neminem patricium Manlium Marcum vocari licet* (it is forbidden for any patrician member of the Manlian clan to be named "Marcus") (*Phil.* 1.13.32). Joyce noted this bit of traditional Roman name lore in an archival entry (VI.B.15.76) and embedded it in a discussion of HCE's criminal past: "arrah, sure there was never a marcus at all at all among the manlies" (*FW* 96.6).

There are numerous references in the *Wake* to various models of the venerable Roman custom of divination, some details and mechanics of which are discussed in pages 99–104. The most extensive ancient sources of information about such matters are Cicero's two works *De Natura Deorum* (On The Nature of the Gods) and *De Divinitatione* (On Divination). He presents an immense (but often skeptical) fund of theory and example about the observation of birds in flight, the inspection of the inner organs of animals, and the placement of lightning bolts. Since he himself was a member of the College of Augurs, Cicero sometimes takes these omens and the science of their interpretation seriously—especially when the supranatural message favored his client or political position. Joyce is less reverent about the entire enterprise. He specifically attacks (in Latin, so the message cannot be missed) the *haruspices,* Roman priests whose specialty was the examination of the entrails of sacrificial animals: "(*En caecos harauspices! Annos longos patimur!*)" (Look at the blind entrail-inspectors! We suffer for long years!) (*FW* 100.18).

Joyce's interest in preternatural portents is not limited to the *Wake.* Immediately after the recitation of the mystical villanelle in *Portrait,* the young Stephen Dedalus reveals that he is adept at augury: his ashplant is like a Roman priest's "curved stick," as he watches the flight of birds and hears "their shrill two fold cry." After two pages of continued observation and contemplation, Stephen realizes that he has "felt the augury he had sought in the wheeling darting birds," but he is unable to refine the message: "Symbol of departure or of loneliness?" (*P* 224–26). The implicit connection between literary inspiration and religious ritual was also noted, with a conspiratorial comment, in the 1905 letter to Stanislaus that I cited in the introduction. Flitting just beneath the surface of those references to divination—and many other Joycean passages—is Marcus Tullius Cicero, premier Roman orator, eclectic philosopher, and skeptical augur.

6

Vergil

Publius Vergilius Maro, the poet of Augustan Rome's national epic, was a favorite of Victorian and Edwardian authors. His "stateliest measures ever molded by the lips of man" and imperial themes have the appropriate moral and political overtones for these eras. The line-by-line scrutiny brought to bear on his works in secondary-school classrooms also contributes to the frequency of allusion to the *Aeneid* in the literature of that period. James Joyce's fictional re-creation of his own times and academic experience reflects that Vergilian gloss.[1] When Stephen Dedalus hears a note of anguish and despair in the voices of his younger brothers and sisters, his reflexive frame of reference is literary:

> And he remembered that Newman had heard this note also in the broken lines of Virgil *giving utterance . . . to that pain and weariness.*[2] (*P* 164; Joyce's emphasis)

In *Ulysses* the Roman poet is explicitly mentioned twice. First, at the conclusion of "Aeolus," Professor MacHugh's comment on the "Parable of the Plum" is encapsulated in the headline "VIRGILIAN, SAYS PEDAGOGUE" (*U* 7.1053). Later, in "Oxen of the Sun," the archaicizing phrase "as Virgilius saith" is adduced to support a contention that conception can be caused by the west wind (*U* 14.242–44). This odd bit of gynecological lore is, in fact, proposed in Vergil's *Georgics* 3.272–75. There, however, the effect is limited to mares, and even this claim is qualified by the poet's admission that the statement is *mirable dictu* (an astounding thing to say).

There are also several covert references to Vergilian material in *Ulysses*. In his *Hamlet* dissertation, Stephen refers to Shakespeare as "a lord of language" (*U* 9.454). Actually the phrase was applied to Vergil in a poem by Tennyson that was commissioned by the citizens of Mantua for the nineteen-hundredth anniversary of the Roman poet's death. These Victorian verses with their final apostrophe, "I salute thee, Mantovano," still appear in the introductions to fourth-year Latin tests.[3] At one time they were an obvious assignment in interdisciplinary memorization.

Another unattributed reference to Vergil in *Ulysses* is accompanied by a slightly modified quotation, which Joyce would have expected most of his readers to pick up. The scene is "Eumaeus"; the panhandler Corley has just put the touch on Stephen, whose drink-fogged memory comes up with an appropriately classical reaction: "However *haud ignarus malorum miseris succurrere disco etcetera* as the Latin poet remarks" (*U* 16.175–76). In the first book of Vergil's *Aeneid*, Queen Dido of Carthage tells the shipwrecked Trojans that her own exile from Tyre assures a sympathetic reception for the refugees: *non ignara mali miseris succurere disco* (not unacquainted with evil myself, I have learned how to help the wretched) (*A* 1.630). This eleemosynary line seems to have been a favorite in the entire Dedalus/Joyce family. The verse just cited is used (without the *Ulyssean* change in gender of the adjective modifying the subject) in a 1909 telegram with money sent by John Joyce to Nora, who was facing insistent creditors in Trieste (*JJII* 306). Corley, therefore, receives not only a hexameter's worth of Vergilian compassion but also a half crown (erroneously surmised as a penny) to succor his miseries.

Throughout "Eumaeus," Leopold Bloom is at the side of Stephen Dedalus. Joyce acknowledges a comrade's loyalty by calling Bloom "*fidus Achates*" (*U* 16.54–55) right at the start of that chapter. The allusion, of course, is to Aeneas' faithful companion on every step of his adventures from Troy to Italy, *fidus Achates* (*A* 1.188, 6.158, 12.384).

There are several references to the medieval custom of seeking guidance in important matters by a haphazard stab at the text of Vergil; this type of bibliomancy is called *sortes Vergilianae* (*sors, sortis* [choice by lot]).[4] If, for example, the collective finger of a group of hesitant Crusaders should have lit on *solvite corde metum* (banish fear from your heart) (*A* 1.562), they could then confidently sail off to the Holy Land. In "Wandering Rocks" Bloom, perhaps inadvertently, practices *sortes* on a less classical text, *Sweets of Sin*. When "[h]e read where his finger opened," he came upon a memorable, but scarcely prophetic passage that includes the passionate apostrophe "*For Raoul!*" (*U* 10.607–9). This custom is also more specifically alluded to in the *Wake*: "*O'Mara Farrell* . . . volve the virgil page and view" (*FW* 270.L2, 25); "volve" is Latin for "turn" and "*O'Mara*" is meant to echo Vergil's *cognomen* Maro. (The Sanskrit root of that word is *smar*, which means to "to be thoughtful" and is connected with memory.) A similar play on the poet's names is heard in "Wirrgeling and maries" (*FW* 88.33–34). In "Night Lessons" there is another example, this time with an amorous twist: "SORTES VIRGIANAE" (virginal choices by random selection) (*FW* 281.R2). Both the literary and the romantic aspects of this phrase, which occurs just after one of the Quinet-passages, are confirmed by "Margaritomancy" (*FW* 281.14), the word that the marginal Latin phrase is intended to gloss. The suffix "-mancy" is derived from the Greek noun meaning "divination," "prophecy," "oracle." *Margarita* is Latin for both "pearl" and "daisy." Here the bilingual compound is meant to designate a classically adept ingénue playing "He loves me. He loves me not."

Not one of the titles of Vergil's genuine works (*Eclogues, Georgics, Aeneid*) appears on any of Joyce's pages. There is, however, a line of Wakean doggerel: *Or Culex feel etchy if Pulex don't wake him?* (*FW* 418.23). *Culex* (Gnat) is the title of a short verse piece that may be the product of Vergil's youth, or (far more likely, in the opinion of scholars) an inconsequential effort by a later author falsely attributed to the poet. At any rate, Joyce's *Culex*, in the midst of the insect-infested "Ondt and Gracehoper" episode, performs no august literary function. It merely balances the *Pulex* (Flea) later on in the line.[5]

Although the titles are neglected, the first lines (and they served as a work's "title" in antiquity) of all three of Vergil's works are embedded into the *Wake*. Joyce's "*arma virumque romano*" (*FW* 389.19) is very close, with an interpolated patriotic twist, to *arma virumque cano* (I sing of arms and the man) (*Aeneid* 1.1). There are also two interpretative renditions in English of this memorable line: "virgils like Armsworks, Limited!" (*FW* 618.2) and the more literal "weapons, warriors bard" (*FW* 277.F3). The later allusion is reinforced by Joyce's wordplay, in the next footnote, on the title of Macaulay's once popular series of versified tales of early Roman heroism: "the lays of ancient homes" (*FW* 227.F4) (see pages 58–59).

The first line of Vergil's collection of pastoral poems cannot be missed: "Titubante of Tegmine—sub—Fagi" (*FW* 403.9) is meant to sound a bit like *Tityre, tu patulae recumbans sub tegmine fagi* (Tityrus, you are lolling beneath the shelter of spreading beechtree) (*Eclogues* 1.1). More carefully camouflaged is a third opening line, "foster wheat crops" (*FW* 76.35). I read these words as an adequate, but not very inspired translation of one of the topic questions that begin Vergil's verse encomium to Italy's fields and flocks: *quid faciat laetas segestes* (what makes grainfields flourish) (*Georgics* 1.1).[6] There is another, even more cryptic reference to the same line in "over his *face* which I *publicked* in my bestback *garden* for *laetification* of *sidero*dromites" (*FW* 160.20–21; my emphases). The italicized words direct attention to Joyce's sound-for-sense transfer of *faciat laetas*; his domestication of *segestes* (grainfields) into "garden"; and, to jog the allusive fancy of less ardent Vergilians, the Roman poet's *praenomen* (Publius) has been expanded into the past tense of an English verb. The first element in "*sidero*dromites" comes directly from the next clause in the opening line of the *Georgics: quo sidere terram* / *vertere* (under which star to turn the earth) (*G* 1.1–2). In the *Wake* passage under scrutiny, Joyce typically carries the allusive process one step farther. A Latin word for "star" is *sidus, sideris;* an unrelated Greek adjective, *sidēros,* means "iron." The *Wake's* "siderodromites," therefore, is probably meant not merely to echo Vergil's promise of astronomical information, but also to delight the etymological fancy of those who travel (*dromos* is "track" in Greek) on the railroads. This bit of translingual punning is immediately reinforced by the phrase that completes the primary passage cited above: "and to the irony of the stars" (*FW* 160.21–22).

This same type of deeply buried "quotation" of a Vergilian text (and there are also earlier examples from *Ulysses*) can be unearthed in another passage: "*Capellisato*, shoehanded slaughterer of the *shader* of our *leaves* (*FW* 255.1–2; my emphases). This heroic epithet from the end of the *Wake's* "Mime" is probably addressed to the aroused HCE. Its literary source, while definitely Vergilian, does not come from the Roman epic; rather, the italicized words are clearly meant to recall the final two lines of the *Tenth* (and last) *Eclogue*. Here, after he has praised the poet Gallus, Vergil brings his series of pastoral verses to a close by urging the kid goats to return to home pastures before night falls: *nocent et frugibus umbrae. / Ite domum saturae, venit Hesperus, ite capellae* (The shadows are bad for the crops. Go home after a full day of grazing; go home, kidlings. The Evening Star has come) (*E* 10.76–77).

If a casual reader of *Ulysses* wished to show that he could accurately quote something between "Stately, plump . . . Buck Mulligan" and Molly's terminal "Yes," he might come up with the awesomely high-toned, "Ineluctable modality of the visible" (*U* 3.1; compare 3.13, 3.413, 3.425, and 15.3630–31). The initial adjective, "ineluctable," begs for comment, especially in the face of Joyce's frequent etymological wordplay. Its association with the "visible" is a false clue—but one that is characteristically Joycean. The "-luc-," that is, has nothing to do with the Latin word for "light"; but tantalizing suggestions of verbal delusion of this sort need to be examined. The potential confusion can be illustrated by a brief excursus to examine the ramifications of a Latin maxim, *lucus a non lucendo.* This phrase would be a perfect motto for parts of *Ulysses* and all of *Finnegans Wake.* It is the classic example of the inspired perversity of many attempts by lexically naive native speakers, before the dawn of professional philology, to explain the origins of their words. The Latin noun *lucus* means "forest glen," "grove." Though the word originally denoted a *clearing* in the woods into which light could shine, it is frequently found in contexts where the natural meaning is a "shady spot, "thicket"—the sort of place that might be described in impure Wakese as a "bosky old delltangle" (*FW* 465.3). Even the ancient Romans appear to have been puzzled by the fact that the root for this word was *lux, lucis* (light). They quite sensibly overcame the paradox, however, by adding a negative and asserting that *lucus* is derived from *non lucendo* (not emitting light).

Joyce might well have been introduced to this odd maxim in one of his early lessons in Latin at Clongowes Wood College. The first issue of the school paper includes a review of "A Clongowes Novel." Its author is commended for his accuracy in capturing local detail. He described a room that "was square in shape, and lighted from above; which room I afterwards learned was known, apparently on the *lucus of non lucendo* principle, as the 'Round Room'."[7] Finally, Joyce's abiding interest in this type of off-kilter etymologies is confirmed by an archival entry: "Lucan a non lucendo" (IV.B.19.56). Lucan was a first-century A.D. poet whose epic, the *Pharsalia*, is notorious for its baroque rhetoric and laborious constructions. Thus, in recording the Notebook entry, Joyce registered his awareness of the paradoxical maxim and engaged in some incidental literary criticism (see page 213).

In a similar way, I suspect, more than one reader of *Ulysses* has been momentarily fooled by the presence of "visible" as the object of "ineluctable modality." The apparent root *-luc-* must somehow be connected with "light"; and "ineluctable" must mean something like "unable to be darkened." As pop epistemology that definition makes surface sense; as scientific etymology it is all wrong.[8] The Latin verb at the root of "ineluctable" is *lucto*, which means "to wrestle," "to grapple with." Thus "ineluctable modality" is a condition of seen things that cannot be evaded, a function of the visible that sends direct signals, unmediated by analysis: "Signatures of all things" (*U* 3.2) that one perceives in a flash and need not wrestle to a comprehensive fall.

The upshot of the foregoing mini-exercise in Latin word-origins is to elucidate Joyce's source for the archetypically Ulyssean adjective "ineluctable." It comes, with no visible mediation, from Vergil's *Aeneid*. During Aeneas' tale to Queen Dido about the fall of Troy, the hero tells that a priest of Apollo had solemnly announced that the city's end was at hand: *venit . . . ineluctabile tempus* (time that could not be wrestled away has come) (*A* 2.324).[9] This four-element adjective (negative prefix, preposition, root, potential suffix) is an exotic word-choice, even for portentous statements to the hero of a nation's foundation epic. Except for obvious imitations in later Roman poetry, Vergil's two examples of *ineluctabilis* are the only notable uses of the word in ancient literature. There can be little doubt, therefore, about Joyce's model for his own lightly Englished imitation, which leads off "Proteus": "The ineluctable modality of the visible" (*U* 3.1). Certainty in assignment of this particular source is provided by another Vergilian citation, in Latin, later in *Ulysses*. Commenting on the recitation of John F. Taylor's typological speech in "Aeolus" in favor of the primacy of the Irish language, Professor MacHugh says to Stephen, "It has the prophetic vision. *Fuit Ilium!* The sack of windy Troy" (*U* 7.909–10). MacHugh's Latin quotation comes directly from the next verse in the prophet-priest's speech in the *Aeneid: venit summa dies et* ineluctabile *tempus / Dardaniae. fuimus Troes, fuit Ilium* (the final day has come, the time that the land of Dardanus cannot struggle out of. We used to be Trojans. Ilium once was) (*A* 2.324–25).

In his self-inflating biography, Oliver Gogarty reports that "Joyce had 'a nose like a rhinoceros for literature'." In addition to quotations from Dowland, Jonson, and Mangan, he would compare Vergil's *procumbit humi bos* (the ox falls flat out to the ground) (*A* 5.481) to a line from Dante with similar rhyth-mic effects.[10] Impressive; but the following example of intertextuality from the *Aeneid* and *Ulysses* takes Gogarty's report of virtuoso citation to the outer limits of credibility. During 1918 when Joyce was working on the first third of *Ulysses,* he made notes on useful material from his readings. These notes have been edited by Phillip Herring and can most conveniently be consulted in his transcription.[11] The first two entries cited below occur, one after the other, on the same page; the third is found eleven pages later:

> Vergil I.52 conical isle
> $\quad\quad$ Aoelus = high
> [b]brazen walls $\quad\quad$ (VIII.A.5.15)

> Hades $\quad$ α ἰδειν
> $\quad\quad$ un seen (maker of) (VIII.A.5.26)

Early in the *Aeneid* (1.52) the goddess Juno arrives at the island homeland of Aeolus, where "the lord of the winds sits on a lofty citadel" (*celsa sedet Aeolus arce*) (*A* 1.56). In his note Joyce presumably followed Bérard's ety-mology and reduced this scene to "Aoelus [*sic*] = high." The "brazen walls" are not Vergilian, but probably reflect a line from Horace, *murus aeneus* (*Odes* 3.3.65). At any rate, the phrase is meant to refer to the basaltic cliffs which Bérard reports are found on the island of Aeolus. The final entry has nothing to do with epic geography; it is a typical example of ancient folk etymology. The name of Hades, lord of the Underworld, is here explained (with no basis in linguistic fact) as composed of the prefix *a-* (not) and the Greek verb *idein* (to see). In Joyce's shorthand, this bit of traditional folk etymology becomes "un seen (maker of)." Thus, the king of the realm of the dead has a name that reflects his role as the one who takes all mortals out of sight.[12]

Apart from the obvious fact that all of these entries involve some aspect of classical antiquity, even the most ingenious critic would be hard pressed to find a connection between a Vergilian high place, brazen walls, and the (spurious) etymology of the Underworld. It is true that Aeneas' wanderings are framed in the epic by Aeolus' storm and the hero's descent into Hades—but what about those walls? Joyce, however, with his incredible nose for literary connections, found a way to link those notebook entries in *Ulysses*. During the final scene of "Wandering Rocks," the viceregal carriage passes near a park where a Scots band is playing "My Girl's a Yorkshire Girl." The military performers are *"Unseen brazen highland* laddies" (*U* 10.1249; my emphasis). Narratively, each of the italicized words makes sense: the band is *"unseen"* because the carriage is progressing along Nassau Street without a clear view into College Park. The bandsmen are *"brazen"* because they are part of a drum-and-bugle corps that "blared and drumthumped" the song. As Scots, the "laddies" are naturally *"highland."* At the same time, it is beyond the wildest coincidence that the three archival adjectives spontaneously grouped themselves together in Joyce's imagination. Rather, the triple modifiers of the "laddies" come from entries that were recorded in and retrieved from—"brazen walls" was crossed out with blue crayon—the 1918 Zürich notebook. Though one would never suspect it, Joyce's interest in Aeolus' lofty citadel and the geography of the *Aeneid* was the impulse behind this bizarrely concocted and ridiculously introverted classical allusion.

There is another, brief passage in *Ulysses* that indicates that this collocation of notebook entries was carefully planned and cleverly exploited. In "Circe," the chapter in which so many episodes are re-created in auditory and visual *déjà vu,* Edy Boardman accosts Cissy Caffrey: "You *never seen* me in the mantrap with a married *highlander*" (*U* 15.93–94; my emphases). The italicized words account for two of the original adjectives; the third ("brazen") can be inferred from the fact that the putative lover is known to be married and any connection between him and Miss Boardman would be shameless on her part.[13]

In the primary *Ulysses* Notebook mentioned above, there are six entries that cite the *Aeneid*, and a seventh that refers to "Virgil 3 days bora—bonaccia" (VIII.A.5.20). The later is probably a reference to the three days of storm (*bora*, or *borea*, meaning "north wind" in Italian), followed on the fourth day by a "calm sea" (*bonaccia* in Italian). This weather pattern is reported in *Aeneid* 3.203–7. These seven archival entries would seem to offer reliable evidence that material from the wandering and descent sections of Vergil's Roman epic, as well as from the primary Homeric source, were part of the structural framework of *Ulysses*. Strictly speaking, such a conclusion would not be justified. Not one of the specifically Vergilian entries in the Zürich notebook comes directly from the *Aeneid* itself. Each is a secondhand reference taken from the volumes of Bérard's *Les Phéniciens et l'Odyssée* or from volumes 1 and 3 of Roscher's comprehensive *Lexikon [of Greek and Roman Mythology]*.[14] These two works (which are the sources of the majority of the entries in this Notebook) supplied Joyce with almost all of the detailed Odyssean background—including the parallel citations from the text of the *Aeneid*—to which he referred while composing *Ulysses*. Thus, the same archival evidence that revealed the Vergilian inspiration of "unseen brazen highland" undercuts a claim that this marvelously kaleidoscopic phrase is a *direct* result of Joyce's methodical reading of the original text. In balance, there is a big gain for critical insight into Joyce's methods of composition, and a minor correction in an estimate of the scholarly depth and research originality of his display of classical finesse.

The scrupulous exclusion of the material in Notebook VIII.A.5 from being tallied as firsthand allusion to the actual text of Vergil does not mean there are no direct echoes of the *Aeneid* in *Ulysses*. The passages discussed below will demonstrate that the Roman epic was frequently and ingeniously incorporated by Joyce into his works.

THE UNDERWORLD

A cluster of undoubted examples appear in "Hades"; all come from Aeneas' tour of the Underworld. In the *Aeneid* a steep, deep cave serves as the entrance to the nether regions. There Aeneas and his guide, the Sibyl, sacrifice four black bullocks after cropping the tufts of hair between their horns (*A* 6.243–49). On the drive to the cemetery, Bloom's carriage is momentarily blocked by a "drove of branded cattle. . . . Springers. . . . Roast-beef for old Ireland. . . . all that raw stuff, hide, hair, horns" (*U* 6.385–95).[15]

As Paddy Dignam's funeral cortège passes the stonecutter's yard on the "[l]ast lap" to the cemetery, the narrator reports:

> Crowded on the spit of land silent shapes appeared, white, sorrowful, holding out calm hands, knelt in grief, pointing. Fragments of shapes, hewn. In white silence: appealing. (*U* 6.459–61)

The pieces of funereal statuary are described in terms that Vergil applied to crowds of the recently dead who rush to the banks of the infernal rivers and beg to be ferried across into the Underworld itself: *stabant orantes primi transmittere cursum / tendebantque manus ripae ulterioris amore* (They were standing there appealing to be first to cross the passage and they were holding out their hands in desire for the farther shore) (*A* 6.313–14).

In *Finnegans Wake* Issy occasionally interrupts Shaun's apology in "The

Mookses and the Gripes." In one such instance, she seems to be surrounded by companions who are described in terms reminiscent of the just-quoted lines of Vergil:

> The siss of the whisp of the sigh . . . and shades began to glidder along the banks, greepsing, greepsing, duusk unto duusk, and it was glooming as gloaming could be. . . . citherior spiane an eaulande, innemorous and unnumerose. (FW 158.6–13)

Now, back to *Ulysses* and "Hades." As the mourners of Paddy Dignam enter Glasnevin Cemetery they pass the "Murderer's ground. . . . Wrongfully condemned" (U 6.476–78). The Underworld in the *Aeneid* also includes an area in which are found "falso damnati crimine mortis" (those condemned to death on a false charge) (A 6.430). Not far are *Lugentes campi* (Mourning Fields) (A 6.441); Joyce calls the entire burial ground "the dismal fields" (U 6.877). In the *Aeneid*, the wraith of Dido "errabat silva in magna" (was wandering in a large wood) (A 6.451) and other souls are "shaded by a myrtle grove" (*myrtea circum / silva tegit*) (A 6.443–44). In *Ulysses,* statues once again serve as manifestations of the shades of the dead: "Dark poplar, rare white forms. Forms more frequent, white shapes thronged amid the trees" (U 6.487–89). Finally, after all the graveside ceremonies for Paddy Dignam have been completed, Bloom prepares to leave the cemetery: "The gates glimmered in front: still open" (U 6.995). In Vergil's Underworld *sunt geminae Somni portae . . . / quarum altera fertur / cornea . . . altera candenti perfecta nitens elephanto* (there are twin gates of Dream . . . one is said to be made of horn . . . the other glistens, since it is made from shining ivory) (A 6.893–95). In *Finnegans Wake* the material of both of these Vergilian gates, through which dreams pass into the upper world, is specifically and most appropriately combined: "hornmade ivory dreams" (FW 192.27).

The Ulyssean parallels and echoes cited in the previous two paragraphs are fairly well recognized; the *mise en scène* of "Hades" and Bloom's reverie as he explores Dublin's largest cemetery almost invite an elegiac mood. Dreams, the realms of the dead, an epic return from the Underworld are equally congenial topics for *Finnegans Wake.* Thus, direct references to the Latin text of the sixth book of the *Aeneid* make several otherworldly appearances in that work. When Aeneas wishes to visit Avernus, the Sibyl instructs him to pluck the Golden Bough as their passport through the forbidden regions. The somewhat passive hero is led to the location of this branch by a pair of doves, whom he recognizes as the totem birds of his goddess-mother, Venus (A 6.187–204). All of this was condensed by Joyce into "venuson . . . dovetimid" (FW 93.17). The presence of the *Aeneid* here is confirmed by a later and more expansive treatment of the same epic scene:

> Bright pigeons all over the whirrld will fly with mistletoe message round their loveribboned necks and a crumb of my cake for each chasta dieva. (*FW* 147.22–24)

Vergil's twin doves also arrive with a whirl of Latin alliteration: *venere volantes / et viridi sedere solo* (they came flying along and settled on the green ground) (*A* 6.191–92). Aeneas recognizes his mother's omen and thanks his "diva parens" (goddess parent) (*A* 6.197). In Roman mythology (as opposed to Wakean fantasy), amorous Venus cannot be called a "chasta di[e]va" (chaste goddess).[16]

In another epic episode Aeneas' divine mother is able to equip her son with new armor from the Olympian forge, precisely because she does not concern herself with chastity. The goddess of sexual rapture approaches Vulcan in his golden sleeping-chamber and arouses his divine love; the armorer of the gods accepts his "old flame" (*A* 8.370–94). To Joyce Venus' maternal manipulation of the production schedule of the blacksmith god suggested the following generalization: "Venuses were gigglibly temptatrix, vulcans guffawably eruptious" (*FW* 79.18). This is an adequate summary, with a pair of adverbs interpolated for postclassical (and precoital) comic relief, of the sexual politics of the Olympian maternal-military complex in the *Aeneid*.

From the famous Vergilian simile, which describes the Golden Bough in terms of a parasitic vine that thrives in winter frost, scholars deduce that the poet may have some sort of mistletoe plant in mind.[17] Joyce noticed and exploited this item of mythological botany. To those whose ears are attuned not only to omnipresent scatology, but also to the possibility of classical allusion in the *Wake*, the rustling of Vergil's preternatural talisman can be heard in "let her be peace on the bough" (*FW* 465.13–14; compare *FW* 248.18, "boughpee"). Here the hallowed branch is being sacrilegiously doused by a golden shower. Moreover, the immediately preceding part of the same sentence is also perversely festive: "Let us be holy and evil." This exhortation must be an allusion to the Christmas song "The Holly and the Ivy." Another Yuletide (and Vergilian) plant, the mistletoe, must be hidden somewhere in this same general area of text. The adjacent presence of "frankincensive" (*FW* 465.12) would then join myrrh and the Bough's gold to constitute a reference to the Magi's three Epiphany gifts.

An important aspect of Aeneas' tour of Hades is his visit to the area around the River Lethe where the souls of the yet-to-be-born congregate. There his father, Anchises, shows his son the ranks of the heroes of Roman history. From the poet's perspective, this era of the nation's future has passed, but from the epic perspective it is still to come. Anchises summarizes the civic purpose of their mutual review of patriots, in the famous Roman mandate:

> tu regere imperio populos, Romane, memento
> (hae tibi erunt artes), pacique imponere morem,
> parcere subiectis et debellare superbos. (*A* 6.851–53)

> (Roman, remember that you will rule the nations—this will be your forte—to impose abiding peace, to spare the beaten and to devastate the arrogant.)

In Shaun's defense of his conduct late in the *Wake*, the twin son catalogues his many benefits to society. The list includes a Vergilian boast: "on my siege of my mighty I was *parciful of my subject* but in street wauks that are darkest I *debellendem superb*" (*FW* 545.28–29; my emphases). The "Eleventh Question" of I.6 is the locus for another allusion to Aeneas' trip to the Underworld. This time Shaun appropriates (and perhaps repudiates) the Vergilian lines quoted just above. As if to emphasize its epic source, a modified version of the final imperative (*parcere*) can be detected in the midst of the twin's bloated rhetoric:

> In need not anthrapologize for any obintentional (I must here correct all that school of neoitalian or paleoparisien schola of tinkers and spanglers who say I'm wrong *parcequeue* out of revolscian from romanitis I want to be) downtrodding on my foes. (*FW* 151.7–11; Joyce's emphasis)

Some of the contributions from the *Aeneid* to establishing a ghostly aura for Joyce's "Hades" episode have been noted in commentaries on *Ulysses*. On the other hand, no critic has seen a connection with this epic episode and the discussion of Shakespeare as reported in "Scylla and Charybdis." Joyce apparently made just such an allusive link. In a recently published (and fragmentary) memoir, Thomas MacGreevy, an Irishman who knew Joyce in Paris during the late '20s and '30s, writes that the author himself said

> that I was the first person who had ever sensed its [the relationship between fathers and sons in the National Library scene] significance for him and apropos of it, referred to the importance of the descent into the underworld of Aeneas searching for his father.[18]

The Hairy Monster

There is another equally extensive series of Vergilian allusions that seem to have completely slipped through the source nets of the annotators. The title itself of "Cyclops" demands attention to the ways that the Homeric monster Polyphemus influenced Joyce's description of the Citizen, the barkeep at Barney Kiernan's. The Linati schema includes "Prometeo" (Prometheus) and "Galatea" (a sea-nymph whom the Cyclops loves) in the list of persons associated with this episode. I find no traces of either in the text, but there is ample evidence of a significant and appropriate Vergilian analogue for the Citizen.[19]

In the *Aeneid* the primary example of gigantic barbarism is not the Homeric Cyclops, but a native Italian monster, Cacus. The etymology of the name is significant: in Greek the adjective *kakos* means "bad," "evil," "ugly"; the verb *kakkō* means "to defecate," "to crap." In Latin, *caco, -are*, has the same meaning and tone. Thus, Vergil's giant is literally an evil shit. His deeds in the epic resonate the twofold derivation of the name. When Aeneas visits Pallenteum in the second half of the epic, the Trojan hero is told how Cacus had long terrified the village (which is the site of the future city of Rome). The mountain-dwelling monster once slaughtered numerous helpless inhabitants of the area. Aeneas' arrival coincides with the annual celebration by the local people of their deliverance from this cruel ogre. Their savior was the mighty Hercules. In their ritual the people tell of the crime that brought about Cacus' downfall. He stole four magnificent bulls and four lovely cows from Hercules' herd, while the hero was returning from one of his labors. To punish this audacity, the avenger ripped off the top of the monster's mountain cave and strangled the fire-breathing rustler. There are distinct traces of these Herculean feats in Joyce's "Cyclops" episode.

First, the Citizen reacts to the news that one of Dublin's mayoral candidates is meeting with "the cattle traders":

> Hairy Iopas, says the citizen, that exploded volcano, the darling of all countries and the idol of his own. (*U* 12.828–830)

"Hairy Iopas" is rightly glossed as an awkward translation of Vergil's description of the bard who sings at the banquet that Queen Dido gives to welcome the Trojan refugees to Carthage. Vergil specifies that he is *crinitus Iopas* (*crinitus* is more appropriately translated as "long-haired") (*A* 1.740). But neither Iopas nor the focus of his cosmological song seems to have any connection with the Dublin mayoral candidate or Irish cattle traders. And a Vergilian epithet as an expletive is not what one expects to roll off the Citizen's lips. The phrase, then, is probably meant to be heard as nothing more than a local euphemism for "Holy Jesus," like "Hokey jasons" (FW 89.34) or "hosy jigses" (FW 375.26–27). Blasphemy aside, there is another problem of reference here: Who or what is "that exploded volcano" (U 12.829)? That last epithet has nothing to do with Iopas, or with Jesus. I suggest that "that exploded volcano," like the phrase that immediately follows it ("the darling of all countries and the idol of his own"), does not modify "Hairy Iopas." It is meant to refer to the speaker himself, the Citizen, who is most definitely a volcanic type. An "exploded volcano" is one in which an eruption has created a huge, circular crater, a feature of the landscape that some mythographers associate with the single large eye in the forehead of a cyclops (kyklos is "round"; ops is "eye" in Greek). The description is even more appropriate if it is meant to recall the Homeric monster's loss of his eye and the gaping socket that is left after Odysseus' visit. The second phrase ("darling . . . idol . . ."), then, is also to be taken as a recognition of the Citizen's athletic fame as the "champion of all Ireland" (U 12.881–82). This interpretation, in summary, hears the two descriptive phrases as gratuitous comment on the speaker, spoken by the chapter's anonymous Narrator. (Or, with even greater narratological probability and force, these comments should be heard as a minor intrusion of the "Arranger.")[20]

Reinforcing such an "arrangement" is the difficulty of imagining any way that either description could be applied to Vergil's Iopas. On the other hand, an "exploded volcano" would be a nicely synoptic metaphor to capture what happens to Cacus in his fatal encounter with Hercules, as narrated in the *Aeneid*. This suggestion is not meant to nullify the primary assignment of both qualifiers to the Citizen. Rather, the Citizen's apparently unmotivated "Hairy Iopas" sets off a chain reaction of literary associations in the imagination of the Narrator. He is the one who makes the leap from "Iopas" to "volcano"—and he does so precisely because Joyce has already established, earlier in the chapter, the basis for just this type of identity glide. Joyce foreshadows the comment by means of two explicit and scene-setting statements that are also spoken by the Narrator. Each of these is followed by a detailed interpolation that is set in place as a mock-epic expansion of the remark by the Arranger.

The textual evidence to support this interpretation is presented in the following paragraphs. Before that, it is necessary to establish the presence of the Italian monster in the action of the early sections of "Cyclops," then to return to the explicit connection that Joyce makes between Cacus and the Citizen. That connection is mediated by "Hairy Iopas."

The Narrator begins the chapter with an account of the bad-debt suit between Michael E. Geraghty, purchaser, and Moses Herzog, vendor. One of the thirsty comrades is reported to have commented on this matter at law: "*I dare him,* says he, *and I doubledare him.* Come out here, Geraghty, you notorious bloody hill and dale robber!" (*U* 12.100–101; Joyce's emphases). This challenge to the allegedly rustic thief is followed by a catalogue of "herds innumerable," composed of every type of four-footed farm animal. They are heard "trampling, cackling, roaring, lowing, bleating, bellowing," and so on (*U* 12.102–10).

In the *Aeneid* the fatal encounter between Cacus and Hercules has taken place years before Vergil's hero visits the battle site. On the anniversary of the event, Evander tells the newly arrived Aeneas the entire story in great and gory detail.[21] In keeping with the laws of epic hospitality, Aeneas' host begins his tale only after his guest's flagon has been filled and the servants are attending to the rites of the wine god (*Bacchumque ministrant*) (*A* 8.181). As mentioned above, Hercules was returning through Italy from his Tenth Labor, the slaying of the royal Erythean herdsman: *tergemini nece Geryonae spoliisque superbus* (triumphant with his booty after the slaughter of three-formed Geryon) (*A* 8.202). Even a first-time reader of *Ulysses* would be struck by the Latin name of the vanquished king-shepherd in the line just cited; "Geryon" sounds remarkably like the name of the Citizen's "bloody mangy mongrel, Garryowen" (*U* 12.119–20), who is introduced immediately after the parade of livestock mentioned above. The detail is incidental, but it is not coincidental. It is just the sort of wordplay, especially involving proper names, that would surprise no reader of *Finnegans Wake*. Since the impact of the classics on *Ulysses* has involved other examples of typically Wakean techniques, why not a bit of Hiberno-Herculean name-twisting here?

After the drink orders have been filled in traditional epic fashion, the Narrator in *Ulysses* continues his tale of what the Citizen did: "And with that he took the bloody old towser [Garryowen] by the scruff of the neck and, by Jesus, he near throttled him" (*U* 12.149–50).

This eye-witness account of the Citizen's abuse of his animal is followed by a two-paragraph aside. In them, according to one critic, the monstrous and cruel barkeep is described in terms that are "irished Rabelais or simply hyperbolic Irish revival (heroic)."[22] The following are selected elements in that volcanic description, each matched with a parallel passage from the Hercules-Cacus episode in the *Aeneid:*

From shoulder to shoulder he measured several ells. . . . [a body] covered . . . with a strong growth of tawny prickly hair (*U* 12.155–57):
villosaque saetis / pectora (*A* 8.266–67) (a chest shaggy with bristles)

A powerful current of warm breath issued at regular intervals from the profound cavity of his mouth (*U* 12.163–64):

faucibus ingentem fumum (mirable dictu) / evomit (A 8.252–53) (he spews forth a mass of smoke from his jaws—an incredible sight); *illius atros / ore vomens ignis* (A 8.198–99) (spewing forth dark fires from his mouth).

From his girdle hung a row of seastones . . . on these were graven . . . the tribal images of many Irish heroes and heroines of antiquity [here follow the names of ninety such stalwarts] (U 12.173–99):
foribusque adfixa superbis / ora virum tristi pendebant pallida tabo (A 8.196–97) (attached to the mighty doors [of Cacus' cave] were hanging the heads of heroes, faces ghostly pale with gore).

The similarity of these monstrous details (hairy torso, fiery breath, trophy images) argues, definitively in my judgment, that Joyce had his eye directly on Vergil's text while composing this section of "Cyclops." Corroboration is offered by a comparison of the Citizen's mistreatment of Garryowen ("by Jesus, he near throttled him") and Hercules' method of dispatching Cacus: *et angit inhaerans / elisos oculos et siccum sanguine guttur* (and he stuck to him and squeezed his eyes out of their sockets and his throat dry of blood) (A 8.260–61). In prehistoric Italy, this was the way that a "hill and dale robber" was punished because he tried to engage in the illegal cattle trade at the expense of a wandering hero. Thematically significant details of that epic vengeance are applied to Joyce's Citizen—but with no hint that Bloom is destined to play the role of Hercules.

In his "hyperbolic Irish" emphasis on the barbarity of the Citizen, Joyce also calls attention to the "strong growth of tawny prickly hair," and even the "bristles of the same tawny hue" projecting from his nostrils (U 12.157–59). Like Esau in Genesis 27:11, the Citizen is "a hairy man."[23] So is Vergil's Iopas, who is evoked in the Citizen's oath (A 1.740 and U 8.829); so is Cacus, the cattle-rustler in the *Aeneid* 8.266–67. These are the allusive links that contribute a Vergilian aspect to Joyce's portrait of the Citizen as a past-his-prime Irish Cyclops. And there is one final connection. Iopas and the Citizen are both somehow involved with "that exploded volcano." Vergil reports a genealogical detail about Cacus: *huic monstro Volcanus erat pater* (Vulcan was the father of this ogre) (A 8.198). Vergil's volcanic Cacus is so much a part of the makeup of the Citizen that he surely can be forgiven, especially if he'd been sipping a bit of his own "Wine of the Country" (U 12.144), for a bit of momentary confusion involving hairy Iopas, also from the *Aeneid*. It would also be a safe bet that none of the customers in Barney Kiernan's would have been likely to detect either the allusive error or its integrative purpose.

Cacus also makes an incidental, but apt appearance in the *Wake*. In one of the many versions of what HCE did in the park, his alleged crime is compared to what "nobodyatall [did] with Wholyphamous and build rocks over him" (*FW* 73.9). Odysseus (as "Noman") and the cyclops Polyphemus are clearly present here. The "rocks"—and others are all over this page: "rochelly" (*FW* 73.23), "chambered cairns" (*FW* 73.29), "rocks" (*FW* 73.33), "skatterlings of a stone" (*FW* 73.34)—are more appropriate to the mountain cave in which the Italian monster tried to hide from Hercules. Its monumental remains are shown to Aeneas: "a craggy cliff . . . a pile of rubble torn far away from the mountain" (*A* 8.190–91). In the *Wake,* an oath is added to reinforce the validity of the comparison, "be Cacao Campbell" (*FW* 73.10). I hear a narratively and allusively appropriate Latin *campus belli* (field of war) here—and, even in the secondhand account, the characteristic stutter ("Ca-ca") before "Campbell." The verbal imitation of this speech problem is repeated in HCE's own reference to his foul nemesis, "The caca cad!" (*FW* 534.26). The rocks, the Greek and Latin monsters, the pattern of scatological etymology cannot be pushed aside as a fanciful mound of intertextual debris.

Miscellaneous Allusions

The trip to Hell and back and the throttling of Cacus are not the only episodes in the *Aeneid* that attracted Joyce's thematic attention. The Trojan refugees are forced to trace their way to a new homeland in Italy because the gods have decreed that Troy must fall. The city's fate is succinctly stated by Vergil in a phrase that was taken, as is, directly into *Ulysses:* "*Fuit Ilium!*" (Troy used to be) (*A* 2.325 and *U* 7.910). At the start of the *Wake,* the fate of HCE is compared to the fall of the King of Troy in similar terms; but the words only approximate real Latin or genuine Vergil: "Belling him up and filling him down. He's stiff but he's steady is Priam Olim!" (*FW* 6.22–23). *Priam(us) olim* would mean "Priam once [was]." In the *Aeneid* the fall of Priam is equally clipped: *haec finis Priami fatorum . . . / . . . iacet ingens litore truncus* (this was the end-point of Priam's destiny . . . the trunk of his huge body lies on the sea shore) (*A* 2.554–57). Joyce also reports that the grief at "Fillagain's chrissormiss wake" rolled out in a "profusive plethora of ululation" (*FW* 6.14–17). In his *Georgics,* Vergil describes another example of the consternation of a nation at the death of its leader. When Julius Caesar was assassinated, the "cities resounded with howling (*ululantibus*) wolves" (*G* 1.486); and the citizens prayed to "the native gods of the fatherland and Romulus and Mother Vesta" (*di patrii Indigetis et Romule Vestaque mater*) (*G* 1.498). That Latin ritual invocation lies behind Joyce's "his ville's indigenous romekeepers, homesweepers (*FW* 6.4–5). The terminal jingle in this line also reminds the *Wake*'s readers that Vesta is the indigenous goddess of the city's collective hearth and home.

The most detailed and pathetic narrative of the fall of Troy is book 2 of Vergil's *Aeneid*. In it the hero recounts the last hours of the city when he is at a banquet in Carthage. Joyce was certainly thoroughly familiar with the circumstances of this famous epic flashback. In a 1928 letter to Harriet Shaw Weaver he offers to elucidate some of his literary problems to his patron:

> Though I shall feel like Eneas [*sic*] when invited by Dido to tell his tale *"Infandum, regina, iubes renovare dolorem."* Nevertheless *he told it.* (*Letters* III.73)

The Latin is a direct quotation (You order me, Queen, to make new unutterable sorrow) of a line at *Aeneid* 2.3.

Troy's doom is sealed when its defenders fail to heed the premonition of the city's seer-priest: *timeo Danaos et dona ferentis* (I fear Greeks, even when they are bringing gifts) (*A* 2.49). The *Wake* repeats that warning twice: "timid Danaides!" (*FW* 94.14); "doraphobian" (*FW* 478.32). The two lexical roots of the second example not only refer to Greeks, they are Greek: *dōra* (gifts), *phobia* (fear). In the legendary accounts it was Ulysses who led the Greek commandos out of the wooden horse; then Troy was engulfed in a fatal firestorm. Aeneas recognized these divine omens and the inevitability of the Greek assault. Spurred by his goddess-mother Venus, he fled to save whatever remnant he could from the doomed city and guided the refugees to a new homeland.

In the *Aeneid* the hero's obedience to the demands of the gods and his acceptance of the responsibilities of command earn him the epithet *pius*. For the Romans the attribute *pietas* was only marginally connected with our concept of "piety"; rather, a person was *pius* because he did not shirk shouldering the duties imposed by his obligations to the gods, his country, his family, his comrades. In the *Wake*, immediately after Shem has revealed the alchemical formula (in appropriately medieval Latin) for the concoction of ink (*FW* 185.14–26), there is a paraphrase (more or less) for those whose vocabulary does not encompass the original-language terms for that fluid's organic components. The passage begins with an allusion to the hero of Vergil's epic: "Then, pious Eneas, conformant to the *fulminant* firman which enjoins on the *tremylose terrain*" (*FW* 185.27–28; my emphases). The initial vocative clearly imitates the formulaic *pius Aeneas* (*A* 1.220, and seventeen other *loci*). His loyalty and fidelity are shown by the fact that he repeatedly conforms to mandates that the lightning-god transmits to a trembling earthling. The Latin roots (italicized for emphasis in the citation) should now fall into place, especially if one remembers that Jupiter is known to fulminate. What is not so easily perceived is the fact that Joyce's passage is lifted directly from Vergil's *Georgics*. There the poet reminds farmers that *ipse pater . . . / fulmina molitur dextra, quo maxima motu / terra tremit* (the Father of the gods himself . . . wields lightning bolts in his right hand, and at their crash the most solid earth trembles) (*G* 1.328–30).

There is another passage that conceals a similar adaptation of some Vergilian lines. Lightning is also at the center of the second echo—a fact that will not surprise those who remember Joyce's lifelong fear of thunderbolts and the role of these natural phenomena in Vico's scheme of the evolution of civilization.[24] From the well-known account of the "abnihilisation of the etym" (*FW* 353.22), I isolate (and emphasize) the following three pseudonuclear terms: *explodo*tonates . . . fragor*omboassity* . . . mole*tons*" (*FW* 353.23–26). Even though Joyce injects "empyreal Rome and mordern Atems" (*FW* 353.29) into the pile, there is no hint whatsoever of a genuinely classical source for the three emphasized morphemes. But there is such a model. In the second half of the *Aeneid*, Prince Turnus, leader of the native Italians, breaks into the Trojan fortress and smashes a defensive tower: *procubuit subito et caelum* tonat *omne* fragore. / *semineces ad terram, immani* mole *secuta* (suddenly [the tower] collapsed and the entire sky rings with the crash—halfdead men [fall] to the ground, and a huge mass of stone followed) (*A* 9.541–42).

The previous two examples of Vergilian allusion strongly suggest that Joyce had a Latin text of the poet's works on his desk when he was putting together *Finnegans Wake*.[25] The parallels are too close to have been quoted from memory. Neither passage is likely to have been anthologized, nor is there anything in them even to suggest that they might have been assigned as schoolboy memory exercises. The only common denominator between the lines on the storm from the *Georgics* and the lines on the collapse of a tower from the *Aeneid* is their mutual emphasis on violence, divine and human. Why Joyce should have sought—and reproduced so closely—a specialized Vergilian vocabulary for his scenes of turbulence cannot be explained in terms that normally apply to literary criticism. But their use is a fact, and this aspect of eccentricity in Joycean allusion is confirmed by another item of evidence from the *Aeneid*.

In the same paragraph of Shaun's defense of his civic virtues that was cited earlier, he calls himself "magmonimoss" (*FW* 545.32). This adjective is an adaptation of another of the epithets of *magnanimus* (greatminded) *Aeneas* (*A* 1.260 and elsewhere). The Wakean spelling also suggests "magma," the molten rock at the earth's core. This geological angle is corroborated by the immediately adjacent text, in which Shaun itemizes additional benefits: "as staidy lavgiver I revolucanized by my eructions" (*FW* 545.32–33). If the technical details of volcanology are a bit shaky here, the problem is not entirely Joyce's. In the *Aeneid,* it is Cacus, the monstrous son of god Vulcan, who spews forth dark fires: *illius atros / ore vomens ignis* (*A* 8.198–99). Joyce chose an even more revolting verb to assign to Shaun in the *Wake* passage just cited. It too has its origins in the Latin epic. Vergil uses participial forms of *eructo* twice: once to describe an actual eruption of Mt. Aetna (*eructans* [*A* 3.577; compare *A* 6.297]) and another time to make as graphic as possible the Cyclops' regurgitation of his cannibal feast (*eructans* [*A* 3.632]).

None of these echoes of the Vergilian vocabulary for the visual and sonic effects of thunder, lightning, and volcanic eruption was designed to be detected. But Joyce did have a reason for this type of hypercryptic intertextuality. That motive responds to my own personal experience in the same sort of classically oriented schools and their venerable academic rationale. In the international fraternity of Jesuit schools, the language curriculum certainly did not isolate grosser and more violent passages from the *Aeneid* for special emphasis in the classroom. Such official attention would merely have underscored the marginal comments already added to the texts by vicarious student combatants. These notes were our way of injecting a little blood and guts into a string of comments about ablative absolutes or deponent verbs. This was necessary, since the standard textbooks did not include an elaborate apparatus of cross-references that highlighted half-dead warriors being crushed by a falling tower, the earth quivering at repeated lightning strikes, or hairy monsters vomiting ill-digested human flesh. Rather, Latin teachers tended to stress Roman *pietas* or Aeneas' magnanimity not merely as matters of grammatical or metrical finesse but also as contributions to their students' moral formation. Thus, I can imagine empathically the gleam in Joyce's eye as he returned to schoolboy Latin texts years later during the composition of his works. This time part of his purpose was to redeploy those passages that portray the darker side of Roman heroism: the submission of individual choice to divine tyranny, the conviction that it is a fit and pleasing thing to kill for one's country, the recognition of ineluctable power of merciless destiny. As mentioned in my general introduction, this seriocomic inversion of the contextual emphasis in hallowed texts is a variation on the literary ploy that I call the "Parser's Revenge." Thus, when Joyce returned to the *Georgics* and the *Aeneid,* he selected elements that suited his purposes as a mature writer who was, as his own work progressed, reading Vergil not to prepare for an inspiring exam essay, but to exploit an ancient source for covert quotation both contorted and comic.

In this spirit, Joyce gathered several other major clusters of epic excerpts from the *Aeneid.* The first of these allusions pivots around the hero's tragic encounter with Dido, queen of Carthage. Just after the Trojan refugees have been driven ashore in North Africa by a divine storm, Aeneas meets Venus, his disguised goddess-mother. He relates his latest suffering and says that his steadfast loyalty to his mission "has spread his fame beyond the heavens" (*fama super aethera notus*) (*A* 1.379). This phrase was appropriated by Joyce to ensure worldwide coverage of HCE's great fall: "Big went the bang: then wildewide was quiet: a report: silence: last Fama put it under ether" (*FW* 98.1–3).

Venus then hides her son in a cloud and leads him safely into the presence of Queen Dido. Aeneas' entrance line, as he breaks cover, is memorable: *coram, quem quaeritis, adsum / Troius Aeneas* (Right here—the one you seek, Aeneas of Troy—here I am) (*A* 1.595–96). The key verb (*adsum*) was remembered by Joyce and transferred to HCE to announce his resurrection, at his own wake. Joyce has *his* hero not only report his revival but also request another touch of the whiskey that inspired it: "Add some" (*FW* 74.7).[26]

In his same speech of revelation to Dido, Aeneas praises the queen of Carthage for her kindness and begs the gods to reward her, "if there is a divine mind which regards right action" (*mens sibi conscia recti*) (*A* 1.604). Again, it is HCE who echoes Aeneas' words, this time in one of his groveling apologies near the end of the *Wake*—and in the original Latin: "*mens conscia recti*" (*FW* 581.17–18).

The entire pageant of Aeneas' welcome to Carthage (including the Queen's offer of succor) serves as an epic preface to Dido's death in book 4 of the *Aeneid*. The Trojan refugee's preparations to sail away to Italy, after a year at Dido's side, were immediately detected by the queen: *quis fallere possit amantem?* (who can deceive a lover?) (*A* 4.296). Joyce placed a restatement of that pathetic rhetorical question in Molly Bloom's final soliloquy: "but you cant fool a lover" (*U* 18.355). Dido's regal suicide is also parodically commemorated in the *Wake*: "she is deeply sangnificant. *Culpo de Dido!* Ars we says in the classies. *Kunstful*, we others said" (*FW* 357.15–16). The suicide wound (*colpo* in Italian) of the Carthaginian queen was struck to erase her shame (*culpa* in Latin, *colpa* in Italian) for loving and losing Trojan Aeneas. That blow was certainly bloody itself (*sanguis* in Latin). In historical terms, Dido's death was also fated to stir up significant bloodshed between her descendants and the Romans in the Punic Wars. Moreover, the queen regarded her failure to conceive a son for Aeneas as another fatal flaw. In the *Aeneid*, Dido's primary epithet is *infelix*. And, in fact she *was* literally *infelix* ("infertile," as well as "ill-starred," "unhappy").[27] Joyce, a dedicated student of Latin vocabulary, Vergilian nuance, and menstruation, did not pass up this opportunity to parade his own cleverness in the classics by means of an obscene Germano-English pun.[28]

Dido is not the only female character from Vergil's epic to leave a carefully disguised mark on the *Wake*. In one of the earliest Notebooks, Joyce made the following entry: "singe-set △'s hair afire / ⌐nefarious" (VI.B.1.122). Just before he welcomes the Trojan refugees to Italy (and offers the hand of his daughter to Aeneas), King Latinus observes a terrifying omen: *astat Lavinia virgo, / visa (nefas) longis comprendere crinibus ignem* (the maiden Princess Lavinia stands near, her long hair is seen to catch fire, a dreadful thing to watch) (*A* 7.72–73). The key word, "nefarious," which is crossed out in the Notebook, reappears without change as "nefarious" (*FW* 389.24) in a passage packed with Latin and Vergilian allusions. The specific reference to an awe-inspiring portent in the *Aeneid* would not be suspected without the archival hint. The Vergilian omen is, moreover, picked up and used by Joyce in I.6 in the "Second Question," which elicits a description of ALP (△): "she's flirty, with her auburnt streams" (*FW* 139.23–24).

There are a number of other brief echoes to the works of Vergil in the *Wake*, and one in *Ulysses*. The most ingenious of these is "rearin antis" (*FW* 450.7). McHugh cites a source in *rari nantes* (a few, scattered men swimming) (*A* 1.118). These survivors are the crew members who escaped the sinking of several of Aeneas' ships off the coast of Carthage. One page later in the *Wake*, Shaun pledges fidelity to his "sow-white spouse" (*FW* 451.20–21). This may have something to do with Snow White, but I suspect the primary referent is Vergil's *sus . . . alba* (white sow) (*A* 8.43–45), whose prophetic presence, with her thirty offspring, marks the site of the Latin city of Alba Longa (compare *U* 14.191, 233).

The phrase "as bare as a Roman altar" (*FW* 409.19) sounds like a Latin proverb. But, as far as I can determine, it is neither ancient nor sectarian. Thus, I propose a radical distortion of Vergilian intent and syntax as its source. In his verse-handbook on all phases of agriculture and herding, the *Georgics*, Vergil did not mince words in describing the rigors of climate that a farmer must face: *nudus ara, sere nudus* (you must plow your fields stripped naked, stripped naked you must sow your seeds) (*G* 1.299). Here the verb form *ara* is a singular imperative, "plow." To an unprepared student, that word could easily be confused with the Latin noun *ara* (altar). I suspect that Joyce heard one of his urban comrades at Belvedere take a stab at Vergil's *nudus ara*, and come up with "bare altar." No dedicated parser would ever forget that magnificent howler. Hence its memorialization in the *Wake*.

Just after the ceremonial parade of prelates, clerics, and saints and their symbols in "Cyclops," there is an extended simile in which the coordinated swimming of sea-nymphs is compared to the union of spokes and hub in a wheel. The nymphs then "laughed, sporting in a circle of their foam: and the bark clave the waves" (*U* 12.1772–82). When Aeneas sails up the Tiber to visit the site of Rome, the Magna Mater of the gods begs Jupiter to change the Trojan fleet into sea-nymphs. Her prayer is answered, and *qualis Neriea Doto / et Galatea secant spumantem pectore pontum* (and like Doto, Nereus' daughter, and Galatea, they cut the foaming sea with their breasts) (*A* 9.102–3). Why these Vergilian nymph-ships appear in Barney Kiernan's pub is totally unclear. Nor can I come up with any explanation as to how an animal omen, Trojan refugee swimmers, or a naked altar contribute to the plot or aura of the works in which Joyce placed them.

Equally perplexing is "an oldest ablished firma of winebakers, Lagrima and Gemiti" (*FW* 290.26–27). Literally, the pair's pseudo-Latin names mean "Tear and Groans," which is not very upbeat for a dealer in spirits. Nevertheless, the firm definitely borrowed its venerable title from Vergil: *gemitum lacrimasque* (*A* 10.465) or *gemitu lacrimisque* (*A* 10.505) or *gemitus lacrimabilis* (*A* 3.39).

The sites of HCE's construction projects range from "eldorado" to "ultimate thole" (*FW* 134.1–2). In the *Georgics* Vergil praises the power of the Emperor Augustus by citing *ultima Thule* (*G* 1.30) as one of the ends of the earth that will acknowledge his rule. The first line of the catalogue of HCE's achievements as a master builder contains the twin epithets "myther rector and maximost bridgemaker" (*FW* 126.10–11). Spanning both of these phrases is a divine invocation from the *Aeneid*: *et divum tu maxime rector / Iuppiter* (and you, Jupiter, supreme ruler of the gods) (*A* 8.572–73). Joyce's coinage "myther" acknowledges that a mythological slant is part of the play here. Viewed in the same perspective as "*mithyphallic*" (*FW* 481.4), the word also suggests that HCE's epic effort is *ithyphallic* (*ithys* means "upright," "straight" in Greek), the Latin for which is *rectus*, as in the root of "rector" and "erection." A Roman "bridgemaker" was a *pontifex*, an archaic term that was transferred, metaphorically, to the members of the city's most august priestly college. The leader of this politically and religiously influential group was the *pontifex maximus* (see pages 95–99).

In the midst of the inquiries about the entire domestic history of HCE and ALP, a series of replies, some in semi-authentic Latin, are given. One of them is the following: "*Nascitur ordo seculi numfit*" (*FW* 512.36). The model sentence for this statement is a famous line (transferred to the back of a U.S. one-dollar bill) from Vergil's so-called "messianic" *Eclogue*: *magnus ab integro saeclorum nascitur ordo* (a grand order of ages, from an unblemished origin, is being born) (*E* 4.5). Joyce has, as usual, made some adjustments to both the medium and the message. If the final element of his phrase is separated into "*num*" and "*fit*," then the Wakean reply itself becomes a cynical rhetorical question: "The [new] order of the ages—it never takes place, does it?"

Discounting the reliability of the speaker, that last rhetorical ploy strikes an appropriately pseudo-Vichian note on which to wind up the presentation of textual evidence from the works of Rome's great national poet. The material examined revealed a remarkable—and remarkably diverse—series of apt Vergilian allusions in the works of Joyce. The analyses of the selection and the discussions of how this material was used by Joyce offer a new angle of insight on his sources and methods of composition. The "highland lassies" and the elaborate "Iopas-Cacus-Cyclops-Citizen" identity-glide are examples of distinctly Wakean techniques at work in sections of *Ulysses* that do not appear, comparatively speaking, narratively or stylistically exotic. The transfer to Glasnevin Cemetery in "Hades" of funereal components of the Vergilian Underworld, on the other hand, might be expected in any author of Joyce's educational background; but the disguised references are hellishly clever.

The series of previously unsuspected (and quite literal) citations from the *Aeneid, Eclogues,* and *Georgics* are impressive evidence that the classical material in *Finnegans Wake* is far more than an attempt to impart a patina of pseudoantiquity on a slab of futuristic fiction. The parallels between the fall of Troy and HCE's catastrophes and Joyce's grotesque adaptation of material from Queen Dido's Carthaginian court are masterstrokes. The choice and placement of such excerpts show that a search for significance and design in Joyce's deployment of classical material may be frustrating, but rarely in vain. The Vergilian components, in Latin or English, show a controlling allusive hand behind every stage in the composition.

7

Horace

When he was fourteen or fifteen years old, James Joyce translated an ode of Horace, *O fons Bandusiae* (*O* 3.13), into decent English verse—a commendable but not uncharacteristic exercise for a young student who had already won several prizes for his examination scores, especially in Latin.[1] More than forty years later in the autumn of 1938, the sight of swans swimming in the lake at Montreux prompted Joyce to recite appropriately valedictory verses from Horace:[2]

> tempestivius in domum
> Pauli purpureis ales oloribus,
> comissabere Maximi. (*O* 4.1.9–11)

> ([Venus], with your flying escort of gleaming swans, you will far more appropriately direct your procession to the house of Paulus Maximus.)

In a paragraph of *Portrait* that bristles with Latin phrases, Joyce's fictional alter ego, Stephen Dedalus, muses that "The pages of his timeworn Horace never felt cold to the touch even when his own fingers were cold: they were human pages." Then, in a moment of pretentious modesty, Stephen adds that "even for so poor a Latinist as he, the dusky verses were . . . fragrant" (*P* 179–80). Near the end of this novel, Stephen Dedalus caps a catalog of his father's occupations with "at present a praiser of his own past" (*P* 241). The phrase echoes Horace's *laudator temporis acti / se puero*, the final stage in his "ages of man" in the *Ars Poetica* (lines 173–74). Stanislaus Joyce remembers his brother's "Horace in the thick, brown second-hand volume with abundant notes."[3]

The purpose of this chapter is to identify and discuss quotations from or references to the poems of Horace in Joyce's works. By far the most numerous and cryptic of these allusions are embedded in *Finnegans Wake*, but faint Horatian echoes can be heard on isolated occasions in the earlier publications.

The devotion to Horace attributed to Stephen Dedalus above is the sole explicit reference to the Roman poet from *Portrait*, perhaps because in his first novel Joyce consciously avoided the tendency of Victorian and Edwardian authors to display their education by interlarding their prose with frequent snippets from *literae humaniores*. In his 1903 review of several forgettable novels by A. E. W. Mason, Joyce devotes one of his four paragraphs of dismissal to noting that "a minor phenomenon is the appearance of Horace in each story" (*CW* 131).

In the text of *Ulysses* there is scarcely more: a tag phrase from *Satire* 2.2.26, *rara avis* (rare bird), is included, totally out of context, in a passage so replete with clichés that even Leopold Bloom recognizes its "blandiloquence" (*U* 16.231). In "Oxen of the Sun" after Mrs. Mina Purfoy has, at long last, delivered her baby, the medicals and the amateurs who have been keeping watch propose a toast: "Per deam Partulam et Pertundam nunc est bibendum!" (*U* 14.1439). The archaic goddesses of childbirth (Partula) and the loss of virginity (Pertunda) are saluted in the same words as Horace's invitation to the Romans to celebrate the defeat of Cleopatra, *Nunc est bibendum* (now it is the time to drink) (*O* 1.37.1).

Arranged along the left-hand margins of almost two pages at the conclusion of the "Night Lessons" section in *Finnegans Wake* is a list of names of classical writers and leaders, biblical and mythological figures (*FW* 306–8). The entry *"Horace"* is faced by the essay topic "Advantages of the Penny Post" (*FW* 307.1–2). The link is Horace's two books of *Epistles*, verse letters addressed to various "correspondents."

Early in the *Wake*, the twin sons of HCE are introduced by the words "'Twas two pisononse Timcoves" (*FW* 39.14). The allusive basis of this phrase is a covert reference to the two sons of Piso (in Latin, the *Pisones*), to whom Horace addressed the longest and most famous of his *Epistles*, letter three of book two, more popularly known as the *Ars Poetica*.[4] In the midst of his literary advice on the techniques of narrative poetry, Horace suggests to the brothers that they occasionally snatch their readers *in medias res* (into the middle of things) (*Ars Poet.* 148). Joyce plays clever games with this maxim: "in midias reeds" (*FW* 158.7) and "in medios loquos" (*FW* 398.8).[5]

There are two other adaptations of Horace's literary advice to the Piso brothers in the *Wake*. The poet warns against the introduction into a narrative of an incongruous spate of "fine writing," usually in the form of a gushing description of a natural scene: a *purpureus . . . pannus* (*Ars Poet.* 15–16). Appropriately enough, Joyce uses an exact translation of the two Latin words "patchpurple" (*FW* 111.2; compare "paupers patch" [*FW* 316.23]) in a passage in which the primary topic is the hen's unearthing from the middenheap a copy of an incriminating letter. With direct reference to the search for this crucial document, it is reported earlier in the work that "there was in nillohs dieybos [*in nullis diebus* (on none of the days)] as yet no lumpend papeer in the waste" (*FW* 19.31–32). Joyce immediately comments on this state of affairs with a Horatian axiom: "mightmountain Penn still groaned for the micies to let flee" (*FW* 19.32–33). The familiar original of this phrase is *parturient montes, nascetur ridiculus mus* (the mountains will be in labor, a ridiculous mouse will be born) (*Ars Poet.* 139). The obstetrical note is reinforced by the next sentence, "all was of ancientry" (*FW* 19.33), which combines a near pun on *enceinte* (French for "pregnant") and an irreverent reminder of the source, an old-time literary effort. There is an echo of the mountains' labor when a woman "with that rarefied air of a Montmalency. . . . her ancient of rights regaining. . . . greater grown then in the trifle of her days, a mouse, a mere tittle, trots off with the whole panoromacron picture" (*FW* 318.2–9).

Another Horatian allusion is almost immediately adjacent to the last citation. "The Annexandreian captive conquest" (*FW* 318.11) may represent Joyce's reworking of Horace's *Graecia capta ferum victorem cepit* (Greece, although defeated, conquered her crude victor) (*Epist.*2.1.156). At the same time, the phrase is also meant to suggest a couplet from Dryden's "Alexander's Feast." In this ode, Alexander the Great enjoyed elaborate Hellenistic postcombat debauchery, mitigated by some civilizing music; then "At length, with Love and Wine at once oppress'd, / The vanquish'd Victor sunk upon her breast."

Giordano Bruno's motto, *In tristitia hilaris hilaritate tristis* (in sadness be joyful, in joy be sad), is usually cited as the source for the *Wake*'s frequent use of phrases like "Tristopher and Hilary" (*FW* 21.12). Equally plausible as a classical model is a verse from Horace: *oderunt hilarem tristes tristemque iocosi* (sad men hate the happy person, and lighthearted people hate the sad man) (*Epist.* 1.18.89).

Several other passages from Horace's *Satires* and *Epistles* that have left their mark on the *Wake* require mere citation.[6] Each is brief and self-evident; none seems to contribute anything more than an antique glow to the content in which it occurs:

> *FW* 116.16 "*Est modest in verbos*" and *FW* 523.19–20 "The Mod needs a rebus"[7]: *est modus in rebus* (there is a middle ground in things) (*Sat.* 1.1.106).
>
> *FW* 128.14–15 "quid rides": *quid rides?* (What are you laughing at?) (*Sat.* 1.1.69).
>
> *FW* 444.21–22 "as cheap as the niggerd's dirt (for sale!)": *sale nigro* (caustic wit; literally coarse, dark salt) (*Epist.* 2.2.60).
>
> *FW* 455.13 "crass, hairy": *crasso . . . aera* (thick weather, dense air) (*Epist.* 2.1.244); as well as *cras, heri* (tomorrow, yesterday).

FW 466.21–22 "so sedulous to singe always if prumpted, the mirthprovoker!": *sedulitas autem stulte quem diligit, urget* (overblown zeal pushes beyond limit the poet who foolishly cherishes his subject) (*Epist.* 2.1.260).

FW 553.2 "countrymouse": *rusticus . . . mus* (*Sat.* 2.6.80).

Throughout the *Wake*, there are numerous allusions to Horace's shorter, polymetric Odes. For clarity of presentation these echoes are divided into two categories: in section I are those examples that Joyce has translated, at least partially, into something like English (that is, "Traduced into jinglish janglage" [*FW* 275.F6]); in section II are those phrases that Joyce has left more or less in the original, though with occasional adjustment of the "latten tintacks" (*FW* 183.20).

I.

FW 54.5–6 "Favour with your tongues! *Intendite!*": *favete linguis* (keep holy silence) (*O* 3.1.2).

FW 244.11–12 "let's stay chez where the log foyer's burning!": *dissolve frigus ligna super foco / large reponens* (melt the cold by generously piling more wood on the grate) (*O* 1.9.5–6).

FW 336.21 "*qua* golden meddlist": *auream quisquis mediocritatem / diligit* (whoever chooses the golden mean) (*O* 2.10.5–6).

FW 408.19 "I can seeze tomirror in tosdays": *carpe diem, quam minimum credula postero* (seize today, place as little as possible on deposit for tomorrow) (*O* 1.11.8).

II.

FW 37.22 "Arvanda always aquiassent": *aquosus Eurus arva radat* (the water-filled east wind scours the fields) (*Epode* 16.54).

FW 38.11 "no persicks and armelians for thee": *Persicos odi, puer, apparatus* (I dispise Persian geegaws, boy) (*O* 1.38.1).

FW 49.13 "Cornix inauspiciously": *aquae nisi fallit augur / annosa cornix* (unless the predictor of rain, the old crow, is wrong) (*O* 3.17.12–13; compare Pliny *NH* 10.14.30).

FW 57.22 "exegious monument, aerily perennious"[8]: *exegi monumentum aere perennius* (I have erected a monument more lasting than bronze) (*O* 3.30.1).

FW 58.18 "Eheu, for gassies!": *eheu fugaces . . . / labuntur anni* (alas, the fleeing years are slipping by) (*O* 2.14.1–2).[9]

FW 280.32 "fount Bandusian shall play liquick music": *O fons Bandusiae. . . . unde loquaces / lymphae desiliunt tuae* (O spring of

Bandusia. . . . from which your babbling streams leap down) (*O* 3.13.1, 15–16).

FW 328.8 "zones asunder"; compare "melt my belt" (*FW* 450.3–4: *solutis / . . . zonis* (with sashes unfastened) (*O* 1.30.5–6).

FW 551.13 "*pelves ad hombres sumus*": *pulvis et umbra sumus* (we are dust and shadow) (*O* 4.7.16).

A number of other Horatian references require more comment. During Yawn's inquest by the Four Old Men in the *Wake,* the defendant is accused of betraying his comrades and evading the truth: "the massstab whereby Ephialtes has exceeded is the measure, *simplex mendaciis,* by which our Outis cuts his thruth" (*FW* 493.23–24, Joyce's emphasis). Ephialtes is the Greek who showed the Persian invaders how to circumvent the defended pass at Thermopylae; he is the archetypical traitor of ancient history. "Outis" ("Nobody" in Greek) is the name Odysseus/Ulysses used to outwit the Cyclops in the one-eyed monster's cave. It is, of course, the most famous onomastic stratagem in all world literature. The italicized words *simplex mendaciis* are Joyce's compact conflation of two well known Horatian phrases. *Simplex munditiis* (simple in her elegant accessories) (*O* 1.5.5) is the poet's description of the studied artlessness of the flirt Pyrrha; also note "her prytty pyrrhique" (*FW* 20.32). *Splendide mendax* (the illustrious liar) (*O* 3.11.35) is Horace's oxymoronic praise for the only one of the fifty daughters of Danaus who broke a pledge to her father and refused to slay her husband on their wedding night. She was "magnificently mendacious." As adapted by Joyce, the words indict Yawn/Shaun for his utter mendacity.

In the "Lestrygonians" chapter of *Ulysses,* one of Barney Kiernan's barmaids is named "Lydia Douce" (*U* 11.562); she is advised to apply borax "with the glycerine" (*U* 11.122) to her sunburnt hands. In rapid succession in "Oxen of the Sun," there are references to Phyllis (*U* 14.1133), Lalage (*U* 14.1143), and Glycera and Chloe (*U* 14.1156). These names are typical of those adopted by Roman lyric and elegiac poets lightly to disguise the objects of their love; Horatian examples include *Lydia* (*O* 1.8.1, 1.13.1, and so on), *Glycera* (*O* 1.19.5, 1.30.3), *Chloe* (*O* 1.23.1), *Phyllis* (*O* 2.4.14). Lalage is, of course, memorably presented by Horace: *dulce ridentem Lalagen amabo / dulce loquentem* (I will love Lalage, who laughs sweetly and chats sweetly) (*O* 1.22.23–24). The last verse of that quotation also appears in "prettily prattle a lude" (*FW* 337.9). Horace originally claimed that Lalage's love would protect him even in the African kingdom of Juba, that *leonum arida nutrix* (dry wet nurse of lions) (*O* 1.22.15–16). That location contributes to a lowercase appearance of Joyce's sweet-voiced woman, who made "melodi of malodi, she, the lalage of lyonesses"

(*FW* 229.10–11). Several of these typically Horatian *amicae* (girlfriends) also appear in a Wakean reprise, each with alluring accessories: "Charmeuses chloes, glycering juwells, lydialight fans and puffumed cynarettes" (*FW* 236.1–2). The final thinly camouflaged name in that series is a reference to Cinara, whose exotic "reign" Horace evokes as a faded memory of the distant past (*O* 4.1.1–4, 4.13.22–23).

In a poem that catalogues the unpredictable process by which Venus yokes, then uncouples mortal lovers, Horace advised his friend Albius to stop mourning his loss of *immitis Glycerae* (*O* 1.33.2). The phrase is an elegant example of both *figura etymologica* (wordplay involving similar roots from different languages) and paradox: *immitis* is the Latin adjective for "harsh," "bitter"; *glycera* is a Greek adjective meaning "sweet." Thus, the young woman who has spurned Albius is neatly characterized as "bitter sweetie." I detect a faint Joycean echo of both the name-play and the jilted lover's sobs in "immitiate my chry!" (*FW* 535.3).

Horace devoted a portion of one of his odes to a series of descriptions of the power of gold: bribes open a besieged city's gates and cause naval commanders to defect in combat. The most telling mythological instance of gold at work, however, is Jupiter's penetration of the brazen tower in which the virgin Danae was immured.[10] The king of the heavens and his accomplice Venus laughed in scorn at the walls, guards, and locks. Then Jupiter turned himself into a shower of gold to gain his amorous objective: *aurum per medios ire satellites / et perrumpere amat saxa potentius / ictu fulmineo* (gold loves to go right through the middles of sentries and to smash stone ramparts with greater force than a lightning bolt) (*O* 3.16.9–11). Joyce seems to be alluding to this startling weapon and tactic in "ejaculations of aurenos" (*FW* 253.27), a potent example of "that ligtning lovemaker's thender appeal" (*FW* 335.11).

In another Horatian phrase, with overtly sexual connotation, Joyce turns things topsy-turvy. The poet advised a friend who had been badly smitten by a very young girl: *tolle cupidinem / immitis uvae* (cast aside the desire for an unripened grape) (*O* 2.5.9–10). Among some gifts that ALP presents to her favorites are "the grapes that ripe before reason" (*FW* 212.16–17) for her sons. In the Latin poem the unready-for-picking grape is a metaphor for the immature girl. In the *Wake,* the plural "grapes" have changed gender. They have metaphorically become the "ripe," just-post-puberty testicles of Shem and Shaun—and the twins' immature "reason" will certainly not deter them from attempting to "devide the vinedress" (*FW* 212.17).

After Joyce composed *Watching the Needleboats at San Saba* (*CP* 48) in September 1913, he mailed a copy of that eight-line poem to his brother Stanislaus (*Letters* II.323–24). The enclosed letter included a line from Horace, *quid si prisca redit Venus?* (What if that old vistor Venus returns?) (*O* 3.9.17). The verse may have some specific reference to the poem's occasion (a Puccini aria at the end of a boat race), or more likely it is a general comment about the possible return of an urge to write poetry.

Very early in the *Wake* Joyce sets the scene for Finn's fall. It occurs in the midst of the urban clamor of dear, dirty Dublin, where "the noobibusses [are] sleighding along . . . and the fumes and the hopes and the strupithump of his ville's indigenous romekeepers . . . thurum and thurum" (*FW* 6.1–5). There is a lot going on here, but the basic details of the description have been lifted directly from a poem by Horace. The poet urged his patron, Maecenas, to flee the magnificence—and hubbub—of the capital to spend some time in the country. As translated into English, Maecenas is specifically advised to leave "his palace that towers into the clouds" and "the smoke and wealth and uproar of Rome." In Latin, the ablative "clouds" are *nubibus* (*O* 3.29.10), which Joyce transliterates into "noobibusses." The second Joycean-Horatian verse that I have cited above has barely been altered in its transformation into Wakese: *fumum et opes strepitumque Romae* (*O* 3.29.12) becomes "the fumes and the hopes and the strupithump" (*FW* 6.3–4). Joyce, however, expands Horace's mention of Rome by indicating that the city's inconveniences are caused by "his ville's indigenous romekeepers" (*FW* 6.4). McHugh correctly points to an allusion to Dublin's "Sick and Indigent Roomkeepers' Society"; but he misses a concurrent echo of Vergil's *Georgics* 1.498: *di patrii indigetes et Romule Vestaque mater* (native gods of our ancestors and Romulus and mother Vesta).

Another passage in the *Wake* contains an equally covert and convoluted reference to Horace. In the programmatic second poem of his first book of odes, the Roman poet addresses Augustus. In almost priestly terms, Horace asks the emperor to deflect the wrath of the gods from a Rome that has seen too much recent violence and civil unrest: "Father Jupiter has flung bolts from his 'fire-red right hand' (*rubente dextra*) at the sacred temples and he has terrified the City" (*O* 1.2.2–4). In a *Wake* passage that imitates the terminology of a medieval scriptorium, Joyce depicts "those ars all bellical . . . wrasted redhandedly from our hallowed rubric prayer for a truce with booty, *O'Remus pro Romulo*, and rudely from the fane's pinnacle tossed down" (*FW* 122.7–10). The presence of civil wars and Jupiter's red hand are obvious here; in fact, both "rubric" and "rudely" reinforce the first reference to that bloody color. Joyce's "prayer for a truce" is almost a paraphrase of Horace's appeal for Jupiter to stop tossing down lightning bolts at the "fane's [temple's] pinnacle." Finally, both the site and the language of Horace's appeal are evoked in Joyce's royal perversion of the traditional Roman Catholic formula for a call to prayer "*O'Remus pro Romulo*" (*FW* 122.9). The attentive reader cannot miss either *oremus* (let us pray) or Romulus and Remus.

Joyce parades his recall of Roman roads, especially the best-known of them, the Appian Way: "Opian Way" (*FW* 448.18), and "Affrian Way" (*FW* 497.12).[11] This famous road may stretch beneath "their three drummers down Keysars Lane. (Trite!)" (*FW* 61.27). Horace wrote *et Appiam mannis terit* (and he wears down the Appian Way with his ponies) (*Epode* 4.14). To justify this speculative bit of verbal archaeology, it is necessary to point out to the reader that Horace here is referring, with immense scorn, to a former slave, now a staff officer who wears down the roads with his high-speed chariot. The Appian Way may not be Caesar's private lane, but the triumvir's policies helped to open doors for this type of military parvenu. The word "drummer" is an English racing term for an off-pace horse; three horses drew the standard Roman chariot. Perhaps, then, it is the erratic drive of the vehicle that "wears away" (*terit*) the ancient paving. At any rate, not only is the topic of a uppity freedman a late-Republican cliché ("trite"), but also every Latin student knows that the perfect passive participle of the key verb here, *tero, terere*, is *tritum*.

While he was collecting material for *Ulysses*, Joyce noted that there were at least two ancient proposals to restore the devastated city of Troy: "Alex to revive Troy / Augustus. Horace mocks" (*UNBM* 106: 32–33). Although the verb "mocks" is entirely too strong, Horace did oppose any putative plans to repopulate Priam's ruined capital. In the midst of an ode in praise of Augustus, the goddess Juno is introduced. She delivers a fifty-line invective against Troy and vows that if its ramparts rise again, the city's captive wives will again weep for their husbands and sons (*O* 3.3.18–68). Neither Horace's version of this divine wrath nor Augustus' proposal has left any trace in *Ulysses*.

During the seven-month period he was working in a bank in Rome in 1906–1907, Joyce wrote to Stanislaus that he had been reading the recently published *Grandezza e decadenza de Roma* by Guglielmo Ferrero (*Letters* II.165). The five volumes of this work put special emphasis on psychological and sociological aspects of the past, seen as a way of understanding contemporary issues. Such an approach would naturally have appealed to Joyce, especially since the academic specialists were attacking Ferrero's work for its irreverent, liberal slant. Joyce explicitly comments on one section of this work: "Ferrero devotes a chapter in history of Rome to the Odes of Horace: so, perhaps, poets should be let live" (*Letters* II.190).

Joyce's concluding clause is ambiguous. Is he deferentially commenting on the value of poetry, even its function as a witness to history? Or, in the context of the impending publication of *Chamber Music*, is there an offhand note of autobiographical pride here? At any rate, in his section on the sociopolitical importance of Horace, Ferrero wrote, "No one realized more profoundly than Horace the immense moral vacuum upon which the vast edifice of the empire rested."[12] Commentators point out that such statements reflect Ferrero's (and

Horace's) opposition to war. True enough, but that opposition did not exclude necessary praise for individual courage in war. That attitude is summarized in Horace's most frequently memorialized verse (the one Wilfred Owen called the "old lie"): *dulce et decorum est pro patria mori* (it is sweet and fitting to die for one's country) (*O* 3.2.13). Joyce exercised the vengeance of a parser on this line. At the end of a 1927 letter to Harriet Shaw Weaver, sent the day before he was to begin a vacation on the beach in Holland, Joyce wrote, "*Dulce et decorum est prope mare sedere*—boglatin for it is a sweet and seemly thing to sit down by the sea" (*Letters* I.254).

As a comparative aside to this discussion of Horace in the works of Joyce, I include the following two references involving the Roman poet and a pair of poet-critics who were contemporaries of Joyce. In one of the Buffalo notebooks the following entry appears: "Odes / IV.6 / I.21 / influential / WBY" (VI.B.37.27). I detect a reference to two Horatian odes, *O* 1.21 and 4.6. These poems are an obvious pair; in each, choruses of Roman boys and girls are invited to sing the praises of Apollo and Diana. I have not, however, been able to find anything similar to either ode, formally or thematically, in the collected works of William Butler Yeats (WBY). Perhaps Joyce's archival note is meant to be a generalized implication that Yeats tends to repeat himself, lyrically.

In a letter written to Joyce in 1917 by Ezra Pound, the American writer deprecates one of his own "beastly long" poems and concludes by stating "As for mellifluous archaism, I am reduced to mistranslating Horace." The Roman poet's ode 4.10 (*O crudelis adhuc*) follows in twelve occasionally rhymed lines.[13] There is no surviving record of Joyce's reaction to Pound's avocation or to the quality of his translation.

A final brief exhibit of Horace's influence on Joyce's writing comes from a passage that, in fact, did not work its way into the text of *Finnegans Wake*. In an October 23, 1928, letter to Harriet Shaw Weaver, Joyce complains that the treatment for his eye problems has brought his literary production to a near halt. He also says that he is sending "the only thing I have written in the last four months, a short description of madness and blindness descending on Swift." That fragment of his recent composition is accompanied by a commentary that is "just fortyseven times as long as the text." Joyce's four lines of text, composed in typical Wakesque vocabulary, naturally includes many color and sight terms, such as the phrase "Atrahora, Melancolores." The author glosses the second capitalized word as "(Greek, Latin, Spanish ending) black, colour, sorrow." The first, "Atrahora," is explained as: "(Latin) black hour. c.f. [*sic*] Horace—*post equitem sedet atra cura*, black care sits behind the horseman" (*Letters* I.273–74). The Latin verse cited by Joyce is from one of

Horace's famous "Roman Odes"; in it the poet uses the personification to remind the over-ambitious citizen that he cannot escape "Black Worry" (*O* 3.1.40). It is not likely that the annotator needed to consult Horace's text for the personified figure or for the glossing verse, since Joyce surely read and perhaps memorized this ode during his last year at Belvedere. As stated above, however, the brief passage on Swift in which the reference to "Atrahora" was embedded apparently became one of the "discards" in the composition of the *Wake*. It does not appear in any of the drafts for or in the final text of that work.

In conclusion, the textual evidence, especially from *Finnegans Wake*, supports the claim that James Joyce (like Stephen Dedalus) never allowed the pages of his Horace text to grow cold to the allusive touch of his fingers. Translated into English or left in Latin, well more than a score of echoes—and there are certainly others that have not been detected—from the Roman poet contribute to Joyce's inexhaustible *lusus verborum*. A major component in that ultimate "game of words" is its mass of neologisms. Here Joyce was following the advice of Horace himself. In the *Ars Poetica* (lines 47–48) the Roman poet urged the two young Pisones to search for the *callida iunctura* (clever verbal connections) that would transform diction by placing familiar words in arresting and extraordinary collocations. *Finnegans Wake* can be read as a multiglottal, polydimensional response to that challenge. Should anyone doubt this fact or belittle the Horatian component of the endeavor, "*Sacer esto*" (Let him be damned) (*Sat.* 2.3.181 and *FW* 168.13).

8

Ovid

Publius Ovidius Naso, known in the English-speaking world as Ovid, lived during the Augustan Age at roughly the same time as Vergil and Horace. Unlike them, however, he never won the emperor's patronage. Rather, he wound up in bitter exile, a sentence imposed for some unspecified affront to imperial dignity, perhaps involving an imputation that his verse encouraged sexual laxity. His most enduring work is the *Metamorphoses,* a poem of epic dimensions that records every sort of transformation in shape, from the formation of the universe out of chaotic prime matter to Julius Caesar's posthumous ascension into the sky as a star. Between these two cosmic events, Ovid presents hundreds of instances of change: a reflection-obsessed youth into flower (Narcissus), a reluctantly pursued maiden into a tree (Daphne), and once pale mulberries stained permanently crimson by lovers' blood (Pyramis and Thisbe).

There are many references to Ovid and his works in Joyce's fiction. A few (like the epigraph to *Portrait*) are acknowledged; others were embedded in various levels of the text, especially during the complex formation of *Finnegans Wake.* The exercise in literary archaeology in this chapter will, therefore, involve several approaches. My first objective is to establish the presence of Ovid in the texts, then to trace the Joycean exploitation of several important strata of allusion to his mythological tales and characters (Phaethon, Deucalion and Pyrrha, Midas, Narcissus). Sometimes I will explore areas of the text that appear to contain Ovidian material, which, on close scrutiny, comes from other (usually classical) sources. Even these false leads are valuable indicators of Joyce's methods of composition and the range of his allusive resources.

The primary Ovidian reference in Joyce is "Dedalus," the surname of the hero of *A Portrait of the Artist as a Young Man* and *Ulysses.* Daedalus (*daidalos* is "skilled," "cunning" in Greek) is the famous inventor-craftsman of the *Metamorphoses.* His arcane skills are commemorated on the title page of *Portrait:*

Et ignotas animum dimittit in artes. (Ovid, M 8.188)

Exactly how Stephen Dedalus/James Joyce "applies his mind and soul to un-known arts" has been the topic of a library of critical studies from every possible perspective. From an expansively philological point of view, the most impressive discussion is by Fritz Senn.[1] His fact-filled, text-centered pages provide a complete analysis of Ovid's epigram-verse and its application to Joyce's enterprise.

In the final sentence of *Portrait* there are two invocations. Both can also be read as allusions to Ovid's Daedalus: "Old father, old artificer, stand me now and forever in good stead" (*P* 253; compare "Fabulous artificer" [*U* 9.952]). In the previous entry in his valedictory diary, Stephen has determined to leave home, "to forge in the smithy of my soul the uncreated conscience of my race" (*P* 253). That emphatic metaphor, followed by "artificer," is certainly meant to pick up on the term that Ovid himself applied to Daedalus in the genetic episode in his *Metamorphoses*; there the Roman poet called mythology's master craftsman an *opifex* (*M* 8.201). Joyce's use of the term "artificer" (from the Latin *artifex*) might be seen as nothing more than a more readily comprehended synonym for Ovid's *opifex*. Not necessarily so. The following is the beginning of a long entry in a standard Latin dictionary:

> artifex, -ficis, *m.* [ars-facio]. I. *Subst.* A.1 One that is master in the liberal arts (while *opifex* is a master in the *artes sordidae* [trades that get one dirty]).[2]

From 1879 until very recently Lewis and Short's massive dictionary was *the* source of lexicographical information about Latin in the English-speaking world. Without doubt Joyce knew and used this work. I suggest that the dictionary's contrast in the definitions of *artifex* and *opifex* contributed to Joyce's precise discrimination in his choice of terms to describe his vocation. The "smithy's forge" on which *he* will create new literary wings for the human race will be founded in the arts, both liberal and arcane.

A final reference to Ovid in the *Portrait* involves Stephen's recollection of the priest at his Jesuit school in Dublin, Belvedere College:

> who had taught him to construe the Metamorphoses of Ovid in a courtly English, made whimsical by the mention of porkers and potsherds and chines of bacon. (*P* 179)

The allusion is to the tale of Baucis and Philemon in the *Metamorphoses*. They are a pious couple who welcome the disguised gods Jupiter and Mercury into their sparse cottage and offer them supper. The meal includes small slices from their "mottled rack of smoked pork" (*sordida terga suis*) served on a table steadied by a "scrap of pottery" (*testa*) under an uneven leg (*M* 8.648, 662). The pair is even prepared to sacrifice their pet goose, if either they or the guest-gods can capture him. For their generosity Philemon and Baucis become custodians of the nearby temple, into which their house is changed, for the rest of their life. At the moment of death they are simultaneously transformed into leafy, side-by-side trees, which can still be seen today, next to the shrine.[3]

Joyce's Father Rector obviously tried to make Ovid's charming tale of generosity and conjugal fidelity more relevant to a class of adolescents by finding suitably homey, vernacular equivalents for the Latin neuter plurals and ablatives of means in the Latin text. Evidence for Joyce's memory of—or intertextual zeal for—this sort of pedagogy can be seen in the *Wake*: "yet am I *amorist*, I love him. I love his old *portugal's nose*" (*FW* 463.18–19; my emphases). The italics signal the covert presence of Ovidius *Naso's Amores* (The Loves) and recall Stephen's claim that he learned "the laws of Latin verse from a ragged book written by a *Portuguese* priest" (*P* 179).

Just as characters from the *Metamorphoses* appear at significant junctures in *Portrait*, so too do other Ovidian episodes make minor contributions to the Ulyssean transformation of the realistic novel. The "Oxen of the Sun" chapter takes place in a maternity hospital, where Stephen Dedalus joins a group of "medicals" who are momentarily at ease, but not off duty. Among the obstetrical curiosities that they discuss is "the theory of copulation between women and the males of brutes." Documentary support for this theory is the tale "of the Minotaur which the genius of the elegant Latin poet has handed down to us in the pages of his Metamorphoses" (*U* 14.992–96). The plot of this squalid affair is complex. Neptune sent a magnificent bull to Crete and instructed King Minos to sacrifice it in his honor.[4] When the King could not bear to slaughter such a splendid animal, Neptune retaliated by infecting Queen Pasiphae with an insatiable lust for the bull. She begged Daedalus, the Athenian-born master technician of the palace, to construct a hollow wooden cow, in which she positioned herself so she could be mounted by the bull. Thus she consummated her passion, "by deception and the beastly disguise" (*dolis et imagine vaccae* [Ovid *M* 9.739]). Joyce compactly recreates this episode in "Circe." Stephen begins with a mocking quote from Psalm 75.10: "Et exaltabuntur cornua iusti" (the horns of the just man shall be raised high). He then supplies a classical example in the vernacular: "Queens lay with prize bulls. Remember Pasiphae for whose lust my grandoldgrossfather made the first confessionbox" (*U* 15.3864–67).

Ovid, who is rarely squeamish in his presentation of gory details, is quite straightforward, even moralistic, in his presentation of the result of Pasiphae's passion for the bull:

The disgrace of the conception grew and the hideous adultery of the mother was revealed by the grotesque appearance of the monster, part human, part bull. King Minos decides to banish this stain on his marriage chamber. (*M* 8.155–57)

The royal shame must be concealed. Thus a labyrinth, in which the Minotaur could be hidden, was designed and constructed by Daedalus. Its many twists and turns were, in fact, so deceptive that even its architect was scarcely able to find the exit. This series of outrageous royal commissions impelled Daedalus to devise a way to escape from Crete. He made two sets of wax-and-feather wings so that he and his son, Icarus, could flee to Sicily. Joyce alludes to the tragic outcome of this plan in *Ulysses*. First, he captures the moment of Icarus' exuberant disregard of the paternal flight plan: "Icarus. *Pater, ait.* Seabedabbled, fallen, weltering" (*U*. 9.953–54). Then, in a burlesque reprise of this motif in "Circe," Stephen speaks: "No, I flew. . . . World without end. (*he cries*) *Pater*! Free!" (*U* 15.3935–36).

The revised Gifford-Seidman annotations gloss both passages with mention of Ovid's *Metamorphoses*, but for *U* 9.953 there is an additional reference to Christ's final words on the cross (Luke 23:46). The Latin text of this evangelical support-passage reads *ait: Pater* (he says "Father"), the key words in both of the Ulyssean citations. The annotators, then, presumably include the New Testament verse because they are aware that *pater ait* is not, in fact, found in Ovid's *Metamorphoses*. In that poem the emphasis is on the father's grief, not the son's panic. What Gifford-Seidman miss is Ovid's other (actually composed first) version of the Daedalus-Icarus tale. The story is embedded in the *Ars Amatoria* (The Art of Loving) as a paradigmatic digression on how hard it is to control winged creatures: just as King Minos could not keep Daedalus in Crete, so too is flitting Cupid unable to be pinned down by reluctant lovers.[5] Icarus' realization of the consequences of his carelessness is specifically expressed in this version of the tale:

> decidit atque cadens "pater o pater auferor" inquit;
> clauserunt virides ora loquentis aquae. (*AA* 2.91–92)

> (He plummeted and as he fell he said, "Father, O Father, I'm going down";
> the sea-green water closed over his mouth as he spoke.)

Those Ovidian lines are the Latin source of Icarus' cry to his father (*pater*) and the encompassing sea of the *Ulysses* passages.

In *Portrait* there is a passage that may well contain a parody of Icarus' farewell. After the retreat and his "conversion," Stephen contemplates his destiny:

> Now, at the name of the fabulous artificer, he seemed to hear the noise of dim waves and to see a winged form flying above the waves and slowly climbing the air. . . . An ecstasy of flight made radiant his eyes and wild his breath and tremulous and wild and radiant his windswept limbs.

The odd word-order and the rush of bathetic adjectives in those sentences suggest (at least in narrative recall) a bit of self-conscious mockery. At any rate, Stephen's comrades refuse to allow him the luxury of prophetic reverie. One of them calls out "—O, cripes, I'm drownded!" (*P* 168–69).[6]

In the "Night Lessons" chapter of *Finnegans Wake* the students have diligently annotated the margins of their book. Names of important figures in world history and culture are placed next to potential and appropriately sophomoric essay topics. "*Ovid*" appears at *FW* 306.L2. The name of the Roman poet is keyed to the thematic phrase "The Voice of Nature in the Forest" (*FW* 306.20–21). This topic commemorates the scores of his human characters who are transformed into flora and fauna in the *Metamorphoses*. Joyce's scholarly apparatus includes a footnote: "Where Lily is a Lady found the nettle rash" (*FW* 306.F4). If Ovid transformed one of his women into either a lily (*lilium*) or a nettle (*urtica*), I have not been able to locate the tale in his works—or those of other classical poets.[7] Joyce is, however, well aware of Ovid's primary plot-device: "metamorphoseous" (*FW* 190.31), "martimorphysed" (*FW* 434.31), "metandmorefussed" (*FW* 513.31). The first two words appear in homosexual contexts, perhaps because Joyce imagined expository same-gender sexuality as an erotic turnaround. This point of view certainly underlies his use of one of Ovid's most florid examples of love gone awry: "You have homosexual catheis of empathy between *narcissism* of the expert and steatopygic invertedness" (*FW* 522.30–32; my emphasis). The repeated presences of Narcissus (and his conversion into a psychoanalytic paradigm) in the *Wake* will be discussed later in this chapter in my review of Joyce's adaptations of specific tales from the *Metamorphoses*.

Before that parade of legendary characters, there are several other direct allusions to Ovid or his works in the *Wake*. The poet's cognomen, Naso, appears in an impossible plural form "nasoes" (*FW* 403.7) on the same page as allusions to two other Augustan Age authors, Vergil and Sallust. The *Wake* also includes deeply camouflaged references to the titles of two less well known works by Ovid, the *Fasti* and *Ars Amatoria*.[8] The first allusion is found in the catalogue of Shaun's noble deeds for human betterment. It is couched in the form of a rhetorical question: "did not I *festfix* with mortarboard my *unniversiries* wholly rational and gottalike" (*FW* 551.28–29; my emphases). At the core of this boast I see and hear the presence of Ovid's *Fasti.* That work is an elaborate, day-by-day explanation of the origin, purpose, and ritual for the many *feasts* of the Roman religious calendar. All of these *annual* celebrations were *fixed* to a certain date, and Ovid supplies a legendary theological and anthropological context for their exotic details.

Another allusion to Ovid's *Fasti* occurs in the midst of HCE's account of what happened in the park, the scene of his alleged crime. His explanation includes a Latin phrase that appears to be entirely in keeping with the plot of this episode: "*regifugium persecutorum*" (*FW* 51.31). If the first word is read as a distortion of *refugium,* then it is possible to see and hear it as a parody of one of the invocations in the Litany of the Blessed Virgin. The canonical *refugium peccatorum* (refuge of sinners) is apologetically twisted into "refuge of the persecuted." On the other hand, there is a genuine Latin word *regifugium.* It means the "flight of the king," and refers to an ancient Roman feast celebrated annually on February 24 (*Fasti* 2.685–856). An Ovidian tale supplies an origin and reason for this feast. Its annual celebration commemorates one of the legendary events that were adduced to provide a hallowed setting for the establishment of a republic at Rome. The banishment of the last Etruscan king, the arrogant Tarquin, is usually explained as a reaction to his son's rape of the Roman matron Lucretia (see page 57).

The primary ancient source for the *religious* ramifications of this tale (with its attendant nationalistic, political, and sexual aspects) is Ovid's *Fasti.* There is, however, specific archival evidence in one of the early *Wake* Notebooks that points to a secondary document: "regifugium / fugalia / 24/2" (VI.B.8.137). These two technical terms from Roman religion require some explanation. In commentaries on the *Fasti* and in discussions of the Roman religious calendar, the feast celebrating the expulsion of the Etruscan kings is called the *regifugium;* but that Latin word is not used by Ovid himself. The second entry in Joyce's notebook, *fugalia,* appears nowhere at all in Latin literature and does not merit inclusion in the largest lexicons. Its meaning, "celebration of the flight," is clear from its roots *fuga* (flight) and *-alia,* an adjectival suffix frequently found in words dealing with feasts, as in Luperc*alia,* Saturn*alia.* I suspect that Joyce picked up both of these technical terms from an old standby, the *Encyclopaedia Britannica* (11th edition). Its article on "Feasts and Festivals" includes this information: "on the 24th [of February] the *Regifugium* or *Fugalia*" (*EB* 10.221). Thus, even though its route into the *Wake's* text is indirect (and, without the Notebook entry, untraceable), an obscure feast in Ovid's *Fasti* can be added to the long list of classical trivia in Joyce.[9]

A final allusion to an Ovidian work is also deeply buried in the *Wake.* The "Eleventh Question" in book I.6 includes a paragraph that sums up the preoccupations of a seamstress-ingénue, who worries about clothes only "when she is not sitting on all the free benches avidously reading about 'it' but ovidently on the look out for 'him'" (FW 166.10–12). In addition to the play on the poet's name ("*ovid*ently"), the topic of this sentence reads as if were directly translated from the Ars Amatoria (The Art of Love). This work, briefly mentioned above in my review of the function of Daedalus and Icarus in Ulysses, is a 2,333-line verse-handbook. It provides explicit suggestions on how to fall in love by really trying. After a long section of advice for males, its third book is devoted to practical hints and mythological precedents that are especially appropriate for Roman women on the make. Although its language and setting are ancient, Ovid's handbook is intended to be part of the amatory arsenal in Joyce's modern, self-improvement reading material for a "demitilery young female" (FW 166.4–5).

The passages discussed above show that Ovid's poetry was a component in the literary raw material that Joyce forged into new shapes on the smithy of his genius. The most significant example is the role of Daedalus and Icarus in Portrait. The rest of this chapter is dedicated to demonstrating how various Ovidian figures played a role in Joyce's fiction. There are four larger sections (Phaethon, Deucalion and Pyrrha, Midas, Narcissus) and a final portion, in which miscellaneous cameo characters are introduced.

PHAETHON

In all of the works of James Joyce there is nothing that can match the thematic reverberations of Tim Finnegan's fall. The fatal descents of Adam, Lucifer, Icarus, Humpty Dumpty reverberate to that event, but without the bricklayer's miraculous recovery. In the lists of literary and historical analogues the name of another mythic plunger receives almost no notice. Yet the celestial exploits of Phaethon are cosmic in scope and epic in emphasis. The Metamorphoses of Ovid devotes over three hundred lines (M 2.1–339) to Phaethon's attempt to prove himself a true son of the Olympian lord of the Sun. Like Icarus, Phaethon's filial enthusiasm and naiveté propel him from the sky into the sea.[10]

The plot of the episode is simple. As a token of the Sun's paternity, Phaethon asks to be allowed to guide the god's chariot for one dawn-to-dusk circuit of the heavens. The father's reluctant promise seals the son's doom, since it is clear that Phaethon cannot manage the solar team of immortal horses. There is a typical Ovidian touch of pathos here: the Sun-king pleads with Phaethon by appealing to his desperate worry about the trip's outcome as absolute proof of his paternal responsibility. When the chariot careens out of control, Jupiter aborts the mission with a lightning-bolt. Joyce summarizes the fatal ride across "joepeter's gaseytotum" (*FW* 426.21) and through the constellations and Milky Way:

> sidereal . . . by the sirious pointstand of Charley's Wain (what betune the spheres sledding along the lacteal and the mansions of the blest turning on old times) as erewhle . . . like a flask of lightning over he careered (O the sons of the fathers!). (*FW* 426.24–30)

The starry (*sidereus* in Latin) points of reference, death by lightning, the disastrous test of fatherhood are all found in the Latin source. The odd phrase "along the lacteal and the mansions of the blest turning on old times" strongly suggests another Ovidian model from an earlier section of the *Metamorphoses*. In his description of the realms of the Immortals, there is a heavenly road, called the "Milky Way" (*via sublimis . . . lactea nomen habet*).[11] On this celestial boulevard the palaces of the Thunderer and other top-rank gods are located (*M* 1.168–72).

One of the many consequences of Phaethon's off-course ride is the sun's extraordinary scorching of many regions of the earth. The orbital deviations do not spare Ireland, "whose verdhure's yellowed therever Phaiton parks his car" (*FW* 110.9–10). Until its "pramaxle smashed" (*FW* 214.24), the radiant chariot's "navel, spokes and felloes hum like hymn" (*FW* 447.4). This last citation is usually glossed as an echo of *Hamlet:*

> Break all the *spokes* and *fellies* from her [Fortune's] wheel,
> And bowl the round *nave* down the hill of heaven,
> As low as to the fiends! (*Hamlet* 2.2.495–97; my emphases)

There can be little doubt of a Shakespearean presence here; but behind it lies an Ovidian source.[12] In Arthur Goldling's translation (1567) of Ovid's *Metamorphoses* there are two passages from the Phaethon episode that most probably served as the model for the bard's use of wheelwright vocabulary here:

> The axeltree was a massie golde, the Buck was massie golde,
> The utmost *fellies* of the wheeles, and where the tree was rolde.
> The *spokes* were all of sylver bright. (2.144–46)

> The Extree plucked from the *Naves:* and in another place
> The shevered *spokes.* (2.401–2; my emphases)

Another passage from a famous Tudor-Jacobean translation is also relevant here. In the Authorized Version (King James, 1611) of the Old Testament, the following verse describes the wheels on the ten bronze stands that supported ten bronze basins in Solomon's temple: "Their axletrees, and their naves, and their felloes, and their spokes, were all molten" (1 Kings 7:33). The decidedly odd spelling of "felloes" (not "fellies") in both the *Wake* and the Bible would seem to argue that Joyce modeled his phrase on the Authorized Version. This deduction, however, cannot be accepted without qualification.

The following is the complex evidence to support that genetic *caveat*. Just before the "navel, spokes and felloes hum" in the *Wake*, this phrase appears: "Meliorism in massquantities" (*FW* 447.2–3). The wheels of the chariot that Phaethon rode were gold not bronze. Goldling translates Ovid's *aureus* (golden) twice in *Metamorphoses* 2.107 as "*massie* golde." This description lies behind Joyce's "meliorism" (*mel* is "honey" in Latin; *or* is "gold" in French) and his semitautological "*mass*quantities." Thus, even if Joyce borrowed his spelling "felloes" from the Bible, he was at the same time aware of Goldling's English metamorphoses of Ovid's original Latin. *Hamlet* cannot be the pivot text here, since it was written around 1601, a decade before King James' scholars published their new version of the Old Testament. Furthermore, there is no hint of a mass of gold in Shakespeare's verses. Scrupulous terminology, therefore, would label Goldling as Joyce's "source"; *Hamlet* and 1 Kings as "parallels." For "felloes" a footnote suggesting "contamination" of texts would be in order. All of which goes to show that Joyce read widely and that it is not inconceivable that he deliberately covered—or confused—his tracks here.

Phaethon's fall is clearly the reason for the incredulous youth's incidental appearance in Joyce's *Finnegans Wake*. What was the justification for his major role in Ovid's *Metamorphoses*? What changes did he cause? I have already briefly touched on the "yellowing" of Ireland's green fields by too close a contact with his fiery chariot. This and other ecological consequences of the apprentice driver's lack of control are given in detail in Ovid's account. The face of the globe was changed and the course of many rivers was affected. Calculations on the number of river names worked into the "Anna Livia Plurabelle" section of text vary from eight hundred to over a thousand. No one seems to have mentioned the following classical parallel to this cascade—and one for which there is oblique evidence of Joyce's familiarity. Ovid's list of fountains, lakes, streams, and rivers that were dried up during Phaethon's ride (*M* 2.239–59) is perhaps the most extensive catalogue in Roman literature. The thirty-two sites specifically named in the Latin poem are limited to the world known, in legend or fact, by Romans of the Augustan Age. Nevertheless, Phaethon's trajectory touched several Joycean rivers, including the Ganges: "gangres" (*FW* 196.18); Ister/Danube: "histereve" (*FW* 214.1); the Tagus: "tagus" (*FW* 208.2);

and naturally the Tiber: "tibertine" (*FW* 211.5). I do not suggest that Ovid is necessarily Joyce's direct source here; rather, that the Roman poet's Phaethon desiccated a specific spate of rivers and that this "change" in the shape of the environment might have influenced Joyce's flood of Wakean waterways.

A second, and minor, list of rivers also occurs in Ovid's *Amores* 3.6.23–24. In this work a lover, who has been separated from his beloved by a storm-swollen river, curses the stream. To emphasize his point, he cites as *amici curiae* the names of about ten rivers that mythology records as helpers of those in love. Only one of these Ovidian rivers shows up in the *Wake*, but it does so in full flood: "—Xanthos! Xanthos! Xanthos!" (*FW* 235.9). The River Xanthus flows on the plain near Troy; it is also called the Scamander, which not only appears in the *Wake* but is also hallowed there: "Holy Scamander" (*FW* 214.30).

There is another, only slightly less conspicuous Joycean catalogue for which there is an Ovidian analogue. In *Ulysses,* twenty-nine appropriately sylvan guests and the two attendants are present at the wedding of "Miss Fir Conifer of Pine Valley," solemnized at "Saint Fiacre in Horto" (*U* 12.1266–95). This technique is repeated, less obviously, in a passage in the *Wake* that is introduced by "what's nicest and boskiest of timber trees in the nebohood" (*FW* 235.15–16). A roster of a dozen or so trees follows; "incense palm edcedras" and "Larix ['larch' in Latin] U' Thule" (*FW* 235.17, 19) are typical examples. A second Wakean catalogue of trees appears in long parentheses between "The Mookse and The Gripes" and "Burrus and Caseous" (*FW* 159.34–160.14).[13] Here the arboreal puns are fairly feeble and the trees seem to be introduced only to supply an audience for the two debates: "*Vux Populus,* as we say in hickory-hockery and I wish we had some more glasses of *arbor vitae*" (*FW* 160.13–14). The compound "hickory-hockery" is a fairly demonstrative rein-forcement of the italicized Latin phrases. One does not, in fact, have to be an advanced student of *hic-haec-hoc* to see "*Populus*" doing double duty as the Latin noun for a poplar (*populus,* feminine) and the people (*populus,* masculine). It is not much of a linguistic leap from *arbor vitae* (tree of life) to *aqua vitae* (water of life), alias whiskey for the Irish or aquavit for Scandinavians.

In an analogue-episode in Ovid's *Metamorphoses,* twenty-four enchanted trees come to the open plain to listen and offer shade to Orpheus, after the master-singer has lost his wife to the Underworld (*M* 10.86–105). Ovid's trees are limited to those from the Mediterranean world; Joyce's come from the forests of several continents. This difference is far more likely the result of the latter's incessant search for pun material than it is a factor of cross-cultural literary dendrology.

A coda to my discussion of Phaethon's appearances in the *Wake* involves an archival clue that, as it turned out, was misleading. Stuart Gilbert's papers are now on deposit in the Harry Ransom Humanities Research Center at Austin, Texas. A small spiral notebook, probably compiled in 1928, includes some items assembled for potential use in the composition of the *Wake*. Other entries involve inquiries that Gilbert had about *Ulysses*, since he was in the process of composing his commentary on that book. Among these notes are what seem to be nearly adjacent references to Ovid's *Metamorphoses:* "Phathuse & Lampetie / comment the Oxen / . . . Met. II. 41."[14] The terminal reference to Ovid's text is to the beginning of the scene that describes the Sun-god's welcome of Phaethon to his heavenly palace. I can find no trace of this line in the *Wake* or *Ulysses*. The significance of the initial two-line entry is more complex—and illustrates the rashness in underestimating the scope and depth of Joyce's use of classical allusion.

In Ovid's *Metamorphoses*, two of the Heliads (children of the Sun) are cited as the primary mourners at Phaethon's sepulchre; they are the sisters Phaethusa and Lampetie (*M* 2.340–66). In fact both become so rooted to the vicinity of their brother's tomb that they are transformed into trees. Gilbert's notebook entry (which may well have been an answer by Joyce to one of his queries) indicates the presence of the two sisters in "Oxen [of the Sun]." And so they are, as we learn in Gilbert's book:

> Trinaria (Sicily), the triangular island was dedicated to Helios [Sun]. His seven herds of sacred oxen were guarded by his daughters, Phaethusa and Lampetie, to whom correspond, in this episode ["Oxen"], the two nurses, "white sisters in ward sleepless . . . for Horne holding wariest ward."[15]

The mythological names and bucolic duties of the sisters have been lifted right from the text of Homer's *Odyssey* (12.127–36). The sentence indicating the transfer of their duties to a maternity ward in *Ulysses* occurs in the initial section of "Oxen" (*U* 14.76–79).

Gilbert attaches a footnote to the explanatory passage cited above from his book. In it he explains the presence of "white," used to describe the sisters and throughout this episode of *Ulysses*. They are the "daughters of . . . daylight itself, 'seeds of brightness' (*U* 14.243), the white house of life contrasted with the 'tenebrosity' (*U* 14.380) of the nether world."[16] As far as Ulyssean symbolism goes, Gilbert's footnote makes perfect sense. As far as classical sources go, it does not cover all possibilities. When the two sisters of the Sun appear in Ovid's *Metamorphoses* at Phaethon's tomb, Lampetie ("Shining" in Greek) is modified by the Latin adjective *candida* (*M* 2.349). This word can be translated as "shining white" or "gleaming white." In no other ancient source is the etymology of Lampetie's significant name so emphatically underscored. Ovid's display of *figura etymologica* here is typical of his rhetorical technique, which was frequently imitated by Joyce. I suggest, then, that, in addition to selecting two Odyssean women to serve as guardians of his maternity ward in "Oxen," Joyce was also aware of Ovid's radiantly "white" description of one of the sisters—and that this Latin adjective from the *Metamorphoses* made its minor contribution to the thematic "colour" of the episode in *Ulysses.*

DEUCALION AND PYRRHA

References to global floods are found in both the *Metamorphoses* and the *Wake.* Ovid's version of the deluge tale starts with an inspection tour of earth by Jupiter, who is disguised as a mortal. A notorious scoffer, Lycaon, commits the ultimate sacrilege by attempting to serve a meal of human flesh to the supreme god and by threatening to murder him. For these crimes he is transformed into a wolf (*lykos* in Greek). Despite the provocation, Jupiter is reluctant to cast his thunderbolts and burn the entire earth—the smoke pollution on Olympus would be unbearable. So he sends a flood. Only Deucalion and his wife Pyrrha are selected to survive on a small raft. After the waters recede, the aged pair see no way to restore the human race. The oracle of Themis instructs them "to throw the bones of their great mother behind them." The pious couple are horrified, but obey when they realize that the "great mother" is the earth and that her "bones" are stones. This bizarre tale of repopulation by lapidation is based on the phonetic similarity in Greek between the words for "stone" (*laas*) and "people" (*laos*). Ovid cannot resist making a moral point out of this genealogy: thanks to our origin, we humans are a flinty race (*M* 1.414–15).

Several chips from this Ovidian narrative can be detected in the *Wake.* First there is a handful of references to the names of Deucalion and Pyrrha, in situations in which they seem to be ancient manifestations of HCE and ALP. The pair is invoked, "para Saom Plaom," for a vaguely Roman "convocacaon" of authorities "in the names of Deucalion and Pyrrha" (*FW* 179.9–12). Both are present in "Like *Jukoleon,* the seagoer, when he bore down in his *perry* boat" (*FW* 367.20–21; my emphasis). Pyrrha's connection with fire (*pyr* in Greek) is evident in "Sparks' pirryphlickathims" (*FW* 199.35). On the same page the same word-root in "pyrrakness" (*FW* 199.21) is, anatomically, a pair of knees and, topographically, the Pyrenees. In a Wakean list of the four seasons, the heat of Summer is emphasized in "*Pyrrha Pyrrhine*" (*FW* 548.28). The husband and Wellington blend their names in "the famous eld duke alien" (*FW* 197.3).

An interlude in the "Mime" involves almost all the components of the

Deucalion and Pyrrha tale, more or less integrated into the fantasy plot. It is night. The children must return to their snug roost, "when the wildworewolf's abroad" (*FW* 244.10–11). The rain falls in the darkness, and as the world is "circumveiloped by obscuritads. Man and belves frieren" (*FW* 244.15–16) (*belve* are "wild beasts" in Italian). It is cold. The children shudder "Drr, *deff coal lay on* and, pzz, call us *pyrress!*" (*FW* 244.17–18).[17] Pyrrha is the "salutable spousefounderess" (*FW* 244.18–19), inasmuch as she deserves to be both "hailed" and "saved" (*saluto, salutare* in Latin). Another Latin root embedded in the heart of the adjective also commemorates her rescue from the "briny" (*sal*) waters and her sharp "insight" (*sal*) into the meaning of the oracle's odd instruction. "Rockdops" (*FW* 244.23) summarizes the couple's bizarre obedience to Themis to ensure the perpetuation of the race. In case the mime's audience has not caught the classical allusion here, Joyce gives them a cross-cultural prod from Genesis: "Ark!? Noh?!" (*FW* 244.26). (For another interpretative slant on this passage, see pages 204–5.)

The repopulation theme is also part of HCE's defense of his own character later in the *Wake*. The alleged offense that permeates this section of the work is sexual. Here the defendant is asserting the primacy of his natural, heterosexual drives, so unlike the shamefully exposed conduct of Oscar Wilde. The (im)proper name "Deucollion" is repeated three times in very close proximity (*FW* 538.29, 30, 33) as part of the testimony. "Deu," when pronounced, sounds the standard Latin prefix (*du-*) or the basic Romance word (*deux, due*) for "two"; "collion" is archaic English for "testicle." To make a long exposition short, the suspect in question here is defending himself on a charge involving his two stones.[18] He states they are "pigstenes" (*FW* 538.32), which "testify to my unclothed virtue by the longstone erectheion of our allfrist manhere" (*FW* 539.2–4). No explication beyond some rudimentary etymology should be necessary here. *Testis* is both "testicle" and "witness" in Latin. Joyce's awareness of this connection is confirmed by "BLOOM (*placing his right hand on his testicles, swears*)" (*U* 15.1483–84). "Virtue" is derived from *vir*, the Latin word for "man," "warrior," "husband." The "erectheion" is both an Athenian temple on the Acropolis in honor of the city's earthborn king, Erechtheus, and an English-Latin play on "erection"; "manhere" completes HCE's oath with a German appeal to "mein Heer," as in Doubting Thomas' acknowledgment of "*my Lord* and my God" (John 20:28).

MIDAS

Focus now shifts from the flood tale and its consequences to another Ovidian story, which, in its Wakean metamorphosis, is subjected to several moralizing twists. Midas is primarily remembered as the mythological king with the self-destructive touch of gold. Joyce makes incidental reference to this aspect of the myth, but his primary emphasis falls elsewhere. After Midas renounced and purged his power to transmute anything into gold, he served as a member of a panel to judge a music contest between Apollo's lyre and Pan's pipes. When Midas, characteristically, made the wrong choice, Apollo transformed the king's ears into the ears of an ass. Joyce signals his awareness of this aspect of the myth in "Circe," where Leopold Bloom appears *"with asses' ears"* (*U* 15.1885). Midas hid them under a turban, but his barber knew. Afraid to reveal the royal secret, but unable to keep total silence, the barber whispered his news into a hole in the ground beside a marsh. There, even today, the breeze-rustled reeds sound the news: "Midas has ass's ears." An archival entry specifically refers to the king's final humiliation: "Secret of Midas from moaning reeds" (VI.B.1.63). These are the details of Ovid's Midas tale that Joyce selected to reincorporate in the *Wake*. Most of these transformed passages have been discussed by Senn in an article in which the presence of Midas is detected in the phrase "in midias reeds" (*FW* 158.7). These three words are seen and heard as an allusion to the well-known narrative technique found in epic poetry, *in medias res.*[19] Critics use that Latin phrase to point out that Homer or Vergil often begin their tales "in the middle of things."

The most conspicuous example of the Midas motif in *Finnegans Wake* begins with an invocation of the Trinity's Third Person in a breezy parody of the traditional Christian benediction: "spiriduous sanction!" (*FW* 482.2). In those two words it is just possible to hear a Latin *spiritus* (wind, breath) and, instead of a "Holy (*sanctus*) Ghost," a sanction laid on the tone-deaf monarch. This introduction is followed by a question and answer that seek to identify HCE in his role as Earwicker and to suggest his affinity to Midas:

—Breeze softly. Aures are aureas. Hau's his naun?
—Me das has or oreils. Piercey, piercey, piercey, piercey! (*FW* 482.2–4)

Ovid's last word about Midas in the *Metamorphoses* is *aures* (ears) (*M* 11.193). Joyce takes the oral-aural aspect of the tale one step farther by modifying HCE's ears with "aureas," the Latin adjective for "golden." There is also a muted hint of a Latin "breeze" (*aura*) here. The wordplay with similar sounding roots is repeated in the answer: "or" is French for "gold" and "oreils" is very close to "oreilles" (ears). And *perce-oreille* is French for "earwig," which is the base of HCE's last name, Humphrey Chimpden *Earwicker*.

The moral tale that Ovid assigned as the cursed consequence of Midas' metamorphosis is retold, in highly compact form, in another *Wake* passage: "the big ass, to hear with his unaided ears the harp in the air, the bugle dianablowing . . . so 'tis said, the bulbul down the wind" (*FW* 475.35–476.1). That statement is made during the Four Old Men's inquisition of Yawn-Shaun in III.3. They have convened to get to the bottom of his alleged shenanigans and, it seems, they have brought their ass as a witness. The brute will listen to a "harp" (Apollo's lyre) and a "bugle" (a wind instrument that makes its music when blown, like Pan's pipes). I suspect that Joyce chose the bugle instead of a more strictly appropriate reed instrument here, because there are some reeds blowing in the breeze a bit later in the passage. "[B]ulbul" doubles (for the plural) "bul," which is the Danish word for "stem"—as in the sort of *bul*-rushes that grow beside marshes. (It is also the Persian word for "nightingale.") The "down" from the seedpods of these reeds is being broadcast, downwind, by the breezes. Finally, Joyce works some of the refrain from American folksong into his re-creation of the punishment of Ovid's asinine Midas: Dinah blows her horn.[20]

Sonic effects are also paramount in Joyce's final transformation of the Midas motif: "The siss of the whisp of the sign of the softzing at the stir of the ver grose O arundo of a long one in midias reeds" (*FW* 158.6–7). The "siss" in this passage is Issy, and it is her voice in the previous line that announces its erotic context: "—I see, she sighed. There are menner" (*FW* 158.5). Not only are there males (the Mookse and the Gripes) around, but they are aroused: "ver grose" can be divided into "verg(e)" ("rod," "wand," "stem" in French) and "rose"; the erection can also be judged as sizable ("gros(s)e" in French or German). This interpretation is strengthened by the exclamation "O arundo," which points to the girth ("around") of the rod, which is immediately followed by a comment on its length ("a long one"). Moreover, *(h)arundo, (h)arundinis* is the Latin word for "reed." Ovid used it as a plural ablative of description (*harundinibus* [*M* 11.190]) in his disclosure of King Midas' secret disfigurement. The presence of that specific literary source is confirmed by "in the midias reeds." In short, that phrase does triple duty: it specifies the original tale; it translates "arundo"; and it locates (in the middle of things) the big "menner's" wand that prompted Issy's (the "siss's") original sighs.

After this graphic Franco-Latin exposition of the twin brothers' growing excitement, the other Joycean references to Midas are somewhat of a letdown. In the same episode ("The Third Watch of Shaun") as two of the previous passages from the *Wake*, there is a discussion of Shaun's gigantism, which seems to be a trait he inherits from his father, HCE. At any rate, he appears as a "cataleptic mithyphallic" (*FW* 481.4); this is metrical-medical-mythical jargon in the service of anatomical motor response. The introduction of interdisciplinary technical terms continues with the use of the vocabulary of anthropology and physics. The twin is next asked a question about his ancestral heritage: "Was this *Totem Fulcrum est*" (*FW* 481.4). The pseudo-Latin phrase could be twisted two ways. First, into *tota pulchra est* (she is totally beautiful), which is lifted from a liturgical source, the Gradual sung on the feast of the Immaculate Conception.[21] Second, into *totum fulcrum est,* which is Joyce's own composition; it means "the whole thing is a bedpost"—and it does not have any obscene connotations, at least in ancient Latin. Nevertheless, the son seems to be concerned about his father's phallus in this passage. Shaun's father is everywhere on this page, and his presence is threatening: "Gun, the farther. . . . Bap! Bap! —Over Tad, Hellig Babbau" (*FW* 481.19–20). Next we are told that the man whom he fears "could be all your and *my das*" (*FW* 481.33; my emphasis). The italics added in the last citation should be comment enough to make the point here.

In summary, then, in the *Wake* it isn't Midas' gold that is the primary concern; rather, it is the metamorphosis into the asinine ears that hints at some secret shame. But most of all, for Joyce's characters the emphatic allusion to Ovid's doubly unfortunate king revolves around a series of threatening reeds that stand out in the middle of things.

NARCISSUS

The next Ovidian figure to be discussed is Narcissus, the self-obsessed youth who faded into a flower in the *Metamorphoses.* His primary Joycean venue is the last sections of *Ulysses,* in which he appears as a small statue. The reflections of Molly and Leopold Bloom on this minor work of domestic art are significant. The textual evidence leads gingerly into several pages of psychological speculation, a paragraph or two on comparative anatomy, and several comments on possible images of Narcissus on the rippled surface of the *Wake.* In a final section, I return to Narcissus as a psychoanalytic paradigm; but this time the guiding authority is Sigmund Freud, whose essay on "An Infantile Neurosis" ("Wolf Man") left undeniable traces on Joyce's composite Wakean portrait of Yawn/Shaun.

Narcissus is introduced into *Ulysses,* anonymously, in one of Bello's sadistic fantasies. The madame of the Nighttown brothel warns Bloom that the sanctity of his home is at risk; she threatens that the women he has propositioned "will deface the little statue you carried home in the rain for art for art' sake" (*U* 15.3185–86). Two chapters later, in "Ithaca," this artifact reappears. Its subject is now specified and the statue offers Bloom consolation:

The candour, nudity, pose, tranquility, youth, grace, sex, counsel of a statue erect in the center of the table, an image of Narcissus. (*U* 17. 1427–28)

Later in the same chapter, when Bloom gets into bed, the following "play of forces" is noted:

> the anticipation of warmth (human) tempered with coolness (linen), obviating desire and rendering desirable: the statue of Narcissus, sound without echo, desired desire. (*U* 17.2032–34)

In her soliloquy Molly remembers that Milly once broke the "hand off that little gimcrack statue with her roughness" and that it cost two shillings for "that little Italian boy to mend so that you cant see the join" (*U* 18.1014–16). All of this leads up to Molly's desire, on her own part, for "some consolation" (*U* 18.1349). She has been wondering about Bloom's cocoa-drinking companion in the kitchen. She would like to meet a poetic "university student sort," like those she has seen swimming and sunbathing "naked like a God or something." That drift of Molly's reverie is a response to the following line of fantasy:

> why arent all men . . . like that lovely little statue he bought I could look at him all day long curly head and his shoulders his finger up for you to listen theres real beauty and poetry for you I often felt I wanted to kiss him all over also his lovely young cock there so simple I wouldnt mind taking him in my mouth if nobody was looking as if it was asking you to suck it so clean and white he looks with his boyish face. (*U* 18.1348–54)

The "consolation" which both husband and wife find in contemplating a "gimcrack" Narcissus can be examined in terms of what Joyce, its verbal "sculptor," writes about the statue. For Bloom, the "counsel of a statue erect" is that of cathexis, the concentration of his psychic energy on an object that, in this case, acts as a surrogate for his own sexuality. The "play of forces" cited when he gets into bed with Molly is a series of neutralizing oppositions: "warmth-coolness," "obviating-rendering," "sound-[silence] without echo," [passive] "desired"-[active] "desire."

In Ovid's *Metamorphoses* Narcissus is destined to have a long life only if he never knows himself. The verb in the tale's original augury is *noverit* (*M* 3.348), which can also be translated as "recognizes." The precise ambiguity of the Latin thus predicts Narcissus' tragic fate. Of all his hopeful lovers, Echo is the most persistent. When she is repeatedly spurned, her body completely wastes away, and in the forest and the mountains, she can be heard but not seen. Meanwhile, Narcissus is faced with a parallel fate: he has been captivated by an insubstantial image in the still waters of a sylvan pond—of himself. He does not recognize the reflected features, but sees that they display the same tortures of frustrated love that he feels. Finally, Narcissus, too, wastes away, and what was once his beautiful body is transformed into a yellow flower surrounded by white leaves.

There is every indication that Joyce intended the considerable attention given to the statue of Narcissus in *Ulysses* to be emblematic of the sexual situation of the Blooms, husband and wife. For Leopold, the choices made by the youth in the myth reflect his own qualified abnegation of sexuality. For both men, that is, there is a decision *not* to respond: desired desire without satisfaction. In "Circe," Bello's threat to "deface the little statue" is, on one level, an obvious threat of castration as a punishment for Bloom's action in the brothel—but he has done nothing. On another level, it is a reminder that Bloom's homelife with Molly is not "art for art' sake," and that she will not fade away like Echo. The reality and necessity of choice threaten to smash his fantasy of indecision and inaction— precisely because Leopold is a man capable of sexual arousal, not a statue in a pose of perpetual "tranquility."

In "Lotus Eaters," Bloom's epistolary romance with Martha Clifford is conducted at a distance, but her latest letter contains a pertinent (if unintended) omen: "A flower. I think it's a. A yellow flower with flattened petals" (*U* 5.239). Even if Bloom's strategy is to keep Martha a pen's length away, Molly *is* present, and he will be faced with choices: "No roses without thorns" (*U* 5.277–78). At the end of the same section of *Ulysses* from which the two citations have just been taken, there is another ominous floral allusion to the consequences of Narcissus' inability to face his sexual destiny. The following is a description of Bloom as he lolls in the water of the bath:

> He foresaw his pale body reclined in it at full . . . lemonyellow. . . . and saw the dark tangled curls of his bush floating, floating hair of the stream around the limp father of thousands, a languid floating flower. (*U* 5.567–72)

It cannot be proved that Joyce intended this emphatic final paragraph at the end of his chapter to be a direct allusion to Narcissus. But Stuart Gilbert definitely thought so, and his study of *Ulysses* was prepared in close and detailed consultation with Joyce. In the episode outline that precedes Gilbert's analysis of each chapter, the "technic" listed for "Lotus-Eaters" is "Narcissism."[22]

Molly's fantasies, on the other hand, leap with synecdochical logic from a recognition of young Stephen (the poetic student) to "his lovely young cock." The pronoun "his" requires some comment, involving a switch from figures of speech to figures of argument. Joyce has constructed an erotic enthymeme here—a line of reasoning that does not offer proof or evidence to justify each intermittent step. Mediating, indeed directing Molly's fixation on the phallus is "that lovely little statue," which she does not specifically identify as Narcissus. But she repeatedly muses in immortal terms: "Id like to meet a man like that God" [Is "God" a muted exclamation or the object of the preposition?] (*U* 18.1344–45). The swimmers, in her reverie, are also "naked like a God or something" (*U* 18.1347). "His," therefore, refers, not directly to Stephen, but to that statue which she "often felt" she wanted to kiss. Of course, Molly's identification of her desires with the statue are far more explicit than Bloom's, and, at the end of her paragraph, she is most definitely focusing on Stephen. But, just as her "desired desire" finds idealized, divinized expression and dimension in a statue, so too do Molly's fantasies lead (and have led) to decision and action. Mythologically speaking, there are two ways of expressing this difference between the Blooms: one man's Narcissus is another woman's Priapus. Or, in the real world, some sexually frustrated wives may not choose to fade away, without sound, like Echo.

The last comments cited above on the little statue of Narcissus in *Ulysses* came from Molly. There is, however, another, life-size, classical statue in the work that involves Leopold Bloom as its primary spectator. The narrative context that surrounds this artistic monument also has mythological, Ovidian overtones. While having lunch in Davy Byrne's, Bloom remembers Molly's "all yielding" kisses of sexual compliance on Ben Howth. Then he jumps from this recollection to "naked goddesses" in the museum. Even in his unpunctuated fantasy, however, Bloom deprecates himself:

Suppose she [a goddess] did [speak as in the tale of] Pygmalion and Galatea what would she say first? Mortal! Put you in your proper place. (*U* 8.924–25)

Recollection of the staples of the diet of the immortals, "Nectar . . . drinking electricity," moves Bloom to wonder about the digestive process of goddesses:

Immortal lovely. And we stuffing food in one hole and out behind. . . . They have no. Never looked. I'll look today. . . . See if she. (*U* 8.928–32)

At the National Museum, Buck Mulligan has spotted Bloom hovering near the statue of "foamborn Aphrodite"; he warns Stephen:

He [Bloom] knows you. . . . he is Greeker than the Greeks. His pale Galilean eyes were up her mesial grove. Venus Kallipyge. (*U* 9.614–16)

In "Circe" there is, naturally, an even more graphic reprise of Bloom's circumspect exercise in comparative anatomy and diet:

THE NYMPH

(*loftily*) We immortals, as you saw today, have not such a place and no hair there either. We are stonecold and pure. We eat electric light. (*U* 15.3391–93)

Bloom's dedication to the back side of Aphrodite's kallipygic statue is primarily a mark of his innate scientific curiosity. It is also emblematic of the orientation of his sexual attention to Molly during the "10 years, 5 months and 18 days" (*U* 17.2282) since Rudy's death.

Before returning to Narcissus, it is necessary to take a final glance at statues, large and small, in *Ulysses*. The textual evidence comes from a portion of Molly's soliloquy. She moves from thoughts about her own breasts to breasts as symbols of beauty to a comment on the "modesty" of sculptured poses:

like those statues in the museum one of them pretending to hide it with her hand are they so beautiful of course compared with what a man looks like with his two bags full and his other thing hanging down out of him or sticking up at you like a hatrack no wonder they hide it with a cabbageleaf. (*U.* 18.540–44)

There is nothing at all like this in Ovid or in any other classical work on mythology. This sort of crude anatomical realism is a world removed from the sylvan nymphs and mortal youths and maidens (however introverted) that are the objects of Ovid's metamorphoses. Yet there is a connection between Narcissus and the Blooms. Joyce's Ulyssean statue motif begins with what appear to be sentimental recollections of a cheap, classical statue of Narcissus—the plaster equivalent of the paintings and reproductions of Homeric scenes that crowded Victorian and Edwardian galleries.[23] The polarization of the reactions of both the Blooms to this artifact, however, is part of the novel's larger design, especially as it impinges on the psychological aspects of their sexuality. In layman's terms Leopold sublimates his failures with Molly by withdrawing from, but not totally abnegating desire. For him, Narcissus embodies "candour . . . tranquility . . . grace," attributes that are essentially passive. This does not mean that Bloom wishes to deny his manhood; the statue that consoles him is "erect in the center of the table." Rather, as far as Molly is concerned, his exercise of natural heterosexual intercourse has been suspended until further notice.

Molly has compensated, physically and psychically, for her husband's prolonged abstention from vaginal intercourse. In her soliloquy she recalls both her recent encounter with Boylan ("Hugh the ignoramus that doesn't know poetry from a cabbage" [U 18.1370–71])and a previous visual assault by a pair of exhibitionists: "that disgusting Cameron highlander . . . or that other wretch with the red head" (U 18.545–46). These events have understandably warped—or at least too narrowly focused—her view of the impulses behind male sexuality. This opinion is corroborated by her observations of the strategically artistic differences between the poses of male and female nude statues in the museum. Nevertheless, the conclusions reveal that Molly too has an amateur's interest in comparative anatomy, and that her comparisons do not favor the male specimens in her experiments. The only evidence that runs counter to her denigrating descriptions of male genitalia is her comment on the "lovely young cock" of the statue of Narcissus. Molly also remembers his "curly head and his shoulders his finger up [its purpose not to tickle like Boylan], to listen theres real beauty and poetry for you" (U 18.1350–51). What these last remarks indicate is not so much Molly's sexual compulsiveness, but a romantic wish for a new fantasy life, into which the young student-poet, Stephen Dedalus, could be introduced as a fleeting image of "desired desire."

There is, then, a basic and overarching difference between the "play of forces" that husband and wife display as they react to the statue of Narcissus in *Ulysses*. The issue is not primarily aesthetic, although each uses terms of fundamental artistic judgment: "grace," "beauty," "lovely." The field of response is more one of volition, choice, psychic energy, as symbolized by the statue—and here I emphasize the object as such, because there is no indication on Molly's part that she is aware of the myth behind the figure. Bloom, who is more reconciled to the conjugal consequences of his choices, opts for static tranquility, no repercussions, without echo. Molly, volatile, hopes for and is willing to initiate action, with its turbulent but possibly "poetic" consequences.

It is impossible to leave this discussion of aesthetics and Greek statues without noting a comic foreshadowing of these *Ulyssean* elements in the midst of the collegiate debate recorded in *Portrait*. Stephen Dedalus and Lynch are discussing Aristotle's definition of tragedy; Stephen refines his terminology:

You see I use the word *arrest*. I mean that the tragic emotion is static. . . .
The feelings excited by improper art are kinetic, desire or loathing. . . .
—You say that art must not excite desire, said Lynch. I told you that one day I wrote my name in pencil on the backside of the Venus of Praxiteles in the Museum. Was that not desire? (P 205)

This is the sort of evidence that one hopes to find to support claims of a tran-scendent intertextuality of all of Joyce's fiction.[24]

Several forms (usually distorted) of Narcissus also glimmer across the sur-face of the *Wake*. But neither this youth who was enchanted by his own im-age in the water nor his frustrated lover Echo makes a deep impression on that text, although some of the verbal ornamentation is extremely clever. The pri-mary reference comes from one of the Liffey washerwomen, who works the names of a number of prominent seventeenth- or eighteenth-century Dubliners into her scrubbing song. Jonathan Swift is represented by his two Esthers (the real first names of his beloved "Stella" and "Vanessa") in "estheryear's" (*FW* 212.31). Henry Dodwell appears in the clear as "dodwell" (*FW* 212.33). Wedged between these two is Bishop Narcissus Marsh, whose names are reversed to mirror the image reflected from Ovid's forest pool, "marsh narcissus" (*FW* 212.31–32). Each of the three Dubliners mentioned above was Protestant. Two were clergymen, whereas Dodwell was a theologian who refused ordination. This stringently righteous sectarian affiliation may have something to do with making the accused "recant his vanity fair" (*FW* 212.32). That last phrase, in addition to alluding to Thackeray's *Vanity Fair*, specifies the cause for Narcis-sus' metamorphosis. Joyce, typically, has more to offer here. Though he is distinctly English, Thackeray is included in this list of Irish authors because he published *The Irish Sketch-book* in 1844 under the pseudonym of "Michael Angelo Titmarsh." The surname is the link between both Bishop Narcissus *Marsh* and "the tittles" that are drawn on the adjacent "tattle-page" (*FW* 212.34).

There may also be a lightly limned Narcissus hiding in "Be me punting his reflection we'd begin his beogrefright in muddyass ribalds. Digteter! Grundtsagar!" (*FW* 423.17–18). I suggest that Joyce intends his readers to glimpse Narcissus' blurred reflection, in "beogrefright": *bio-* (life), *graphō* (to write, to paint in Greek). Thus, the Wakean word is a life portrait as well as a written biography. The image that is drawn appears "in muddyass ribalds," which approximates *in mediis rebus* (in the middle of things in Latin), and thus may also be connected with that muddled ass Midas. There is, however, an equally relevant Ovidian phrase. It is the poet's graphic description of Nar-cissus' actions as he tries to grasp his own reflected image: he pushes his arms *in medias . . . aquas* (into the middle of the waters) (*M* 3.428–29). Joyce's "in muddyass ribalds," read with the appropriate Ovidian accent, is a phonetic transformation of the original Latin phrase into something like "into the middle of the ripples." As McHugh suggests, the "Digteter" in the passage just cited could conceal a *Dichter*, the German word for poet. One can extend this hint by linking it with the next word, "Grundtsagar" (*FW* 423.18), which sounds like *Grundsage,* German for myths about the origins of things. Ovid's *Meta-morphoses* are packed with etiologies of every sort, including the origins of the echo and the narcissus.

Another allusion to Narcissus may lie just beneath the surface of "the squidself which he had squirtescreened from the crystalline world" (*FW* 186.6–7). Here the youth's murky self-portrait darkens the clear surface of the pond on which it is reflected. A tragically persistent Echo may also be faintly heard in the preceding phrase, "each word that would not pass away" (*FW* 186.6).

Despite his expressed skepticism about the psychoanalytic enterprise, Joyce occasionally combines Roman mythology with Viennese case history. Several scholars have discussed the impact of Freud's famous "Wolf Man" on the *Wake*.[25] The most recent and thorough of these studies is Ferrer's essay, which cites incontrovertible archival evidence that Joyce read and used the 1925 English translation of this case history, "From the History of an Infantile Neurosis." Most of the verbal echoes occur in III.4 as the voyeuristic Four Old Men observe HCE and ALP making love in the bedroom above their Chapelizoid pub. This is Joyce's variation on the primal scene that lies at the bottom of the complex series of problems that incapacitated Freud's patient. In addition to this basic instance in which the "plots" coincide, there are three distinct allusions to Freud's text in other places in the *Wake*. The first two involve Narcissus; the last is mixed into a passage that I have already associated with Midas' erection.

When the inquisitor wishes to put the pressure on Yawn-Shaun, he interlards his vocabulary with jargon that suggests a contemporary source: "You have *homosexual catheis* of empathy between *narcissism* of the expert and *steatopygic* invertedness. Get yourself psychoanalised!" (*FW* 522.30–32; my emphases).

The Freudian passage on which this citation is directly modeled is the following mouthful of conclusion and *obiter dicta:*

> The *narcissistic* masculinity which attached to his genitals, being opposed to the *homosexual* attitude, was drawn in, in order to assist the ego in carrying out the task. Merely to avoid misunderstandings I will add that all *narcissistic* impulses operate from the ego, and that repressions are directed against libidinal object-*cathexes.*[26]

The similarity of the italicized words in the two passages leaves no room for doubt, in my judgment, about Joyce's model here. It is therefore fitting that he not only rejects (and turns upside down) Freud's basic point, but also scrambles his terminology. Joyce sees a "one-for-one" (*katheis* in Greek) connection between narcissism and inversion, whereas Freud asserts that narcissism is a masculine attachment, opposed to "the homosexual attitude." "Steatopygic" (*stear, steatos* is "hard fat," "firm flesh"; *pygē* is "buttocks" in Greek) refers both to a confirmed anal preference and to what Freud called "the permanent seat of narcissistic impulses in the ego." Moreover, in the analysis of the "Infantile Neurosis" from which the quotation comes, the perspective from which the subject viewed his parents' intercourse is crucial. Part of the boy's problem is his infantile reaction to the fact that their *coitus* was *a tergo* (from the rear), with the consequently exaggerated illusion of the father's penis being engulfed between the mother's buttocks. From the child's point of view it is inconsequential whether these buttocks were "kallipygic" or "steatopygic"— he certainly did not know the difference. My interest here, however, is not idle speculation about anatomy or psychoanalytic theory, but Joyce's attention to narcissism and its possible link to Ovid's version of the tale of the youth whose self-recognition was fatally askew. In this passage from the *Wake,* his clinical observation has been mediated by an inverted passage from Freud, with typical awareness (by both parties) of the sometimes ambivalent force of word-roots, German, English, and/or Latin.

A nearby sentence is also relevant to this topic: "Nircississies are as the doaters of inversion" (*FW* 526.34–35). The adage about necessity and maternal invention has been twisted to connect narcissism and homosexuality, which, in the language of the times, was often termed "inversion." The punning presence of "doaters" reinforces the theme of self-admiration; and the suffixed "-sissies" are homosexuals being taunted for their lack of manliness. The next sentence also features a potentially narcissistic phrase in "laughing classes" [looking glasses], through which Issy and her reflected image will become "poolermates in laker life" (*FW* 526.35–36). Here one can also hear "polarities" that have been joined at some later time, perhaps on the shore of a glassy Ovidian lake.

In an earlier passage, Shaun has been criticized for his concern with his appearance: "inwreathed of his near cissies . . . with looiscurrals" (*FW* 234.14–15). The curly head garlanded with narcissuses may not be a direct quotation from Ovid, but the pun on Lewis Carroll invites inspection through more than one looking glass. Thus, I propose an unexpected source inspiration for the phrase "hevnly buddhy time" (*FW* 234.13–14), which occurs immediately before the first citation. In Ovid's Latin text Narcissus considered his reflected "eyes to be a twin star" (*geminum, sua lumina, sidus* [*M* 3.420]). At least part of Narcissus' body, then, has become heavenly. It is probably prudent to regard an Ovidian parallel here as mere coincidence. But "Infantile Neurosis" supplies a direct source in a footnote to the analysis. Freud indicates that his patient had dreams "representing the coitus scene as an event taking place between *heavenly bodies.*"[27] In the next paragraph in this section of Freud's discussion, it is asserted that, just as the boy saw his father's penis disappear during the primal scene, so too did he feel sympathy, and "rejoiced at the reappearance of what he thought had been lost." The entire analytic section is summarized by this sentence: "Moreover, the narcissistic origin of sympathy (which is confirmed by the word itself) is here quite unmistakably revealed." Two entries in a *Wake* Notebook unmistakably confirm the presence of Freud here: "look for me in the sky"/"coitus between heavenly bodies" (VI.B.19.90.)[28]

Since Yawn has been identified with Narcissus in several of the previous passages, I add a final, fading reference. The first lines of III.3 describe the twin's exhausted sleep: "Lowly, longly, a wail went forth. Pure Yawn lay low. On the mead of the hillock lay" (*FW* 474.1–2). When Ovid's Narcissus expired, "he dropped his wearied head on the green grass." Just before this, he bade the world farewell, and Echo returned his cry: *dictoque vale, "vale" inquit et Echo* (When "Farewell" was heard, Echo also said "Farewell") (*M* 3.501–2). The two passages display some affinity in tone and sonic echoes, but a judgment of definite allusion here would be rash. On the other hand, one page later in the *Wake,* Yawn still lies asleep "amongst the daffydowndillies, the flowers of narcosis" (*FW* 475.9–10). Joyce's thematic etymology is right on the mark here; the root of the word "narcissus" is connected with *narkē* ("numbness," "stiffness" in Greek).

Miscellaneous Metamorphoses

The allusions to Phaethon's fall, the re-creative piety of Deucalion and Pyrrha, Midas' outstanding reeds, and Narcissus' statuette and psychosis are the clusters of Ovidian material for which it is possible to establish a significant thematic link to the Joycean contexts in which they occur. There are a number of other references to characters from the *Metamorphoses,* but most of them are the sort of general cultural artifacts that Joyce used as the bases for name puns or isolated echoes of key phrases. A few throw minor shimmers on the immediate surface of the text; most are merely additional displays of the author's congenial deployment of classical elements in *Ulysses* and the *Wake.*

Joyce demonstrates that he has thoroughly read Ovid's tale of the career of Daedalus. The master craftsman was exiled from Athens to Crete because he murdered his nephew Perdix. The youth had been apprenticed to Daedalus, and he soon displayed inventive skill that made his uncle envious. Thus, Daedalus pushed him off the Acropolis; but Minerva/Athena transformed the plunging boy into a partridge (*perdix* in Latin), a bird that never flies too high. The metamorphosed victim is a witness to the fall of Icarus—and he beats his wings and sings for joy at the tragedy (*M* 8.236–59). The core name-play here is packed into a single Joycean sentence: "I am perdrix and upon my pet ridge" (*FW* 447.28–29).[29]

The Argonaut (perhaps "argaumunt" [*FW* 8.25]) Jason is duly commemorated in "*Jason's Cruise*" (*FW* 123.26), a phrase that is placed in the midst of a roster of ancient mariners. He is also clearly part of the play in the irreverent exclamation "Hokey jasons" (*FW* 89.34). Medea, the alien woman whom he abandoned, puts in a far less distinct appearance in "medears" (*FW* 348.7). The "First Question" of I.6 ascribes the following mythic feat to the prodigious HCE: "[He] threw peblets for luck over one sodden shoulder and dragooned peoplades armed to their teeth" (*FW* 134.4–6). There is a contamination of several folklore motifs here: some superstitious grains of salt and the "backward toss" (*post tergum* [*M* 1.383]; *post vestigia* [*M* 1.399]) of the stones assigned by the oracle to the flood-drenched Deucalion and Pyrrha. The dominant element, however, is from the Jason-Medea tale. So that he could safely approach the shrine of the Golden Fleece, Medea had instructed Jason to sow "dragons' teeth" (*vipereos dentis* [*M* 7.122]) on the open field. From them, she promised, would miraculously spring a fully armed population of siblings who would slaughter one another while he made off with his booty.[30] Thus, some of the many strange birth transformations that are so typical of Ovid's work glide together to form one of the many characterizations of HCE.

Among the catalogue of tree names that identify the women who "graced the ceremony" of the wedding of "Miss Fir Conifer of Pine Valley" in *Ulysses* is "Miss Daphne Bays" (*U* 12.1268–70). Joyce's dendrological terminology is accurate: "laurel" is *daphne* in Greek, *laurus* in Latin. The tale of the tree's origin—and why its leaves are sacred to Apollo—is most memorably told in Ovid's *Metamorphoses*. After Apollo had mocked Cupid's child-sized bow and arrows, the love godling selected two barbs from his quiver. With his first arrow (the one with the gold tip) he wounded Apollo, who immediately lusted after Daphne. The maiden in turn was hit with a lead-tipped shaft, which caused her to flee from the panting, love-stricken god. When it looked as if she would be caught, Daphne prayed to her father for perpetual virginity. Her prayer was granted and she was transformed into a laurel tree.

In *Finnegans Wake*, Joyce indicates he knows Ovid's version of that tale: "laurals" and "daphdaph" appear almost next to each other (*FW* 203.30). On the same page that contains a long allusion to Deucalion and Pyrrha, Joyce records the beginning of a love prayer to a lord: "Panther monster. Send leabarrow loads amorrow" (*FW* 244.34). I hear not only a perverted *Pater Noster*, but also Cupid's shot of the lead arrow, loaded with a rejection of love, (*amor* in Latin), into Daphne's marrow. In Ovid, the maiden's prayer is addressed to *genitor carissime* (dearest father) (*M* 1.486); and Cupid's gold arrow "pierces deep into Apollo's bones": *traiecta per ossa medullas* (*M* 1.473).

Another human victim of divine sexual predation is Clytie. After the Sungod found another, mortal lover, she revealed his shameless philandering. Ovid reports that Clytie's punishment-metamorphosis is made to fit the crime. She is changed into a flower that perpetually turns to follow the course of her betrayed and betraying lover: Clytie becomes a heliotrope (*helios* [sun]; *tropos* [turning in Greek]). Heliotropes spring up all over the *Wake,* but none of them seems to have a detectable Ovidian influence. The exception is a "Klitty of a scolderymeid" (*FW* 239.18), who might be related to the mythical Clytie (see "^{g}clytia / nymph" [VI.B.4.275] and "heliotrope ᗰ" [VI.B.21.229]). At any rate, her Joycean appearance occurs near another echo of a verse from the Lord's Prayer. That passage can be twisted into an allusion to the Sun's sexual desires and his celestial mission of global warming: "eat on earth as there's hot in oven" (*FW* 239.17–18).

"*Procne, Philomela*" (*FW* 307.L) commemorates the sisters who were betrayed by Tereus. In Ovid's narrative, Philomela ingeniously weaves a report to her sister of the rape and mutilation by her brother-in-law. She uses this medium of communication because he has cut out her tongue. Procne gets revenge by serving Tereus the flesh of their son at a royal banquet. Procne is transformed into a swallow, Philomela into a nightingale, Tereus into a hoopoe. The names of the two occur in the margin of "Night Lessons," keyed to the entry: "Meditations of Two Young Spinsters" (*FW* 307.6–7). This phrase reduces Ovid's gory tale to a little more than Philomela's woven message and Procne's considered interpretation of it.[31] In another allusion to this myth, the juxtaposition of "toutes philomelas as well as magdelenes" (*FW* 237.36–238.1) signals the mirror image of the pure and the promiscuous aspects of Issy. The mythical victim and her slurred debaucher are also found in the conclusion of an alphabetical list of the Rainbow Girls, with a pair of aspirated initial consonants (*ph* and *th*), "philomel, theerose" (*FW* 248.2). There are in the *Wake* assorted swallows, nightingales, and a single hoopoe (*FW* 449.27), but all appear in contexts in which the tenor is avian not Ovidian.

Another of the marginal topics of a heroic life in the "Night Lessons" episode mentioned above is *Tiresias* (*FW* 307.L). His metamorphosis is fascinating. He came upon two snakes copulating and killed the female; for this act of impiety he was transformed into a woman. Years later (and wiser) in similar circumstances, Tiresias killed the male snake and was restored to his former sex.[32] The suggested essay topic for this legendary mortal is wonderfully appropriate: "Is the Co-Education of Animus and Anima Wholly Desirable?" (*FW* 307.3–4). Here Joyce pokes some fun at the pretentious terminology of

Jungian psychology, and reasserts his command of the fundamental conjuga-
tional distinctions in Latin gender endings: -*us* (masculine) and -*a* (feminine).

Ovid's Hyacinth is a Spartan youth, loved by Apollo, who was accidentally
killed by a rebounding discus that the god had thrown. Apollo inscribed his
immortal cries of grief on the flower into which the dying victim was transformed: *ipse suos gemitus foliis inscribit, et AI AI / flos habet inscriptum*
(Apollo himself writes his own groans on the petals, and the flower is inscribed with "Alas, alas") (*M* 10.215–16). In a *Wake* paragraph packed with
references to scribes and their writing equipment, Hyacinth is traced out, in a
florid hand: "whyacinthinous riot of blots and blurs and bars and balls and
hoops and wiggles and juxtaposed jottings" (*FW* 118.28–30). In another passage involving writing, the Latin color of the Hyacinth's marking (*purpureus,*
"crimson" [*M* 10.213]) is altered to more conventional tints of ink: "And with
steelwhite and blackmail *I ha'scint* for my sweet an anemone's letter" (*FW*
563.16–17; my emphasis). My italics here are designed to call attention not
only to the flower, but also to Apollo's cry, which would be pronounced like a
long "i" in English. The pathetic transformation is clearly signaled in "leaves
alass! Aiaiaiai" (*FW* 293.22). A final appearance of the metamorphosed youth
is in a small nosegay, beside another tragic victim of divine attraction: "Hyacin-
ssies with heliotrollops" (*FW* 603.28).

In the *Metamorphoses,* Pomona (fruit, apple in Latin) is successfully wooed
by a lover who assumes many disguises. Joyce recreates part of this tale in "an
unknowable assailant (masked) . . . Lotta Crabtree or Pomona Evlyn" (*FW*
62.32–34).

Leander, who drowned in a storm while trying to swim the Hellespont to
be with his beloved, is discovered washed ashore near her house by Hero. This
tragic tale does not form part of the *Metamorphoses,* since neither of the two
lovers is changed into another shape to haunt Roman mythology as a shore
flower or seabird. But the doomed love of Hero and Leander was memorialized in another work by Ovid. They are the "writers" of a pair of letters in his
Heroides, a series of fictional epistles by mythic lovers to their beloved. Thus,
for example, Dido writes a last lament to Aeneas over his betrayal just before
she commits suicide, and Penelope addresses over a hundred petulant lines to
Ulysses: Where is he, now that Troy has fallen? The two verse letters by Hero
and Leander (*Heroides* 18 and 19) are, in fact, the earliest and the most extensive classical treatment of the story. Joyce's allusions to this legend are mainly
onomastic and give no hint of his source of information. Only the principals
are present in "my hero and lander" (*FW* 466.14); the site and cause of the
swimmer's death are mocked in "Out of my name you call me, Leelander. But
in my shelter you'll miss me" (*FW* 487.30–31). The geography of the affair is

compactly, but erroneously (Leander is European) summarized in "his birthspot lies beyond the herospont and his burialplot in the pleasant little field" (*FW* 135.17–18).

The most expansive passage involving Hero and Leander makes a bizarrely logical connection between the two lovers and a series of unique annual boat races at Oxford. Near the university city, the River Thames[33] is too narrow to permit crews to race side-by-side. Therefore, the various colleges' eight-man shells compete by pursuing and "bumping" the rival boat ahead (note "Bumping races" [*FW* 437.3]). The annual champion is the boat that has bumped its way to "the head of the river." The best collegiate oars and those who have won "dark blues" for competing against Cambridge are tapped for the prestigious all-University rowing club, Leander. The following is what Joyce quizzically made out of this mishmash of Oxonian lore and classical myth: "Or where Neptune sculled and Tritonville rowed and leandros three bumped heroines two?" (*FW* 203.12–14; also see page 82 in this volume). The presence of two sea-gods, Neptune and Triton, in the passage imparts a lightly classical sheen to it, but nothing that points to a direct source in a specific text.

In a 1921 interview with the American writer Djuna Barnes, Joyce gave early and eccentric proof of his mastery of Ovidian etiological myth.[34] He explained how the great hunter Orion got his name. The original tale is told in the *Fasti* (5.493–544) for May 11 (when the stars in the constellation Orion set). Once upon a time, Jupiter, Neptune, and Mercury visited earth, where they were amply wined and dined by a poor widower. In exchange for his hospitality the man asked for a son—but not a new wife. The gods then showered the hide of the ox that had been served at their feast with Olympian piss (*urina* in Latin; *orina* in Italian). From that divinely "impregnated" hide Orion was born. Later, the "ancient sound" of the first letter of his name was transformed to "O" and he became a guardian of Diana, the goddess of the hunt. She is responsible for his metamorphosis into a constellation. This extraordinary tale of a hero's origin and name does not seem to have left a mark on the *Wake*, beyond the fairly obvious "eternal chimera*hunter* Orio*lopos*" (*FW* 107.14; my emphases).

In one of the final descriptions of the resurgent HCE, his acrostically rounded shoulders ("the hullow chyst excavement") hint at the presence of another typical means of legendary salvation for an infant destined to become a great hero. Perseus, for example, was set adrift on the sea in a chest; yet he survived to ride Pegasus and to rescue Andromeda. The suggestion of an Ovidian allusion in the HCE acrostic cited just above is supported by the immediately adjacent phrase in the text: "astronomically fabulafigured" (*fabula* is tale, myth, drama in Latin) (*FW* 596.28–29). If the foregoing constellation of conjecture seems too ethereal, there is highly charged archival testimony to the fact that some of Joyce's compositional raw material was, in no small measure thanks to Ovid, radically "myth elated" (VI.B.36.70, as two words; *FW* 266.9–10, as a single unit).

During the late Middle Ages and the Renaissance the influence of Ovid, especially his *Metamorphoses*, on the literature and art of Europe was immense. Sometimes his more salacious or potentially sacrilegious tales were "moralized" to accommodate them to new standards, but generations of artists were inspired by the prolific Roman poet. The evidence in the preceding pages shows that James Joyce, hardly scandalized, readily "metandmorefusses" (*FW* 513.31) the Latin verses into character paradigms and portmanteau puns. Phaethon, a sleek statuette of Narcissus, and the reedy witness to Midas' shame are the primary examples here. Beside these are numerous other adaptations that demonstrate the presence of every sort of Ovidian gimmick throughout Joyce's extended "methylogical mission" (*FW* 373.21).

9

Miscellaneous Authors,
Classical and Medieval

Previous chapters, dealing with the impact of Vergil, Horace, Ovid, and Cicero on Joyce's fiction, were packed with examples of acknowledged and camouflaged allusion. Since those authors have for centuries received the heaviest attention in schools, that emphasis is not surprising. Many of the references and original-text citations from major works have been shown to be thematically active (and sometimes activating) components of the passages in which they occur. These integrated parallels supply additional evidence to show that Joyce's polyglot coinages and snippets from Latin literature are more than ornamental displays of a resolutely classical and Jesuit education.

References to a number of less well known Roman authors—ones not necessarily covered in the regular school curriculum—are the topic of this chapter. Separate headings signal the discussions of Hadrian, Catullus, the Priapic poems, Petronius, Martial, and Plautus. A case for thematic allusion can be made for almost all the examples cited here in this portion of the chapter. The same sort of contextual relevance is more difficult to maintain for the names and works that conclude the survey of literary references in Joyce's *opera*. Most of the final items are arranged in what is little more than an annotated catalogue of authors or titles, including a few Christian and medieval notices. This format both completes the record of citation from the entire range of Latin literature and challenges the inquisitive reader to discover missing links between the reference and the context.

Hadrian

The first exhibit involves a unique, Imperial-age Roman poem. Even though the allusions to this work have been woven into the text of the *Wake* without obvious traces, its explication is fairly straightforward. In the midst of the swarm of insects which surround "the casus . . . of the Ondt and the Gracehoper" (*FW* 414.18–21), there flutter several allusions to a Latin epigram by the Emperor Hadrian (A.D. 117–138). The poem, addressed to his soul as he is dying, is brief enough to be quoted in full:

Animula! vagula, blandula
hospes comesque corporis,
quae nunc abibis in loca—
pallidula, rigida, nudula
nec, ut soles, dabis iocos?

A fairly close translation, allowing for some ornamental expansion in lines 3 and 4, is this early-nineteenth-century version:

Ah! gently, fleeting, wav'ring sprite,
Friend and associate of this day!
To what unknown region borne,
Wilt thou now wing thy distant flight?
No more with wonted humor gay,
But pallid, cheerless, and forlorn.

Initially, the most obvious Joycean echo is "animule" (*FW* 417.35). In Latin, *animula/us* is a diminutive of *anima/us* and literally means something like "little soul"; metaphorically it is a term of affection. Joyce modifies this word with the adjective "featherweighed" (*FW* 417.34), an acceptable, but a bit pugnacious, Wakean translation of *blandula*. A crossed Notebook entry, in the midst of other references to insects, is to the point here: "ᵇfeatherweight / animule" (VI.B.4.298). The presence of the exaggeratedly Latinate "veripatetic imago" (*FW* 417.32) in the immediate vicinity of "animule" suggests two things about Joyce's vocative addressee: it is both a wanderer (peripatetic in Greek) and therefore *vagula* (fleeting), and something that "reveals a genuine image" (*verus*, true; *pateo*, to lie open). That creature is also *very pathetic*, which nicely fits the tone of the epigram. Moreover, *imago* is one of several Latin words regularly used, if not specifically for "soul," then generically for "ghost," "shade," "spirit," as in Vergil's *Aeneid* (4.654) when the dying Dido sighs *et nunc magna mei sub terras ibit* imago (and now my great soul/spirit will go beneath the earth). McHugh's *Annotations* indicate—and, as a professional entomologist, he should know—that *imago* is also a term for an adult insect.

In the spirit of this twofold denotation, then, one should note the "psyche" on the previous page (*FW* 416.6). This Greek noun means "soul," "spirit," "ghost,"—and "butterfly" or "moth," as in the entomological term, Psychodidae: moth midges. In his attempt to catch and pin into the text as many references to butterflies as possible, Joyce would not have missed those polyvalent possibilities. Next to "psyche" in the text is the exclamation "laus!" (*FW* 416.6), which is both the Latin noun for "praise," "honor" and a Wakean distortion of the word "louse." One final intertextual echo of the Latin poem's first verse: the "animule" has just completed a journey "sinctfying chronic's despair" (*FW* 417.36). I suggest that this phrase can be paraphrased to signify death, which is the end of hope, time's despair. If so, these words are also thematically linked to the cluster of allusions from a deathbed poem.

The second verse of the Latin also makes its appearance in this *Wake* episode. The Gracehoper has "jingled" through his life seeking, without effort or expense, to make merry, to drink and eat. That final ambition is expressed as his hope "to sirch for grub for his corapusse or to find a hospes" (*FW* 416.14–15). McHugh glosses "sirch" with "sirse," Lithuanian for "wasp"; "grub" (larva) is obvious; "corapusse" suggests both "carapace" (the bonelike covering of the thorax and abdomen of some insects) and the Latin word for "body" (*corpus*); "hospes" may seem to yield only "hospice," since the Gracehoper presumably and presumptuously wants bed with his board. *Hospes* is in fact the Latin word for both "host" and "guest"; as such it can carry the etymological force of a "host" of a parasite. Thematically all of these multilingual suggestions fit the fable well. There also can be no doubt that the appearance of "corapusse" and "hospes," in the same line of the *Wake*, is Joyce's conscious echo of Hadrian's Latin phrase *hospes, comesque corporis*. There is additional archival evidence to support my etymological-entomological speculations: "[b]curapass / (corpus)" (VI.B.4.248).

If additional evidence is necessary, line 3 of the English translation cited above asks to "what unknown region" Hadrian's soul is about to fly. The *Wake* phrase that follows "hospes" is "he wist gnit!" (*FW* 416.15). Here there is a play on "gnit/gnat," and more; the words are also phonetic Dutch for "he does not know," which sounds like an allusion to the "unknown region" in the English version.

So much for the verbal echoes flitting between the Latin epigram and the *Wake*. What about the English translation of Hadrian's verse quoted above? Its author is George Gordon, Lord Byron. His works are memorably honored by Joyce.[1] In *Portrait*, the hero is challenged:

—And who do you think is the greatest poet? asked Boland, nudging his neighbour.
—Byron, of course, answered Stephen. (*P* 80–81)

At the end of "A Little Cloud" from *Dubliners*, Little Chandler opens a "volume of Byron's poems" and begins "to read the first poem in the book." Though not called by its title in the story, this poem is "On the Death of a Young Lady" from the *Hours of Idleness*: Joyce goes on to quote six verses from it in the text (*D* 83–84). On the overleaf of the page on which that poem is printed in Byron's first collection of poetry is his translation of "Adrian's Address to His Soul When Dying*," as cited above.[2] The asterisk in Byron's text is the poet's indication that just beneath his version of the epigram is a footnote. It contains the Latin text also printed above.

Before releasing my grip on Hadrian's butterfly, I wish to point out that Joyce had frequent occasion to be reminded of this poem during his years at University College. *St. Stephen's* was an undergraduate journal that appeared there at irregular intervals from June 1901 to June 1906. A number of the early issues contained a column written by "Chanel," the pseudonym of Arthur Clery. The December 1901 issue of *St. Stephen's* notes "sundrye rioutuous and sedytious publications under the names of one Skeffington and one Joyce." The reference is to a privately printed pamphlet containing two "censored" papers by Skeffington (on university education for Irish women) and by Joyce (on the parochialism of Irish drama).[3] Clery's column was entitled "Parvula Blandula," which can be paraphrased into English as "Unspicey Itemettes." This title is not precisely the *vagula blandula* of Hadrian's poem, but (since *blandula* occurs nowhere else in all Latin literature) an allusion to that work is obviously intended. It is highly likely, then, that Joyce remembered not only a childhood favorite (Byron), but also a collegiate nemesis (Clery), when he set about alluding to the Latin poem in the *Wake*. As a matter of high-probability conjecture, I also push for a covert procedure, of similar ingenuity and with characteristic cunning, in a much earlier work. Arthur Clery, the penman of "Parvula Blandula," does not appear as a member of Stephen's coterie in *Portrait*. Nevertheless, I hear a memento of both the unctuous collegiate columnist and the poetic Emperor in the pair of adverbs that Joyce chose to describe the gaze of another University College comrade: "blandly and vaguely" (*P* 226).

CATULLUS

The reputation of Catullus as an x-rated poet has been reinforced by countless school editions of his works in which occasional lines are silently excised and whole series of poems are missing. This type of censorship drives serious students to larger library editions, in which (until recently) the taboo material was translated into Italian. Unfortunately, the next level of scholarly resource, a comprehensive Italian dictionary, usually defined the essential terms in Latin. (This method of language-learning recirculation is one of the hallowed pedagogical ploys of a classical education.) Many of Catullus' poems are, by any standard, quite offensive, primarily because of their open and repeated threats of ramrod violation of every bodily orifice. Just the sort of source, one would think, to crop up all over the place in *Finnegans Wake*, a work that shares some of the same tendencies of sexual invective. After a thorough search for allusion and quotation, however, I find very little of Catullus in any of Joyce's works. What does occur is an exception that proves the rule.

The poet's name, as Glasheen suggests, is probably present in "over-*cautelous*ness" (*FW* 111.20; my emphasis) and "Gotellus" (*FW* 527.1). The traditional autobiographical reading of Catullus' poems centers on the ups and downs of his heart-wrenching love affair with "Lesbia," the poetic pseudonym for Claudia / Clodia, the wife of Quintus Metellus. All these designations appear: "Lesbia" (*FW* 93.27), "lispias" (*FW* 348.26); "Cloudia Aiduoclis" (*FW* 568.10); "Metellus" (*FW* 252.15). In none of these citations do I detect any thematic reason for the presence of a Catullan character.

Clodia also appears, this time as the target of unremitting invective, in a long speech delivered by Cicero in defense of a young client who had been allegedly led astray by this jaded seductress. To avoid giving direct offense to Clodia's influential family, Cicero conjured up one of her own ancestors to excoriate her for staining the chastity of Roman matrons.[4] The prudent orator delicately notes that this resurrected "spokesperson," Appius Claudius, was blind, so that he will not have to see the sluttish appearance of his descendant. Since this Appius Claudius was noted for his strict morals, he cannot positively be identified with Joyce's "happyass cloudious" (*FW* 581.22–23), but the perversion of the censor's august *praenomen* is a nice touch (also see pages 55–56 and 117–18).

When Catullus' affair with Clodia/Lesbia was at its ecstatic peak, he addressed two poems to his love on the topic of kisses. In the first, after a famous, upbeat opening, *Vivamus, mea Lesbia, atque amemus* (Let us live, my Lesbia, and let us love), he has a request:

> da mi basia mille, deinde centum,
> dein mille altera, dein secunda centum, etc. (5.1, 7–10)[5]

> (Give me a thousand kisses, then a hundred, next another thousand, then a second hundred, etc.)

In another poem Catullus has his beloved ask the following question:

Quaeris quot mihi basiationes
tuae, Lesbia, sint satis superque. (7.1–2)

(You ask, Lesbia, how many of your sweet little kisses are enough and
more than enough for me.)

These two short poems—the one with its cascade of numbers, the other in
which the lover's question gives rise to an epic simile in the reply—are ancient literature's most memorable tributes to the kiss.

On the bottom half of a single page of the *Wake* a Joycean surplus of
postscripted Latin kisses appears:

three *basia* or shorter and smaller *oscula* . . . and then that last labiolingual
basium might be read as a *suavium* if whoever the embracer then was
wrote with a tongue in his (or perhaps her) cheek. (*FW* 122.21–34; Joyce's
emphases; my ellipsis)

Joyce's Latin amatory vocabulary in this passage is impressive.[6] He demonstrates the distinction between *oscula* and the longer and passionate *basia*. He
knows that a kiss involving lips and tongue (*labia, lingua*) brings the entire
puckered mouth (*suavium*) into foreplay.

That lexical finesse is admirable, but it is not necessarily evidence for direct
Catullan influence here. There are, however, two other passages on the same
page of the *Wake* which point quite explicitly to that Roman poet and his
literary revelations of his heart-wrenching problems with Clodia/Lesbia. Just
before the elaborate description of "tongue-kissing," Joyce indicates that in
such circumstances "two is company when the third person is the person darkly
spoken of" (*FW* 122.30–31). Catullus' notorious rival for Lesbia's love was a
friend, Marcus Caelius Rufus. He was the one into whose arms the poet claimed
his beloved had strayed from him. (As mentioned above, Cicero defended this
young man-about-town against serious charges lodged by Clodia after their
passion had, in turn, cooled.) As far as Catullus was concerned, Caelius was
the ultimate betrayer of friendship and trust. The poet wrote at least one darkly
bitter epigram excoriating the deceit of his former comrade. Its emphatic first
word addresses Caelius in the familiar (and dismissive) vocative form of his
cognomen: *Rufe* (77.1). With typical wordplay on the meaning of the Latin
adjective *rufus* (red), Joyce alludes to the fact that this treacherous friend-
rival stole the kisses of Catullus' *inamorata*: "his ruddy old Villain Rufus"
(*FW* 122.16–17). Finally, in the first Latin poem cited in the second-last paragraph, Catullus urged Lesbia to multiply their kisses and to disregard the "gos-

sip of puritanical old geezers" (*rumoresque senum severiorum*) (5.2). The Joycean context of the passage in which Rufus and the Latin kisses occur does not involve the Four Old Men. Nevertheless, in other venues this quartet of senile busybodies *will* definitely observe the trysts and attempt to put a hex on the kisses of various Wakean lovers. Thus, it is not too far-fetched to suggest that the avatars of these tongue-wagging gaffers may lurk "in the marginal panels" (*FW* 122.25) of this highly Catullan passage.

Joyce may well have intended an allusion to another Catullan poem in an earlier passage in the *Wake*. The Latin source is a witty scenario in which the poet plays with the Roman proverb *sexagenarios de ponte* (sixty-year-olds off the bridge). This phrase most probably refers to the fact that after they reached the age of sixty, citizens could not vote in the assemblies and were pushed away from the bridges leading to the tally-areas.[7] In one of his only mildly risqué poems, Catullus introduces an old man who has problems, not with his civic franchise, but with his wandering wife. She is "friskier than a scrumptious goatling," yet he allows her "to sport around as she likes" (*ludere hanc sinit ut libet*) (17.15–17). The poet suggests shock-therapy to bring the superannuated husband back to his senses and marital responsibilities: "off the bridge head over heels into the mud with him" (*quendam municipem meum de tuo volo* ponte / *ire praecipitem in lutum per caputque pedesque*) (17.8–9). I hear reverberations of this primitive bit of folk fun in the following string of Wakean verbs: "to attax and abridge, to derail and *depontify*" (*FW* 97.22–23; my emphasis). These four hostile verbs appear in a passage in which the Four Old Men are discussing ways to stop HCE's flight to avoid punishment for his sexual offenses. They assert that he needs "reeducation of his intestines" (*FW* 97.18–19), instruction that has a phallic-gonadal as well as alimentary aspect. At any rate, the episode appears on the same page as "the triduum of Saturnalia" (*FW* 97.33). This is a three-day Joycean recelebration of the ancient Roman feast on which presents were exchanged, rules of decorum relaxed, and slaves allowed temporary freedom to do what they wanted. There is, then, a Wakean context for some decidedly unrestrained activity, including the possibility of Catullan rustic sex therapy involving a tumble from a bridge into the mud.

There are several other related items in the *Wake* that may also be rooted in Joyce's memory of one of Catullus' poems; or, if they originally sprang from another source, they have been selected or modified to echo a Latin model. In the series of battles that erupt after HCE's dream burial, recruits are mustered from "both Celtiberian camps" (*FW* 78.25). The Romans regarded the Celtic inhabitants of the Iberian peninsula as rugged warriors in their own land, but barely civilized rubes in the larger world. In two poems Catullus levels insults at a certain Egnatius, who flashes a dazzling smile on every possible occasion, even at the cremation of a widow's only son. Catullus explains this odd behavior by pointing out the curious Spanish custom of brushing one's teeth with urine. That is state-of-the-art dental hygiene in Celtiberia— and smiling Egnatius is a prototypical ugly *Celtiber*. In fact, he is the "son of Celtiberia renowned for its cute little bunnies" (*cuniculosae Celtiberiae fili*) (39.17 and 37.18). The barrage of scatological and sexual innuendo here seems to me to be just the sort of thing Joyce would have appropriated from an ancient author and covertly inserted into the *Wake* in the guise of what appears to be merely an outdated ethnic tag.[8]

In the discussion of the rivalry between Gogarty-Mulligan and Joyce-Dedalus, I mentioned the Roman custom of *ad hoc* poetic competition, especially at drinking parties during which an adept "rhymer" would try to outwit his comrades. The Latin verb for this verse sport is *ludo, ludere, lusi, lusum* (to play, to mess around). Catullus uses it on several appropriate occasions; one example is *multa satis lusi* (I have sported around enough [in making up] many [love-poems]) (68.17). I hear a compressed echo of this phrase in "*Multalusi*" (FW 290.19; compare "Lludillongi" [FW 519.8]).

Another Catullan echo involves a Latin phrase that is familiar even to readers who know nothing about that language or its literature. Catullus' brother died and was buried in the Troad, the area in what is today western Turkey near the traditional site of Troy. The poet visited his brother's tomb and crystalized his grief in verse: *atque in perpetuum, frater, ave atque vale* (and for all time, brother, hail and farewell) (101.10). Joyce has at least five imitations of this line, all in the more-or-less original Latin:

Aves Selvae Aquae Valles! (FW 147.6–7)[9]
Ave! And let it be to all remembrance. Vale. (FW 305.27–28)
Ave . . . Vale. (FW 420.25)
once we lave 'tis lave and vale. (FW 600.7)
So. Avelaval. (FW 628.6)

The impetus behind my final identification of Catullan material in Joyce's work comes from three related sets of archival notes. Among the papers of Stuart Gilbert is a notebook labeled "folder of notes about working on *Ulysses* and *Finnegans Wake* with James Joyce."[10] (The presence of "*Ulysses*" in that description is somewhat misleading, since it refers to Gilbert's 1930 *Study* of the novel, not to the novel itself.) In between pages 20 and 21 of his notebook Gilbert placed a slip of paper on which he wrote that "*Penelope* Mrs Bloom" is somehow connected with the "worship of Cybele, Tellus." On page 31 of the same C14 notebook there is a series of entries that deal with several elements in Catullus' poem on Attis, and their connection with the song "My Girl's a Yorkshire Girl" near the end of the "Circe" episode of *Ulysses* (*U* 15.4026–27).

As far-fetched as it may seem, there is a Latin least-common-denominator that reconciles these apparently disparate elements. Before citing that key Catullan factor, however, it is necessary to take a fast look at the poem in which it occurs. Catullus' poem on Attis (63) is about a young Greek man who castrates himself to serve at the Phrygian shrine of the great mother-goddess Cybele. The devotee almost immediately regrets his self-mutilation and, in a long soliloquy, bemoans everything that he has lost: everything. The work's 93 lines were composed in the syncopated Galliambic meter, designed to imitate the rhythm of kettledrums and cymbals. The diction is equally eccentric, with numerous "strange and harsh compounds." The pathos of the poem is reinforced by Latin grammar: Attis is frequently modified by adjectives that are feminine (not masculine) in gender. One of the tasks of Cybele's servants is to perform the goddess's ritual dance, the *tripudium*. That Latin noun is the unifying factor that underlies the cluster of entries in Gilbert's notebook. He cites two lines from Catullus' poem:

quo nos decet citatis celerare tripudiis.
simul haec comitibus Attis cencinit notha mulier. (63.26–27)

(where it is proper that we whirl in the frenzied three-beat dances. As soon as Attis, the false female, sang these instructions to the comrades.)

In both these preparatory notes for and in his completed *Study* of *Ulysses*, Stuart Gilbert directs the reader to "[c]ompare the change in sex in the *Attis* poem of Catullus" with the passage in "Circe" depicting Bloom's metamorphosis when he is tapped by Bello's fan: "Bloom is tortured, becomes a light woman." And throughout this episode Bloom is referred to in feminine pronouns (*U* 15.2770 and following). Gilbert follows his reference to Catullus' poem by stating that in it, "as here, the ritual dance of the *tripudium* is mentioned. (*My Girl's a Yorkshire Girl* is in *three-time, a tripudium*)."[11] The phrase "as here" is not quite accurate. Bloom, male or female, does *not* dance in "Circe" and the "Yorkshire Girl" is not played in *Ulysses* for another forty pages. When that performance does take place at *Ulysses* 15.4004, Zoe claps her hands and commands "Dance! Dance!" Stephen Dedalus responds: "Quick! Quick! Where's my augur's rod? (*he runs to the piano and takes his ashplant, beating his foot in* tripudium)" (*U* 15.4012–13; my emphasis). Then the drums and the pianola begin to play "*in waltz time the prelude of* My Girl's a Yorkshire Girl" (*U* 4026–27).

What Gilbert has done is to contaminate the two *Ulyssean* episodes (Bloom's sex change and Stephen's *tripudium*) by relating both to Catullus' Attis poem. There can be no doubt that Gilbert is correct in pointing out Joyce's source here. In presenting the evidence, however, it was necessary to make the connection in his notebook entry and textual footnote a bit more explicit for readers who are not fully initiated into the rituals of Joycean classical allusion. In fact, in a notebook entry that was not incorporated into the final text of his *Study*, Gilbert passes on additional information about Joyce's complex methods of composition. Gilbert indicates that Stephen's *tripudium* in "Circe" "was prepared for in the Proteus episode."[12] Absolutely correct. In "Proteus" Stephen walks on Sandymount strand and contemplates his borrowed boots "wherein another's foot had rested warm. The foot that beat the ground in tripudium, foot I dislove" (*U* 3.447–49). The phrase "another's foot" refers to that of Buck Mulligan; but it is left unclear where or when the "[s]tately, plump" pseudopriest had beat the ground in a ritual three-beat.

The foregoing explication of the studied use of Catullus' Attis poem in *Ulysses* demonstrates the intricacies of Joyce's methods of composition. Revelation of the details of this process was possible only through a comparison of notebook material in the Stuart Gilbert archive and a footnote in his *Study* of *Ulysses*. Even there, considerable extrapolation was necessary to link Boom as a *notha mulier* (pseudo-female) (Catullus 63.27) and the *tripudium* of "My Girl's a Yorkshire Girl." As the recipient of an honors degree in *literae humaniores* at Oxford, Gilbert had the books at hand in which to check out esoteric details. For example, in another notebook Gilbert wrote: "For W in P see Catullus p. 120 for / ἅπαξ λέγομενα in language."[13] The page reference is to Elmer T. Merrill's standard edition of the poems of Catullus, first published in 1893 and frequently reissued. On page 120 Merrill points out that the Attis poem is packed with "strange and harsh compounds"; the Greek phrase just cited means "[words] read only once." Some of Catullus' Latin vocabulary in this poem, in short, is quite exotic, with compound coinages not unlike the portmanteau words Joyce was inventing for the *Wake* in progress.

Another entry in the same notebook reads: "Penelope Tellus see Lucretius II 600 (Catullus)." This entry was used by Gilbert in his comment on Molly, in "Penelope," as "Gaea-Tellus, the Great Mother, Cybele."[14] A bit later in the same paragraph of Gilbert's commentary, Cybele is reported to be "always attended by lions." Joyce used this bit of classical arcana by having Molly Bloom compare Blazes Boylan to a lion as a bedfellow; but, she rather scornfully, adds, "Im sure hed have something better to say for himself an old Lion would" (*U* 18.1377–78). Without Joyce's hint to Gilbert (which clearly sent him back to Merrill's edition of Catullus), few commentators—and fewer readers—would ever have picked up the following allusions: in Catullus, the chariot of the

Great Earth Mother is "yoked to lions"; in Lucretius, the goddess "whips her yoked-in-tandem lions into action."[15]

PRIAPEA

Among the series of notes, mainly on mythological and classical material, that Joyce made for *Ulysses* is the following entry: "Priapea Pen (vetula) sits smutty talking / amg the Freier" (VIII.A.5.10).[16] The "Pen" in that citation is an abbreviation for Penelope, and the rest of the note records that she sits, talking dirty, among the suitors (*Freier* in German; in contemporary idiom the term can also mean pimps). Obviously Joyce is referring to a source that presents a heterodox version of what happened at Ulysses' palace in Ithaca before the master returned. That source, a comprehensive German handbook on classical mythology, supplied him with the information, and both of the Latin words in his entry. Roscher's *Lexikon* here cites the *Priapea*, a collection of poems written about or in some way involving the ithyphallic god, whom the Greeks and Romans called *Priapos/us*.[17] Many of these brief works are outrageously obscene. The primary collection is a group of eighty Latin epigrams traditionally entitled *Carmina Priapea* (Priapic Poems) or simply *Priapea*.[18] Poem 68 of that anthology includes this couplet:

> ad vetulam tamen ille suam properabat, et omnis
> > mens erat in cunno, Penelopea, tuo. (*Priapea* 68.27–28)

> (Nonetheless that man [Ulysses] was rushing to his little old wife, and his whole mind, Penelope, was in your cunt.)

The substantive *vetulam* (little old woman) certifies that *this* poem is the one referred to in Joyce's note. And in it Penelope does in fact sit around speculating which of the suitors is the man best equipped—literally—to take Ulysses' place. The god Priapus concludes the poem by volunteering that *he* could have stood in for the missing husband, but he had not yet been created at the time of the Trojan War (*Priapea* 68.37–38).

The only reference in all of Joyce's *Ulysses* to something that is specifically "priapic" is a technical term from botany cited in "Circe" by the sexologist Virag: "priapic pulsatilla" (*U* 15.2395). The *Anemone pulsatilla* is a flowering herb once used for sundry medicinal purposes and as a reputed aphrodisiac. As it appears in the novel, this phrase appears to have nothing to do with the collection of Latin epigrams. On the other hand, Virag's phrase could be interpreted to foreshadow—however fleetingly—a later moment in the novel. There the "Penelope" of Joyce's *Ulysses* does at least contemplate some "smutty talking"; but Molly's potential audience, near the end of her monologue, is her husband, not the suitor(s): "Ill tighten up my bottom well and let out a few smutty words" (*U* 18.1530–31).

If one wishes to speculate about other parallels between the Penelope of the *Priapea* and Molly of *Ulysses*, there is some minor evidence at the start of the novel's final monologue. Molly makes a general comparison about the adequacy of Boylan's penis, which she terms a "crowbar": "no I never in all my life felt anyone had one the size of that to make you feel full up" (*U* 18.148–50). In the Latin poem, Ulysses' wife awards the palm to her husband: *nemo meo melius nervum tendebat Ulixe* (nobody used to stretch out his sinew better than my Ulysses) (*Priapea* 68.33). There is a clever pun here: *nervus* can mean "bowstring," as well as "sinew," "tendon." And *nemo* (nobody) is Odysseus' famous name stratagem in the cave of the Cyclops. Thus, Penelope, herself a woman of many turns, not only praises her husband's heroic proportions, but also predicts his revelatory means (in the archery contest) of punishing the suitors for their attempts at sexual poaching. Finally, for the sake of textual thoroughness, I should mention that the *Priapea* poem cited above reads an obscene meaning into the μῶλυ (*mōly*), the talisman-herb that protected Odysseus from the sexual voodoo of Circe: *quem cum "moly" vocat, mentula "moly" fuit* (although he calls [the magic plant] "moly," the "moly" was his prick) (*Priapea* 68.21).

The parallels discussed in the last few paragraphs are meant to suggest that Joyce knew more about *Priapea* 68 than might be suggested by the mere précis of one of its topics in a notebook entry that was cited from a scholarly source. Definitive judgments are impossible here, because visions of epic-sized penises are recurrent features of male-generated pornographic fantasy, whether it be ancient Roman or modern Joycean. There can be no question, however, that the startling motif of a "smutty" Penelope is countervalent enough to be traced to a written source. The most conspicuous treatment of a vocally unchaste wife of Ulysses is the *Priapea* poem that was specifically identified in one of Joyce's pre-*Ulysses* notes.[19] There are also a number of other possible allusions to other poems from this Latin collection. All occur in *Finnegans Wake*; some involve fairly close echoes of the original text.

Before presenting these comparative passages, it is necessary to discuss the literary (and pedagogical) status of the Priapic corpus. A scholarly, yet completely accessible new edition—with straightforward translations of every word—covers the ground with verve. The editor writes:

[The Priapus of the *Priapea*] is nasty: aggressive, arrogant, crude, cruel, cynical, egocentric, exhibitionist, filthy-minded, foul-mouthed, lewd, sadistic, sarcastic and selfish, yet self-pitying. But he is witty—and this itself, together with the elegant and technically-perfect Latin in which he is described, would have attracted a large circle of readers who would delight in such entertaining excellence.[20]

That synopsis seems to me to capture the tone and the potential appeal of these poems quite well.

Next, a bit of multi-(horti)cultural background about the central figure in these poems. In sculpture or on vase paintings Priapus was normally depicted as a mature male displaying a penis of extraordinary size. Romans frequently placed a wooden statue of Priapus in their gardens to protect the fruit from thieves. There is a *Wake* Notebook entry that indicates that Joyce was aware of this custom: "park statue / of Priap ⊓ " (VI.B.9.4). The guardian-god's all-purpose, gender-unbiased weapon was his prize prick—and he threatened potential violators of his rural sanctuary with every imaginable sort of penile retaliation. These graphic poems, in short, leave almost nothing to be filled in by the imagination of even the most fantasy-prone schoolboy.

The Latin text of the *Priapea* was most often printed as a complement to another "underground" work, *The Satyricon* of Petronius. A standard nineteenth-century edition (the one Joyce would most probably have used) is that by Buecheler, first published at Berlin in 1862. Its sixth edition (1922) includes the *Satyricon, Priapea*, the fragments of Varro's satires, the *Apocolocyntosis* (The "Pumpkinification" of the Emperor Claudius), and a few other related documents. This edition, totally in Latin, except for a few Greek cross-references, was the scholarly equivalent of a book in "plain brown wrappers"—for those whose Latin was up to the challenge.

The identity of the author of the only pre-twentieth-century translation of the *Priapea* into English verse confirms the status of this work. That 1890 version was prepared by "Outidanos" (Good-for-nothing in Greek), the pseudonym of Captain Sir Richard Burton, the ubiquitous explorer and translator of exotic pornography from several languages.[21] The *Priapea*, then, most assuredly never appeared in the curriculum of any Jesuit school or university. This does not mean that enterprising young Latin scholars did not acquire texts, and, with a little bit of lexical ingenuity, stun themselves and their classmates with excesses of priapic grossness.

If Joyce were even casually acquainted with the text of the *Priapea* at any time while he was working on the *Wake*, he would have been delighted by this epigram:

ED si scribas temonemque insuper addas,
     qui medium vult scindere, pictus erit. (*Priapea* 54)

(If you would write ED and include a shaft in addition, there will be a picture of what wants to split you in the middle.)

This couplet is an example of a "figure-poem": its components are designed, graphically, to *show* as well as to *tell* the "plot." Commentators differ on the exact outline of the "picture" described in line one, but consensus sees an erect phallus: the E is the organ's head which is connected to the scrotum, D, by the *temon*, a "shaft." One astute scholar visualized a schematic outline in the form of "a graffito like those scrawled on the walls at Pompeii": E⎯D. As far as the *Wake* is concerned, what is most significant here is not the anatomical accuracy of the figure, but the presence of the component letters, "E" and "D." If both were to be transliterated from the Roman into the Greek script then HCE (E) and ALP (Δ) would be emphatically and appropriately depicted. Neither McHugh's thorough study of the *Wake* sigla nor any archival material hints at a Priapean influence on the source for these omnipresent symbols. But the temptation of seeing a classical influence here is too great to resist initial mention of the Latin "figure" couplet.[22]

There is another Priapean couplet that pivots around an analogous rhetorical ploy. It is a "letter-poem," in which the pronunciation and/or combination of syllables produce a clear, but parasyntactic message.

cum loquor, una mihi peccatur littera: nam te
  pe-dico semper blaesaque lingua mihi est. (*Priapea* 7)

(My tongue sputters and when I speak, one
letter gets screwed up: I always bugger "U".)

The final clause of my English version is a gross paraphrase of the equally obscene original. The Latin text manipulates a dental "*te*" and a plosive "*pe-*," which (so he claims) Priapus' tongue can't keep straight. Thus, the Latin *te pe dico* (as three units) means "I say 'tee' for 'pee'"; whereas, *te pedico* (as two units) means "I bugger you."

Throughout his works, to capture idiosyncratic speech patterns and for just plain fun, Joyce plays around with different letter pronunciations. In the *Wake*, for example, the Gaelic "L/R" Interchange and the "P/K" Split are linguistic phenomena of some importance.[23] On a less elevated level, in a journal article a number of years ago, I suggested that a common, obscene, second-person singular command lurked in the letter-titles of Stephen Dedalus' soon-to-be-written books: "Have you read his F? O yes, but I prefer Q. Yes, but W is wonder. O yes W" (*U* 3.139–40).[24] A closer parallel to the thrust of the Latin couplet cited in the previous paragraph is the ditty sung by "THE PRISON GATE GIRLS":

If you see Kay
Tell him he may
See you in Tea
Tell him from me. (*U* 15.1892–96)

The first and third lines phonetically spell out two of the most common English four-letter words.

A number of Priapean poems and other verses inspired by them play the
same sound-sense games, from several different sexual and linguistic angles.
That sort of phonetic substitution, with barbed results, is part of the verbal
machinery that makes the *Wake* go round; but I have not been able to locate a
direct echo of the Latin poem in Joyce's text. The best analogue I can offer is
an unsubtle "Gobugga ye, sez I! O breezes!" (*FW* 95.18–19). Here the Roman
god's threat is supported by a wind-muffled Christian blasphemy. As a priapic
coda, I also note "Lankyshied!" (*FW* 95.18), immediately prior to the exple-
tives just cited. This single word can operate on at least three levels:
"Lancashire," "Danke schön!," and "lanky Scheid" (*Scheit* is log in German),
the last to warn that Priapus' long log is poised to penalize all garden thieves.

There are innumerable local and generalized erections in the *Wake*. And
cross-cultural phallic metaphors tend to transcend the lexical limits of individual languages so routinely that it would be preposterous to claim direct
influence of the *Priapea* on Joycean passages that are merely similar. Even
"*hereditatis columna erecta*" (*FW* 131.30) probably has far more to do with
HCE's fraudulent claim to represent the "upright pillar of his heritage" than
with Priapus' warning that he is ready, willing, and able to deploy *adstans
inguinibus columna nostris* (the pole which stands out from my loins) (*Priapea*
10.7). The Roman god repeatedly threatens to snag, gag, or thump the bad
boys and girls who dare to steal his fruits: *pedicare volo, tu vis decerpere poma*
(I want to bugger you, you want to swipe my apples) (*Priapea* 38.3; compare
15.5, 23.2, 35, 44). Something like this sort of thing may be going on early in
the *Wake*: "cargo of prohibitive pomefructs" (*poma* is Latin for apple or for
fruit in general; the Romans also used *fructus* for the latter word). The con-
traband delivery is apprehended by "Paddy Wippingham" who "cotched the
creeps of them pricker than our whosethere outofman" (*FW* 19.15–17; compare *FW* 52.9–10 for another combination of a "garden" and "whipping").
Much later, the following parenthesis pops up as the Tailor speaks to the Norwegian Captain, "(buthock lad, fur whale)" (*FW* 311.33). I direct the reader's
attention to a key word in those phrases: *fur*, which is Latin for thief. That
short noun is shot throughout the *Priapea*, especially when the watchman-
god grabs, then wales the buttocks of thieving apple pickers with his big wooden
harpoon.

Priapus boasts that he wields *et falx lignea ligneusque penis* (both a wooden sickle and a penis of wood) (*Priapea* 6.2), and that his apparently "useless stick of wood" (*inutile lignum* [*Priapea* 73.3]) is ready for instant action. This ancient Roman wooden weapon may be connected, in Joyce's imagination, with another, and distinctly beneficial, wooden instrument found in an entirely different religious environment. In *Finnegans Wake* HCE runs into trouble in the park with an "uncertain weapon of *lignum vitae*" (*FW* 84.5). The primary allusion here is to the arboreal instrument of the fall of the human race in the Old Testament. The *lignum vitae* and the *lignum scientiae boni et mali* (the tree of life and the tree of the knowledge of good and evil) grew in the middle of the Garden of Eden (Genesis 2:9). Adam and Eve were forbidden to eat the fruit of the latter tree. Christian legend reports that Christ's cross, the New Testament instrument of redemption from the Fall, was built out of the wood from this once paradisical tree. At any rate, Joyce was well aware of the intertestamental metaphor of the "wood of life," most especially in its manifestation in the Good Friday ceremony at which the cross was venerated. During this Roman Catholic ritual a Latin hymn was sung: *Crux fidelis, inter omnes arbor una nobilis . . . / dulce lignum* (Loyal cross, the one noble tree among all the others . . . sweet wood).[25]

My suggestion of the possible parquetry of the sacred wood of the Christian cross and the priapic wood of a pagan statue may seem far removed from the textual evidence in *Finnegans Wake*. Not necessarily so. In the Garden of Eden, the fruit of a tree caused Adam's fall; atonement for that offense took place on the wood of the cross; the abiding force of this redemption is perpetuated in the ritual words and actions of the church. In the Roman gardens over which Priapus stood guard, the theft of fruit merited swift punishment; those who abused the tree underwent stiff humiliation from a wooden rod; the *Priapea* are the Latin poems that memorialize that inflexible fact of arboreal crime and punishment. In composing his cosmic tale of the fall and rise of HCE, Joyce incorporated aspects of these two mythoritualistic systems; and the *Wake*'s various threatening poles, columns, shafts, and so on are manifestations of that conflated vision. To support that suggestion, I point once again to the presence of an "uncertain weapon of *lignum vitae*" (*FW* 84.5) at the scene of HCE's primeval crime. (A mythological reason for the description of this weapon as "uncertain" could be its lack of discrimination in selecting an object of attack. Just as is the case with Priapus' ramrod, HCE's tool is not gender-specific.) The claim for Joyce's creative grafting of sacred and/or profane woods is based on his awareness of parallel terms and customs. Joyce certainly knew about the function of Roman priapic statues and that there was a collection of Priapean verse; he might well have incorporated congenial phrases from it into the burgeoning *Wake*. But, thus far, my argument for influence has not been bolstered by textual or archival evidence (one early and secondhand reference to "priapea" aside) for direct citation of the Latin poems themselves. At this point in the process, then, it is necessary to present some evidence from the *Wake* itself for a tentative claim for specific quotation.

The first exhibit involves an exotic—or sacrilegious—combination of three texts, from the *Wake*, the *Priapea*, and the Gospels:

1. —*Tris tris a ni ma mea!* Prisoner of Love!
   Bleating Hart! Lowlaid Herd! Aubain Hand! Wonted
   Foot! *Usque! Usque! Usque! Lingnum in . . .* (*FW* 499.30–32; ellipsis and emphases are Joyce's; also see *FW* 301.15–16)
2. Tristis est anima mea usque ad mortem. (Matthew 26:38; Mark 14:34; compare Psalm 41:6)
   (My soul is saddened all the way to death.)
3. ergo qui prius usque et usque et usque
   furum scindere podices solebam. (*Priapea* 77.8–9)
   (therefore I who once was accustomed to splitting—all the way up, all the way up, all the way up—the bottoms of thieves.)

There is a lot going on in the primary passage from the *Wake*. The fall of HCE is being recreated in, by, and through language that refers to the passion and death of Christ. The chopped syllables of the initial gospel phrase in Latin— with a deliberate misquotation of the second syllable of *tristis* and the elimination of *est*—and its continuation in the repetition of *usque* suggest the syncopation of some sort of musical-vocal presentation. The passion chapters from Matthew's gospel were chanted on Palm Sunday; the similar (but briefer) section from the gospel of Mark is assigned to be sung in the liturgy on Tuesday of Holy Week. In the Palm Sunday ceremony, the gospel was traditionally chanted by three deacons; the change of roles and voices was designed to make the "parts" (Christ, Pilate, the crowd) as dramatic as possible. But this type of liturgical chant was *not* a polyphonic production, with repetition and/or musical elaboration of phrases.

There was, however, another opportunity on which Joyce, certainly and frequently, heard a similar verse in a similar setting. In the "Gradual" (the short prayer intoned by the priest and the choir before the reading of the gospel) for Holy (Maundy) Thursday, a verse from the Epistle to the Philippians was chanted: *Christus factus est pro nobis obediens* usque ad mortem, *mortem autem crucis* (on our behalf Christ became obedient *all the way to death,* death that is on the cross) (Phil. 2:8; my emphasis).[26] This prayer *was* cantilated, with frequent repetition of the words for melodic musical effect. I suggest that the Gradual for the Holy Thursday Mass is relevant here, because the primary *Wake* passage contains another, incomplete Latin phrase: "*Lignum in . . .*" (*FW* 499.32; ellipsis and emphasis are Joyce's). The Latin noun *lignum* (wood) does not occur in Matthew's gospel or in Philippians; but that word was a prominent and repeated part of a memorable Good Friday liturgical ceremony, the solemn Veneration of Holy Cross. I quote from a 1925 missal:

> [The priest] uncovers, before all the people, first, the head of the crucifix, next the right arm, and lastly the entire cross. While doing so, he advances . . . ever uplifting higher the cross, and *thrice* (my emphasis here) chanting, each time on a higher note: *Ecce lignum crucis in quo salus mundi pependit* (Behold the wood of the cross on which the salvation of the world hung).[27]

That chant accounts for the "*lignum*" and the elliptical preposition "*in*" with which the *Wake* passage terminates. It was the repetition of "*usque*" in the chanted Gradual, I suggest, that reminded Joyce of the triple repetition of "*lignum*"—and the presence of "*in*"—in the similar Good Friday chant. All of these sung texts were memorable parts of Joyce's favorite rituals, those of Holy Week.[28] This series of liturigical ceremonies concludes with the grand awakening on Easter Sunday.

Why interject a line from an obscene pagan poem into this neat little Christian package? Because *Priapea* 77.8 is the only place in all Roman literature where there are three *usques* lined up in a row. I am willing to wager that *Finnegans Wake* 499.31–32 is the only place in all English literature with the same triple Latin adverb. And the Gradual for Holy Thursday is the only section of the Roman Catholic liturgy to feature repeated *usques*, there to emphasize the extent of Christ's obedience. Being suspicious of coincidence in such Wakean matters, I accept the high probability that a line from the *Priapea* has been evoked here as a far-fetched, studied counterpoint to the two solemn Christian texts.

Now for something which, while slightly less grotesque, is equally convoluted. In the initial poem in the Priapean collection, the reader is warned to lay aside prudery and "drop the raised eyebrow" (*pone supercilium* [*Priapea* 1.2]). The titular god indicates that he is about to unfurl his outsized *ruber hortorum custos . . . inguen* (ruddy prong, the guardian of the gardens) (*Priapea* 1.5–6). At the start of the "Mime," HCE "luked upon the bloomingrund" (*FW* 223.31); only eight lines later "he was an injine ruber" (*FW* 224.3). The presence of "goodda purssia" (gutta percha) (*FW* 224.2) confirms the Asian raw material for a western American "India-rubber" in these two words. There is definite archival evidence for Joyce's source of that last term: a 1923 popular biography of P. T. Barnum.[29] That genetic inspiration, however, hardly stands in the way of a shaping contribution from another source, especially if the second influence also reinforces the use of the Latin adjective *ruber* for "red" Indian. If Joyce scanned the texts of the *Priapea*, he could hardly keep from noticing this programmatic poem and its admonitory *ruber . . . inguen*. The noun *inguen* is one of the standard terms for the *membrum virile*; the adjective *ruber* is an indication of its agitated state. If one accepts this sort of multiple causality—and numerous other examples in the *Wake* make it impossible to reject the temptation to do so *a priori*—then the *Priapea* supply a reason for HCE to be looking and lurking over the "bloomingrund." That is, the Latin poem explicitly identifies him and his ruddy prong as "the guardian of the gardens" (*hortorum custos*).

The final exhibit in this discussion of an influence of the *Priapea* on Joyce's work pivots around a pair of Notebook entries: "ʳirruminatio" and "ʳmolimen" (VI.B.31.33). The Latin noun *ruminatio* means "chewing the cud"; *molimen* means "great exertion," or "maximum effort." Neither of these two terms (both of which are open to metaphorical extension into "pondering," "deep intellectual consideration") would seem to have any connection with matters priapic. On the other hand, scattered throughout the *Priapea* and the poems of Catullus is a word that sounds quite similar to the first entry; moreover it begins with the same prefix as the word in Joyce's note, *irrumatio*. This term (and its verbal form *irrumo, irrumare*) is always found in obscene, usually threatening contexts; it means "ramming a penis into someone's mouth." This is exactly the force of Catullus' promise of retaliation to an enemy: *nam insidias mihi instruentem / tangam te prior irrumatione* (if you set up ambushes for me, I'll slap you in the teeth beforehand—with my ramrod) (21.7–8).

The second Notebook entry cited above, *molimen*, is derived from the Latin verb *molior, moliri* (to exert effort, to work to accomplish). Another verb, which sounds somewhat similar, is *molo, molere* (to grind); it is frequently found in sexual situations, usually involving adulterous intercourse. When Joyce inserted "molimem" into the *Wake*, he slightly altered its spelling to "moliman" (*FW* 240.27). Maybe the change in form is meant to imply that the grinding is homosexual. The implication is bolstered by the fact that the Latin adjective *mollis* (soft, effeminate) is often used in sexual invective.[30] There is, however, nothing in the Wakean context of the two crossed words which indicates that either of them is sexually (homo- or hetero-) marked. In the final text of the *Wake*, "irruminatio" has been converted into the verb in a highly Latinate, partly liturgical, partly physical passage: "the tantum ergons *irruminate* the quantum urge" (*FW* 167.6–7; my emphasis). "Moliman" is found in a passage in which there are several terms from Melanesian pidgin—and a pseudo-Homeric epithet, "Anaks Andrum" (King of Warriors) (*FW* 240.27). What then is the connection between these Notebook entries and the *Priapea*?

A short poem in that collection presents the phallic god announcing a scale of penalties for anyone who dares to steal the fruit he guards:

> For the first offense, you'll be buggered;
> If you're caught twice, I'll ram it in your mouth.
> For your third attempt, double jeopardy:
> Back and front, down and up, in and out. (*Priapea* 35.1–5)

The lexical link betwen that nasty bit of Roman verse braggadocio and *Finnegans Wake* is the pair of Latin verbs that ends adjacent lines in the original text of the poem: *irrumabo* (I shall ram) and *molieris* (you will endeavor). As my analysis has tried to indicate, neither of the two Notebook entries ("irruminatio" and "molimen") is *per se* sexual, much less obscene. In a Priapic and Joycean context, however, both are definitely capable of being so manipulated. Numerous parallel examples of a similar sort, especially when Latin roots come into play, lead me to the conclusion that these exotic and similar word pairs and their Notebook juxtaposition are not a case of etymological coincidence.

PETRONIUS

Petronius' *Satyricon*, a long Menippean (occasional verse passages inserted in the prose) satire, would appear to be an obvious model for parts of *Ulysses* and all of *Finnegans Wake*. This first-century A.D. work is raunchy, irreverent, colloquial, hilarious—a picaresque *Odyssey* in Latin. Its fragmented plot involves the adventures in and around southern Italy of several on-the-road youths. They escape the clutches of Quartilla (a Bella-type madam), attend a dinner party staged by Trimalchio (a fabulously rich ex-slave), sail on the yacht of Lichas, mount a legacy-hunting scam that involves cannibalism, and so on. One of the heroes is persecuted by Priapus, who causes him to become impotent just as he meets the ravishing Circe. There is an attack on "modern" Roman education, in which rhetoric has become the media of MBA's in togas; the conventions of epic poetry are parodied in a *Capture of Troy* and a *Civil War*.

The famous "Tale of the Ephesian Woman" (*Satyricon* 111–12) is alluded to in "Oxen of the Sun" (*U* 14.886). At the brothel in "Circe," Boylan informs Bloom that "You can apply your eye to the keyhole and play with yourself while I just go through her a few times" (*U* 15.3788–89). In the *Satyricon*,

Quartilla cuts a slit in a door panel so she and the two heroes can peek "with lecherous curiosity" at the sex play of their youngest companion and his Lolita-like bedmate (*Satyricon* 26). Since this type of voyeurism is a commonplace in pornography, I do not claim the one passage was a model for the other. There is, however, another pair of episodes in which the parallel details are too similar—and too bizarre—to be written off as an instance of two zany imaginations coming up with the same outlandish details.

At Trimalchio's banquet in the *Satyricon,* one of the guests entertains the party with a ghost story. Two comrades on a trip come to a cemetery (*venimus inter monimenta*); one man heads off toward some gravestones to do his business (*homo meus coepit ad stelas facere*). When his buddy looks around, he sees a pile of clothes next to the road and the other man pissing in a circle around them (*at ille circumminxit vestimenta sua*). Then he suddenly becomes a wolf (*et subito lupus factus est*); he howls and runs off into the woods. The pile of clothes turned into rocks (*lapidea facta sunt*). The friend rushes to his girlfriend's house, where he is told that a wolf has just attached the farm—but a slave pierced his neck with a spear. Terrified, the second man rushes back to the pile of his friend's clothes. There is nothing there but blood. Meanwhile, back at home the comrade is lying in bed while a doctor tends to his neck wound. The narrator concludes: *intellexi illum versipellem esse* (I understood that he was a werewolf) (*Satyricon* 61–62).

In *Finnegans Wake* there are three primary passages in which there can be found the same curious collocation of burial places, wolfmen, and pissing:

> Ni, he make peace in his preaches and play with esteem. Werewolf! Olff! Toboo! So olff for his topheetuck the ruck maid raid, aslick aslegs would run. (*FW* 225.6–10)

> when the wildworewolf's abroad. . . . drr, deff, coal lay on and pzz, call us pyrress! . . . Isegrim under tolling ears. Far wol! . . . The trail of Gill not yet is to be seen, rockdrops. (*FW* 244.10–26)

> He'll umboozle no more graves nor horne nor haunder, lou garou, for gayl geselles in dead man's hills. (*FW* 352.30–32)

A few basic annotations (with the help of McHugh) are necessary: "Ni" is Chinese for "to urinate"; "topheet-" is probably meant to refer to *tophet*, the Semitic term for a Phoenician-Carthaginian place of sacrifice and ritual burial; the rocks cast by Deucalion and Pyrrha became people; "Isegrim" is an allusion to Isengrim, the wolf in the Reynard the Fox tales; "Gill" attacks HCE and lets stones fall out of his pocket to mark the road; "loup garou" is French for "werewolf"; "Kayl" is Armenian for "wolf"; "Geselle" is German for "comrade." These details seem to me to establish, beyond any doubt, that Joyce carefully designed a graveyard-rockspissing-werewolf scene to be part of the weird adventures in the *Wake*. The classical source of these improbable elements is the ghost story in Petronius' *Satyricon*. That work, like the *Priapea* with which it was frequently published in a single volume, was another x-rated ancient work. Thus, though the text was certainly never assigned in one of his Latin classes, there were other opportunities—in Trieste, Zürich, and Paris—for Joyce to read and remember this episode.

MARTIAL

Selections from the first four books of Martial's *Epigrams* were on the Latin examination syllabus for Joyce's second year at University College. The witty and often ribald verses of this first-century A.D. Roman poet, however, seem to have had relatively little impact on Joyce's work. In a previous chapter on Gogarty/Mulligan as a *grammaticus gloriosus,* I discussed the thematic contribution of an epigram by Martial on the preference for eunuchs as lovers by Roman matrons. Those droll two lines also left minor traces in the *Ulysses'* notesheets, "Oxen of the Sun," and *Scribbledehobble* (see pages 36–37 and notes 26 and 27 on page 258).

In *Finnegans Wake* there is only a single detectable echo from Martial—and it is a familiar phrase that might have been remembered from an occasional essay or the grandiose "address" of someone's Dublin residence: *rus in urbe* (country in the city) (*Epigrams* 12.57.21). That hybrid venue works its compounded way into the Cad's report of HCE's crime: "the tale of the evangelical bussybozzy and the *rusinurbean*" (*FW* 40.7–8; my emphasis). Variations on the phrase reappear in "Grander Suburbia . . . ruric or cospolite" (*FW* 309.9–10) and "suburbiaurealis in his rure" (*FW* 332.34).

The last two books of Martial's *Epigrams* are composed of a series of two-line verses that "describe" (sometimes in riddle form, often involving puns or odd associations) things that could be served to guests at a banquet or given to them as mementos of the occasion. The technical terms for this type of distich are taken from the Greek: *Xenia* (hospitality treats) and *Apophorēta* (take-home favors). The following is an example of the first category, the topic of Martial's Book 13:

Capones
Ne nimis exhausto macresceret inguine gallus
    amisit testes. nunc mihi Gallus erit. (*Epigrams* 13.63)

(*Capons*
That rooster lost his balls so that he wouldn't shrivel up from a played-out cock. Now the capon will be my [dinner's] priest-eunuch.)

The wordplay here pivots on the lexical fact that *G/gallus* has three meanings in Latin: a man from Gaul, a castrated devotee of Cybele (see pages 191–92), and a rooster. The rooster in the epigram, then, has been forcibly converted into a plumper, tastier, and liturgically corrected capon for the banquet guests' delight.

A second distich illustrates Martial's crisp technique in describing a luxury party favor, an *Apophorēton* from book 14:

Loculi Eborei
Hos nisi de flava loculos implere moneta
    non decet: argentum vilia ligna ferant. (*Epigrams* 14.12)

(*Ivory Money-boxes*
It is not proper to fill these money-boxes with anything but golden coins: let cheap wood hold the silver ones.)

There are parallels to these party practices in the works of Joyce. In the *Wake*, ALP appears "with a Christmas box apiece for aisch and iveryone of her childer" (*FW* 209.27–28). The list of holiday gifts extends over two pages (*FW* 210.6–212.19). Each present, whether edible or treasurable, is assigned to an appropriately named girl or boy. Since this catalogue is situated in the midst of a chapter dedicated to Anna Livia Plurabelle, a cascade of rivers also runs through it. All of these factors are typical Wakean ways and means of muddying the narrative water. The primary complication, however, is the fact that the description of each of the gifts is couched in the same "riddlilng" form used by Martial in the epigrams quoted above. The first present, for example is "A tinker's bann and a barrow to boil his billy for Gipsy Lee" (*FW* 210.6–7). As McHugh indicates there are three rivers here (Bann, Borrow, Lee); and George Borrow wrote several books about Gypsies, including the highly popular novel *Romany Rye*. Gypsies often earned money as tinkers. In Australian slang, a "billy" is a kettle used for boiling tea water by vagabonds in the outback. Lee is a common surname among Gypsies. Finally, there was a famous American ecdysiast, Gypsy Rose Lee. In fact, I suggest that her (missing) middle name reveals what this gift is: a rose. If so, then this significant omission also supplies the surname of Billy Rose, the entertainment impresario who created many stars like Miss Lee.

Another appropriate gift is the "scruboak beads for beatified Biddy" (*FW* 210.29). According to a standard compendium of saints' lives, Bridget (or Bride), the patroness of Ireland, fled from an arranged marriage into "a grove of oaks once sacred to idol-worship. . . . [Here] she formed the convent of Kildare (or 'place of the oak')."[31] Thus, the saint's namesake receives either some rustic jewelry or a set of rosary beads made from wood specifically dedicated to her patron. The list concludes with two generic gifts for "ilcka madre's daughter a moonflower and a blookvein" (*FW* 212.15–16): the girls begin to menstruate. Their brothers receive "the grapes that ripe before reason" (*FW* 212.16–17): the boys reach puberty.

The epigrams of Martial are not, of course, the only possible model for Joyce's use of this "riddle-label" to link gifts to appropriate recipients. The same type of *xenia* puns are found in Petronius' report of the zodiacal hors d'oeuvres served at Trimalchio's banquet (*Satyricon* 35) and the nabob's guests take home ingeniously described *apophorēta* (*Satyricon* 56). A similar technique is used in an anonymous medieval catalogue of Old and New Testament characters, each of whom brings an appropriate offering (for example, Eve an apple, Isaac a ram, Peter a crowing cock) for Cyprian's banquet.[32]

A more modern parallel to this hospitality custom is a "Christmas cracker," which is part of the yuletide festivities for English and Irish children. These "crackers" are hollow paper cases enclosing a low-power firecracker or some device that "explodes" when a tab is pulled. Inside each of the colorfully decorated cases is a small gift (such as a paper hat) or a strip of paper inscribed with a cryptic promise. These "mottoes" were composed following the same techniques first found in ancient Greek and Latin epigrams. Joyce was aware of this custom. In *Portrait* Stephen remembers a party and the "children, wearing the spoils of their crackers" (*P* 68). In "Circe" Bloom and Mrs. Breen flirt and reminisce about Christmases past: "After the parlour mystery games and the crackers from the tree we sat on the staircase ottoman. Under the mistletoe" (*U* 15.461–63). There is, in fact, eye-witness testimony that Joyce himself practiced this custom. Lucie Noel, Paul Léon's wife, reports that "Joyce's gifts were often in the nature of a pun." For example, he once sent Léon ("Lion" in French) a large porcelain lion, and a blue and white striped necktie to match the book jacket of the first edition of *Ulysses* and the national colors of Greece.[33]

The long catalogue of ALP's gifts to her offspring is not the only place in the *Wake* in which analogous riddle techniques are used. The three pages of titles proposed for the "Mamafesta" of "Annah the Allmaziful" (*FW* 104.1–107.7) are full of cryptic allusions to literature and history. In the essay topics section of "Night Lessons" the marginal names of fifty-six classical and biblical figures are keyed to adjacent themes (*FW* 306.15–308.1). "Prometheus" the fire-giver, for example, is classical mythology's prime benefactor of the human race. His name suggests an essay on "Santa Claus" (*FW* 307.L and 16).

In short, the epigrammatic concision of Martial's verse is generically far removed from the scope of Joyce's later works. Except for the "Roman-matrons-and-eunuch" entry in the Notesheets and *Scribbledehobble*, there is no firm evidence of direct allusion to the poet. The extraordinarily cryptic form of the list of the children's presents in the "Anna Liffey" section of the *Wake* may owe something to techniques used by Martial in composing couplets to accompany poetic gifts in the last two books of his *Epigrams*. Even if there is no direct influence here, the repeated use of the form in the *Wake* is significant enough to have merited an extended discussion.

PLAUTUS AND ROMAN COMEDY

There appears to be only one possible allusion—and it is muted—to Plautus in *Ulysses*. About halfway through "Oxen of the Sun," one of the "medicals" adopts the prose style of the eighteenth-century satirist Junius to comment on the double standard of male promiscuity: "It ill becomes him to preach that gospel. Has he not nearer home a seedfield that lies fallow for the want of the ploughshare?" (*U* 14.928–30). Emphatically to reinforce the earthiness of the metaphor Joyce assigns, a bit later in "Circe," the following stage direction and dialogue to Leopold Bloom: "*(his eyes wildly dialated, clasps himself)* Show! Hide! Show! Plough her! More! Shoot!" (*U* 15.3815–16).

The same sort of agrosexual metaphor appears in Roman comedy, "couched in terms as straightforward as they are bucolic" (*U* 14.927–28). A husband's conjugal neglect and infidelity are indicted in one of Plautus' plays: *fundum alienum arat, incultum familiarem deserit* (he plows another's bottom land, and leaves his own personal field uncultivated) (*Asinaria* 874).[34]

Despite the lack of direct citation, there can be no doubt that Joyce was familiar with the general structure and stock roles of Roman comedy. In *Ulysses* there is an unspecified reference to Terence's *Autontimorumenos* (The Self-tormentor) (*U* 9.939), but the "Mime" chapter of the *Wake* clearly displays an awareness of the genre on its first page. The production's characters are introduced: The ingénue—*virgo* (Issy), the wife—*matrona* (ALP), two types of young bucks—*adulescentes* (Chuff and Gluff), the old goat—*amator senex* (HCE), and the typical servants—*servus servaque* (Saunderson and Kate) (*FW* 219–21). The "benediction of the Holy Genesius Archimimus" (*FW* 219.8–9) is invoked: he is an actual Roman comic actor who was martyred for refusing to perform a burlesque of Christian baptism on stage. There is an allusion to Terence's "Adelphi [*The Brothers*] by the Brothers Bratislavoff" (*FW* 219.14).

Finally, as the chapter winds to a close, the standard appeal by a Roman actor for applause is heard three times: "Upploud!" (*FW* 257.30), "Uplouderamain!" (*FW* 257.33), "Uplouderamainagain!" (*FW* 258.19). Just after the first call for audience approval, we learn that "The play . . . , Game, here endeth" (*FW* 257.31). The Latin word for both "play" and "game" is *ludus,* which is also one of the standard terms for a Roman comedy and the civic festivals at which the plays were presented. The troupe of actors in this type of popular drama is called the *grex* ("herd"; compare "the Grex's molten mutton" [*FW* 170.34]).

There is considerably more textual evidence to support the claim that HCE is sometimes cast in the role of a rutting billy goat in the *Wake.* The clearest statement is also the most comprehensive: he's "a big rody ram lad at random" (*FW* 28.36). Two acrostic phrases reinforce the point: "*Hircus Civis Eblanensis!*" (*FW* 215.27) and "Erin's hircohaired culoteer" (*FW* 275.1–2). The first HCE reference just cited is Latin for "The Goat Citizen of Dublin"; the second is geographically more expansive and combines the noun *hircus* (buck goat) with an English indication of his hairiness. Indeed, in Anna Livia's final reverie HCE is evoked in a pair of scrambled acrostics: "ever complete hairy of chest, hamps and eyebags" (*FW* 616.14). The Latin adjective for "hairy" is *pilosus,* the goatish presence of which can be detected in "Hirculos pillar" (*FW* 16.4) and "pilluls of hirculeads" (*FW* 128.36).

If one grants that HCE is hirsute, there is still reason to inquire "*Quare hircum?*" (Why a goat?) (*FW* 89.27). I believe that Joyce purposely framed that question in Latin to convey a hint to the initiated reader that HCE is not merely hairy; he is also (in contemporary idiom) horny. In the literature of the ancient Romans, especially in comedy and verse invective, goats are notoriously lecherous animals, so much so that the mere thought of sexual contact with a randy buck should disgust any right-thinking Roman woman.[35]

Plautus' comedy *Mercator* (The Merchant Mariner) is a handy source of information about this attitude. The plot involves a son who has returned from a trading trip with a young woman whom he purchased for his pleasure in Rhodes. The merchant's sexagenarian father sees the girl and is sexually rejuvenated. His next-door neighbor reacts with scorn: *anima foetida, senex hircosus / tu osculere mulierem?* (Will an old goat like you kiss the girl with your foul breath?) (lines 574–75). Earlier in the play the same neighbor gives one of his slaves some instructions about the farm: *profecto ego illunc hircum castrari volo* (I want that hegoat castrated immediately) (line 272). The lusty father, who overhears this line, correctly interprets it as a most unfavorable omen. As a matter of fact, the neighbor compounds that inauspicious sign; just prior to calling the father on old goat, he mockingly addresses him as *vervex* (wether, castrated sheep) (line 567). Joyce displays a verbalized form of this word in "berbecked" (*FW* 64.31). Phonetically the "v/b" shift is as typical in Latin as it is in Joyce's Wakean language; morphologically, the ersatz perfect passive participle form is a clue that the word is meant to be translated as "castrated."

In his life of Tiberius, Suetonius reports that a noble Roman matron committed suicide after she had been forced to cater to the Emperor's lusts. She curses him as *hirsuto atque olido seni* (a hairy, stinking old geezer) (*Tiberius* 45). The Emperor's sexual tastes are also mocked in a gross line from farce produced soon after the scandal: *hircum vetulum capreis naturam ligurire* (The old goat goes for the does with his tongue) (*Tiberius* 45). Joyce was well versed in the rich vocabulary of Latin obscenity and scatology; and there are other allusions to Plautus and Suetonius in his work. Hence, I suggest that Joyce was drawing a specific and sharp parallel between the sexual rivalry of HCE and Glugg-Shem by referring to the randy father in terms of a stock character in Roman comedy, the *senex libidinosus* (the raunchy gaffer), who in the language of ludic abuse is frequently and typically labeled a hairy old goat.

In the light of its slightly risqué plot (a father and son as rivals for the love of a fairly compliant young woman), it is not likely that Joyce read Plautus' *Mercator* at Belvedere College. Indeed, no Roman comedy was assigned on the examination syllabi during Joyce's time at the school or during his three years at University College. The "*senex hircosus*/old goat" trope was, however, a staple of Roman comedy and invective; indeed, Joyce might have run across the term in a history of Latin literature or in a dictionary. Nevertheless, there is one verbal parallel that causes me seriously to speculate that Joyce *did* actually have the original text of the *Mercator* in hand when he wrote the following Latinate description of HCE: "to live all safeathomely the pre*senile* days of his life of opulence, *ancient* ere *decrepitude* . . . till stuffering stage" (*FW* 78.1–3; my emphases). In Plautus' play when the Old Father asks his neighbor what image he projects, the friend replies frankly: *Acherunticus / senex vetus, decrepitus* (Bound for the pains of hell, [you are] an ancient, decrepit, old dotard) (lines 290–91). The close conjunction of the key words in both brief passages argues against—but does not firmly negate—pure coincidence. There is more. In *Scribbledehobble* (74 [251]), the entry "Stinking goat M.L." appears. Who (or what) is "M.L."? I can find no candidates in part V of *A Portrait of the Artist as a Young Man* to which these notes supposedly correspond. Could the "M.L." be an abbreviation for "Mercator Lysymachus"? Lysymachus is the sarcastic neighbor in Plautus' play, the one who repeatedly calls the amorous father a decrepit, foul-breathed, goatlike old geezer.

To complete this discussion of HCE's goatish behavior, I include two references to the Emperor Tiberius that appear in passages quite close to each other:

And, speaking anent Tiberias and other incestuish salacities among gerontophils. (*FW* 115.11–12)

The unmistaken identity of the persons in the Tiberiast duplex came to light in the most devious of ways. (*FW* 123.30–31)

The imputation of incest is obvious; "salacities" has its roots in the Latin *salax* (from *salire* "to leap"), an adjective usually applied to lecherous animals, as in Ovid's *salax aries* (a randy ram) (*Fasti* 4.771). The compound "gerontophils" here does not mean a "lover of old people"; it is the Greek equivalent of the *amator senex*, the *senex libidinosus,* the "horny old gaffer" of Roman comedy. All of these qualities are consistent with the picture of the unbridled, kinky, and geriatric lust that Suetonius paints in his life of Tiberius. The Emperor's bisexuality (to some "a devious way" of doing things) is suggested by "duplex" and reinforced by "bisexycle" (*FW* 115.16). Tiberius' pleasure palace was on the Isle of Capri (Goat Island), where Suetonius reports:

He devised little nooks of lechery in the woods and glades, and had boys and girls dressed up as Pans. . . . The island was openly called "Caprineum" [the place of goatlike behavior]. (*Tiberius* 43)[36]

Again, these connections of vocabulary and theme strongly suggest an immediate link between the text of Suetonius and the *Wake.* There is one additional remark to be made about the career of the Emperor and its possible influence on Joyce's portrait of HCE. Suetonius reports that even as a young officer Tiberius Claudius Nero was such a heavy boozer that he became known by the nickname "Biberius Caldius Mero," which roughly means "Drinker of Undiluted Hot Wine" (*Tiberius* 42). Here a Notebook entry strongly suggests that Joyce knew about this ingenious pun: "Tiberius Biberius" (VI.C.7.204).

That completes the review of Plautine references in Joyce. The identification of HCE, an archetypical dirty old man, with the ludicrous *hircocus senex* of Latin comedy makes sound narrative sense, and is balanced by the darker side of the general Roman association that brings the sadistically decadent Emperor Tiberius on stage. Once these members of the cast have appeared, however briefly, in their initial scene, they (or equally qualified stand-ins) tend to pop up all over the script of the *Wake.*

Miscellaneous Writers

In the early first century b.c. Lucretius wrote a long philosophical poem, *De Rerum Natura* (On the Nature of the Universe). Its topics range from an atomic theory as an explanation of the composition of the world to an attack on the horrors performed in the name of "religion." In the discussion of the Roman gods, a passage from Lucretius' invocation to Venus was cited as a probable source for several odd terms in the *Wake* (see pages 80–81). There are two other certain allusions, both in "Night Lessons." In a footnote the poet is blended into a legendary violation of Lucretia: "And a ripping rude rape in his lucreasious togery" (*FW* 277.F2). Across from the marginal name "*Lucretius*" is a suggested essay topic: "The Uses and Abuses of Insects" (*FW* 306.L4 and 30). That association springs from a (possibly apocryphal) report in St. Jerome's *Chronicle* that Lucretius experienced "periods of insanity brought about by his use of a love-potion" (*amatorio poculo in furorem versus*) and that he later committed suicide (*propria se manu interfecit*).[37] Joyce extrapolates from the Latin love potion to the conventional "Spanish fly," and from it to the misuse of insects.

No less than seven Latin authors appear in a single omnibus sentence:

> While *Pliny the Younger* writes to *Pliny the Elder* his calamolumen of *contumellas*, what *Aulus Gellius* picked on *Micmacrobius* and what *Vitruvius* pocketed from *Cassiodorus*. (*FW* 255.18–21; my emphases; see VI.B.46.98 and Rose, *Index Manuscript*, 210–14)

Pliny the Younger is famous for his letters on many topics of current interest. For example, he reported to Tacitus the details of the death of his uncle, Pliny the Elder, during the eruption of Mount Vesuvius. The elder Pliny's best-known work is a comprehensive, thirty-seven book encyclopedia, *Natural History*. Atherton spots a quotation from that work in one of ALP's name riddles: "a drowned doll to face downwards" (*FW* 210.23–24).[38] He traces that piece of scientific trivia to Pliny's report that drowned men float face upwards, women face downwards (*N.H.* 7.17).

Columella composed a systematic treatise on all aspects of agriculture, *De Re Rustica* (note "rarerust" [*FW* 430.6]); he (and his rough contemporary Pliny the Elder) are memorialized in the *Wake* in the elegiac "Quinet" passage (*FW* 281.4–13) and its five variations.[39] Incidentally, the phrase "calamolumen of contumellas" (*FW* 255.19) involves several thinly disguised Latin words: *calamus* is a "reed" usually used as a pen; *lumen* means "light"; *calumnia* is "a slanderously false accusation" and *contumellia* is another legal term meaning "verbal abuse," "scornful insult." Thus, while indicating that a writer's pen can shed light, Joyce also draws technical attention to the fact that the spoken or written word can maliciously darken another's reputation.

In the mid-second century A.D. Aulus Gellius composed *Attic Nights*, in which he recalls and rehearses the interests of his student days in Athens. The chapters deal with history, literature, grammar, law, philosophy, and they are packed with hundreds of quotations from Greek and Latin writers. Joyce's "Micmacrobius" (*FW* 255.20) initially diminishes the name of Macrobius. He was the fifth century A.D. author of a commentary on Cicero's *Somnium Scipionis* (Scipio's Dream), a visionary piece that is naturally commemorated in the *Wake:* "some somnione sciupiones" (*FW* 293.7–8). His major work is the *Saturnalia*, a long and tedious holiday symposium on a wide range of topics, the central panel of which is an eccentric compendium of Vergilian criticism. Many of Macrobius' philological and "scientific" facts and bits of antiquarian data were cribbed from Aulus Gellius. Joyce reverses this process by making Gellius the subject and Macrobius the object of the verb "picked on" (*FW* 255.20).

Vitruvius (first century B.C.) is the author of *De Architectura*, the only treatise of its kind to survive from the ancient world. There seems to be no citation of this work, however, in the description of the marvels of construction by HCE.[40] The last name in the group is that of Cassiodorus, a Roman civic official, scholar, and, after a mid-career change of vocation, the founder of a most important early monastery in southern Italy. His writings include a summary of Roman (and world) history and the *Institutions*, a guide to every aspect of monastic life. Since Vitruvius lived six centuries *before* Cassiodorus and since the learned abbot had no interest whatsoever in engineering or architecture, it is hard to explain why Joyce wrote that the former "pocketed from" (*FW* 255.20) the latter.

In the sentence that immediately follows the passage just discussed there is perhaps an eighth allusion to a Roman author. Among other things, "Buke of Lukan" (*FW* 255.21) may be meant to conjure up the epic poet Lucan. His *Pharsalia* is about the civil war between Caesar and Pompey; Joyce distorts this title into "Parsuralia" (*FW* 353.24) in a paragraph that resounds with Latin vocabulary (see pages 124–25). Another minor poet of Roman epic, Silius Italicus (first century A.D.), is commemorated in "numerose Italicuss" (*FW* 407.17). The Latin adjective *numerosus* (prolific, rhythmical) is more properly a comment on the length of his major work (the 12,200-line *Punica*) than on its negligible poetic qualities.

"Ausonius Audacior" (*FW* 267.6) looks like a Latin name. An obvious candidate is Ausonius, a fourth-century A.D. Gallo-Roman teacher and poet from

Bordeaux. Why he should be called "the Bolder" (*Audacior*) is unclear, unless there is a covert allusion to his outrageously obscene epigram mentioned above in a note to an earlier topic in this chapter. On the other hand, as the next line in the *Wake* indicates, he was a "gall" (*FW* 267.7), whose "holy presumption" is cited in a footnote (*FW* 267.F3). There may be another evocation in "Ausone sidulcis" (*FW* 209.35); there the second element would refer not to Ausonius' audacity, but to the "sweet" (*dulcis*) flow of his verses. Two pages before the preceding citation is the exclamation "I mosel hear that!" (*FW* 207.23). Since the context is the Anna Livia Plurabelle chapter with its spate of rivers, an allusion to the Moselle causes no surprise. At the same time, Ausonius' most important poem is the 483-line *Mosella*, in praise of the river and its environment.

The words "*Coactus volui*" (Having been forced, I was willing) are put into the mouths of two unstable characters in *Ulysses*. Cashel Boyle O'Connor Fitzmaurice Tisdall Farrell mutters them in "Wandering Rocks" (*U* 10.1113); later Virag Lipoti repeats them in "Circe" (*U* 15.2553). This legal formula comes from the Emperor Justinian's *Digest* 4.2.21.5. In this sixth-century A.D. compendium of Roman law, the effect of fear on the validity of a contractual action is under discussion. An opinion is cited:

> Si metu coactus adii hereditatem, puto me heredem effici, quia quamvis si liberum esset noluissem, tamen *coactus volui* (my emphasis).

> (If I have been forced by fear to accept a legacy, I judge that I am made a legatee, because although I would not have been willing had it been freely offered, nevertheless, having been forced, I was willing.)

Roman Law was (and is) a standard subject in the curriculum of English and Irish universities; but Joyce never enrolled in such a course, and it is highly unlikely that this quite technical passage would have been assigned reading in other subjects. How then could these Latin words have entered Joyce's vocabulary? I suggest that sometime during his education, from his readings, or in a conversation with a solicitor, Joyce came across this legal formula adduced to lend quasi-antique support to an argument. Until very recently, Jesuit professors punctuated their lectures with authoritative phrases such as "*sub specie aeternitatis*" (under the aspect of eternity), "*ars est celare artem*" (art is to conceal the art), "*operatio sequitur esse*" (action follows essence). In my semi-cloistered youth, for example, I heard a stunning demonstration of the hallowed principle of the "double effect." An august Rector dispensed his guests from their Lenten fast by urging a free hand with the smoked Japanese oysters at a cocktail party, *"ne potus noceat"* (lest the drink cause harm). And lawyers, of course, have always been liberal in their professional invocation of Latin: *"separatio a mensa et a thalamo"* (separation from board and bed [*U* 9.716)], *"res ipsa loquitur,"* et al.[41]

Near the end of *Portrait* Stephen invokes the sympathetic patronage of Thomas Aquinas, not in his role as a philosopher of aesthetics, but a poet. Aquinas wrote *Pange lingua gloriosi,* which is said to be "the highest glory of the hymnal." Stephen disagrees with this judgment: "[T]here is no hymn that can be put beside that mournful and majestic processional song, the *Vexilla Regis* of Venantius Fortunatus" (*P* 210). Lynch picks up the cue and begins to sing a stanza of this hymn, which is quoted, in Latin, in the text.

Venatius Fortunatus was a sixth-century bishop of Poitiers, at the intersection of the Gallo-Roman and Frankish worlds. Stephen's high estimation of his hymns was seconded by the Church. During Joyce's lifetime, *Vexilla Regis* (The Battle Banners of the King) was sung immediately after the solemn veneration of the cross on Good Friday. It was, therefore, a memorable part of the same ceremony that was discussed earlier in this chapter in connection with the parodic use of *lignum crucis* (the wood of the cross).[42]

Another writer from Roman Gaul was Severus Sulpicius, a late-fourth-century ecclesiastical historian whose most important work was a *Life of St. Martin of Tours.* Although he was thoroughly familiar with a modern biography of the saint that is deeply in debt to that *vita,*[43] Joyce cited Sulpicius only as the author of *Historia Sacra* (also known as *Chronica*).[44] This work is an attempt to give a concise account of world history from the creation until his own day, A.D. 400. The *Wake* alludes to this project as follows:

> Clios clippings, which the chroncher of chivalries is sulpicious save he scan, for ancients link with presents as the human chain extends. (*FW* 254.7–9)

Saxo Grammaticus was a thirteenth-century Danish historian. His rough Latin prose is the ultimate source of information for the Hamlet legend, a fact that would certainly have been familiar to Joyce. He is invoked twice in the *Wake:* once as "By Saxon Chromaticus" (*FW* 304.18) where the "teacher" (*grammaticus*) has been renamed "the Colorful" (*chrōma* is Greek for "color"); and again as a grouchy "sexon grimmaticals" (*FW* 388.31). Another medieval Latin source for Shakespeare (perhaps with an oblique reference to Prince Hamlet) is cited in the same section of the text: "Cease, prayce, storywalkering around with *gestare romanoverum*" (*FW* 361.32–33; my emphasis). The *Gesta Romanorum* (Deeds of the Romans) is a prose anthology of tales, ancient and medieval, that was compiled in the early fourteenth century in England. It was immensely popular throughout all of Europe and served as the basis for exotic plots in many subsequent works.

There are, of course, other Latin writers whose works were known and used by Joyce. Almost without exception, however, the works were resolutely postclassical, thoroughly Christian in tone and topic. As such, Augustine, Jerome, Aquinas—to name the major figures—fall outside the scope of my study. There is, moreover, an excellent introduction to this important field of influence in Atherton's chapter "The Fathers [of the Church]" in his *Books at the Wake*.[45]

A great scholar of Christian hymnography argued that Venatius Fortunatus, cited above as the author of *Vexilla Regis*, should be regarded "not as the last of the Roman, but as the first of medieval poets."[46] That judgment and the cultural parameters it sets are a just and fitting place to conclude this long survey of Latin authors and their presence in the works of Joyce.

10

Joyce's Own Latin

In *Portrait* there are several brief sentences couched in grotesque schoolboy "dog Latin": "—*Credo ut vos sanguinarius mendax estis*" (I believe that you guys are a bloody liar [*sic*]) (*P* 195); "—*Nos ad manum ballum jocabimus*" (We'll play around at handball) (*P* 198). One of his comrades from the University College days recalls that Joyce and John Byrne ("Cranly") often carried on long conversations in this personal—and perverted—version of the language of the ancient Romans. Sheehy goes on to speculate that "these talks [may have been], on Joyce's part, the first intimation of the vocabulary of *Finnegans Wake.*"[1] The citations from *Portrait* and others like them in *Stephen Hero* (*SH* 106–15) are Joyce's earliest surviving fragments of original (however corrupt) Latin. The purpose of the chapter that follows is to identify and examine other significant examples.

The complex pseudo-Ciceronian passage in *Ulysses,* with its climactic result clause, has already been gone over in detail on pages 33–39. There are a few other Ulyssean Latin items that came from or were deliberately altered by Joyce's own pen; they are discussed below in the context of the recent heated controversies about the "correct" text. *Finnegans Wake* contains two fairly long Latin passages that were certainly composed by the author himself. Both appear in "writerly" contexts: the first (*FW* 185.14–26) describes how Shem concocted the ink that was used to inscribe the *Wake*'s central letter; the second (*FW* 287.20–28) is a "Night Lessons" academic display of Latin composition, the purpose of which is a fairly complex synopsis of Joyce's version of a Brunonian-Vichian theory of history.

Scattered throughout the *Wake* Notebooks there are a surprising number of words or phrases in Latin. Those instances that can be traced to a Roman *literary* text have been treated in the chapter in which the ancient author is discussed. Occasional references to Roman history or religion from the Notebooks are also found in the appropriate section above. There is, however, another type of Latin entry in the Notebooks. Presumably these words or phrases are Joyce's personal notes, composed and jotted down in that form, perhaps because the "dead" language most economically captured the gist of his pre-text inspiration or *aide-mémoire*. At the end of this chapter I discuss representative examples of this type of Joycean archival Latin. Some of these apparently original phrases have, in fact, made their devious way into the final text of *Finnegans Wake* and are thus more than just Notebook curiosities.

Since the specifically Latin material in the works of Joyce has rarely been analyzed in context, this chapter is primarily an explication of the grammatical shape and narrative purpose of the original passages. By *original* I mean those phrases that appear to be the product of Joyce's own competence in Latin—or the result of his significant and purposeful manipulation of a citation from a classical or medieval text. Sometimes, obviously, it is difficult to determine the genesis of individual phrases, or to distinguish the Joycean contamination from, say, a Horatian composition. In any ambivalent cases, my guideline has been the utility of explication. That is, if McHugh or O Hehir and Dillon explain the phrase and situate it in its Wakean context, then there is rarely a reason for repeating their insights.[2] On the other hand, where linguistic nuances seem to have been overlooked or narrative contributions missed, I have risked reexamining familiar passages. Those Latin elements that have already been treated in previous chapters are, of course, not reprised—and certainly not reparsed—here.

In the introduction I briefly mentioned the short-lived "canonization" of an early eighteenth-century translation of a popular song into Latin (page 9). Although "Balia" can no longer be attributed to Joyce's pen (he only copied it), in 1932 he did in fact translate a contemporary six-line poem into Latin—and French, German, Norwegian, and Italian. The modest work that Joyce chose to put through those linguistic paces is James Stephens's "Stephen's Green":

The wind stood up and gave a shout.
He whistled on his fingers and

Kicked the withered leaves about
And thumped the branches with his hand

And said he'd kill and kill and kill,
And so he will and so he will. (*Letters* I.317–19 and *JJII* 656–57 for all versions)

Joyce's Latin version and a literal translation follow:

> Jacobi Juncundi Viridiversificatio
> Surgit Boreas digitorum
> Fistulam, faciens et clamorem.
>
> Pes pugno certat par (oremus!)
> Foliis quatit omne nemus.
>
> Caedam, ait, caedam, caedam!
> *Non* ne habeat ille praedam.
>
> James the Joyous' Green-Poem
> The North Wind rises, making a pan-pipe
> of his fingers—and quite a racket.
>
> His foot, ready for a fight, joins the battle (let us pray!)
> He batters every grove with their leaves.
>
> I will kill, he says, kill, kill!
> [I fear] he will have nothing left for booty.

My translation of the last line explains the italics used on *Non*, which I have substituted for the editors' "Nos" (us). That pronoun makes no sense and distorts the original conclusion of Stephens's poem; moreover, without *Non* there would be no reason for Joyce's use of the subjunctive in "*habeat.*" Hence, I suggest that both editors of the Latin translation of this poem misread *Non* for *Nos.* My emendation preserves sense (the wind is utterly ruthless) and syntax (*Non ne* introduces an implied clause of fearing, which requires the subjunctive mood). I am surprised that Stuart Gilbert missed these considerations when he prepared Joyce's May 7, 1932, letter to Stephens for publication.

For a number of years the English Department at the University of Miami has sponsored a short, informal conference on the weekend nearest to Joyce's birthday. The third (1989) gathering was dedicated exclusively to the text of *Ulysses* and featured a face-to-face confrontation between Hans Walter Gabler and John Kidd. The proceedings of that conference do not record a modest, five-minute contribution to the topic, with a congenial Latin twist. That omission is rectified in the following three paragraphs.[3]

Near the end of "Oxen of the Sun" some of the "medicals" repair to a pub for more drink. They address the landlord: "Boniface! Absinthe the lot. *Nos omnes biberimus viridum toxicum, diabolus capiat posterioria nostria*" (*U* 14.1533–34). The dog Latin repeats the group's beverage order, and then some: "We all will drink the poisonous green, let the devil take our hindmosts." In the original 1922 edition of *Ulysses* the final two words were printed in the grammatically correct form, "*posteriora nostra.*" The alteration to the incorrect double "*-ia*" was made in the 1932 edition, presumably to emphasize the linguistic crudity of both the form and matter of the saying.[4]

At the beginning of "Circe," Stephen tells Lynch that they are going to visit "Georgina Johnson, *ad deam qui laetificat iuventutem meam*" (to the *goddess* who brings joy to my youth) (*U* 15.122). This is a sacrilegious perversion of the Vulgate Psalm 42.4, in which the petitioner approaches the altar of *God*, the Heavenly Father (see *U* 1.5), Joyce's change of divine gender from masculine (*deum*) to feminine (*deam*) is not reinforced, in any edition, by the syntactically necessary alteration of the following relative pronoun from "*qui*" (he who) to "*quae*" (she who). Perhaps Joyce scrupulously felt that a single manipulation of a "jot and tittle" of scriptural grammar was sufficient to make his point.

During the same chapter, Stephen displays his arcane knowledge of the musical settings for the Psalms. He cites the first verse of Psalm 18 (Vulgate): "*Coela enarrant gloriam Domini*" (The heavens declare the glory of the Lord) (*U* 15.2089). In all editions the text of *Ulysses* reads "*Domini*" (of the Lord) instead of the Vulgate's "*Dei*" (of God), an indication that the verse was probably quoted from memory. In the proofs for the 1922 edition, Joyce changed "*Coeli*" to "*Coela,*" the form that it has retained through all subsequent editions. Here Joyce's classical training contributed to an error in citation. Throughout the Vulgate the plural form of the Latin word for "sky," "heaven" is declined as a *masculine* noun (with the ending "*-i*"), whereas the classical form is almost always *neuter* (with the ending "*-a*").

The "Ink Passage"

So much for Latin *cruces* (literally "crosses" signaling problems) in the text of *Ulysses*. Next, the *Wake*'s initial extended passage of original Latin. In it, through the medium of decidedly monkish Latin, Shem describes the biochemical process followed in producing a pot of indelible ink:

Primum opifex, altus prosator, ad terram viviparam et cunctipotentem sine ullo pudore nec venia, suscepto pluviali atque discinctis perizomatis, natibus nudis uti nati fuissent, sese adpropinquans, flens et gemens, in manum suam evacuavit (highly prosy, crap in his hand, sorry!), *postea, animale nigro exoneratus, classicum pulsans, stercus proprium, quod appellavit deiectiones suas, in vas olim honorabile tristitiae posuit, eodem sub invocatione fratrorum geminorum Medardi et Godardi laete ac melliflue minxit, psalmum qui incipit: Lingua mea calamus scribae velociter scribentis: magna voce canitans* (did a piss, says he was dejected, asks to be exonerated), *demum ex stercore turpi cum divi Orionis incunditate mixto, cocto, frigorique exposito, encaustum sibi fecit indelibile* (faked O'Ryan's, the indelible ink). (*FW* 185.14–26)

(First of all the Master Maker, the Exalted Seedsower, who positioned himself close to the life-giving and all-powerful earth with buttocks as bare as the day they merged from the womb, lifted up his raincoat and unfastened his underpants, weeping and groaning, but without any shame or anyone's by-my-leave, and loosened his bowels into his hand; next, after he had been relieved of this dark blast and was trumpeting a call to action, he deposited his own shit (that is what he terms his droppings) into a receptacle which once was the respectable urn of grief; then, into that same urn, with an invocation to the twin brothers Medardus and Godardus, he joyfully and mellifluously pissed, while chanting in a loud voice the Psalm which begins "My Tongue is the Pen of a Scribe who Writes Speedily"; finally, from the foul crap that had been mixed with the sweet essence of godlike Orion, and baked and exposed to the cold, he created indelible ink for himself.)

The passage quoted and translated above has been thoroughly explicated and discussed in an accessible article by Father Robert Boyle.[5] He goes over the meaning and ramifications of each phrase with considerable verve and skill. There is little that I can add to his professional commentary, and less that I can amend or correct.

At the time when he wrote, the Garland edition of the drafts, typescripts, and proofs of the *Wake* had not appeared, but Father Boyle did refer to Hayman's pioneer study, *A First-Draft Version of Finnegans Wake*. There is, however, almost nothing that one need say about the textual development of the passage; its *incipit* is found on an early 1924 draft: "Sing hymn Lingua mea calamus scribae velociter scribentis" (*JJA* 47.331). As the passage evolved, there were additions and expansions, but very few substitutions: "denique" (then, next) shortly became "demum" (finally) (*FW* 185.24); "vas" (urn) (*FW* 185.19) first appeared as "poculum" (cup), then "vasum" which is an archaic variant of "vas."

I have detected only one minor slip in Joyce's Latin in the passage. The form "fratrorum" (*FW* 185.20) should be *fratrum*. In grammatical terms, Joyce has substituted a genitive plural of the second declension (*-orum*) for the correct third declension (*-um*). The word *"fratrorum"* remains unchanged in all drafts. Perhaps, Joyce originally intended the word to be an adjectival form, *fraternorum* (fraternal). If so, this latter word is always spelled in the same way as it has just been presented. Moreover, the common classical term for twin brothers is *fratres gemini*, not *gemini fraterni*. In fact, Joyce's precise plural genitive form, *fratrum geminorum*, appears correctly spelled in Horace (*Epistles* 1.18.41); also see Vergil's *gemini fratres* (*Aeneid* 7.670).

There are only several other minor additions I can make to Boyle's commentary. The phrase "animale nigro exoneratus" (*FW* 185.18) is certainly intended to be ambiguous. With respect to its Latin root (*anim-*) the initial noun could be either a "living creature"—here a "black monster"—or "something connected with the wind." Since the context is blatantly excremental, one is faced with a choice between a turd and a fart. My translation opts for the latter ("relieved of this dark blast") only because of Joyce's partiality, throughout his *oeuvre,* for elaborate expressions of individual and cosmic flatulence. This Wakean phrase may, in fact, be intended to be a Latin echo of the Ulyssean "A black crack of noise in the street. . . . Loud on the left Thor thundered" (*U* 14.408–9).

Father Boyle missed an opportunity to suggest a New Testament analogue for one of the phrases in the passage. In his second epistle to Timothy, St. Paul warns his disciple to avoid false teachers and pointless philosophical arguments: "Whoever cleanses himself of such faults will become *a vessel of honor,* useful to his lord and master" (2 Tim. 2:21; my emphasis). The Latin version of the italicized words is *vas in honorem,* fairly close to Joyce's *vas olim honorabile,* which is, however, destined for squalid use by its master.

The next comment involves a matter of a bit more substance: Joyce's initial Latin term for his ink-maker, "opifex" (master craftsman) (*FW* 185.12). That word may indeed have been picked up as an echo from Ovid's description of Daedalus (see page 155). There is, however, another possible literary source for this fairly rare term. It occurs twice in a 612-line poem, *Hisperica Famina,* composed most probably in the sixth century A.D., undoubtedly in Ireland by native monks.[6] These "Westerly Declamations" (as the title might be rendered) are, according to a distinguished scholar of medieval culture, the unique product of

Irish exuberance [which] in the early Middle Ages needed a new Latin, flavored with Greek, Hebrew, and native Irish, private inventions and distortions of glossaries. Nothing like that was yet known in our day . . . but now Mr. James Joyce [and his "Work in Progress"] has appeared.[7]

Most of the topics treated in these wild and woolly verses deal with nature ("The Rule of the Day," "On the Sea," "About the Wind"), but two sections are devoted to the art and craft of a scribe: "De Taberna" (On the Container for a Book) and "De Tabula" (About the Writing Tablet). In each of these short poetic essays—and only here in the entire work—the Latin word *opifex* appears. In line 522 the "craftsman" cuts out the book-satchel from "hairy hide" already flayed by a "butcher" (*carnifex*). In line 539 another "craftsman" cuts off a tree branch; and then hews, carves, polishes "the embellished writing tablet," which is carried around by scholars. There is absolutely no evidence— *pace* Professor Rand's prescient parallel—that Joyce read the Latin text of his native land's *Hisperica Famina*.[8] Thus, it is probably prudent to assign to coincidence these three scribal appearances of *opifex:* two in a medieval poem, the last in the *Wake*. Prudence aside, however, maybe a case for lexical imitation from another source *can*, in fact, be made here.

The following two entries appear on adjacent pages in one of the *Wake* Notebooks: "Hiberno-Latin" and "ᵇAltus Prosator" (VI.B.2.12–13); compare "prosator" (VI.B.33.142). The former Notebook was written in July through November 1923, just in time for the crossed second entry to be identified as the certain and immediate source for the insertion of "altus prosator" (*FW* 185.12) into the drafts of this section of the text.[9] Also without doubt is the ultimate *literary* source for Joyce's phrase. *Altus Prosator* is a 276-line poem marked by an A-Z acrostic. It is traditionally attributed to St. Columba (also known as St. Columcille), the sixth-century founder of numerous monasteries throughout Ireland, at Iona, in Scotland, and on at least some of the northern islands. The diction of this poem is not nearly as linguistically contorted as *Hisperica Famina;* nonetheless, even modest anthologies would categorize *Altus Prosator* as an example of "Hiberno-Latin," with the lexical and syntactical eccentricities that that designation implies.

If one could locate the source from which Joyce lifted the phrase "Hiberno-Latin" as well as the title (which is also the first two words) of Columba's poem, then it might also be possible to point to some extended comment, in that hypothetical source, on the even more exotic Irish verse, the *Hisperica Famina*—and perhaps to detect a citation there from one or the other of the scribal uses of *opifex*. But that link is pure speculation and any claim for definite connections between the pair of early Irish-Latin poems and Joyce's choice of the two Latin terms for his ink-maker cannot (and should not) be carried any farther.

There is something else that deserves mention before the end of the review of the "Ink" passage and the archival-textual presence of "*altus prosator.*" The first clause of St. Columba's poem mentioned above celebrates the "Exalted Seed-Sower," whose temporal scope is inscribed by three Latin verbs, *erat* (the past), *est* (the present), and *erit* (the future) (lines 3–5). The creator of the universe, so the Irish monk proclaims, always *was,* and *is,* and *will be* for all ages. Joyce uses exactly the same verbs, in identical order: "*Erat Est Erit*" (*FW* 140.4–5). The two contexts share nothing in common, and the rhetorical figure of using verbal tense as an indicator of the span of time is hardly rare. (For a classical parallel, see page 255, note 5.) Immediately after these three staccato verbs appear in the *Wake,* however, there is a second Latin phrase: "*Non michi sed luciphro*" (Not for me but for the light-bearer) (*FW* 140.5). Lucifer, the rebel angel, appears momentarily in St. Columba's hymn: *superbiendo ruerat / Lucifer, quem formaverat* (Lucifer, whom [the Creator] had shaped, fell because he was arrogant) (lines 29–30). But again, coincidence, or, more probably, the Irish writers' shared familiarity with the narrative clichés of Christian prehistory should negate too hard a push for direct quotation from St. Columba's *Altus Prosator* by Joyce here.

The "Historiology" Passage

Next, the second long passage of original Joycean Latin in the *Wake.* This time, the topic is a pseudoacademic discussion of human history and time:

> *venite, preteriti, sine mora dumque de entibus nascituris decentius in lingua romana mortuorum parva chartula liviana ostenditur, sedentes in letitiae super ollas carnium, spectantes immo situm lutetiae unde auspiciis secundis tantae consurgent humanae stirpes, antiquissimam flaminum amborium Joardani et Jambaptistae mentibus revolvamus sapientiam: totum tute fluvii modo mundo fluere, eadem quae ex aggere fatuta fuere iterum inter alveum fore futura, quodlibet sese ipsum per aliudpiam agnoscere contrarium, omnem demun amnem ripis rivalibus amplecti.* (*FW* 287.20–28)

(Men from past generations, come, without delay and while the tiny scrap of second-best "Liffey" papyrus is on display. It is inscribed, quite fittingly, in the Latin language of those who have passed away, concerning happenings which are yet to take place. While we are happily sitting over the flesh-pots and observing (yes indeed) the site of Paris from which, under favorable omens, so many branches of the human race will emerge, let us turn over in our minds the most ancient and wise theory of the pair of priests Giordano Bruno and Giambattista Vico. They saw that the entire world flows smoothly, like a river; and that the same things which have been screwed away from the bank will once again be within the bed of the river; and that each thing recognizes itself through its opposite; and that every river has two banks which embrace the same stream.)

The passage cited and translated above is found just a bit more than half-way through the "Night Lessons" chapter. It introduces almost six parenthetical pages (*FW* 287.18–292.32), which interrupt the primary "centered and marginalized" format of this episode. The topic of this excursus seems to be a trumped-up *curriculum vitae*, which is designed to establish the scholastic and intellectual credentials of Shem, who is the instructor and diagrammer in the up-coming geometry lesson. The Latin preface to this academic parenthesis was composed by Joyce in one long sentence in which the auditors are exhorted to rise above mundane matters (eating and drinking in Paris) to contemplate a philosophy of history (as distilled from Bruno and Vico). In my translation I have divided Joyce's periodic clauses into four independent sentences to emphasize and clarify the flow of the thought and the rhetoric. Since this Latin sentence has never been subjected to close analysis—and since the "translations" in several of the standard works on the *Wake* are less than pellucid—I will go through its constituent parts in order and comment on both presentation and proposition.

The initial "venite" (All of you, come) (*FW* 287.20) was originally "venito," an affected "Future Imperative," which does not work because it is singular, and, clearly, a group of reader-hearers are being addressed here. The vocative "preteriti" (more correctly *praeteriti*) (*FW* 287.20) is a perfect participle, which literally means "those having been passed over"; by logical extension it refers to events or people of the past, as I have translated it. Perhaps, however, Joyce intended the invitation not to be a general call to those of the past who had an interest in history, but a specific admonition to the three young scholars in the "Doodles family" (*FW* 299.F4) who have not been paying attention in their classrooms. Hence, since they have been "passed by"—or better, "left behind"—they need remedial instruction in their history lessons. This night-time tutorial session begins, "quite fittingly" ("decentius" [*FW* 287.20–21]) with a mini-essay in the traditional but dead language of academic discourse ("in lingua romana mortuorum" [*FW* 287.20–21]).

The three primary temporal perspectives of history (past, present, and future) that were noted in the previous passage also appear here. There are three designedly distinct forms of Latin participles, which Joyce carefully positioned in the first line (*FW* 287.20) of this passage: "preteriti" is perfect (completed in the past); "entibus" is present (happening now); "nascituris" is future (about to come into being).[10] As a matter of strict morphology, *nascituris* is not a genuine Latin form; the correct future participle of *nascor* is *naturus*. Joyce has made up this form, which *looks* and *sounds* as if it were correct, to reemphasize the element of futurity in both the meaning of the word and its tense. In the context of the historiological theme of the passage, the shape and word-choice of its introduction are no accident: following the lead of Roman orators and poets, Joyce habitually uses grammar and syntax in the service of rhetoric.

The medium of presentation for this academic exercise is "parva chartula liviana" (the tiny scrap of second-best "Liffey" papyrus) (*FW* 287.21). If the wise thoughts propounded here are to be transcribed in a dead language, it follows that the writing surface should also be suitably antique. At this juncture, Joyce got his technical terminology, secondhand, from Pliny the Elder's first-century A.D. compendium, *Natural History*.[11] In his discussion of various exotic Eastern trees and bushes, the Roman encyclopedist reviews the ways and means of manufacturing "paper" from papyrus stalks. The best quality product is called "Augustan" by the Romans, in a spirit of imperial flattery. The second grade, following the same procedure, is known as "Livian" papyrus, after the name of the emperor's wife. In the light of Joyce's frequent references to ALP, particularly in her riverine manifestation, as "Anna Livia" (for example, *FW* 196.3–5) and since the River Liffey is called *Livia* in Latin, I have no hesitation in combining both the Roman and the Irish connotations in my translation.

The next phrase "in letitiae" (*FW* 287.22) contains the only definite error in Latin syntax present in this extended sentence. And here it is certain that the error is not Joyce's. In all drafts the correct ablative form, "letitia," is used after the preposition "in" (*FW* 287.23). The erroneous ending (*-ae*) first appears as a late "correction" on an early 1937 typescript, 47478–91 (*JJA* 53.237). There is an obvious paleographical principle to account for this mistake: the proofreader's eye wandered to "lutetiae," which appears seven words after "letitia." The absolutely correct genitive ending (*-ae*) for the latter word was incorrectly applied, I suggest, to the former. The handwriting of the revisions here is not Joyce's, but neither he nor anyone else seems to have noticed the error or restored the required grammatical form.

All the commentaries point out that the phrase "sedentes super ollas carnium" (sitting over flesh-pots) (*FW* 287.23) is taken directly from the Vulgate version of Exodus 16.3. The Hebrew people have escaped from Pharaoh's slavery, crossed the Red Sea, and are wandering in the desert of

Sinai. They are hungry, and they complain to Moses and Aaron that, had they died in Egypt, at least there they "sat by the pots of flesh" and ate bread to the full. Yahweh then comes to the rescue of his liberated people with miraculous supplies of manna and quails. My translation extends the biblical sense of the phrase to its common use as a moral admonition.[12] The implication is that those who are being exhorted to contemplate the lessons of history here are quite comfortably supplied with food and drink, and more concerned with carnal than intellectual matters.

The Latin proper noun *Lutetia, -ae*, is the ancient name for the Gallic settlement beside the Seine that became Paris.[13] Hence, "situm lutetiae" (the site of Paris) (*FW* 287.22) incorporates allusions to the city where Joyce resided, to the rival banks of its defining river, and to its reputation as a locus of gourmet restaurants and the site of an early center of Latin scholastic education. Early in *Ulysses* there is a passage in which these elements are combined. As Stephen wanders along Sandymount strand he recalls his "Latin quarter hat. . . . *physiques, chimiques et naturelles*. Aha. Eating your groatsworth of *mou en civet*, fleshpots of Egypt. . . . when I was in Paris, *boul'Mich*'" (*U* 3.174–79).

The incorrect spelling of "*amborium*" (*FW* 287.24) crept into the text very late in the publishing process. The correct form is *amborum*, which Joyce himself wrote in the second draft of this section of the "Night Lessons" in July 1926 (47482a.70v [*JJA* 53.18]). That spelling remained unchanged in the ink fair copy and typescript, through all stages of the preparation for its initial publication in *transition* 11 (January–February 1928), every version of *Tales Told of Shem and Shaun* (August 1929), and the revision of that piece (c. 1934–1937). The first time that the incorrect *amborium* entered the text was in an early-1937 typescript prepared for the printers of *Finnegans Wake* (47478.97 [*JJA* 53.238]). That error in spelling was not detected on subsequent galley and page proofs (February–September 1938) nor was it listed for correction on the "Buffalo Errata" (VI.H.4.B.17 [*JJA* 53.418]).

The presence of "auspiciis secundis" (favorable omens) (*FW* 287.23) to mark the emergence of significant portions of the human race is entirely consistent with established Roman traditions to ensure the propitious foundation of any enterprise. The antique flavor of the passage is reinforced by Joyce's choice of the historically inaccurate term "flaminum" (*FW* 287.24) to describe the two Italian philosophers Bruno (who was a Dominican friar for a while) and Vico (who was never in clerical orders). A *flamen* was a member of the Roman college of priests who were responsible for the ritual purity of sacrifices to major gods (see *FW* 242.34 and my discussion on pages 98–99).

The vivid main verb of the entire sentence, "revolvamus" (let us turn over) (*FW* 287.24), has been delayed until halfway through the passage. Grammatically, this form is a first-person plural present active subjunctive. It is used to exhort those addressed in the first line to give serious attention to the hallowed wisdom of Bruno and Vico.

The remaining three and a half lines of the passage are comprised of four parallel constructions, each of which expounds a part of the wise discovery of those two men. In Latin, indirectly reported statements are not introduced by "that," although that is exactly the English conjunction which I have used to begin each clause in my translation. The usual way of reporting something in Latin is to recast the statement's grammatical subject into the accusative (that is, objective) case and to convert its verb into an infinitive form. This preliminary excursus into Latin syntax has been necessary, because I suspect (and will demonstrate my reasons for the suspicion) that there is an important unrecognized problem with both the original composition and the subsequent interpretations of the first of these final four clauses.

The published text of the unit under discussion reads: "totum tute fluvii modo mundo fluere" (FW 287.25). The words *totum* (singular accusative) and *fluere* (present infinitive) are the key syntactical elements; they can be translated as "that the whole thing flows." The next word, *tute*, is an adverb meaning "safely," "securely." McHugh, in the most accessible annotation of the text of the *Wake*, has construed *fluvii* as a partitive genitive to be taken with *totum* to form the phrase "the whole *of the river*." McHugh also links *modo* with *mundo*. The first word is a noun in the ablative case, meaning "in the way," "with the manner"; modifying it is an adjective from *mundus, -a, -um* (clean, refined, elegant). The entire clause, following the lexical and syntactical steps outlined above, is translated by McHugh as "the fact that the whole of the river flows safely, with a clear stream."

In my judgment, there are three closely related problems with the foregoing analysis of Joyce's text. The first involves *fluvii*. I do not think that this genitive form is meant to be taken as defining *totum* (the whole *of the river*). The basis of my objection here is grammatical: in Latin the accusative form of "the whole of the river" is *fluvium totum*—the adjective agrees with the noun; the genitive case is not used. This being the case, then the genitive *fluvii* is surely to be construed with the following *modo* to form the naturally idiomatic phrase meaning "in the way *of a river*," "with a *river's* manner." There is another significant reason for preferring "like a river." Twelve lines before the beginning of the Latin passage under consideration, Joyce inserted into the text a preview of his theme: "A.I. *Amnium instar*" (FW 287.8). This phrase (first presented in its initial letters, then in full form) is Latin for "like rivers," "corresponding to rivers." It announces the central metaphor of the longer Latin passage to come. It also adumbrates the *Wake*'s final narrative flow when

ALP, now consubstantial with the River Liffey, runs toward the sea at Howth. That terminal goal and the more proximate geometry diagram (*FW* 293) are both presented in the sentence that immediately follows "Amnium instar." Note the Latinate choice of "locus" as a more or less technical term to indicate the set of points at which it is possible to get a bearing on the object: "And to find a locus for an alp get a howlth on her bayrings as a prisme O and for a second O unbox your compasses" (*FW* 287.8–11).

My second objection is more logical than grammatical. Why would Joyce—or Bruno or Vico—specify that the metaphorical river of history is "clean," "clear," or "refined"? The following three clauses in their mutually wise statement imply some turbulence in the flux of things, with rival river banks and the alternating movement of the stream stirring up mud from bank to bed. The word-choice of *mundus* modifying the way the river flows is definitely odd.

The third (and most significant) problem with the accepted interpretation centers on the logical and rhetorical core of Joyce's programmatic initial clause. It does not seem emphatic enough or clear enough merely to state that *totum* (the whole) flows, or even that "the whole river flows." (In fact, I suspect that this is the reason why McHugh erroneously links the two words.) Rather, I suggest that Joyce, in the synthesis of his view of history, intended the first clause to be read as "that the whole *world* flows safely, like a river." If that conjecture has any merit, then the key word *mundo* is not a form of the *adjective* meaning "clear," although that word is used correctly in "mundamanu" (with a clean hand) (*FW* 364.33). Rather, it is a *noun* from an unrelated root, *mundus, -i* (the world, the universe). It is the "whole world," in short, that flows, and establishes the metaphorical link between human history and the natural modes of a river. Thus *totum*—as an adjective, not a noun-substantive—modifies the world, rather than being ungrammatically connected to the river.

So much for vocabulary and rhetorical punch. What is a far more crucial factor for the validity of my conjecture is Latin grammar. If Joyce intended some form of *mundus* to be, as I suggest, the indirect-statement subject of the infinitive *fluere*, then that noun must be in the accusative case: *mundum* not *mundo*. The evidence of the draft manuscripts and all subsequent versions of the text is clear: Joyce wrote *mundo* and did not alter its form throughout all the stages right up to the final publication. This paleographic fact represents what might appear to be an insurmountable obstacle to my conjecture about the grammatical shape and logical thrust of the clause.

Perhaps, however, paleographical considerations have more to offer here. First, in the initial draft 47482a–70v (*JJA* 53.18) the *mundo* is written in almost directly above the *modo* (which precedes it in the printed text). I suggest that Joyce intended to create a "subject-bracket" of "totum . . . mundum" here, with the adverbial elements inside the bracket. That structure would emphasize the basic grammatical form of the essential clause: an accusative-with-infinitive ("totum . . . mundum fluere" [that the whole world flows]). Somehow, however, Joyce's eye was attracted by *modo*, and he wrote *mundo*. In subsequent editorial reviews of the Latin passage (there were very few additions), neither Joyce nor any of his assistants noticed or corrected this commonplace variant of scribal "dittography."

Second, there are many other instances of self-conscious word-sound play in this passage: *letitiae—lutetiae* (which also involves the introduction of a definite and uncorrected ending error into the text); *totum—tute; flaminum—fluvii—fluere; fututa fuere—fore futura; omnem—amnem; ripis—rivalibus.* The abiding presence of similar forms of *modo* and *mundo* could have been caused by inattention to grammar and by a desire to create this sort of jingle.

Third, the proofreading in this entire Latin passage was less than scrupulous. I have already referred to the mistake in "letitiae" (*FW* 287.22) and to the intrusive and incorrect spelling of Joyce's "amborum" as "amborium" (*FW* 287.24). There is another minor error in the form of "demun" (*FW* 287.27). This adverb (meaning "finally") is always spelled *demum*, as in the other extended passage of Joyce's original Latin, "demum" (*FW* 185.24).

Fourth—and I almost blush to bring it up—there is another passage in the *Wake* in which Joyce used the word *mundo*. It occurs in a passage lamenting the loss of Finnegan and all good men and true. Their wives are urged to begin a new life in a new world: "Fikup, for fresh nelly, el mundo nov" (*FW* 34.32). McHugh indicates that "Fikop" is Africa in the artificial language Volapuk; "Nelij" is England in that same tongue. The third element is Spanish-cum-Latin (with a final "o" missing from "nov") for the New World. I do not argue that Joyce, whose formal acquaintance with genuine Spanish was minimal, allowed the later Romance form "mundo" to intrude on his ancient Roman composition in "Night Lessons"; but it is entirely possible that one of Joyce's proofreaders might have confused the two words and allowed *mundo* instead of *mundum* to stand in the final text.

These paleographic considerations have been presented to bolster my suspicions that commentators have failed to grasp the key syntax of Joyce's Latin statement of what purports to be a Brunonian-Vichian view of history. In the end, however, the overriding argument in support of my suggested alteration of *mundo* to *mundum* is its necessary logical and metaphorical contribution to the statement in which the word appears: "that the whole world flows safely, like a river."

In addition to the purely textual considerations that have been discussed at some length above, there is another matter that is important here, and that is Joyce's grand design in composing *Finnegans Wake*. In his memoir, Eugene Jolas recalls a moment from the late summer of 1932 when he and Joyce were together in the small Alpine town of Feldkirch, Austria:

> "There really is no coincidence in this book," he said during one of our walks. "I might easily have written this story in the traditional manner. . . . Every novelist knows the recipe. . . . It is not very difficult to follow a simple, chronological scheme which the critics will understand. . . . But I, after all, am trying to tell the story of this Chapelizod family in a new way. . . . *Time and the river* and the mountain are the real heroes of my book."[14] (my emphasis, Jolas's ellipses)

In my judgment, Joyce's heroic characterization of "Time and the river" is directly keyed to the letter and the spirit of the Latin passage on page 287 of the *Wake*.

Is there a *literary* model or source for Joyce's fluminal metaphor? Neither Bruno nor Vico seems to have used world-time-river as an emphatic image in the presentation of their theories of history. This specific figure may appear here or there, but it certainly is not a memorable motif in their own works, nor is it a feature of subsequent commentaries on their historiography.[15] Samuel Beckett's lead essay in *Our Exagmination, etc.* (1929) is, for example, entitled "Dante . . . Bruno. Vico. . Joyce."[16] The language and allusive scope of Beckett's piece are far more lush and extensive than is usual with his prose; but in his nineteen pages there is only one reference that even suggests the world as a river. Beckett contrasts the "'barbarous' directness" of the opening line of Dante's *Divine Comedy* with the "suave elegance" of "*Ultima regna canam, fluido contermina mundo*" (I shall sing of far-away kingdoms, located at the edges of the watery world). Part of the contrast intended here is between Dante's definitive use of "vulgar" Italian and a Latin hexameter verse that clearly situates its poet-author in an antique, classical tradition.[17] Beyond that, there is nothing fluminal in Becket's essay.

Stuart Gilbert also contributed an essay to *Our Exagmination*. He devotes three pages to the importance of Vico's *Scienza nuova* on the subject and scope of Joyce's *Work in Progress*. But once again there is no mention in this discussion of Joyce's conception of an "ideal history" that "the world flows like a river." In another of Gilbert's commentaries on Joyce's work, however, there is a significant clue to a possible—indeed, likely—source of the fluminal figure in the *Wake*'s Latin passage. In 1930 Gilbert published his study of *Ulysses*. In the introduction he cites Vico as an exponent of "the theory of recurrence in the affairs of men and nations," and he specifically stresses the significance of this sort of "historical speculation" for *Finnegans Wake*.[18] Then Gilbert quotes, from the King James version, several verses from the opening chapter of Ecclesiastes, concluding with

> All the rivers run into the sea;
> yet the sea is not full: unto the
> place from whence the rivers
> *come, thither they return again.* (Ecclesiastes 1:7)

Joyce often directed Gilbert's critical discussion of *Ulysses* into channels in which he himself was particularly interested or for which he was the principal source of information. The Old Testament verse cited above may have been pointed out by Joyce to Gilbert as an appropriate literary synopsis of Vico's theory about recurrent cycles in human progress. Indeed, some of the Latin vocabulary for the passage may have been cribbed from the Vulgate text of the verse:

> Omnia flumina intrant in mare,
> Et mare non redundat;
> Ad locum unde exeunt flumina
> Revertuntur ut iterum fluant.

The passage from Ecclesiastes is not, of course, the only "source"—or even the primary reason—for Joyce's use of a riverine figure in his Latin statement of cyclic patterns in history. Another highly plausible candidate for considerable influence here is the Roman poet Ovid. In the final book of his *Metamorphoses* Ovid dedicates over four hundred lines to the philosophical-religious instruction that Pythagoras gives to the second king of Rome, Numa. The key concept in the Greek philosopher's teaching is *omnia mutantur, nihil interit* (all things change, nothing passes away) (*M* 15.165). (Readers of *Ulysses* will be familiar with one aspect of this doctrine, metempsychosis, the transmigration of souls.) Ovid's Pythagoras illustrated his teaching with the following simile:

> nihil est toto, quod perstet, in orbe.
> cuncta fluunt, omnisque vagans formatur imago.
> ipsa quoque asiduo labuntur tempora motu,
> non secus ac flumen. neque enim consistere flumen
> nec levis hora potest, sed ut unda impellitur unda,

urgeturque eadem veniens urgetque priorem,
tempora sic fugiunt pariter, pariterque sequuntur,
et nova sunt semper; nam quod fuit ante, relictum est,
fitque quod haud fuerat, momentaque cuncta novantur. (M 15.172–85)

(There is nothing in the entire world which is permanent. All things
flow, and every outward appearance that is formed is unstable. Even time
itself glides in perpetual motion, not unlike a river. For neither a river
nor a fleeting hour is able to stand still; but, just as a wave is pushed by
another wave and just as the wave washing ashore is both a roller and
itself rolled, so too does time, at one and the same instant, both pursue
and follow. And time is always something new. For what once was has
been left behind, and it becomes something different from what it had
been and every moment is made new.)

There are no direct verbal parallels between the *Wake* passage and Ovid's verses.
At the same time, the figurative similarities—from a poem that Joyce studied
closely—are striking.[19] These Latin lines merit citation, since (above and beyond the historiological passage) the initial, centrally repeated, and final image in *Finnegans Wake* itself is that of a river. One of Joyce's compositional
techniques was to inscribe as much as possible of the whole of a work into its
constituent parts. Hence, even a Latin accusative-with-the-infinitive clause in
the "Night Lessons" episode may participate in the cosmic "riverrun ... [which]
brings us by commodius vicus of recirculation" (FW 3.1–2) through Anna
Livia's "Reeve Gootch . . . and Reeve Drughad" (FW 197.1), "[b]eside the
rivering water of, hitherand thithering waters of" (FW 216.4–5), "moyles and
moyles of it" (FW 628.3), "So. Avelaval" (FW 628.6). And then the world-
river cycle begins again: "Sim. Time after time. The sehm asnuh" (FW 620.15–
16).

Now we return to more mundane matters of the vocabulary and syntax of
the three related clauses that conclude this extended Latin passage.

In the second clause of the final section of this passage, the parallel and
chiastic elements are verb forms: *fututa fuere* and *fore futura*. The first is a
perfect passive indicative; the second is a future active infinitive.[20] It seems to
me that the major problem here is lexical, not grammatical. McHugh's translation indicates that he considers that both of these verb forms come from the
same root, which has been formally manipulated to yield different tenses and
voices: in English, his gloss reads that "those things which *were to have been*
. . . *would later be*" (my emphasis). This translation would be remotely possible (but from a grammatical perspective, highly improbable), only if McHugh

were to have silently altered Joyce's "fututa" (*FW* 287.26) to "futura," so that both verbs were some type of future forms of *sum, esse, fui, futurum,* the Latin verb for "to be." The manuscripts, typescripts, proofs, and text, however, are clear here: from first to last, Joyce wrote and let stand, not "futura," but "fututa." This second form (with a penultimate "*t*" rather than "*r*") is not from *sum* (to be), but from *futuo, futuere, futui, fututum* (to fuck, to screw).

Joyce could have run across this vulgar verb in one of Catullus' obscene invectives, or in the crude threats that punctuate the *Priapea*, or in his *Scribbledehobble* citation of Martial. Indeed, a similar participial form is found in the Priapic poem that impugns Penelope's chastity: Her house is filled with dinner guests who have been fucked (*fututorum*) (*Priapea* 68.30). Whatever the precise literary source might be, it is certain that he *did* know this verb and knew how to decline it: "Federals' Uniteds' Transports' Unions' for Exultations' of Triumphants' Ecstasies" (*FW* 66.8–9; my emphases) modestly conceals (or coyly reveals) the acrostic "F-U-T-U-E-T-E." In Latin, *futuete* is a plural active imperative meaning "You all, fuck," or allowing for idiomatic reflexive usage, "you all, get fucked."[21] In the "Historiology" passage, then, "*fututa fuere*" must mean "things which have been screwed." I have so translated this correct perfect passive form. It cannot mean "which were to have been," for two reasons: vocabulary (*fututa,* not *futura*) and grammar (there is no hypothetical form *futura fuere* in anything like standard Latin).

The image in this verb obviously was intended to portray the thrust of the river's current, which twists material from the banks in between which it rushes. Before leaving the clause, it is also necessary to point out that McHugh's translation of "those" does not do justice to Joyce's "*eadem,*" which means "the same things." Thus, and in conclusion, the second clause should correctly be rendered as "that the same things which have been screwed away from the bank will once again be within the bed of the river." Joyce himself supports the foregoing interpretation, which emphasizes the fluvial renewal and riparian permanence of human history. That affirmation is stated with two markers of thematic significance, an ALP acrostic and the Latin language: "*Amnis Limina Permanent*" (Alluvial Limits Persist; that is, a river's source, banks, course, delta, mouth endure) (*FW* 153.2).

That completes the discussion of Joyce's two displays of original Latin in *Finnegans Wake*. Before moving to the next topic, however, it is necessary to say something in summary about the style of those passages. The first, "Ink," has a distinctly medieval, almost monastic ring. It begins with what is probably an evocation of the title and topic (*altus prosator*) of a famous Hiberno-Latin hymn; invokes Joyce's version of the twin-brother patrons of growth, St. Medard and St. Godard; quotes the first line of the very psalm that a monk might chant as he picks up his pen in a scriptorium; and, finally, displays a prescientific (almost alchemical) faith in transmuting dross to ink. Grammatically, this highly paratactic passage has five indicative verbs and only one (quite obvious) subjunctive. The humor in it is straightforwardly scatological: word-play involving "natibus . . . nati" and the semiclassical link between the mythical hunter Orion and "urine," and "O'Ryan's" in the adjacent English "paraphrase" (see page 182 for Orion's odd birth tale).

The "Historiology" passage, on the other hand, displays complex structure. It is composed of a single independent verb (itself a hortatory subjunctive), a *dum*-clause, two participles (the second triggering an indirect question), and four terminal indirect statements. This is classical periodic syntax, with frequent subordination. As mentioned above, there is considerable (and ingenious) sound-sense play in the choice and placement of words. Although the Latin of this passage is acknowledged to be a "dead language," it has been quickened by Joyce's use of a diminutive (*chartula*) for the papyrus fragment, which is neatly given a Hiberno-Augustan patent. Finally, the carefully channeled rhetoric and exaggerated tense contrast (*fututa fuere* and *fore futura*) of the thematic statements testify, once again, to Joyce's fluid versatility in what was once regarded as a formidable academic challenge, Latin prose composition.

Miscellaneous Passages

In addition to the two extended passages that have been analyzed above, there are countless short fragments of Latin scattered throughout the text of *Finnegans Wake*. There is scarcely a page in that work which does not contain an overt word or covert phrase that Joyce has composed in or adapted from the language of the ancient Romans. The vast majority of these "original" snippets have been detected in McHugh's *Annotations* or in the *Classical Lexicon* compiled by O Hehir and Dillon. In the following section of this chapter, then, I shall concentrate on two examples that are especially interesting, because their full contribution to significant themes has not been recognized.

Near the beginning of the *Wake,* there is a close echo of the biblical creation formula: "Fiatfuit!" (Let there be/it was) (*FW* 17.32). In the work's final episode the order of the compounded verbs is reversed: "Fuitfiat!" (*FW* 613.14). The analogue in the *Vulgate* is *Dixitque Deus: Fiat lux. Et facta est lux* (And God said: Let there be light. And light was made) (Gen. 1:3). In both Wakean contexts there are other allusions to the creation tale "farbiger pancosmos" (*faber* is "maker" in Latin; *pan cosmos* is close to "the whole universe" in Greek) (*FW* 613.11–12). There is also a hint of its apocalyptic antithesis, the end of the world: "from his Inn the Byggning to whose Finisthere Punct"

(*FW* 17.22–23). Since the spirit behind these events is Joycean-Vichian, not Judeo-Christian, the world created out of nothing is not destined to be obliterated at end-time. Rather, the cycle of being begins again: "they are in surgence: hence, cool at ebb, they requiesce" (*FW* 17.25–26). "Only is order othered. Nought is nulled" (*FW* 613.13–14). In short, the juxtaposed contrast of Latin verbal mood (subjunctive/indicative) and tense (present/past) fully participates in Joyce's restatement of the cycle of world history.

Throughout the *Wake* the question "How are you today, my dark sir?" is repeatedly asked, and in a number of different languages.[22] The Latin version, "commodore valley O hairy, Arthre jennyrosy?" (*FW* 93.6–7), needs to be retranslated into the language of the ancient Romans: *Quomodo vales hodie [??], atrate generose?* Here I have substituted the masculine vocative singular of the thematically necessary adjective *atratus, -a, -um* (clothed in black, in mourning) for McHugh's suggestion of *arator* (plowman). I also suggest that Joyce confused *heri* (yesterday) with *hodie* (today) in his translation of the question into Wakean Latin.

There are many other Wakean passages that display similar linguistic ingenuity; most of them have been discussed in the chapters that deal with excerpts from and burlesque adaptations of the writings of major (and a few minor) Roman authors. The next examples move a bit beyond Joyce's skill in composing Latin. They involve some passages from the *Wake* that are not, strictly speaking, *in* Latin. They are, however, so blatantly constructed *from* Latin raw material that it would be impossible to understand what is going on in them without reference to their models. The models are on display (usually crossed) in the *Wake* Notebooks. Thus, selection of the following items was designed both to provide additional illustrations of Joyce's mastery of Latin and to illuminate several passages in the text, the thrust of which might not have been fully felt without a bit of archival prodding.

In the "Mime," Clugg (Shem) wonders whether life is worth living. His dream answer takes him back through successive generations and branches of a grandly extended family tree:

> all old *Sators* of the *Sowsceptre* highly *nutritius* family histrionic, *genitricksling* with *Avus* and *Avia*, that simple pair, and descendant down on veloutypads *by a vuncular* process to Nurus and *Noverca*, those notorious nepotists, circumpictified in their *sobrine* census, *patriss* all of them by the *glos* on their *germane faces* and the *socerine* eyes like transparents of *vitricus*, *patruuts* to a man, the archimede *levirs* of his ekonome world. (*FW* 230.28–34; my emphases)

The seventeen italicized elements in that passage are taken directly (but not in the same order) from a Notebook index of Latin terms for extended family relationships (for example, *nutritius* means "foster-father"; *avia* is "grand-mother"). These entries appear, one after the other, on VI.B.33.142–44. With a single exception, all of them have been crossed with red crayon. The exception is "patris est filius" (he is the son of his father) (VI.B.33.143). That phrase looks like Joyce's personal gloss on the meaning of an unfamiliar Latin verb; it appears immediately after the Notebook entry "patrissas" (you look/behave like your father). That entry comes into the text of the *Wake* as a slightly truncated "patriss" (*FW* 230.32).

McHugh's annotation of the meaning of the technical terms in the passage just cited is accurate and, as usual, it misses very little indeed. There are only a few things that can be pointed out. Joyce's final entry in the index is clearly "ᵣsusceptrix"; although the feminine suffix "-trix" is morphologically correct, that actual form is not found in Latin dictionaries. Perhaps Joyce wanted to include as maternal a presence as possible in this primarily patriarchal family portrait. The entry "ᵣabavunculus" (great-uncle on the mother's side) is split apart and converted into an adjective for its appearance in the text, "by a vuncular" (*FW* 230.30–31). This procedure, however, permitted Joyce to play around with Latin grammar and vocabulary: the English preposition "by" is *ab* in Latin; thus a Roman *abavunculus* can be plausibly (but incorrectly as far as etymology goes) reduced to a Wakean "*by a* vuncular." There are two terms of affinity in the passage that do not appear in the Notebook index: "Nurus" (*FW* 230.31) means "daughter-in-law"; "nepotists" (*FW* 230.31) comes from *nepos,* which means both "grandson" and "nephew." Both are common enough for Joyce to have added on his own to fit the needs of his narrative.

A final consideration here: what was the source for this index of quite technical terms? The article "Affines, Affinitas" in Smith's *Dictionary of Greek and Roman Antiquities* has many of the items, including the fairly rare distinctions *levir* (brother-in-law) and *glos* (sister-in-law). They, like the *vitricus* (step-father) and *noverca* (step-mother) could not contract lawful marriages within the affinities stated in the words.[23] Several other odd words in the index, however, are missing from both Smith's *Dictionary* and the Daremberg-Saglio *Dictionnaire.* Thus, since I accept as a basic archival principle that Joyce is more interested in jotting down words than pondering their contexts,[24] the question of the specific source must remain open. The key to its secure identification will be, in my judgment, the presence of it in of the extraordinarily rare Latin verb *patrisso, patrissare* (to take after one's father). As I have indicated above, this verb lies behind both the Notebook entry "patrissas" (VI.B.33.143) and the text's "patriss" (*FW* 230.32).

For another passage based on Latin archival material, the Notebook index is compact enough to be cited in full: "vespera / conticinium / concubium /

intempestas nox(-ctis) / gallicinium / lucifer" (VI.B.18.259). These are Latin terms for the time divisions of the night: "evening," "silence-time," "bedtime," "dead of night," "cock-crow-time," "light-bringer." Joyce wove Latin and English versions of these words into two *Wake* passages:

> whiles *even* led *comesilencers* to *comeliewithers* and till *intempestuous Nox* should catch the *gallicry* and spot *lucans dawn.* (*FW* 143.15–17; my emphases)

> It *darkles.* . . . Now *conticinium.* As Lord the Laohun is *sheutseuyes.* The *time of lying together* will come and the *wildering of the nicht* till *cockeedoodle aubens Aurore.*(*FW* 244.13, 31–33; my emphases)

There may be another echo of the Latin terms in the memorable evocation of dawn at the end of III.2:

> The silent *cock shall crow.* . . . Walk while ye have the night for morn, *Light*breakfast*bringer.* (*FW* 473.22–24; my emphases)

The second passage was explicated (probably with Joyce's explicit assistance) by Mercanton in 1938.[25] Atherton has suggested a passage from Macrobius (*Saturnalia* 1.3.12–16) as Joyce's probable source.[26] Macrobius' discussion of the periods of the Roman day does have all of the necessary terms except *lucifer,* for which Joyce would have relied on his own store of knowledge. In my opinion, however, it seems more likely that Joyce picked up these terms from some handbook of classical lore, in which this type of data had been digested for easy reference. My primary reason for the handbook hypothesis is the presence of a "translated" list of the names of the Roman months on the previous Notebook page (VI.B.18.258).[27] That index was built into the *Wake* (*FW* 142.8–11), just before the first "night-hours" passage cited above. It seems improbable that Joyce scoured two widely separated passages in the original Latin of Macrobius for two closely related items of information.[28]

Joyce signed an August 29, 1920, letter to Stanislaus with a royal or pontifical "James," rather than his usual "Jim." A parenthesis below "His Majesty's" signature contains this list: "(Heb. Vat. Terg. Ex. Lut. Hosp. Litt. Angl. Pon. Max.)" (*SL* 268). The abbreviation can easily be expanded and translated: "Jew from the Vatican, Exile to/from Trieste (*Tergestis*), Guest in Paris (*Lutetiae*), High Priest of English Literature." In much the same vein Joyce concluded a May 27, 1927, letter to Sylvia Beach on the occasion of the ninth printing of *Ulysses* as follows:

I hope Ulysses IX will soon ascend to the papal throne. His motto is to be: *Triste canis vulpibus* = This 'ere dog will worry them there foxyboys. (*SL* 324–26)

Joyce supplied a translation but not the model for his mock motto. It is an adaptation of *triste lupus stabulis* (a wolf is a source of sorrow for the henhouses) (Vergil, *Eclogues* 3.80).

ARCHIVAL LATIN

The final two areas explored in this chapter directly and primarily involve archival material. The first topic examines some shorter Latin (or consciously Latinate) entries that made their way into the *Wake:*

1. ᵇtill the juggler veins / stood out on him / scrag *sicut* tightrope (VI.B.12.96; my emphasis)

   the juggaleer's veins . . . in his napier scrag stud out burstright tamquam taughtropes (*FW* 300.31–301.1)

This excerpt comes from a "Night Lessons" passage in which the young scholars are sweating out some problems in higher mathematics. The English slang term "scrag" (neck) is reinforced by "napier," which I take to emphasize (in addition to an allusion to the Scottish mathematician John Napier) the decidedly prominent "nape" of the straining student's neck. Perhaps one of the boys is also more proficient than the other in these exercises, since approximation of the Norwegian word *scragg* (a feeble, stunted person) is immediately counterbalanced by "stud." Joyce then completes his cross-linguistic wordplay with a minisimile: the bursting veins are just like "taughtropes." The latter is the final evolution of the Notebook entry "tightrope." By this word Joyce may signal that he has "taught" himself the "trope," since the text's "tamquam" is nothing more than a synonym for the original entry, "sicut." Both words are Latin for "like," "just as," and are frequently used to introduce epic similes.

2. Deus non alligatur / *sacramentis suis* (VI.B.14.187; VI.C.12.185; my emphasis)

   the divine comic Denti Alligator. . . . Swear aloud . . . promises. . . . sacramental. (*FW* 440.6, 8, 13, 21)

The Latin adage cited above means "God is not bound by his own oaths or promises." Though it remained uncrossed, this Notebook entry was transferred into the text, where it is neatly conflated with an allusion to Dante Alighieri's *Divine Comedy*. And its component parts are spread over several sentences in a way calculated completely to disguise the source and its original language.

> 3. 7 urbes certant a / stirpe [b]Homeri / [b]Smyrna Rhodos /[b]Kolophon, Salamis / [b]Chios, Delos, Athens (VI.B.23.17)

> seven dovecotes cooclaim to have been pigeonheim to this homer, Smerrnion, Rhoebok, Kolonsreagh, Seapoint, Quayhowth, Ashtown, Ratheny (*FW* 129.22–24; also see *FW* 481.21–22)

The Notebook lines are from an anonymous Latin version of a Greek epigram about the traditional claimants to be the birthplace of Homer: "Seven cities argue over being the original root of Homer: Smyrna, Rhodes, etc." Joyce's Wakean version pivots around the poet metamorphosed into a lowercase homing pigeon. The less-than-epic bird's possible roosts are also transferred from the eastern Mediterranean to an Irish urban milieu in seven districts of Dublin.

The last part of this section involves a series of Notebook entries that were never adapted or adopted for use in the text of the *Wake*. In these items the Latin seems to be the occasional medium for incidental notes. They fall into no discernible topical or thematic patterns. Rather, these entries provide another perspective on the many ways that Joyce utilized the language of the ancient Romans: every now and then it appears as "shorthand," as an *aide-mémoire* to capture an emphatic point. This habit is not, of course, limited to the *Finnegans Wake* Notebooks.

In one of the *Ulysses* Notesheets the following item appears: "[b]LB juvenis made fun of jews" (*UNBM* 453: 13). Here Joyce employs the Latin adjective *iuvenis* to indicate that, when he was a "young man" (the Romans used the term, sometimes with *adulescens*, for the years between the late teens and forty), Leopold Bloom mocked members of his own race. Another note for "Ithaca" is a pre-text synopsis of the scene in which Stephen and Bloom relieve themselves in the yard of 7 Eccles Street. Joyce reports the dissimilar trajectory "Bloom's longer . . . Stephen's higher" and the fact that "in his ultimate year at High School (1880) [Bloom] had been capable of attaining the point of greatest altitude against the whole concurrent strength of the institution, 210 scholars" (*U* 17.1192–96). A crossed entry in the same series of notes refers to this feat: "[b]LB & SD pissjets / (LB palmarius)" (*UNBM* 473: 4). The

Latin adjective (which should be third declension *palmaris*) means "deserving the palm," "winning the prize." In *Ulysses* itself Stephen imagines finding one of his school prize books for sale in a secondhand bookshop; on its flyleaf is an inscription to Stephen Dedalus "*palmam ferenti*" (winning the prize) (*U* 10.841).

In what is apparently the earliest outline of the projected plot of II.1 ("The Mime") of the *Wake*, Joyce uses a siglum and a Latin verb to note that "x vident" (The Four Old Men see, look on).[29] There are numerous other examples of this sort of incidental, stenographic Latin in the Notebooks. The following examples illustrate the point:

  1. shy sadist can't piss coram aliis (*Scribbledehobble* [741] 120)

The last two words in this entry mean "in front of other people" in Latin. The archival context is the beginning of some notes that are somehow or other related to "Circe." I offer two possibilities: *either* a dominator/-trix is too embarrassed to display her/his scorn for a "slave" by urinating on the victim *or* an inhibited exhibitionist denies pleasure to voyeurs by being unable to put on a shower show while they watch eagerly. Here Latin is at the service of fantasy scatology; there may be an echo of the entry in "I'm Flo, shy of peeps" (*FW* 248.17).

  2. What is it doing? / Pluit (VI.B.2.176)

Joyce answers the question with a prosaic Latin verb: "it is raining." His purpose may be to suggest the function of impersonal verbs in many languages.

  3. Semper poetis est potius / mori quam foedari (VI.B.5.128; also
     VI.B.5.119)

Several people with whom I have discussed this entry suggest that it might be the author's heraldic extension of the motto of the Joyce family, "Death before dishonor." The two lines cited from the Notebook entry can be translated as "Creative artists have always chosen to die rather than to be dishonored." As a matter of fact, the following epigram is carved in block capitals on the lintel, supported by four Ionic columns, of a large office building at 11 Via Barberini in Rome: *Malo Mori Quam Foedari* (I prefer to die rather than to be dishonored). Joyce might well have seen this imposing inscription—or its predecessor[30]—during his seven-month residence in Rome (August 1906–early March 1907). In a May 1, 1935, letter to Harriet Shaw Weaver, Joyce himself has something to add to this matter: "The motto under my coat of arms, however, is: *Mors aut honorabilis vita*" (*SL* 377).

  4. de mortuis nil nisi bonum / nothing but bone in the dead (VI.B.10.91)

Here the "translation" of the Latin adage ("[Say] nothing but good about the dead") contains an elementary boner. The fault is not Joyce's. At the 1993 Paris Colloque on the *Wake* Notebooks, Vincent Deane identified a documentary source for that entry. In an issue of the *Irish Times* published in January 1923, there appeared a feature article on school-examination bloopers. Although this Latin item is not, strictly speaking, "original," Joyce noted it as potential material for the *Wake*. He had already used a distorted version of the saying in *Ulysses: "De mortuis nil nisi prius"* (About the dead, nothing except [what you've said] before) (*U* 6.794).[31]

   5. AMD nauseam (VI.B.33.173)

Joyce is playing with the familiar (and frequently abbreviated) motto of the Society of Jesus, *Ad Maiorem Dei Gloriam* (To the Greater Glory of God). The substitution of the note's "nauseam" for *gloriam* yields "To God's greater nausea." This irreverent variation does not appear in the text of the *Wake;* but another equally clever twist to the maxim is used. In Jesuit schools, the initials "A.M.D.G." were once written at the beginning of essays, tests, and homework assignments; an example of this pious custom is the first line of the page on which Stephen Dedalus wrote his verses for "E_____ C_____" (*P* 70). A student would sign the completed work with "L.S.D." (*Laus Semper Deo*, meaning "Praise to God, Always"). In the *Wake* Joyce combines these two school phrases with the common Sterling-block monetary abbreviation "l.s.d." (*libra* ["pound"], "shilling," *denarius* ["pence"]). A nice mixture of God and Mammon is thus presented in the following Latin phrase: "Ad majorem l.s.d.! Divi gloriam" (*FW* 418.4). Here, however, the word for God is not the motto's regular *Dei*, but the equally correct masculine singular genitive of *Divus*. The switch is clearly intended to reinforce the link between the divinity and worldly wealth by reminding the Latin-savvy reader of that language's adjective for "rich," *dives, divitis.*

   6. savoir, scire, sapere /
      poids, pondus, pensum /
      doigt, digitus, dictum (VI.B.5.12)

These three entries graphically illustrate Joyce's interest in etymology. Each of the initial French nouns (meaning "learning," "weight," "finger") is traced back to its Latin root, verbal and nominal. These last Notebook examples are, of course, fairly elementary, since they involve closely related Roman-Romance vocabularies. As has been demonstrated on numerous occasions, the *Wake* is packed with far more complex instances of the *figura etymologica*, which was one of Joyce's favorite impulses to engage in wordplay.

In *A Portrait of the Artist as a Young Man* there are several instances of "dog Latin" casually used by students, and Stephen Dedalus cribs resounding terms and phrases from scholastic philosophy to formulate his aesthetic principles. In *Ulysses* Buck Mulligan is skewered on a basic error in Latin syntax. In *Finnegans Wake* there are two examples of Joyce's ability to compose sustained specimens of original Latin (the "Ink" and "Historiology" passages) and many instances of incidental use of that language. There is also archival evidence of Joyce's research into the arcana of Roman consanguinity, time-vocabulary, or distorted mottoes. The preceding chapter, in sum, was designed as a commentary on the Latin elements in passages which, "me absantee" (*FW* 198.16), frequently seem to have passed unnoticed or, if detected, to have raised considerable problems of "translation" and critical application. At the same time, it is always helpful to heed the expert's reminder that, in coping with the intricacies of *Finnegans Wake*, one should not get too carried away by momentary coruscations of classical insight:

But how many of her readers realise that she is not out to dizzledazzle with a graith uncouthrement of postmantuan glasseries from the lapins and the grigs. (*FW* 112.36–113.2)

Appendix I
Joyce's Latin Curriculum

From official records it is possible to compile a quite comprehensive outline of James Joyce's academic engagement with Latin. For the Belvedere College years (1893–1898), lists of the works assigned for examination appear on the annual syllabi of the Intermediate Education Board for Ireland. Similar information is available for the set of four examinations that Joyce took to qualify for the various stages leading to a Bachelor of Arts degree at University College (1898–1902). These data serve as the basis for the chart appended below.[1]

In reviewing the outline, it is necessary to remember that the set texts for external examinations were only one component—however important—of Joyce's classroom exercises in the language and culture of ancient Rome. Selections from other authors' texts were certainly read, and every stage of the process also routinely involved all sorts of drill and competitions.[2] In 1894, for example, Joyce won a £2 prize from Belvedere for his excellence in Latin prose composition. In the national Intermediate exams (as in the University College exams) more was demanded than mere translation of set passages.

Grammatical comment, scansion, and sight translation were typical ways and means of putting students through the paces. Granted the reputation of the Jesuits for emphasis on the fundamental significance of the classical dimension in a liberal education, it can be assumed that students at Belvedere were given a stiff and thorough preparation in all aspects of the material that was appropriate for that level of pre-university study. The range of Joyce's reading in ancient texts and his collateral work in Roman history are very impressive. Comparatively speaking, it was certainly the equal of the best at contemporary American public and private schools. It would, however, fall considerably below the mark for scholarship candidates at the premier English grammar schools or elite public schools.[3] That same mastery would have been the goal, in theory, of Joyce's university courses in Latin, but here the standards could not begin to compare with those at Trinity College or at Oxford or Cambridge.[4] In short, what Jesuit instruction in the classics accomplished in an outstanding way at the secondary level, it could not, and did not (for numerous reasons), duplicate for more mature degree candidates at a university.[5]

Finally, a few remarks are in order about the beginnings of Joyce's study of Latin at Clongowes Wood College (1888–1891). Neither the prescriptions of the *Ratio Studiorum* nor the archives of the Irish province of the Society of Jesus are relevant for mundane matters of elementary language instruction. For this stage of the author's academic career the most accurate evidence is Joyce's own portrait of Stephen Dedalus, the very young artist-as-student, at the same school. The narrative re-creates a classmate's problem with the declension of the noun *mare* (*P* 47) and the pandy penalty for a "bad Latin theme" (*P* 48). Precisely.

In the "Elements" and "Third Line" classes in Latin, the emphasis fell heavily on drill in the rudiments: grammar and vocabulary, recitation and repetition, declension and conjugation. The text used for these purposes was probably a local adaptation of Kennedy's *Latin Primer*, with constant recourse to exercises and practice sentences, all involving heavy memorization of exceptional forms and genders. At a slightly more elevated level, there were paradigmatic paragraphs, then longer prose passages, which were designed to reinforce new constructions and the arcana of the attendant syntax. At this point in the young scholar's linguistic formation, another pair of hallowed pedagogical terms would have entered Joyce's working vocabulary: *prelection,* the teacher's highlighting of significant (and/or tricky) items in a homework assignment; and *parsing,* that quintessential technique for demonstrating mastery of a form in context. Exercises like these are familiar to all students of the classics. Those who learned the basics in a Jesuit classroom can recall all sorts of parochial twists and turns, but the academic goal of Joyce's rudimentary Latin at Clongowes Wood has almost universal textual application: it is the necessary prerequisite for reading Caesar's *De Bello Gallico*—traditionally mocked as *"The Calico Belly"* (*P* 43). That text naturally heads the list of examination material on the following chart.

Examination Syllabi For Latin

Belvedere College
Intermediate Education Board for Ireland

June 1894:	Caesar *De Bello Gallico* [selections??]
(700/1200)[6]	Ovid [selections from *Metamorphoses*??]
	History: Early Republic
June 1895:	Caesar *De Bello Gallico* V
(636/1200)	Vergil *Aeneid* V
	History: Punic Wars-Gracchi

June 1897:   Ovid *Metamorphoses* VIII
(642/1200)   Cicero *De Senectute*
                    History: Gracchi-Marius and Sulla
June 1898:   Livy V
(560/1200)   Horace *Odes* III, selected *Epistles*
                    History: [Fall of the Republic??]

Royal University Of Ireland—University College Dublin
Summer 1899:   Matriculation Examination:
(725/1200)   Livy V
                    Horace *Odes* III (1–6, 15, 22)
                    Horace *Epistles* II.1–2
                    Sallust *Jugurtha*
                    History: 390–27 B.C.
Autumn 1900:   First University Examination:
(756/1200)   Vergil *Eclogues,* Georgics II
                    Horace *Odes* II
                    Cicero *Pro Sulla*
                    History: 241–146 B.C. (Punic Wars)
Summer 1901:   Second University Examination:
(353/1200)   Lucretius *De Rerum Natura* I
                    Martial *Epigrams* I-IV (selections in Stephenson edi-
                    tion)
                    Cicero *Letters* XLI-LXXX (Macmillian Classics Series)
                    History: Mommsen *Provinces of the Roman Empire*
                    I.1–194.
Autumn 1902:   Examination for Bachelor of Arts Degree
                    (Joyce took no Latin for this exam.)

Appendix II
Two "Notebook" Indices

The technical detail and schematic format of genetic research are necessary; but the presentation of these data tends to disrupt the flow of a primarily literary-critical discussion. For that reason, a preliminary analysis of two important "Roman" archival indices has been relegated to this appendix. Even though I have highly abbreviated the analysis, the information provided will permit readers to to see the contours of the points of interest. The first set of Notebook entries involves Joyce's creative manipulation of the Latin names for some of the months of the year; the second set demonstrates that, even in the *Wake*, a large number of ancient vehicles and roads lead to Rome.

Roman "Month-men"

The "Seventh Question" posed in Book I.6 breaks into three parts: the Hiberno-Judeo-Christian names of the twelve apostles (*FW* 142.27–28); twelve districts of Dublin (*FW* 142.12–16); twelve "component partners of our societate," who are specified by occupation or avocation (*FW* 142.8–11). McHugh is on the right track when he hints that several of these persons are associated with the months of the year. I suggest that the significance of the title of the first six "partners" is their association with the Roman calendar. The following are the pertinent terms as they appear in the published text of the *Wake:* "the doorboy, the cleaner, the sojer, the crook, the squeezer, the lounger" (*FW* 142.8–10).

The first term, "doorboy," is certainly related to Janus, the guardian god of gates and beginnings. The "cleaner" is an allusion to *Februa*, the Roman festival of purifications. The third item, "sojer," is connected to Mars, since Roman soldiers, under his patronage, began their spring campaigns in March.

The identity and purpose of the next three members of the list ("the crook, the squeezer, the lounger") require archival reference. In the original Notebook index (which was crossed out with a large blue X), these three "month-men" appear as "priser, courter, lounger" (VI.B.18.258; March–July 1927). When these items were added to Joyce's fair copy (1(AB).*1) of this section, "priser" became "thief" and "courter" became "squeezer" (47473–188 [*JJA* 47.56]; July 1927). In the next (and final) stage of revision, "thief" was re-

249

placed by "crook" (47473–160 [*JJA* 47.72]; late July–early August 1927). The entire process, from primary Notebook entry to final text, was relatively short—five months at the most.

In Ovid's *Fasti*, a verse calendar of Roman religious festivals, the month of April is so named because it is then that Spring "opens" (*aperit*) all things. In Joyce's versions, the illegal opener (the "priser" with his jimmy) evolved into a more obvious "thief," and finally into a burglar-plus-tool ("the crook").

Ovid also indicates that the fifth and sixth months probably took their names from the elder (*maiores,* or May) and the junior (*iuvenum,* or June) citizens of Rome (*Fasti* 5.73–78). I suggest that, when he made his initial Notebook entries, Joyce "translated" this age antithesis into a space-time antithesis; he then expressed the contrast in a pair of Franglish adjective-nouns: "court-er" (shorter) and "lo(u)ng-er" (longer). In the first draft "the courter" was replaced by "the squeezer," perhaps to emphasize that a younger courter tends to be more physically demonstrative than a mature (but patient) lounger. Some support for this mensural *coincidentia oppositorum* may come from a later exhortation to the people of Ireland to pray for the return of Shaun. His exile is a time of trial for all, "the old old oldest, the young young youngest"; their ways will wither until "their Janyouare Fibyouare . . . comes marching ahome on a summer crust of the flagway" (*FW* 472.35–473.5).

There are other genetic considerations here. The "month-men" index appears one page before the list of the six Latin terms for the dawn-to-dusk divisions of the night (VI.B.18.258–59; see pages 237–38).[1] This collocation of Roman time terms argues strongly for some common source, perhaps in a yet-to-be-detected handbook or an encyclopedia article on ancient time reckoning. Several other relevant entries appear on VI.B.18.258: "[b]assideration," a Wakean coinage that means "attention to the stars" (*ad sidera* in Latin); this word is used in the text at *FW* 451.36, beside "shoepisser pluvious." There are two other uncrossed entries. The first, "mensural," which refers both to a month (*mensis*) and to measurement (*mensura*). The last item is "calendar lunatic." It looks like Joyce's personal comment not only on a calendar in which the months are calculated according to the phases of the moon (*luna*), but also to the ridiculously complicated computations involved in reconciling ancient solar and lunar calendars.

In sum, I suggest that the first six months of the Roman year lie behind the January-June "partners of our societate" in *FW* 142.8–11. (The last six months involve other, equally ingenious riddle names.) Thus, as they explore the maze of the text, from Notebook to book, critics must follow the thread of Latin-French-English etymologies and wordplay. The foregoing minor exercise in genetic scholarship has attempted to demonstrate that there are often archival clues to the significance of one interpretation instead of another. Joyce put it nicely: plausibility is rarely a case of "six of one for half a dozen of the other" (*FW* 446.19–20).

ROMAN ROADS AND VEHICLES

In an August 29, 1925, letter to Harriet Shaw Weaver, Joyce wrote "I know that ∧*d* [III.4] ought to be about roads" (*Letters* I.232). In fact, the distribution is considerably wider. Throughout the *Wake* there are four primary clusters of terms associated with the constuction and maintenance of Roman roads: *FW* 81.1–11, *FW* 469.34–473.25, *FW* 478.10–16, and scattered references in *FW* 576–85. There is also an extraordinarily long index of technical terms and names, a number of them in their Latin form, in Notebook VI.B. 8.104–13.[2] The editors of this Notebook judge that it was most probably compiled between July 1925 and April 1926.[3] The first material from this index to enter the text was the III.4 run in late 1925, shortly after the letter mentioned above. A long series in III.2 was added in an August 1926 draft; the compact cluster at *FW* 478 became part of the text in December 1928–January 1929. The paragraph in I.4 was composed in late 1936—it is also the most difficult passage in which to explain a thematic purpose for the references to ancient highways.

These archival data show that the terminology about Roman roads from the original index left a fairly broad, but sometimes hardly visible, track across the *Wake*. I give a single example of how thoroughly covered some of these items are: "⁸Summa crusta" (Latin for "topmost layer") (VI.B.8.110) reappears in the text as part of the "calendar" passage that I cited a page or so ago: "marching ahome on *summer crust* of flagway" (*FW* 473.5; my emphasis). Here the "flagway" is intended, by means of a *figura etymologica*, to translate *summa crusta* into an equivalent English roadway term.

To travel over these networks of carefully constructed *viae*, Joyce has supplied several Notebook indices of appropriate period vehicles: VI.B.8.113 (8 items), VI.B.16.32–35 (19 items), VI.C.1.13 (11 items). The following is an example of how a number of the crossed entries in these three lists traveled into the text. After Issy and her entourage of maidens have listened to Jaun's inspiring farewell sermon, they are shown sitting in carriages. Some watch from a "charabang" and a "sedan chair"; others are in three Roman vehicles, "biga triga rheda" (*FW* 469.34–35). Each piece of equipment has appeared in one of the Notebook lists: "basterna (bank)" (VI.B.8.113); "ʳchar a banc," "ʳsitdown chair △," and "ʳbiga triga / rheda" (VI.C.1.13). The latter three terms are the Latin names for, respectively, a two- and a three-horse chariot and a four-wheeled carriage.

This type of research into the evolving text and the elaborately annotated pre-text of the *Wake*—involving obscure Latin teminology—is just about as esoteric an enterprise as one can imagine. At the same time, this sort of "rheadoromanscing" (*FW* 327.11) is an essential means to an interpretation of the finished work. It is also a task that is congenial to a confirmed philologist who has long recognized that "all roads [lead] to ruin" (VI.B.8.113 and *FW* 566.1).

NOTES

INTRODUCTION

1. The translation is quoted in *JJII* 50–51.

2. Stanislaus Joyce, *Keeper*, 252.

3. Mercanton, "The Hours," 228.

4. Gilbert, Notebook "Big" C31, page 116, in the Gilbert Collection of the Harry Ransom Humanities Research Center, Austin, Texas. I thank the director and staff of the HRHRC for their help in examining this material.

5. The following anecdote is frequently told in Latin or ancient history classes. During the First Punic War, the Roman fleet commanded by Claudius Pulcher was demolished by the Carthaginian fleet at Drepana in Sicily in 249 B.C. Pious Roman citizens claimed that this disaster was caused by Claudius' mockery of the prebattle auspices: when the sacred chickens refused to eat (and thus confirm the gods' favor), the admiral threw them overboard and said, "Let them drink." Claudius was court-martialed and died in disgrace.

6. For the publication history and ritualistic imagery of the story, see Schork, "Liturgical Irony," 193–97.

7. The "little lumps of bread" carried by the boy and distributed by the priest in Joyce's Trieste anecdote are *not* the consecrated bread of the eucharistic service. Rather, at the end of the Orthodox liturgy these blessed loaves are given to the congregation as *antidōra* (return gifts) or *apophorēta* (gifts to be taken home as a favor) after the ceremony.

8. Steppe, "The Merry Greeks," 597–617.

9. For discussions on this topic, from three different decades of Joyce criticism, see Boyle, "The Priesthoods," 29–60; Restuccia, "Transubstantiating," 329–40; Shanahan, "The Eucharistic Aesthetics," 373–86. A refreshing antidote to these sacerdotal studies is Day, "Diacre," 309–17.

10. This phrase is taken from a poem by Peter Viereck, "A Walk on Snow" (1955); its context is not irrelevant:

> Being absurd as well as beautiful,
> Magic—like art—is hoax redeemed by awe.
> (Not priest but clown, the shuddering sorcerer
> Is more astounded than his rapt applauders:
> "Then all the props and Easters of my stage

Come true? But I was joking all the time.")
Art, being bartender, is never drunk;
And magic that believes itself, must die.
(*New and Selected Poems,* 155–56)

11. Schork, "Dedalus at Play," 6–7. A last-minute footnote to that article announced the discovery of Joyce's source for the translation: a popular nineteenth-century music-hall song, "[Unfortunate] Miss Bailey." Wes Davis, a graduate student in English at Princeton, has published the details of his discovery of the work's actual author; see "'Balia' *Inventa*," 738–47.

12. *Horizon* 10.57 (September 1944), 178–89.

13. For the archival references and a discussion of the processes of composition, see pages 126–28.

14. An exception to this general principle is the explicit reference to Cicero's *De Senectute* at the beginning of a fairly long index of words from (or based on) the Latin text of that dialogue (VI.B.2.148–49). These entries are discussed on pages 115–19.

15. See Gillespie, *Trieste Library*, 73–74 [Item #109: Cicero]; 144–45 [Item #276: Pope Leo XIII]; 246–48 [Items #521–22: Vergil].

16. Connolly, *The Personal Library*, 25–28 [Item #191: Matharan] and 33 [Item #257: Sallust].

17. Here it is helpful to repeat a comment by a master explicator:

The better kind of *Wake* glossing has stuck to this rule of thumb: we hardly ever find isolated "allusions" or "references." . . . To be satisfied with an ascription, Atherton looked for reinforcement, for patterns, a cluster or a constellation— sheer common sense, but some later scholiasts have on occasion been less demanding.

That advice is from Senn, "Rereading *The Books,*" 84.

CHAPTER 1: GRAMMAR AND SYNTAX

1. Several systems are used to capture the "proper" pronunciation of Latin. The two most influential can be superficially illustrated by the various ways of saying "Cicero." In the "restored" system "c" is a hard sound, as in English "k"; in the "ecclesiastical" system "c" is a soft sound, as in "ch." A Joycean phrase cleverly emphasizes that phonetic distinction: "I'd perorate a chickerow of beans" (*FW* 425.19). The rhetorical "perorate" (like the finale of an oration by Cicero) is keyed to a classical and internal "-ck" in the phrase's distortion of the name; the "bean" (*chicco* is "bean," "berry" in Italian) responds to the Roman Catholic usage and the initial "ch-." Presumably Father Flynn opted for the ecclesiastical system promoted in Roman seminaries, "whose say is soft" (*FW* 254.29–30). There is a relevant Notebook entry here: "⁸il latino pronunciare dal vaticano" (*Scribbledehobble* 88 [401], the transcription of which I have corrected on the basis of the facsimile in the *JJA*). This crossed phrase may be the archival source of "unify their voxes in a vote of vaticination" (*FW* 142.19).

2. The verb "pandy" is derived from the singular imperative of the Latin verb *pando: pande* (spread out [your palms]); see Garvin, *Disunited Kingdom*, 187. Academic concerns of a similar nature extended to the high end of the Jesuit curriculum. In *Stephen Hero* Cranly has last-minute plans to circumvent his University College examiners in Latin composition. Stephen Dedalus reminds him that "they may not be quite ignorant of Latin grammar" (*SH* 127–28).

3. In *The Merry Wives of Windsor* Shakespeare has the parson Will Page run through his declensions: "*Nominativo, hig, had, hog . . . Accusative, hung, hang, hog*" (4.1.41–47).

4. Early anti-Christian polemic claimed that Jesus was the son of a Roman soldier to whom Mary, a perfume-seller, gave herself; see "*ᵇJesus, S of Pantherus & parfumeuse,*" *UNBM* 297: 20.

5. Ovid used the same tripartite tense-bracket in the *Metamorphoses* 1.517–18. Apollo is trying to convince Daphne that he is a worthy lover. He names Jupiter as his father and claims that *per me quod eritque fuitque/estque patet* (through me he reveals what will be, was, and is); for a medieval parallel see page 224. The Latin temporal adverbs *heri* (yesterday), *hodie* (today), and *cras* (tomorrow) are also embedded in "That's our *crass, hairy* and evergrim life, till one finel *howdie*dow" (*FW* 455.13–14; my emphases).

6. See Rabaté, *Authorized Reader,* 120. For more on "Erse," see Milesi, "Perversions," 98–118.

7. This is the traditional English-Irish order of the principal parts of a Latin verb. Otherwise in this book, I use the standard American order (present, infinitive, perfect, perfect passive participle).

8. For detailed comment on this passage, see Milesi, "Female Grammar," 571–78.

9. Joyce had a copy of this part of the Pope's poetic *opera* in his Trieste collection: see Gillespie, *Trieste Library,* 144–45 (Item #276).

10. The reference is to "the sixteenth-century Jesuit grammarian Manoel Alvarez"; see Bradley, *Schooldays,* 129 and 167, n.201.

11. For this reading (instead of the "Corrected" edition's "acatalectic") see the convincing argument by Hayman, "Unpublished Letters," 187–88; also note Rose, *The Lost Notebook,* xx.

12. See Schork, "Graphic," 335–39.

13. There is early archival evidence of Joyce's interest in the Hebrew alphabet. A photograph of some of Joyce's notes for *Stephen Hero* includes this entry: "*Tenebrae—* . . . the acrostic of Jeremiah: Aleph, Beth, Ghimel, Daleth" (*SH,* facing page 93). The reference is to one of the "Lamentations" attributed to the Old Testament prophet Jeremiah; the first four are marked, in Hebrew, by alphabetical acrostics. *Lamentation* 2 was chanted during the Holy Week service of *Tenebrae;* see Peradotto, "A Liturgical Pattern," 321–26. For additional information on Joyce's use of Hebrew, see Rose, *The Index Manuscript,* 61–79; Glasheen, "Semper," 7–11; Reichert, "Hebrew," 163–82.

14. Joyce probably composed the first draft of this section of the *Wake* during the late summer of 1932 in Feldkirch, Austria. That location may have influenced his selec-

tion of the color of the infantry uniforms of the central powers in World War I for "f" and "g": *feldgrau* is German for "field grey"; see Schork, "Feldkirch," 308.

15. See Schork, "Mnemotechnic."

16. There is an interesting archival variation on this same theme (and the "source" of the *Wake* citation): "⁸tree bisexual / ⁸m form fem gend" (VI.B.3.126). In Latin the generic word for "tree," *arbor,* and the terms for all trees are *feminine* in gender, even though their lexical forms appear to be *masculine.*

17. In "Hammisandivis" and "sodullas" (the first and last terms in the *Wake* passage under discussion) I also hear "Adam and Eve," who were the world's first "mates" (*sodales* in Latin).

18. Leigh, *Comic Latin Grammar,* the doggerel quoted appears on 156–57.

Chapter 2: Buck Mulligan as a "Grammaticus Gloriosus"

1. Gogarty, *That Time,* 26–33, 57–65. For a compact review of Gogarty's schools and universities, including stints at Clongowes Wood and the Royal University (University College Dublin), see O'Connor, *The Times,* 5–7. Class differences and "grammatical precedence" are discussed by Platt, "The Buckeen," 77–86.

2. *Shaw's Plays,* 13; note Joyce's "Sainte Andree's Undershift" (*FW* 147.26–27). Throughout "Aeolus" Professor MacHugh is a parody of a would-be Greek teacher; and he is nicely cut down by Stephen's father: "—And Xenophon looked upon Marathon, Mr. Dedalus said, looking again on the fireplace and on to the window, and Marathon looked on the sea" (*U* 7.254–55).

3. In *Le Rouge et le noir,* for example, Julien Sorel's ascent from sawmill to the guillotine—with a significant stop at the Marquis' hotel—is charted in terms of his command of Latin; see Schork, "Stendhal's Latinitas," 23–38. Pope Leo XIII wrote "Latin poetry" (*D* 167), while William Ewart Gladstone's books on Homer attracted critical attention. It is his lack of Greek that kept Hardy's Jude Fawley out of "Christminster." Although it refers to an earlier era, Ong's "Puberty Rite," 103–24, is worth mentioning here. Also note that in *Ulysses* Stephen Dedalus serves as an ancient-history-cum-Latin master at Deasy's school; the language of the ancient Romans was his classical locus.

4. See Jenkyns, *The Victorians,* 60–86, 155–226; Theoharis, *An Anatomy,* has an excellent chapter on Matthew Arnold's Hellenism and its impact on *Ulysses,* 142–99.

5. See appendix I and Bradley, *Schooldays,* for information about Joyce's curriculum and scores. In a collegiate essay, "The Study of Languages" (1898–1899), Joyce wrote "the writer acknowledges humbly his ignorance of Greek" (*CW* 295).

6. In Joyce's Trieste library there is a copy of Homer's *Odyssey, Book I,* with many notes and an interlinear "translation" into Italian; several pages of this work are annotated (mainly vocabulary) in Joyce's handwriting; see Gillespie, *Trieste Library,* 120 [Item #219].

7. *Ulysses* Notebook VIII.A.5.145, 159, 163, 165; also see *UNBM* 49–57, and *The Lost Notebook,* 28–29.

8. Gogarty, *That Time*, 27.

9. Gogarty, *That Time*, 50–52.

10. Gogarty, *Many Lines*, 11. Gogarty did in fact win the Vice-Chancellor's Prize at Trinity College, Dublin, in 1903 for his poem, "The Death of Shelley." Tradition attributes its final line as a contribution by Joyce (*JJII* 131). That act of collegial composition is alluded to in the *Wake*: "Can you write us a last line?" (*FW* 302.23).

11. Gogarty, *That Time*, 64.

12. Gogarty, *Many Lines*, 88–89.

13. Gogarty, *Perennial*, 10.

14. Gogarty in fact reviewed *Finnegans Wake* in the *Observer* (May 7, 1939); he called it "the most colossal leg pull since MacPherson's *Ossian*," but acknowledged Joyce's "indomitable spirit" and his book's "magnitude" (quoted from *JJII* 722).

15. Gogarty, *Perennial*, 16.

16. Kenner, *Voices*, 15–48.

17. For a more balanced assessment of Gogarty's life and career, see O'Connor, *The Times*, especially the "Joycean" sections, 8–93; Lyons, *Syphilis*, 171–202; and Carens, "Joyce and Gogarty," 8–45.

18. Gogarty, *That Time*, 72, 78–79.

19. This passage escaped Paul Van Caspel's sharp eye in *Bloomers*. It is noted and translated without comment in O Hehir and Dillon, *A Classical Lexicon*, 565.

20. See Burgess, *Joysprick*, 163: "The only sizeable piece of secular Latin we hear in *Ulysses* is this of Cicero's: [*U* 14.707–10]." Cicero aside, there is another claimant for the "inspiration" of this passage; James Henry Tully recalled his "oration," on a visit to the Joyces' house, about the sexual preferences of the Emperor Claudius' consort Messalina. Tully (and the name is significant for this unverifiable anecdote) said that young James jotted down his statements and that they reappeared "all dressed out in classical Latin" in *Ulysses*; see Garvin, *Disunited Kingdom*, 37–41. A taurine adaptation of the vernacular "source" may also appear in the text of *Ulysses*: "He had horns galore . . . so that the women of our island, leaving doughballs and rollingpins, followed after him hanging his bulliness in daisychains" (*U* 14.586–89).

21. See *JJII* 206, for the complete text of what is there entitled "The Song of the Cheerful (but slightly sarcastic) Jesus."

22. Carens, "Joyce and Gogarty," 28–45; the full text of the song is on page 34. Carens also suggests the application of the song's sexual criterion to the Bloom-Boylan rivalry. I wish to thank the Department of Rare Books, Cornell University Libraries, for sending me a copy of this item in its collection (Scholes #523) and permitting me to quote from the letter.

23. "Catalepsis" is a medical term. Perhaps Gogarty meant a nominal form of "catalectic" (lacking a syllable in the final foot); or perhaps he wanted to hoodwink Joyce by employing the wrong term for "catachresis" (the misuse of a word resulting from a misunderstanding of its etymology). If the latter, his fun with fancy terminology was in vain; Joyce's memory for detail is as impressive as his mastery of rhetorical terminology: "A cataleptic mithyphallic!" (*FW* 481.4), with its metrical and sexual ramifications, is part of the fun here.

24. Later, in Molly's monologue in "Penelope," comparisons are drawn between Boylan's size and Bloom's spunk (*U* 18.143–55, 168).

25. See Brown, *Sexuality*, 63–78, and Lowe-Evans, "Birth Control," 803–14, and *Crimes against Fecundity.*

26. See *UNBM* 298: 57.

27. *Scribbledehobble* 117 [721]; see Schork, "Plautus and Martial," 198–200.

28. In "The Holy Office," his 1904 satirical broadside on provincialism and hypocrisy in Dublin, Joyce aimed this couplet at Gogarty: "or him whose conduct 'seems to own' / His preference for a man of 'tone'" (*CW* 150).

29. The characters in the ballad also play a cameo role in the Wake: "a reiz every morning for Standfast Dick and a drop every minute for Stumblestone Davy" (*FW* 210.28–29).

30. "Sublimis" [*sic*] is the adjective modifying "erectionibus" in Joyce's first draft (V.A.12.18); it is crossed out and changed to "excelsis."

31. In the first draft "testibus" is modified by "pergravibus," which is crossed out and changed to "ponderosis." I refuse to speculate about a possible influence of Gogarty's term "gravy" on Joyce's initial choice of "pergravibus" to characterize the ballocks of the rejected centurions.

32. See V.A.12.18 with several initial substitutions; V.A.17.5 and 7; and V.B.12.a–13.

33. The two terms appear side by side in Pliny, *Natural History,* 11.110.263: *idque tertium ab hermaphroditis et spadonibus semiviri genus habent* (halfmen constitute this third category, distinct from hermaphrodites and eunuchs). *Semivir* is found twice in Vergil's *Aeneid* (4.215, 12.99); both instances are insults to "unmanly" Trojans; Fitzgerald translates the first as "half-men," the second as "eunuch." Also note *Scribbledehobble,* 91 [461]: "castrati, all, spadones have balls: thlibiae, balls crushed, thlasiae spermatic cord cut"; none of these Latin anatomical entries seems to have made its way into the final text of the *Wake.*

34. After this chapter first appeared in journal form, it generated some comment. On Joyce's "translation" of his own material, see Ronnick, "Mulligan's Latin," 217–20 and Senn, "In the Original," 215–17 on the "original" use of vocabulary in the passage.

35. In "Circe" a "Libyan eunuch" is cited by Virag (*U* 15.2574); see *"Ulysses" Annotated,* 497, for comment on this person—and the possibility of a variant reading here.

36. Note two examples of similar constructions with the subjunctive: the already quoted clause "*Ut implerentur scripturae*" (*U* 14.1577) and "*Butyrum et mel comedet ut sciat*" (*FW* 163.3; also see *FW* 610.16).

37. Gogarty, *Many Lines,* 29.

38. For another swipe at Gogarty in the *Wake,* see Garvin, *Disunited Kingdom,* 140–41 (on *FW* 56.11–19).

Chapter 3: Roman History and Culture

1. "Peter Parley" was the creation of an American author, Samuel G. Goodrich, who wrote numerous "*Tales*" for a juvenile audience; see Sullivan, *Jesuits,* 43–45.

2. In a gloomy, October 4, 1906, letter to Stanislaus from Rome itself, Joyce wrote: "I wish I knew something of Latin or Roman history. But it's not worth while beginning now. So let the ruins rot" (*Letters* II.171). See Spoo, "Attitudes," 481–97 and *Language of History,* 14–37.

3. I have examined copies of the University College examination papers in the collection of the Zürich James Joyce Foundation.

4. *"Ulysses" Annotated,* 476.

5. Livy 1.54.709; see Schork, "Tarquinius Bloom," 646–48.

6. Dumas, *The Count of Monte Cristo,* 652 (no translator is acknowledged). The original text reads: "pareil à Tarquin abattant avec sa badine les têtes des pavots les plus élevés, M. de Villefort abattait avec sa canne les longues et mourantes tiges des roses trémières" (Dumas, *Le Comte de Monte Cristo,* 1295). Note that the English version omits Tarquin's weapon, *badine* (baton, riding crop).

7. Livy 1.9.10–12; the translation (with key Latin words in brackets) is from *Livy: The Early History,* 28. See Ogilvie, *Commentary,* 69, for a summary of the theories on the etiology and etymology of the word *Thalassius.*

8. At the start of the "Anna Livia Plurabelle" section of the *Wake,* the washerwomen's gossip contains several references to rape as they discuss HCE's alleged crime in the park: "He's an awful old reppe" (*FW* 196.11); "O, the roughty old rappe!" (*FW* 196.24). His suspicious marriage is also evoked with "when he raped her home, Sabrine asthore" (*FW* 197.21).

9. See *Encyclopaedia Britannica* 3.943 or, for more details, *Dictionary of National Biography* 3.656–59.

10. After Caesar's assassination, the last book of the *Gallic War* was completed by Aulus Hirtius, who acknowledges Balbus' encouragement (*Bellum Gallicum* 8, Preface). In one of his letters Cicero reports that the political situation in Rome is desperate, nevertheless *Balbus aedificat* (Balbus builds). This is followed by a sentence in Greek: "What's it matter to him?" (*Letters to Atticus* 12.2.2).

11. *"Ulysses" Annotated,* 409.

12. Gilbert, *A Study,* 298, n.1.

13. For trenchant comment on narrative arrangement of this episode, see Benstock, *Con/Texts in "Ulysses,"* 51–53.

14. Plutarch *Pyrrhus* 34.2–3; Joyce's "beldam" is a "poor, old woman" in the original Greek. If the word-choice here was influenced by an archaic translation of this *Life,* it was not North's famous version.

15. An archival note is of tangential interest here: "parents who had ligits and concub. Jugurtha" (*UNBM* 407: 227). Sallust reports that Jugurtha was indeed the offspring of a royal concubine (*Bellum Iugurthae* 4.6–7) and that he reached the throne by killing the two legitimate sons of the previous king.

16. Ptolemy was a mid-second-century A.D. astronomer and geographer from Alexandria; among his "calculations" in the latter discipline is a description of Ireland.

17. For a discussion of this index and its source (*Encyclopaedia Britannica* 2.222), see Van Mierlo, "Traffic," 109–10.

18. "On Keeping Shop," 3.

19. In a July 22, 1933, letter to Harriet Shaw Weaver, Joyce mentions his father's reputation for "loud elaborate curses (he is quoted on the jacket of an amusing book [Robert Graves'] *Lars Porsena or The Future of Swearing*)" (*Letters* III.250).

20. Cumpiano, "A 'Chin-Chin Chat'," 60–64.

21. There are a number of other early Roman social and political terms in VI.B.18.266–67. For incisive comment on Vichian theories of the importance of *famuli*, marriage rights, and plebeian-patrician conflict, see Rabaté, *Authorized Reader*, 130–31.

22. *The New Science*, 206 (#570), 240 (#638), 388 (#1031). Also see Treip, "Recycled Historians," 61–72, and Hofheinz, "Vico," 89–95.

23. *New Science*, 198 (#558) and 388 (#1030).

24. I realize that my application of the alphabet to Christological controversy may seem absurdly far-fetched. It has a Joycean precedent. When describing the dogmatic differences between the Roman and Eastern Orthodox churches that are debated in "The Mookse and the Gripes" (*FW* 152.15–159.5), Joyce dictates, "All the grotesque words in this are russian or greek [*sic*] for the three principal dogmas which separate Shem from Shaun. When he gets A and B on his lap C slips off and when he has C and A he looses hold of B" (*SL* 367).

25. There is a pertinent entry in a *Wake* Notebook: "deiectio a saxo Tarpeio" (VI.B.1.115), which corresponds to Livy's text: *de saxo Tarpeio deiecerunt* ([the tribunes] threw [him] from the Tarpeian Rock) (6.20.12).

26. See page 120 for Cicero's application of this hallowed example of family dishonor to his invective against Mark Antony.

27. See Bradley, *Schooldays*, 41–43.

28. Joyce offers this explanation in an August 14, 1927, letter to Miss Weaver (*SL* 328); also see Notebook VI.B.6.81.

29. In an October 31, 1925, letter to Dámaso Alonso, the Spanish translator of *Portrait*, Joyce discusses various euphemisms for "shit"; he indicates that French females sometimes use the word "miel" instead of Marshal Cambronne's "merde" (*Letters* III.129–30).

30. See Schork, "Awake, Phoenician," 767–76.

31. Another quotable comment about Joyce's reaction to Rome and its history appears in a 1906 letter to Stanislaus from the Eternal City itself: "Yesterday I went to see the Forum. . . . Rome reminds me of a man who lives by exhibiting to travellers his grandmother's corpse" (*Letters* II.165).

32. McHugh indicates that the motto of one of the Borgias was *aut Caesar aut nihil* (either Caesar or nothing) and links a version of this phrase with the Emperor Caligula. The nearest classical analogue that I can locate for that proclamation of tyrannical monomania is Caligula's *oderint, dum metuant* (let them hate, as long as they fear) (Suetonius, *Caligula* 31.1).

33. Joyce played with versions of the Latin (*augustus*) and Greek (*sebastios*) adjectives for "exalted," "revered" on several occasions: "*The Augusta Angustissimost for Old Seabeastius' Salvation*" (*FW* 104.5–6) and "brather soboostius, in my augustan days? With cesarella looking on" (*FW* 468.3–4).

34. The name "ᵇʳCaligula" is crossed in an entry at VI.B.4.148. Another archival note refers to "Caligula's houseboat / Nemi gold bay" (VI.B.6.36); this is a reference either to two elaborate houseboats found on the western shore of Lake Nemi (*Encyclopaedia Britannica* 19.369) or to Suetonius' report of ten-banked floating palaces on which the emperor cruised along the Campanian coast (*Caligula* 37). Neither of the VI.B.6 entries was used in the *Wake*.

35. The phrase "Copula Felix" is, of course, meant to suggest the famous paradox by which St. Augustine characterized the original sin of Adam and Eve in the Garden of Eden. He called their offense a *felix culpa* (happy fault), since it made necessary the incarnation of Jesus Christ; his death was the penance for the sin that condemned the entire human race. The obscene distortion of the phrase here is a preview of its numerous permutations and perversions throughout the *Wake;* see Montgomery, "The Pervigillium Phoenicis," 470–71.

36. For details, see Birley, *Marcus Aurelius,* 184–91, 224–25, and Ellis, *Irish Mythology,* 85–87, 139–40.

37. Cary, *A History of Rome,* 714. In his 1909 review of *Salome,* Joyce wrote of Wilde's final writings: "his true soul, trembling, timid, and saddened, shines through the mantle of Heliogabalus" (*CW* 205).

38. In a long index of names and terms from early French history the following entries appear: "ᵇʳAttila & Aetius / Geneviere" (VI.B.4.142).

39. There is a relevant Notebook entry that links HCE and Rome: "ᵇm eternal city" (VI.B.23.32). This item seems to have lost its specifically personal note in its transferal to the text: "(one has thoughts of that eternal Rome)" (*FW* 298.32–33).

40. The logo for the Paris-based *transatlantic review* (in which Joyce published the first fragments of "Work in Progress," April 1924) is a sailboat tossed on a giant wave; above the ship is the Latin verb "*Fluctuat.*"

Chapter 4: Roman Gods, Goddesses, and Ritual

1. For a convenient summary of the interplay between Roman history, legend, religion, mythology, and cult, see Gardner's nicely illustrated *Roman Myths.*

2. *Léon Letters,* 19. I thank Vincent Deane for sending copies of the January 15, 1935, letter and Léon's notes for his reply to Joyce.

3. Although the distinction is at times artificial, I have excluded gods whose primary habitat is Greek (such as Prometheus) and tales that came almost exclusively from Greek sources (such as the birth of Venus/Aphrodite). These items will be part of my companion volume on Joyce's use of the language and culture of ancient Hellas.

4. Joyce gave roughly the same explanation in an August 20, 1939, letter to Frank Budgen (*SL* 397–98).

5. Brilliant archival archaeology by Ingeborg Landuyt has revealed the source of a deeply buried allusion to Jupiter. In a late-nineteenth-century history of *La Poste et les Moyens de Communication* by Engené Gallois, there is a reference to oracular questions addressed to Zeus/Jupiter in his ancient shrine at Dodona. These appeals for information were inscribed on lead tablets left in and around the god's temple. In the

Wake this bit of information about esoteric means of communication reappears as "the musics of the futures . . . addressing himself *ex alto* [Latin for 'from on high']" (*FW* 407.33–34). The propriety of this allusion is confirmed by the nearby presence of "anteprepreviousday's pigeons-in-a-pie" (*FW* 407.29); at Dodona the god's oracular answers were derived from the cooings of black doves.

6. Lucretius' *De Rerum Natura I* was on the Latin syllabus for Joyce's Second University Examination (1901) (see appendix I). In one of his notebooks now at the Harry Ransom Humanities Research Center, Stuart Gilbert includes the entry "Lucretius De R.N.I" in some "W in P" material (*Notebook* "Big" C31, page 16); also see another archival reference to Lucretius on page 193–94.

7. See Bergin, *The New Science*, 353 [# 958] and 398 [# 1049].

8. Some Teutonic chemotherapy also lurks here: *mehr* (more), *Kur* (cure, health regimen), *Salz* (salt), all in German.

9. I owe this reference to Zack Bowen; see his *Musical Allusions*, 171. Also note "°myrtle of Venus with Bacchus' vine" (VI.B.45.139).

10. There is archival evidence that Joyce was acquainted with the "art-history" section of Pliny's *Natural History*. The entry "bTimanthes, satyrs with thyrsus measure his thumb" (*UNBM* 114: 42) is a reference to *NH* 35.36.74. There Pliny reports that on a small panel depicting "A Sleeping Cyclops," the Greek painter Timanthes gave his viewers an idea of the scale intended by showing some satyrs at the giant's side. They were measuring the size of his thumb with a ritual wand (*thyrsus*) used in ceremonies in honor of Bacchus.

11. The epic analogies are *Iliad* 1.590–94, and *Paradise Lost* 1.22–48, 229–33; see Schork, "Milton, Blindness," 71.

12. There are several pertinent archival notes: "gherculaneum / gVesuvius / goverthrow / gpompey" (VI.B.13.33); "last daze of pampaying" (VI.B.32.201); "eruption Pompeian" (VI.C.143).

13. The Wakean phrase "it pines for an umbrella" (*FW* 159.35) does not appear to have any connection with the disaster at Pompeii; it introduces a long series of puns on tree names.

14. Treip, "Recycled Historians," 61–72.

15. The term is traditionally connected with the *Pons Sublicius* (Bridge of Wood Beams) built in the time of the kings across the Tiber near the Janiculum Hill. It was later considered so sacred that it could not be repaired until the pontifex had personally offered a sacrifice on the site.

16. In a Notebook entry Oscar Wilde is designated "puntifex maximus"; on the same page another item appears: "pantyfix mixymost" (VI.B.5.107). These notes may have contributed to "Pantifox" (*FW* 293.F2) and "pontofacts massimust" (*FW* 532.9).

17. See Hofheinz, "Vico, Natural Law," 89–95, and *Invention*, 141–81.

18. A brief archival index demonstrates Joyce's awareness of this phenomenon: "°omens / vultures / bees / °statue stumbled" (VI.B.33.12). Romulus claimed the right to found the city of Rome because he saw more vultures than Remus (Livy 1.7.1); Aeneas is welcomed to Latium by King Latinus because a swarm of bees settled on the

sacred laurel tree (*Aeneid* 7.58–70). I can find no stumbling statues in Latin literature or the works of Joyce.

19. In one of Catullus' poems, Amor blesses a couple: *nunc ab auspicio bono profecti mutuis animis amant amantur* (and now, setting out *under a good auspice*, with hearts that are mutually pledged, they love and are loved) (45.19–20).

20. The anecdote is reported by Suetonius, *Augustus* 7.2.

21. The most graphic source for comments on Antony's outrageous behavior in his cups is Cicero's *Philippic II*, pages 109–11.

22. A famous early Roman legend gives the Palatine region as the site of the rustling of Hercules' herd by the abominable monster Cacus (see pages 132–36). The Palatine is also the area in which Romulus and Remus were raised as foundlings. The mature twins began their return to power by raiding the herds of the usurper, their wicked uncle, who had ordered them to be exposed on the banks of the Tiber.

23. Giedion-Welcker, "Meetings," 268–69; also note "Oman nomad" (VI.B.6.112).

24. Gilbert, *A Study*, 143.

25. In the *Ulysses* Notesheets there are two entries about this sort of minor Roman divinity: "Prorsa, Postverta, Nixii, ꞌPartula, Genita Mana" (*UNBM* 169: 104; see Herring's note on page 172) and "deae virginenses, prema, ꞌpertunda: Deus Subigus" (*UNBM* 180: 79; see Herring's note on pages 183–84).

26. See Notebook VI.C.15.245. In "Last Epistle," 731–32, Patrick McCarthy detects an allusion to a minor birth-goddess, Decuma, in the fact that ALP is "still her deckhuman amber too" *FW* 619.19). There is a tenuous reference to Decuma in Aulus Gellius (3.16.9–10). Stuart Gilbert proposed, apropos to "Circe," that in the "domain of Feronia, goddess of forests and fauna," there were neighboring towns named "Setia and Suessa (pigtown)" (*A Study*, 311). Thus, to show that she is capable of numinous word association, Zoe reveals to Bloom that she is from "Hog's Norton" (*U* 15.1983).

27. Gogarty, *Many Lines*, 11, and the memoir by Sheehy, *The Joyce We Knew*, 29.

CHAPTER 5: CICERO

1. Joyce himself provided a guide for that passage: "Names. Buonaparte (Goodbody) Cicero (Podmore) Christ (Doyle) / Racine (root)" (*UNBM* 86: 5–6, and 185: 20–21). Figuring out the bases for these derivations should cause few difficulties, if one remembers that "Christ" (the anointed one) is cognate to the Greek "chrism," and hence to the French "d'huile" and its English phonetic counterpart. In the same series of notes, there is another pertinent reference: "Cicero (Roseberg) 1905" (*UNBM* 115: 81); "Cicero" was the name of Lord Roseberg's horse, winner of the Derby at Epsom Downs.

2. See Matthews, "Puns," 20–24. Cicero records wordplay with *Nobilior* (more noble) and *Mobilior* (more fickle); Joyce follows with "Burke's mobility" (*FW* 235.13).

3. See Fitzpatrick, "*Ratio Studiorum*," 36.

4. One of Joyce's friends from the early years in Paris recalls a discussion about Plutarch's *Life of Mark Antony*, who seemed to him "to be the outstanding figure of the ancient world"; see Power, *Conversations*, 72–75.

5. Browne, *Christian Morals,* 60. Other eminently Ulyssean words from the same work are "parallaxis" (117) and "metempsychosis" (120). In one of the Notesheets for "Oxen of the Sun," "ʳassuefaction" occurs (*UNBM* 218: 64). For the latest on Joyce's use of sources for this chapter, see Janusko, "Yet Another Anthology," 117–31, and his bibliographical notes.

6. In 1903 Joyce reviewed Ibsen's first play, the historical drama *Catilina,* for the London *Speaker* (*CW* 98–101). The review clearly shows that Joyce was more interested in Ibsen's technique and themes than in his historical veracity.

7. Twin verbs from the same root are repeated throughout the *Wake:* "(phiat! phiat!)" (*FW* 34.7), "*Fuitfuit*" (*FW* 50.32), "fooi, fooi" (*FW* 75.7), "fuitefuite" (*FW* 235.10), "*Fuitfiat!*" (*FW* 613.14).

8. These epithets of Jupiter are discussed in more detail on page 77.

9. A more detailed discussion of HCE as a "buckgoat" is found on pages 209–11.

10. Marcus Porcius Cato (234–149 B.C.) was the primary example of stern Roman virtue; he ended each of his speeches with the reminder that the resurgent "Carthage must be destroyed." Joyce also records the fact that, as an old man, Cato began to study Greek (*CW* 219). Publius Cornelius Scipio Aemilianus (185–129 B.C.) was the Roman general at the final collapse of Carthage; he also destroyed the Celtiberians at Numantia in Spain.

11. David Hayman, the editor of the facsimile publication of this Notebook, suggests July–November 1923 for its compilation (*JJA* 29.xii).

12. Cicero himself comments on the four traditional Roman divisions of life: *pueritia* (boyhood: until 17); *adulescentia* (with *iuventus*) (young manhood: until 40); *aetas media* (middle age: over 40); *senectus* (old age: over 60); see *De Senectute* 10.34 and 20.76. Joyce was aware of these distinctions: "to mark the precise point between boyhood (*pueritia*) and adolescence (*adulescentia*)—17 years" (*Letters* II.79).

13. In the synopsis that introduces her *Third Census,* Glasheen significantly refers to Joyce's 1903 review of Lady Gregory's *Poets and Dreamers* (see *CW* 103–4): "The story-tellers are old, and their imagination is not the imagination of childhood. The story-teller preserves the strange machinery of fairyland, but his mind is feeble and sleepy. . . . her book . . . sets forth in the fulness of its senility" (lvi).

14. The following data were first presented, in highly abbreviated form, at the Fourteenth International James Joyce Symposium (1992) in Dublin. Since that time both the decipherment of the Notebook entries and their use in the *Wake* have benefited immensely from the expertise of Wim Van Mierlo (Antwerp) and Vincent Deane (Dublin).

15. An incident recalled by one of Joyce's Belvedere classmates may also have contributed to this phrase. John F. Byrne reports the following vocabulary howler. When a teacher asked for the meaning of "pedestrian," one student replied, "A pedestrian is a Roman soldier, Sir." Joyce's reaction was a "spontaneous shout [not] a laugh— . . . more like a howl of agony" (Byrne, *Silent Years,* 140).

16. I strongly suspect that the "rooster" flopping out of an "ark" in this phrase is also meant by Joyce to recall the unceremonial ditching of the auspical chickens by Appius' son, Admiral Claudius Pulcher (see note 5 on page 253).

17. The most recent editor of Cicero's text discusses this folk belief in his commentary on the passage: Cicero, *Cato Maior*, 149.

18. On the other hand, there is at least one more archival reference to the philosopher: "Carneade skeptic / held laws daughters / of fraud" (VI.B.1.116 and VI.C.3.137).

19. For the latest word on the dating of the *Wake* Notebooks, see Rose, *Textual Diaries*, 41–88.

Chapter 6: Vergil

1. I know of only one, quite limited treatment of this topic: Ramon Sales, "Presencia," 505–10.

2. The quotation is from Newman, *Grammar of Assent*, 78–79.

3. For the complete text of this tribute see Tennyson, *Poems*, 530–31.

4. See Hamilton, "Fatal Texts," 309–30; Katz, "*Sortes*," 245–58; and Arkins, "Further Note," 241–43 (evidence for use of *sortes Vergilianae* by Yeats and Gogarty).

5. See Senn, "The Gnat," 233.

6. In the line immediately after the Vergilian allusion in the *Wake* there is a Joycean verb, "obcaecated" (*FW* 76.36), which is obviously derived from *obcaeco, -are, -avi, obcaecatum* (to make blind, to conceal). In the latter sense practically the same form, *occaecatum*, is used by Cicero in an agricultural passage to refer to a seed "buried" in the soil (*De Senectute* 15.51).

7. The review is cited in Scholes and Kain, *Workshop*, 131–32.

8. There may be a translingual imitation of this sort of wordplay "in the Nichtian glossery which purveys aprioric roots for aposteriorious tongues": "lux apointlex" (*FW* 83.9–11). Here the Latin noun *lux* is modified by a French phrase for "dawn" (*à pointe du jour*) and/or an English-sounding adjective that renders the whole process "pointless."

9. There is another appearance of this adjective in the epic, and in the same emphatic terminal position in the hexameter line: *ineluctabile fatum* (fate that cannot be wrestled away) (*A* 8.334).

10. Gogarty, *That Time*, 73. The analogue from Dante is *E caddi come corpo morto cade* (And I fell the way a dead body falls) (*Inferno* 5.142).

11. Herring, "Notebook VIII.A.5," 287–310.

12. Joyce lifted this etymology from Roscher's *Lexikon* I.2.1778–79; see Senn, "Strandentwining," 103. To Senn's examples add a line from the burial of Paddy Dignam in "Hades": "—Though *lost to sight*, Mr. Dedalus said, to memory dear" (*U* 6.457; my emphasis).

13. See Benstock, *Con/Texts in "Ulysses,"* 140–41. Any connection between the highlander's name ("lance-corporal Oliphant" [*U* 15.96]) and Margaret Oliphant, the author of *Stories Seen and Unseen*, is probably purely coincidental here.

14. See Herring, "Notebook VIII.A.5," 291–92, and "Bedsteadfastness," 54.

15. I owe this observation to John McEliece, a student in a Spring 1995 seminar on "Intertextuality" at University of Massachusetts, Boston.

16. The primary allusion is to the aria "Casta Diva" from Bellini's *Norma*.

17. The Vergilian passage is *Aeneid* 6.205–7. Speculation about the anthropological

ramifications of this sacred tree gave rise, of course, to James G. Frazer's *The Golden Bough.* For a cogent treatment of Joyce's use of that work in the *Wake,* see Vickery, "Rituals of Mortality," 408–23.

18. Dawson, "MacGreevy," 309.

19. Senn proposes another Golden Age Roman poet as a contributor to this episode in "Gigantism," 561–77.

20. For the concept and function of the "Arranger," see Hayman, *Mechanics,* 88–104, 122–25.

21. The Vergilian passages are *Aeneid* 8.185–275 (King Evander's narration) and *Aeneid* 8.285–305 (twin choruses dance and sing the tale before the altar of Hercules).

22. Hayman, "Cyclops," 274.

23. For a discussion of HCE as a "hairy"—and horny—billygoat, see Schork, "Sheep, Goats," 205–7.

24. See the references in "Thunderstorms, J's fear of" in the *Index* of *JJII* (879) and *Letters* I. 241.

25. Joyce owned and read the Latin texts of Vergil's *Georgics* and *Aeneid* while in Trieste; see Gillespie, *Trieste Library,* 246–48 (items #521–22). There are no Vergil texts listed in the catalogue of his Paris library; see Connolly, *Personal Library.*

26. There is a relevant archival entry here; see *Scribbledehobble* 129 [746]: "Ad sum."

27. Examples of the "fertility" denotation of the adjective are Vergil's salty or acidic soil, which is *frugibus infelix* (unproductive of a harvest [of grapes]) (*G* 2.239), or the geographical designation "Arabia Felix" for that portion of the peninsula which is not desert.

28. The menstrual dimension of the *Wake* passage is reinforced in a comment by Senn, "Nausicaa," 297; to gloss the adjective "bloody" as applied to the Virgin Mary, Senn refers to *Letters* II.134 and Gilbert's *A Study,* 259. All of the blood in book 4 of the *Aeneid,* of course, comes from Dido's self-inflicted wound; as does Ovid's vivid adjective *sanguinolenta* (*Heroides* 7.70).

CHAPTER 7: HORACE

1. See Bradley, *Schooldays,* 112, 115, 129, 138–39. Selections from Horace's *Odes* and *Satires* were assigned on examination syllabi (see appendix I). For the translation of Horace's ode, see *JJII* 50–51.

2. Mercanton, "The Hours," 227. Mercanton also reports that "Joyce delighted in Horace, whom he preferred to Vergil because of his minute perfections, his diverse meters, his rarest music" (228).

3. Stanislaus Joyce, *Keeper,* 241.

4. The presence of "the gossiple so delivered in his epistolear" (*FW* 38.23) in the previous paragraph of the text adds another, liturgical (Gospel and Epistle) dimension to the normal Greco-Latin word for "letter." The parenthesis that immediately follows the "two pisononse Timcoves" conceals a scrambled quotation from the Old Testament's Song of Songs: "(the wetter is pest, the renns are overt and come and the voax of the

turfur is hurled on our lande)" (*FW* 39.14–15). I have no doubt that Joyce also meant to signal the exact beginning of this Biblical allusion (chapter 2, verse 11) by the English "two" and the Spanish "eleven" (*once*) in "*two* pison*once*" (*FW* 39.14; my emphasis). For other examples of this sort of cabalistic reference, see Schork, "Haus Citrons," 407–18 (Deut. 28:44), and Halper, "Answers," 11–12 (Num. 17:6–9).

5. See Senn, "In Classical Idiom," 37–38.

6. There is a crossed archival note, "ᵇSD = Horace's deaf donkey" (*UNBM* 97: 120); this is an allusion to Horace, *Epis.* 2.1.199–200, that does not seem to have left its mark on the final text of *Ulysses.*

7. At the bottom of this same page of the *Wake*, Joyce violates his manipulation of Horace's admonition to observe moderation in diction: "Pythagorean sesquipedalia of the panepistemion" (*FW* 116.29–30); "*sesquipedalia*" is taken directly from the *Ars Poetica* (line 97).

8. This phrase and the next (*FW* 58.18) were added to the text of the *Wake* on the same stage of revision in 1936 (*JJA* 45.313); this may suggest that Joyce had a text of Horace's *Odes* in hand as he prepared this section of his work for final publication.

9. Horace addressed this ode to Postumus; compare "Postumus" (*FW* 377.9) and "posthumour's" (*FW* 316.34).

10. For a complete discussion of this ode, see Schork, "*Aemulos Reges*," 515–39.

11. Roman highways and means of transportation (along with their archival origins) are discussed in appendix II.

12. For convenient reference I cite the English translation: Ferrero, *Greatness and Decline* 4.210–11; also see Spoo, *Language of History*, 27–33, and Humphreys, "Ferrero," 239–51.

13. Pound, *Pound/Joyce*, 122–23.

CHAPTER 8: OVID

1. Senn's study is most accessible in the anthology of a number of his most important articles, *Dislocutions*, 73–84. For an interesting discussion of Daedalus and D'Annunzio, see Cope, *Joyce's Cities*, 46–61.

2. Lewis and Short, *A Latin Dictionary*, 168.

3. The presence of an *anser . . . minimae custodia villae* (the goose who was the sentry of their tiny cottage) (*M* 8.684) and the metamorphosis of their house by Jupiter can be seen as a domestic parallel to the warning of the geese at the Capitoline temple during the raid by the Gauls (see pages 46 and 62).

4. There appears to be a reference to this in *Scribbledehobble* 117–18 [721]: "sacrifice a bull (Irish) to Neptune." Another possible classical allusion is to Laocoon's tragic sacrifice on the shores of Troy in the *Aeneid* 2.201–2.

5. For a thorough analysis of the function of this Ovidian passage (but without any Joycean undertones) see Ahern, "Daedalus and Icarus," 273–96.

6. See Halper, "'Hawklike Man'," 312.

7. There is, however, the possibility of Wakean cross-reference here, since St. Kevin's female temptress certainly must have regretted her rash behavior when the chaste

hermit attacked her with a scourge of nettles. The key text is "smoothing out Nelly Nettle and her lad of mettle, full of stings" (*FW* 604.36); see Schork, "Childhood Miracles."

8. Atherton also suggests an allusion to Ovid's works-in-exile, *Tristia* (Sad Things) and *Ex Ponto* (From the Black Sea) in "a song of alibi" (*FW* 190.30; *alibi* is Latin for "in another place"); see Atherton, *The Books*, 271.

9. It is also possible to cite the likely source for the two Latin names of the feast recorded in the *Encyclopaedia Britannica*: Smith, *A Dictionary*, 985. (This reference work was frequently reprinted and widely used, but I detect no firm evidence that it was one of Joyce's habitual sources of obscure classical information.)

10. The two doomed youths are jointly commemorated in an elaborate simile by Dante, *Inferno* 17.106–14.

11. In the final Book of the *Wake* there is a reprise of this motif: "the greek Sideral Reulthway, as it havvents . . . the vialact coloured milk train" (*FW* 604.12–14).

12. See Taylor, "The Fellies," 18–20.

13. The source for Joyce's information here apparently has nothing to do with classical or Renaissance epic poetry. In a late (1938) *Wake* Notebook there is an elaborate index of trees and horticulture, many items of which were transferred into the text. See *The Index Manuscript*, 291–96.

14. Gilbert, small notebook headed "Anna Sequana," 54; also see *UNBM* 191: 33.

15. Gilbert, *A Study*, 297.

16. Gilbert, *A Study*, 297, n.2.

17. My emphases call attention to the modern Greek pronunciation of "*eu*" as "*ef*," as in *efkaristo* for *eucharisto* (thank you).

18. See parallels in *Ulysses* where "MEDICAL DICK AND MEDICAL DAVY" appear on a playbill (text by "Ballocky Mulligan") as "two birds with one stone" (*U* 9.1176–85).

19. Senn, "In Classical Idiom," 37–39; also note the generic archival reference: "ᵇMidas" (VI.B.12.64).

20. See the duet in the minstrel show in "Circe" (*U* 15.420–23) and Bauerle, "American Popular Music," 155.

21. This liturgical chant is loosely based on some parallel phrases in the Vulgate, Judith 11:19, 13:20, 31. In this book of the Old Testament the Israelites celebrate Judith's decapitation of the Assyrian commander Holofernes. The heroic deed takes place in the general's *bedroom*—an intertextual fact that I do not, for one moment, suggest Joyce noticed.

22. See Gilbert, *A Study*, 147, and Ellmann, *Liffey*, [191] in his appendix, which compares the Linati and the Gorman-Gilbert schemata.

23. See Kestner, "Victorian Iconography," 565–94. Also note that the Blooms' statue of Narcissus had "his finger up for you to listen" (*U* 18.1350–51), whereas on the wall of his apartment in Zürich Joyce pinned "a photograph of a Greek statue of Penelope. It represented a woman, drapped, seated, looking at her upheld finger" (Budgen, *Making of "Ulysses,"* 188).

24. The two best studies of this aspect of Joyce's work are Devlin, *Wandering and Return*, and Benstock, *Con/Texts in "Ulysses."*

25. See Ferrer, "Freudful Couchmare," 367–82 and "La Scène primitive," 15–36. At the Fourteenth Paris James Joyce Colloquium (1993), Wim Van Mierlo discussed additional archival material from Freud in Notebook VI.B.9. In Freud's case history of "An Infantile Neurosis," there is an incidental detail that, in terms of the language-learning aspects of this book, is too ominous to be passed by in silence. The wolf phobia of Freud's young patient was exacerbated when he was severely taken to task by his teacher for making a stupid mistake in Latin translation. The harsh master's name was Herr Wolf (Freud, *Standard Edition* 17.39–40). In an astounding coincidence of pedagogical nomenclature, Joyce's 1893 Italian master at Belvedere was Mr. Loup (Bradley, *Schooldays*, 106).

26. Freud, *Standard Edition* 17.111 or *Collected Papers* 3.593.

27. Freud, *Collected Papers* 3.566, n.1.

28. Ferrer, "Freudful Couchmare," 375.

29. Erzgräber seeks to insert Perdix into Joyce's use of the Daedalus-Icarus myth in *Portrait* and *Ulysses;* his arguments are not convincing ("Antike," 321–29, 339).

30. The same mythic motif briefly appears in *Ulysses:* "It rains dragons' teeth. Armed heroes spring up from furrows" (*U* 15.4680–81).

31. McHugh sees an extended allusion to this tragic triangle in the "nightingales" program at *FW* 360.23–361.25 (*Sigla*, 86–87). I am unable to educe from the text the evidence for that claim, but "innocents immutant!" *FW* 361.20–21) could be a reference to Philomela and her tapestry.

32. Ovid re-creates this tale in *Metamorphoses* 3.316–38. The occasion for the story is Jupiter's contention to Juno that women get more pleasure from sex than men. Tiresias is a natural arbiter; he agrees with Jupiter. Juno blinds him as a punishment; but Jupiter counters with the gift of prophetic "second-sight." Joyce certainly knew these details, as recorded in VIII.A.5.29.

33. Thanks to the deference granted to the geographical whim of the elders of the Ancient Universities, the Thames at Oxford is known as the Isis. Joyce seems to have supported this eccentricity of fluminal nomenclature: "floating on a stillstream of isisglass" (*FW* 486.23–24) and "Icis" (*FW* 214.31) in ALP's list of rivers.

34. Barnes, "Vagaries Malicieux," 253; also see Scott, "'The Look'," 157–63.

Chapter 9: Miscellaneous Authors, Classical and Medieval

1. See Gleckner, "Byron," 40–51.

2. I suspect that Joyce actually quoted the epigram from the complete edition, Lord Byron, *The Poetical Works* (London: Routledge, 1880), a copy of which was in his personal collection in Trieste; see Gillespie, *Trieste Library*, 64–66 [Item #92].

3. See Sullivan, *Jesuits*, 209–13.

4. Cicero, *Pro Caelio* 14.33–34. In this famous *prosopopoeia* (dramatic personification) Appius Claudius invokes another of Clodia's ancestors, the heroic vestal virgin Quintia Claudia.

5. Four lines from this poem (without reference to its author) are quoted at the end of his chapter on "Calypso" by Gilbert, *A Study,* 146.

6. As a matter of fact, Joyce's interest in this topic extends at least as far back as *Scribbledehobble.* In that Notebook, under the general heading of "Words," he jotted down: "cosset and caress: [br]osculum (cheek) basium (lips) suavium [br]tongue)"; see *Scribbledehobble* 172 [981].

7. For a compact discussion of the Latin "age-ist" maxim and its application to Catullus' poem see *Catullus,* 146, and Frazer's appendix to Ovid's *Fasti* 425–29 with reference to *Fasti* 5.621–62.

8. In one of his epigrams (12.18.10–11) Martial refers to the *nomina crassiora* (quite uncouth names) one encounters in Celtiberian territory.

9. The novelist George Moore wrote an autobiographical trilogy *Hail and Farewell: Ave* (1911), *Salve* (1912), *Vale* (1914). Tennyson also repeats Catullus' farewell in his poem "Frater Ave atque Vale" (Tennyson, *Poems,* 533).

10. The notebook to which I refer in this section of my study is numbered "C14" in the preliminary catalogue of the Gilbert material. I wish to acknowledge my gratitude to the director, Thomas F. Staley, and staff of the Harry Ransom Humanities Research Center in Austin, Texas, for their courtesy and help during my visit to the collection. The trustees of the estate of Stuart Gilbert also kindly permitted me to obtain photocopies of several documents in the HRHRC archival collection.

11. Gilbert, *A Study,* 334, n.1; the HRHRC notebook material is from C14, 31.

12. Gilbert, *A Study* 315, n.1; the HRHRC notebook is again C14, 31.

13. Gilbert, HRHRC notebook "Big" C31, 98.

14. Gilbert, HRHRC notebook "Big" C31, 51, and *A Study,* 385, which is an explication of *U* 18.1378. As a matter of fact, the phrase is applied to Molly at the end of "Ithaca": "Listener: reclined semilaterally . . . in the attitude of Gea-Tellus" (*U* 17.2312–13).

15. *Catullus,* ed. Merrill, 128; there, the scholarly note to poem 63.76 refers the reader to "Lucr.II.600," which is proof of Gilbert's source.

16. This notebook is analyzed by Herring, "Notebook VIII.A.5," 287–310; that study is reprinted (with a few revisions) in Herring's *Joyce's Notes* 3–33. Joyce's source of information here is Roscher, *Lexikon* 3.1910; also see *UNBM* 393: 9 for another entry on Penelope and the suitors.

17. The term "ithyphallic" is a compound made of the Greek adjective *ithys* (straight, erect) and the noun *phallos* (penis). In the *Wake* Joyce raises the word to legendary dimensions: "mithyphallic" (*FW* 481.4).

18. There is a complete, modern, scholarly edition (with notes and English translations) of these works by Parker, *Priapea.*

19. See Herring, "Bedsteadfastness," 49–61.

20. *Priapea,* 50.

21. The translation, along with a prose version by "Neaniskos" ("Young Man" in Greek), was published in 1890 in Cosmopolis. This information comes from *Priapea,* 56.

22. See *Priapea*, 152–53 and 204–5. There is also a longer and more elaborately graphic "figure" poem on the same general topic (with a female component represented by △) in the epigrams of Ausonius; see *Ausonius* 2.205–7. Wilhelm Füger delivered a brief paper on this topic at the Zürich International James Joyce Symposium in June 1996.

23. See Milesi, "Perversion," 105–13, and O Hehir and Dillon, *A Classical Lexicon*, 650–52.

24. For more comment on this passage, see Schork, "Graphic Exercise," 335.

25. The Latin text is cited from *The Roman Missal*, 495–98. This Passion hymn is the *Pange Lingua* of Venatius Fortunatus—which is *not* the hymn of the same title mentioned at *P* 210. The second *Pange Lingua*, based on the work of Fortunatus, was composed by Thomas Aquinas, and was sung during the procession after Mass on Holy (Maundy) Thursday.

26. There is frequent wordplay with this phrase in the *Wake*: "*Huskvy Admortal*" (*FW* 105.16–17), "*Usquadmala*" (*FW* 184.28), "Whiskway and mortem!" (*FW* 510.33).

27. *Roman Missal*, 491–92.

28. For Joyce's abiding dedication to Holy Week services, see *JJII* 309–10 and Mercanton, "The Hours," 214–15, 246. For the Adoration of the Cross, see Gilbert, *A Study*, 301–2; for the ritual of *Tenebrae*, see Peradotto, "A Liturgical Pattern," 321–26; for the *Exultet* on Holy Saturday, see Day, "Le Diacre," 309–17. For the want of a better place to put it, I add a final, semiliturgical Priapic item here. In one of the recopied *Wake* Notebooks for which the original has been lost, the following entry appears: "27/9 S. Cosme = Priapus" (VI.C.7.164). I am aware of no conceivable connection between Priapus and St. Cosmas, one of the widely honored twin physician-martyrs of the early Church; his feast day is September 27.

29. See Schork, "Barnum," 762.

30. A prime illustration comes from the *Priapea* 64:

quidam *mollior* anseris medulla
furatum venit huc amore poenae;
furetur licet usque: non videbo.

(A certain guy, softer than the pinfeathers of a goose, comes here to steal, because he just loves my penalty; let him steal all he wants—I'll close my eyes.)

31. Greene, *Saints*, 53. This book was in Joyce's personal collection in Trieste; see Gillespie, *Trieste Library*, 109 [Item #199].

32. This elaborate series of biblical jokes and puns is the *Caena Cypriani* (Cyprian's Banquet). This document is effectively adapted by Umberto Eco, *The Name of the Rose*, 427–33.

33. Noel, *Friendship*, 15.

34. Two archival notes are to the point here: "⌐lying fallow ploughshare" and "⌐seedfield nearer home" (*UNBM* 243: 46, 48). For other examples of this trope see

Enk, *Plauti Truculentus* 2.46–47 and Adams, *Sexual Vocabulary,* 151–54. There is also a pseudo-Martial epigram (cited from Pierrugues, *Glossarium Eroticum,* 223) to the same effect:

> Cur sit ager sterilis, cur uxor fertilis, edam:
>> quo fodiatur ager non habet, uxor habet.

> (Why his field is fallow, why his wife is fruitful, I shall explain: the field doesn't have anything to be ploughed by—the wife does.)

35. In one of Catullus' grossest invectives, addressed to the regulars at *salax taberna* (a drinking spot which leaps with lust), the poet rakes the studs who think that they alone have the right to fuck every girl (*quidquid est puellarum / confutuere*) and who regard all rivals as billygoats (*putare ceteros hircos*) (37.1–5). A standard commentary glosses *hircos* with "i.e., creatures detestable to all women." This connotation of crude lechery can also be found in English: "An admirable evasion of whoremaster man, to lay his goatish disposition to the change of a star!" (*King Lear* 1.2.138; compare "kingly leer" [*FW* 398.23]). Also note Stephen Dedalus' postretreat vision of damnation: "stinking, bestial, malignant, a hell of lecherous goatish fiends" (*P* 138) and Leopold Bloom as "A fiendish libertine from his earliest years this stinking goat of Mendes" (*U* 15.1755).

36. I suspect that Joyce may have converted Suetonius' *in silvis quoque ac nemoribus* (in the woods and glades) into the more explicitly sexual Latin phrase "*prostituta in herba*" (prostituted herself on the grass) (*FW* 115.15), which appears just three lines after the initial Tiberius reference cited on the previous page.

37. See Lucretius, *De Rerum Natura,* 5–15.

38. Atherton, *Books,* 273.

39. For a good discussion of these passages see Hart, *Structure and Motif,* 182–200.

40. In the introduction to his general survey of Joyce's work, Parrinder draws a nicely proportioned literary analogy from Vitruvius' *On Architecture:* the term "grotesque" is traced back to wild ornamental designs on Roman buildings constructed during the Augustan renewal of the city (see Parrinder, *Joyce,* 8).

41. See Schork, "Justinian," 77–80.

42. Jacques Mercanton reports ("Hours," 246) that he and Joyce attended Good Friday services in Paris in 1939. After they left the church, Joyce "began to sing softly in a deep slow voice: *Quae vulnerata lanceae*" (Which was wounded by the lance's point). This is the beginning of a stanza from *Vexilla Regis,* but not the same one intoned by Lynch at *P* 210.

43. See Van Mierlo, "St. Martin," 29–41, for a complete report on this source, its archival traces, and its use in the *Wake.*

44. Stuart Gilbert quotes a Latin passage from this work in one of his *"Ulysses"* notebooks (HRHRC "Big" C31, p. 25) and directly refers to "Sulpicius Severus' Sacred Histories"; but I have detected no trace of that entry in Joyce's work.

45. Atherton, *Books,* 137–48.

46. Raby, *Christian-Latin Poetry,* 94. Perhaps the most recondite literary entry in Joyce's Notebooks is "Juventilian cento" (VI.B.8.85). This is a garbled reference to the

fourth-century A.D. *cento* ("patchwork" in Latin) by the Spanish priest Juvencus. His hexameter work retells the Gospels in verses taken from Vergil.

CHAPTER 10: JOYCE'S OWN LATIN

1. Sheehy, *We Knew,* 22. I use the term "dog Latin" to specify this sort of *ad hoc* approximation of the ancient language by students. Some of the vocabulary and grammar might pass muster, but the structure is definitely contemporary, not ancient. Bog Latin (*pace U* 14.628–29) and "japlatin" (*FW* 467.14) have nothing to do with the language of the Romans; see Glasheen, "Secret Languages," 49, and Graham, "Japlatin," 52–53. The point of the second article is confirmed by a Notebook entry: "⁸Jap's latin / spell word in / its sound." (Erethay isay onay Igpay Atinlay inay ethay *Akeway*!)

2. Throughout this book I have assumed that all readers are familiar with McHugh, *Annotations,* and Gifford, *"Ulysses" Annotated.* O Hehir and Dillon, *A Classical Lexicon,* is limited to word-roots, vocabulary, and general linguistic material, but it is a very useful guide to those areas.

3. The *James Joyce Literary Supplement* 3.1 (Fall 1989) is a fairly complete synopsis of the debate and comment at the conference. It does not, however, refer to my contribution, which is summarized below. It is worth noting here that the infamous passage, "Word known to all men . . . *Amor*" (*U* 9.429–31), was *not* addressed in my brief remarks, since it appeared in the "Corrected" text for the first time and thus had been only a marginal part of the "continuous" text under debate at the conference.

4. The passage (with the original spelling) is cited by Gilbert, 304; a variation on the same theme is found in a passage of theological controversy in the *Wake:* "*occupante extremum scabie*" (*FW* 575.36–576.1).

5. Boyle, "Page 185," 3–16; reprinted in *Critical Essays,* 59–72.

6. For an introduction to and text-translation of these poems see Herren, *Hisperica Famina.*

7. Rand, "The Irish Flavour," 141.

8. The archival reference "Hisperica Famina" (VI.B.46.73) comes from Macalister's *The Secret Languages;* see Rose, *Index Manuscript,* 154–56.

9. The phrase first appears in the evolving text on 47474–13 (*JJA* 47.372), which is dated early February 1924; see a February 8, 1924, letter to Harriet Shaw Weaver (*Letters* I.210).

10. Joyce displays his grasp of the pertinent terminology and theoretical distinctions in another passage: "this actual futule preteriting unstant, in the states of suspensive exanimation" (*FW* 143.7–9).

11. Pliny, *NH* 13.12.74 and 80; Joyce's immediate source of information about the various grades of papyrus was undoubtedly the *Encyclopaedia Britannica* 20.744.

12. The moral dimension of the phrase is paramount in its use in *Ulysses.* Bloom muses about an embezzler-gambler who took his earnings to America: "Fleshpots of Egypt" (*U* 546–48). Stephen personifies the allusion: "Cleopatra, fleshpot of Egypt" (*U* 9.883–84). Virag excoriates Bloom for patronizing Bella Cohen's brothel: "Fleshhotpots of Egypt to hanker after" (*U* 15.2365–66).

13. Here one can rely on the authority of Julius Caesar. He dispatched his trusty lieutenant Labienus to *Lutetiam . . . id est oppidum Parisiorum, quod positum est in insula fluminis Sequanae* (Lutetia . . . it is the town of the Parisi that is situated on an island in the River Seine) (*De Bello Gallico* 7.51.1).

14. Jolas, "My Friend," 11–12; for more on the occasion and place, see Schork, "Fedlkirch," 308–11.

15. The figure of speech is not mentioned in any of the essays in *Vico and Joyce,* nor is the Latin passage at *FW* 287.20–28 directly addressed by any of the seventeen contributors to this volume of conference papers.

16. The conventions of punctuation have deliberately been violated here in placing the final full stop *outside* the quotation marks. There is no final full stop in the original title, and I suspect that the number and placement of Beckett's authorial periods may have some latent significance.

17. Beckett, "Dante," 19. I have not been able to identify the source of the Latin line that Beckett cites.

18. Gilbert, *A Study,* 39–40.

19. The relevance of the Pythagoras passage from Ovid was pointed out to me by Jolanta Wawrzycka at the 1995 Zürich Workshop on "Homer and Joyce."

20. The standard form of the future active infinitive is *futurum esse,* with *fore* as an alternative, syncopated form. Thus *"fore futura"* is, strictly speaking, an overemphatic form that was invented by Joyce, probably to balance *"fututa fuere."*

21. A Notebook entry contributes to the pedantic obscenity here: "footootoo is the supine / of the verb to stop to come" (VI.B.17.58). The grammatical term "supine" refers to a relatively rare form of the verb, which functions as a one-word purpose clause. Thus, the supine of *futuo* is indeed *fututu* (phonetically "footootoo"); Joyce's note also supplies a not very subtle euphemism for the literal translation of the form. Also note a bilingual parenthesis "(fouyoufoukou)" (*FW* 320.5).

22. See Hart, *Structure,* 227.

23. *Dictionary of Antiquities,* 28, and *Dictionnaire des Antiquités* 1.128. There are several crossed entries for Roman marriage terminology at VI.B.1.117; They appear in the text as "purchase" (*FW* 365.3) from "ᵣcoemptio-purchase"; "paterfamilias" (*FW* 386.13); "confarreation" (*FW* 390.11).

24. See Lernout, "Radical Philology," 25–34, and Schork, "By Jingo," 115.

25. Mercanton, "L'Esthétique," 44.

26. Atherton, "Four Watches," 39–40.

27. The Roman months Notebook index and its transfer into the text of the *Wake* are discussed in the first part of appendix II. It needs, however, to be noted here that Macrobius does record some of the traditional explanations for the names of the divisions of the Roman year in another section of his compendium.

28. In fact, a passage from the *Etymologiae* of Isidore of Seville (5.31.1–14) has even more parallel detail for the "night-hours" passage than Macrobius. But, in terms of purely verbal "clicks," the closest analogue to the six terms in the Notebook index is an entry in *Dictionnaire des Antiquités* 2.170. If there were other evidence for Joyce's use

of this massive French reference work, I would cite it as the documentary source for the Notebook entries. As it stands, I suspend judgment on this matter.

29. This synopsis is recorded on a sheet written in mid-1926: 47482a.2 (*JJA* 51.3).

30. By total serendipity, I spotted this inscription on my way to the Alitalia office in August 1995. Inquiries did not uncover the date (early twentieth century?) of the construction of this large, five-story building.

31. In his "Annotations of 'Annotations',", 19, Van Caspel claims that the original Latin maxim should read *De mortuis nil nisi bene*. I think he is wrong in substituting an adverb (*bene*) for a parallel neuter noun as the direct object of an understood imperative—but there may be Dutch variations on the maxim with which Joyce was unfamiliar.

Appendix I

1. For Clongowes and Belvedere I have relied on the data given (and fully discussed) in Bradley, *Schooldays,* 112–39; Sullivan, *Among the Jesuits* has fewer technical data, but is still well worth reading. In the archives of the Zürich James Joyce Foundation are printed copies of the University College exam papers for 1899–1902. I thank the director, Fritz Senn, for permitting me to consult this material and to summarize the Latin portions.

2. Examples of typical terms, techniques, and mnemonics have been embedded in Joyce's fiction and are discussed in chapter 1.

3. Here we have the supercilious (but probably accurate) testimony of Gogarty, *That Time,* 27.

4. Although the focus is on a period a decade prior to Joyce's university years, there is an interesting comparative survey in Richmond, "Classical Studies," 145–62.

5. This comparison is not meant to imply that Joyce's University College Latin professors did not make a lasting impression on their student. References to various verbal incarnations to "Browne and Nolan" are scattered throughout the *Wake*. The primary allusion is probably to the well-known Dublin publishing firm, Browne and Nolan. There is a concomitant nod to Giordano Bruno "the Nolan" (of Nola), the reputed heretic whose fiery death was epigrammatically commemorated near the end of Joyce's first novel (*P* 249). Another pair of candidates can be introduced here. In the list of "College Staff for the Session 1898–9" on the University College Matriculation Examination paper for 1899 the following names appear:

Professors
Greek and Latin Languages
Rev. Henry Browne, MA FRUI
Rev. T.P. O'Nowlan, MA FRUI

Also see "ᵒRev. M. Nolann & Brown" (VI.B.44.122).

6. The parenthetical numbers are Joyce's score out of a perfect mark of 1200; a score of 700 was extraordinarily high.

APPENDIX II

1. The terminology of time reckoning is cleverly distorted in at least two other passages: melancholy Anglo-Saxon days of the week (*FW* 301.20–22) and Romance seasons of the year (*FW* 548.28–29).

2. See Van Mierlo, "Traffic," 107–17, for a general discussion of roads in the *Wake* and for the identification of some *Encyclopaedia Britannica* sources for the VI.B.8 index. In "La Poste," Landuyt has shown the documentary source for the construction terms and names of vehicles on VI.B.8.113 and VI.B.16.32.

3. Danis Rose has recently suggested a narrower time range (July–September 1925) in his discussion of this Notebook; see *Textual Diaries,* 82–86.

Bibliography

Abbreviations are used for the following periodicals or annuals:

AFWC   A "Finnegans Wake" Circular
AWN   A Wake Newslitter
EJS   *European Joyce Studies*
JJLS   James Joyce Literary Supplement
JJQ   *James Joyce Quarterly*
JSA   *Joyce Studies Annual*

Adams, James N. *The Latin Sexual Vocabulary.* Baltimore: Johns Hopkins University Press, 1982.

Ahern, Charles F. "Daedalus and Icarus in the *Ars Amatoria.*" *Harvard Studies in Classical Philology* 92 (1989): 273–96.

Arkins, Brian. "A Further Note on the *Sortes Vergilianae.*" *Classical and Modern Literature* 14 (Spring 1994): 241–43.

Atherton, James S. "A Man of Four Watches: Macrobius in FW." *AWN* 9 (1972): 39–40.

———. *The Books at the Wake: A Study of Literary Allusions in James Joyce's "Finnegans Wake."* Carbondale and Edwardsville: Southern Illinois University Press, 1974.

Aubert, Jacques, and Fritz Senn, eds. *L'Herne: James Joyce.* Paris: L'Herne, 1985.

Ausonius. *Ausonius.* Translated by Hugh G. Evelyn White. Cambridge, Mass.: Harvard University Press (Loeb Classical Library), 1961.

Barnes, Djuna. "Vagaries Malicieux." *The Double Dealer* 3 (May 1922): 249–60.

Bauerle, Ruth. "American Popular Music in *Finnegans Wake.*" In *Picking Up Airs: Hearing the Music in Joyce's Text,* edited by Ruth H. Bauerle, 129–69. Urbana and Chicago: University of Illinois Press, 1993.

———, ed. *Picking Up Airs: Hearing the Music in Joyce's Text.* Urbana and Chicago: University of Illinois Press, 1993.

Beckett, Samuel, et al. "Dante . . . Bruno. Vico . . Joyce." In *James Joyce / "Finnegans Wake": A Symposium (Our Exagmination round His Factification for Incamination of Work in Progress).* New York: New Directions, 1972.

Benstock, Bernard. *Narrative Con/Texts in "Ulysses."* Urbana and Chicago: University of Illinois Press, 1991.

Bergin, Thomas G., and Max H. Frisch, trans. *The New Science of Giambattista Vico.* Ithaca: Cornell University Press, 1968.

Birley, Anthony R. *Marcus Aurelius: A Biography.* Rev. ed. New Haven: Yale University Press, 1987.

Boardman, John, Jasper Griffin, and Oswyn Murray, eds. *The Oxford History of the Classical World: The Roman World.* Oxford and New York: Oxford University Press, 1988.

Bowen, Zack. *Musical Allusions in the Works of James Joyce.* Albany: State University of New York Press, 1974.

Boyle, Robert. "The Priesthoods of Stephen and Buck." In *Approaches to "Ulysses,"* edited by Thomas F. Staley and Bernard Benstock. Pittsburgh: University of Pittsburgh Press, 1970.

———. "*Finnegans Wake,* Page 185: An Explication." *JJQ* 4 (Fall 1963): 3–16. Reprinted in *Critical Essays on James Joyce's "Finnegans Wake,"* edited by Patrick A. McCarthy, 59–72. New York: G.K. Hall, 1992.

Bradley, Bruce. *James Joyce's Schooldays.* New York: St. Martin's, 1982.

Brown, Richard. *Joyce and Sexuality.* Cambridge: Cambridge University Press, 1985.

Browne, Thomas. *Christian Morals.* Edited by S. C. Roberts. Cambridge: Cambridge University Press, 1927.

Budgen, Frank. *James Joyce and the Making of "Ulysses" and Other Writings.* Oxford and New York: Oxford University Press, 1972.

Buecheler, Franciscus, ed. *Petronii Saturae et Liber Preapeorum.* Berlin: Weidmann, 1922.

Burgess, Anthony. *Joysprick: An Introduction to the Language of James Joyce.* New York: Harcourt Brace Jovanovich, 1973.

Byrne, John Francis. *Silent Years: An Autobiography with Memoirs of James Joyce and Our Ireland.* New York: Farrar, Straus and Young, 1953.

Byron, George Gordon, Lord. *The Poetical Works.* London: Routledge, 1880.

Carens, James F. "Joyce and Gogarty." In *New Light on Joyce from the Dublin Symposium.* Edited by Fritz Senn, 18–45. Bloomington: Indiana University Press, 1972.

Cary, Max, and Howard H. Scullard. *A History of Rome.* 3rd ed. New York: St. Martin's Press, 1976.

Catullus. *The Poems.* Edited by Kenneth Quinn. London: Macmillan, 1970.

Cicero. *Cato Maior: De Senectute.* Edited by J. G. F. Powell. Cambridge: Cambridge University Press, 1988.

Connolly, Thomas E. *The Personal Library of James Joyce.* Buffalo, N.Y.: University of Buffalo Press, 1957.

———, ed. *James Joyce's Scribbledehobble: The Ur-Workbook for "Finnegans Wake."* Evanston: Northwestern University Press, 1961.

Cope, Jackson I. *Joyce's Cities: Archeologies of the Soul.* Baltimore: Johns Hopkins University Press, 1981.

Cowan, Thomas. "Sacer Esto?" *AWN* 11.3 (June 1974): 39–44.

Culleton, Claire A. *Names and Naming in Joyce.* Madison: University of Wisconsin Press, 1994.

Cumpiano, Marion. "A 'Chin-Chin Chat' of Cincinnatus and Cabbages." *AWN* 17 (August 1980): 60–64.

Cyprian. *Caena Cypriani* (Cyprian's Banquet). In *Monumenta Germaniae Historica: Poetae Latini Medii Aevi* IV.2.1. Berlin: Weidmann, 1914.

Dalton, Jack P., and Clive Hart, eds. *Twelve and a Tilly*. Evanston: Northwestern University Press, 1966.

Daremberg, C., and E. Saglio, eds. *Dictionnaire des Antiquités Grecques et Romaines*. Paris: Hachette, 1877.

Davis, Wes. "'Balia' *Inventa*: The Source for Joyce's Latin Manuscript." *JJQ* 32 (Spring–Summer 1995): 738–47.

Dawson, Hugh J. "Thomas MacGreevy and Joyce." *JJQ* 25 (Spring 1988): 305–21.

Day, Robert Adams. "Le Diacre Dedalus." In *L'Herne: James Joyce,* edited by Jacques Aubert and Fritz Senn, 309–17. Paris: L'Herne, 1985.

Devlin, Kimberly J. *Wandering and Return in "Finnegans Wake": An Integrative Approach to Joyce's Fictions*. Princeton: Princeton University Press, 1991.

Dictionary of National Biography. Edited by Leslie Stephens and Sidney Lee. Oxford: Oxford University Press, 1967–68.

Dumas, Alexandre. *The Count of Monte Cristo*. London: George Routledge and Sons, 1879.

———. *Le Comte de Monte Cristo*. Edited by G. Sigaux. Paris: Gallimard, 1981.

Dunleavy, Janet E., ed. *Re-Viewing Classics of Joyce Criticism*. Urbana and Chicago: University of Illinois Press, 1991.

Eco, Umberto. *The Name of the Rose*. Translated by William Weaver. San Diego and New York: Harcourt Brace Jovanovich, 1983.

Eliot, T. S. *The Complete Poems and Plays, 1909–1950*. New York: Harcourt, Brace and Company, 1958.

Ellis, Peter B. *A Dictionary of Irish Mythology*. Santa Barbara: ABC-CLIO, 1987.

Ellmann, Richard. *Ulysses on the Liffey*. New York: Oxford University Press, 1972.

———. *James Joyce*. New York: Oxford University Press, 1982.

Encyclopaedia Britannica. 11th ed. New York: Encyclopaedia Britannica, 1911.

Enk, P. J., ed. *Plauti Truculentus*. Leiden: Brill, 1963.

Erzgräber, Willi. "James Joyce und die Antike." *Literaturwissenschaftliches Jahrbuch* 33 (1992): 319–41.

Fahy, Catherine, comp. *The James Joyce-Paul Léon Letters*. Dublin: National Library of Ireland, 1992.

Ferrer, Daniel. "The Freudful Couchmare of $\wedge d$: Joyce's Notes on Freud and the Composition of Chapter XVI of *Finnegans Wake*." *JJQ* 22 (Summer 1985): 367–82.

———. "La Scène primitive de l'écriture: Une lecture joicienne de Freud." In *Genèse de Babel: Joyce et la création,* edited by Claude Jacquet, 15–35. Paris: Centre National de la Recherche Scientifique, 1985.

Ferrero, Guglielmo. *The Greatness and Decline of Rome*. Translated by H. J. Chaytor. Freeport, N.Y.: Books for Libraries, 1971.

Fitzpatrick, Edward A., ed. *St. Ignatius and the "Ratio Studiorum."* New York and London: McGraw-Hill, 1933.

Freud, Sigmund. *Collected Papers*. Translated by Joan Riviere. London: Hogarth Press, 1950.

———. *The Standard Edition of the Complete Psychological Works.* Edited and translated by James Strachey. London: Hogarth Press, 1966.

Gardner, Jane F. *Roman Myths.* London: British Museum Press/Austin: University of Texas Press, 1993.

Garvin, John. *James Joyce's Disunited Kingdom and the Irish Dimension.* Dublin: Gill and Macmillan, 1976.

Giedion-Welcker, Carola. "Meetings with Joyce." In *Portraits of the Artist in Exile.* San Diego and New York: Harcourt Brace Jovanovich, 1986.

Gifford, Don, with Robert J. Seidman. *"Ulysses" Annotated: Notes for James Joyce's "Ulysses."* Rev. ed. Berkeley, Los Angeles, London: University of California Press, 1989.

Gilbert, Stuart. "The Latin Background of James Joyce's Art." *Horizon* 10.57 (September 1944): 178–89.

———. *James Joyce's "Ulysses": A Study.* New York: Vintage, 1965.

Gillespie, Michael P. *James Joyce's Trieste Library: A Catalogue of Materials at the Harry Ranson Research Center.* Austin: University of Texas Press, 1986.

Givens, Seon, ed. *James Joyce: Two Decades of Criticism.* New York: Vanguard Press, 1963.

Glasheen, Adaline. "Semper as Oxhousehumper." *AWN* 1.1 (February 1964): 7–11.

———. "*Finnegans Wake* and the Secret Languages of Ireland." In *A Wake Digest,* edited by Clive Hart and Fritz Senn, 48–51. Sydney: Sydney University Press, 1968.

———. *A Third Census of "Finnegans Wake."* Berkeley: University of California Press, 1977.

Gleckner, Robert. "Byron in *Finnegans Wake.*" In *Twelve and a Tilly,* edited by Jack P. Dalton and Clive Hart, 40–51. Evanston: Northwestern University Press, 1966.

Gogarty, Oliver St. John [Mettus Curtius, pseud.]. "On Keeping Shop." *Sinn Fein Weekly,* November 10, 1906, 3.

———. *Perennial.* Baltimore: Contemporary Poetry, 1944.

———. *It Isn't That Time of Year at All.* London: MacGibbon and Kee, 1954.

———. *Many Lines to Thee: Letters to G. K. A. Bell, 1904– 1907.* Edited by James F. Carnes. Ireland: Dolman Press, 1971.

Graham, Philip L. "japlatin, with my younkle's owlseller (467.14)." In *A Wake Digest,* edited by Clive Hart and Fritz Senn, 52–53. Sydney: Sydney University Press, 1968.

Greene, E. A. *Saints and Their Symbols,* rev. ed. London: Whittaker, 1909.

Halper, Nathan. "Answers." *AWN* 1.3 (1963): 11–12.

———. "Note on 'The Hawklike Man'." *JJQ* 17 (Spring 1980): 312.

Hamilton, Richard. "Fatal Texts: The *Sortes Vergilianae.*" *Classical and Modern Literature* 13 (Summer 1993): 309–36.

Hart, Clive. *Structure and Motif in "Finnegans Wake."* Evanston: Northwestern University Press, 1962.

Hart, Clive, and David Hayman, eds. *James Joyce's "Ulysses": Critical Essays.* Berkeley: University of California Press, 1974.

Hart, Clive, and Fritz Senn, eds. *A Wake Digest.* Sydney: Sydney University Press, 1968.

Hayman, David. "Cyclops." In *James Joyce's "Ulysses": Critical Essays,* edited by Clive Hart and David Hayman, 243–75. Berkeley: University of California Press, 1974.

———. *"Ulysses": The Mechanics of Meaning.* Madison: University of Wisconsin Press, 1982.

———. "What the Unpublished Letter Can Tell Us: Or Is Anyone Watching?" *Studies in the Novel* 22 (Summer 1990): 187–88.

———, ed. *James Joyce: A First-Draft Version of "Finnegans Wake."* Austin: University of Texas Press, 1963.

Hayman, David, and Sam Slote, eds. *Probes: Genetic Studies in Joyce.* Amsterdam and Atlanta: Rodopi, 1995 (*EJS* 5).

Herren, Michael W. *The Hisperica Famina: I, The A-Text.* Toronto: Pontifical Institute of Medieval Studies, 1974.

Herring, Phillip F. "The Bedsteadfastness of Molly Bloom." *Modern Fiction Studies* 15 (Spring 1969): 49–61.

———. "*Ulysses* Notebook VIII.A.5 at Buffalo." *Studies in Bibliography* 22 (1969): 287–310. Reprinted in *Joyce's Notes and Early Drafts for "Ulysses": Selections from the Buffalo Collection,* edited by Phillip F. Herring, 3–33. Charlottesville: University Press of Virginia, 1977.

———, ed. *Joyce's "Ulysses" Notesheets in the British Museum.* Charlottesville: University Press of Virginia, 1972.

———, ed. *Joyce's Notes and Early Drafts for "Ulysses": Selections from the Buffalo Collection.* Charlottesville: University Press of Virginia, 1977.

Hofheinz, Thomas C. "Vico, Natural Law Philosophy, and Joyce's Ireland." *JSA* (1993): 89–95.

———. *Joyce and the Invention of Irish History: "Finnegans Wake" in Context.* Cambridge: Cambridge University Press, 1995.

Humphreys, Susan L. "Ferrero, Etc: James Joyce's Debt to Guglielmo Ferrero." *JJQ* 16 (Spring 1979): 239–51.

Jacquet, Claude, ed. *Genèse de Babel: Joyce et la création.* Paris: Centre National de la Recherche Scientifique, 1985.

———, ed. *James Joyce 1: "Scribble 1: Genèse des textes."* Paris: Lettres Modernes, 1988 (*La Revue des lettres modernes* [1988]: 834–39).

Jacquet, Claude, and Jean-Michel Rabaté, eds. *James Joyce 3: James Joyce et l'Italie.* Paris: Lettres Modernes, 1994 (*La Revue des lettres modernes* [1994]: 1173–82).

The James Joyce Archive. Edited by Michael Groden et al. New York and London: Garland Publishing, 1978.

Janusko, Robert. "Yet Another Anthology for 'Oxen': Murison's *Selections.*" *JSA* (1990): 117–31.

Jenkyns, Richard. *The Victorians and Ancient Greece.* Oxford: Oxford University Press, 1980.

Jolas, Eugene. "My Friend James Joyce." In *James Joyce: Two Decades of Criticism,* edited by Seon Givens, 3–18. New York: Vanguard Press, 1963.

Joyce, James. *Finnegans Wake.* New York: Viking Press, 1939.

————. *Collected Poems.* New York: Viking Press, 1957.

————. *The Critical Writings of James Joyce.* Edited by Ellsworth Mason and Richard Ellmann. New York: Viking Press, 1959.

————. *Stephen Hero.* Edited by John J. Slocum and Herbert Cahoon. New York: New Directions, 1963.

————. *Letters of James Joyce.* Vol. I. Edited by Stuart Gilbert. New York: Viking Press, 1957; reissued with corrections 1966. Vols. II and III. Edited by Richard Ellmann. New York: Viking Press, 1966.

————. *Dubliners.* Edited by Robert Scholes in consultation with Richard Ellmann. New York: Viking Press, 1967.

————. *Giacomo Joyce.* Edited by Richard Ellmann. New York: Viking Press, 1968.

————. *"A Portrait of the Artist as a Young Man": Text, Criticism, and Notes.* Edited by Chester G. Anderson. New York: Viking Press, 1968.

————. *Exiles.* New York: Penguin, 1973.

————. *Selected Letters of James Joyce.* Edited by Richard Ellmann. New York: Viking Press, 1975.

————. *Ulysses.* Edited by Hans Walter Gabler et al. New York: Random House, 1986.

Joyce, Stanislaus. *My Brother's Keeper: James Joyce's Early Years.* Edited by Richard Ellmann. New York: Viking, 1958.

Katz, Phyllis B. "The *Sortes Vergilianae:* Fact and Fiction." *Classical and Modern Literature* 14 (Spring 1994): 245–58.

Kenner, Hugh. *Joyce's Voices.* London: Faber and Faber, 1978.

Kestner, Joseph A. "Before *Ulysses:* Victorian Iconography of the Odysseus Myth." *JJQ* 28 (Spring 1991): 565–94.

Landuyt, Inge. "Shaun and His Post: La Poste et les Moyens de Communication in VI.B.16." Forthcoming.

Landuyt, Inge, and Geert Lernout. "Joyce's Sources: *Les grandes fleuves historiques.*" *JSA* (1995): 99–138.

Leigh, Percival. *The Comic Latin Grammar.* London: Charles Tilt, 1840.

Lernout, Geert. *The French Joyce.* Ann Arbor: University of Michigan Press, 1990.

————. *James Joyce: Schrijver.* Leuven: Uitgeverij Kritak, 1994.

————. "The *Finnegans Wake* Notebooks and Radical Philology." *EJS* 5 (1995): 19–48.

Lewis, Charlton T., and Charles Short, eds. *A Latin Dictionary.* Oxford: Clarendon Press, 1879.

Livy. *The Early History of Rome.* Translated by Aubrey de Selincourt. Harmondsworth: Penguin Books, 1960.

Lowe-Evans, Mary. *Crimes against Fecundity: Joyce and Population Control.* Syracuse: Syracuse University Press, 1989.

————. "'The Commonest of all Cases': Birth Control on Trial in the *Wake.*" *JJQ* 27 (Summer 1990): 803–14.

Lucretius. *De Rerum Natura.* Edited by William E. Leonard and Stanley B. Smith. Madison: University of Wisconsin Press, 1961.

Lyons, J. B. *Thrust Syphilis Down to Hell and Other Joyceana.* Dublin: Glendale, 1988.

Macalister, Robert Alexander Stewart. *The Secret Languages of Ireland.* Cambridge: Cambridge University Press, 1937.

Matthews, Victor J. "Some Puns on Roman *Cognomina.*" *Greece and Rome,* n.s., 20 (1973): 20–24.

McCarthy, Patrick A. "The Last Epistle of *Finnegans Wake.*" *JJQ* 27 (Summer 1990): 725–33. Reprinted in *Critical Essays on James Joyce's "Finnegans Wake,"* edited by Patrick A. McCarthy, 96–103. New York: G. K. Hall, 1992.

———, ed. *Critical Essays on James Joyce's "Finnegans Wake."* New York: G. K. Hall, 1992.

McHugh, Roland. *The Sigla of "Finnegans Wake."* Austin: University of Texas Press, 1977.

———. *Annotations to "Finnegans Wake."* Rev. ed. Baltimore and London: Johns Hopkins University Press, 1991.

Mercanton, Jacques. "L'Esthétique de Joyce." *Études de Lettres* (Lausanne) 44 (October 1938): 20–46.

———. "The Hours of James Joyce." In *Portraits of the Artist in Exile,* edited by Willard Potts, 253–80. San Diego and New York: Harcourt Brace Jovanovich, 1986.

Merrill, Elmer T., ed. *Catullus.* Boston: Ginn and Company, 1893.

Milesi, Laurent. "Toward a Female Grammar of Sexuality: The De/Recomposition of 'Storiella as She Is Sung'." *Modern Fiction Studies* 35 (Autumn 1989): 571–78.

———. "The Perversions of 'Aerse' and the Anglo-Irish Middle Voice in *Finnegans Wake.*" *JSA* (1993): 98–118.

Montgomery, Niall. "The Pervigilium Phoenics." *New Mexico Quarterly* 22 (Winter 1953): 437–72.

Moya del Bano, F., ed. *Simposio Virgiliano: Conmemorativo del Bimilenario de la muerte de Virgilio.* Murcia: Universidad de Murcia, 1984.

Newman, John Henry. *An Essay in Aid of a Grammar of Assent.* London: Longmans, Green, 1881.

Noel, Lucie. *James Joyce and Paul L. Léon: The Story of a Friendship.* New York: Gotham Book Mart, 1950.

O'Connor, Ulick. *The Times I've Seen.* New York: Ivan Oblensky, 1963.

———, ed. *The Joyce We Knew.* Cork: Mercier, 1967.

Ogilvie, R. M. *A Commentary on Livy: Books 1–5.* Oxford: Clarendon Press, 1965.

O Hehir, Brendan, and John Dillon, *A Classical Lexicon for Finnegans Wake.* Berkeley: University of California Press, 1977.

Ong, Walter J. "Latin Language as a Renaissance Puberty Rite." *Studies in Philology* 56 (1959): 103–24.

Ovid. *Fasti.* Translated by James G. Frazer. Cambridge, Mass.: Harvard University Press (Loeb Classical Library), 1959.

Parker, W. H., ed. and trans. *Priapea: Poems for a Phallic God.* London: Croom Helm, 1988.

Parrinder, Patrick. *James Joyce.* Cambridge: Cambridge University Press, 1984.

Peradotto, John J. "A Liturgical Pattern in *Ulysses*." *Modern Language Notes* 75 (April 1960): 321–26.

Pierrugues, P. *Glossarium Eroticum Linguae Latinae*. Amsterdam: Hakkert, 1965 (rpt. of Paris, 1826).

Platt, L. H. "The Buckeen and the Dogsbody: Aspects of History and Culture in 'Telemachus'." *JJQ* 27 (Fall 1989): 77–86.

Potts, Willard, ed. *Portraits of the Artist in Exile*. San Diego and New York: Harcourt Brace Jovanovich, 1986.

Pound, Ezra. *Pound/Joyce: The Letters of Ezra Pound to James Joyce, with Pound's Essays on Joyce*. Edited by Forrest Read. New York: New Directions, 1967.

Power, Arthur. *Conversations with James Joyce*. Edited by Clive Hart. Chicago: University of Chicago Press, 1982.

Rabaté, Jean-Michel. *James Joyce: Authorized Reader*. Baltimore: Johns Hopkins University Press, 1991.

Raby, F. J. E. *A History of Christian-Latin Poetry*, 2nd ed. Oxford: Clarendon Press, 1953.

Ramon Sales, Elisa. "Presencia de Virgilio en el *Ulysses* de James Joyce." In *Simposio Virgiliano: Conmemorativo del Bimilenario de la muerte de Virgilio*, edited by F. Moya del Bano, 505–10. Murcia: Universidad de Murcia, 1984.

Rand, E. K. "The Irish Flavour of the Hisperica Famina." In *Studien zur lateinischen Dichtung des Mittelalters: Ehrengabe für Karl Strecker*, edited by W. Stach and H. Walther. Dresden: Wilhelm und Bertha von Baensch Stiftung, 1931.

Reichert, Klaus. "'it's as semper as oxhousehumper': The Structure of Hebrew and the Language of *Finnegans Wake*." *La Revue des lettres modernes* 834–39 (1988) (*James Joyce 1: "Scribble 1: Genèse des textes"*): 163–82.

Restuccia, Frances L. "Transubstantiating *Ulysses*." *JJQ* 21 (Summer 1984): 329–40.

Richmond, J. A. "Classical Studies and Culture in Dublin in the 1880s." *Hopkins Quarterly* 14 (1987–1988): 145–62.

The Roman Missal in Latin and English. 3rd ed. New York: Benziger, 1925.

Ronnick, Michele V. "Buck Mulligan's Latin in *Ulysses*, 14.705–10: Ciceronic not Ciceronian." *Arion*, 3rd ser., 2 (Winter 1992): 217–20.

Roscher, Wilhelm H. *Ausführliches Lexikon der griechischen und römischen Mythologie*. Leipzig: Teubuer, 1902–1909.

Rose, Danis. *The Textual Diaries of James Joyce*. Dublin: Lilliput Press, 1995.

———, ed. *James Joyce's The Index Manuscript: "Finnegans Wake" Holograph Workbook VI.B.46*. Colchester: *A Wake Newslitter* / Edinburgh: Split Pea Press, 1978.

Rose, Danis, and John O'Hanlon. *Understanding "Finnegans Wake": A Guide to the Narrative of James Joyce's Masterpiece*. New York and London: Garland, 1982.

———, eds. *James Joyce: The Lost Notebook: New Evidence on the Genesis of "Ulysses."* Edinburgh: Split Pea Press, 1989.

Scholes, Robert, and Richard M. Kain. *The Workshop of Daedalus: James Joyce and the Raw Materials for "A Portrait of the Artist as a Young Man."* Evanston: Northwestern University Press, 1965.

Schork, R. J. "*Aemulos Reges*: Allusion and Theme in Horace 3.16." *Transactions and Proceedings of the American Philological Association* 102 (1971): 515–39.

———. "A Graphic Exercise in Mnemotechnic." *JJQ* 16 (Spring 1979): 335–39.

———. "Kennst Du das Haus Citrons, Bloom?" *JJQ* 17 (Summer 1980): 407–18.

———. "Joyce and Justinian: *U* 250 and 520." *JJQ* 23 (Fall 1985): 77–80.

———. "Stendhal's Latinitas." *Classical and Modern Literature* 6 (Fall 1985): 23–38.

———. "Liturgical Irony in James Joyce's 'The Sisters'." *Studies in Short Fiction* 26 (Spring 1989): 193–97.

———. "Feldkirch in *Finnegans Wake.*" *Montfort* (Bregenz-Dornbirn) 41. 3/4 (1989): 308–11.

———. "Plautus and Martial in Joyce." *Notes and Queries,* n.s., 36 (June 1989): 198–200.

———. "Awake, Phoenician Too Frequent." *JJQ* 27 (Summer 1990): 767–76.

———. "Barnum at the *Wake.*" *JJQ* 27 (Summer 1990): 759–66.

———. "Tarquinius Bloom the Arrogant." *JJQ* 27 (Spring 1990): 646–48.

———. "Dedalus at Play: Joyce's 'Balia' Ballad." *JJLS* 5.1 (Spring 1991): 6–7.

———. "Buck Mulligan as a *Grammaticus Gloriosus* in Joyce's *Ulysses.*" *Arion,* 3rd ser., 1 (Fall 1991): 76–92.

———. "Sheep, Goats, and the *Figura Etymologica* in *Finnegans Wake.*" *Journal of English and Germanic Philology* 92 (April 1992): 200–211.

———. "'Nodebinding Ayes': Milton, Blindness, and Egypt in the *Wake.*" *JJQ* 30 (Fall 1992): 69–83.

———. "By Jingo: Genetic Criticism of Finnegans Wake." *JSA* (1994): 104–27.

———. "Sheep, Bones and Nettles: St. Kevin's Childhood Miracles." Forthcoming in *James Joyce 4.*

Scott, Bonnie Kime. "'The Look in the Throat of a Stricken Animal': Joyce as Met by Djuna Barnes." *JSA* (1991): 153–76.

Senn, Fritz. "The Gnat." *JJQ* 2 (Spring 1965): 233.

———, ed. *New Light on Joyce from the Dublin Symposium.* Bloomington: Indiana University Press: 1972.

———. "Nausicaa." In *James Joyce's "Ulysses": Critical Essays,* edited by Clive Hart and David Hayman, 277–311. Berkeley: University of California Press, 1974.

———. "The Challenge: *ignotas animum.*" In *Joyce's Dislocutions,* edited by John P. Riquelme, 73–84. Baltimore: Johns Hopkins University Press, 1984.

———. *Joyce's Dislocutions.* Edited by John P. Riquelme. Baltimore: Johns Hopkins University Press, 1984.

———. "In Classical Idiom: *Anthologia Intertextualis.*" *JJQ* 25 (Fall 1987): 31–48.

———. "Ovidian Roots of Gigantism in Joyce's *Ulysses.*" *Journal of Modern Literature* 15 (Spring 1989): 561–77.

———. "Rereading *The Books at the Wake.*" In *Re-Viewing Classics of Joyce Criticism,* edited by Janet E. Dunleavy, 82–89. Urbana and Chicago: University of Illinois Press, 1991.

———. "In the Original: Buck Mulligan and Stephen Dedalus." *Arion,* 3rd ser., 2 (Winter 1992): 215–17.

———. *Inductive Scrutinies: Focus on Joyce.* Edited by Christine O'Neill. Dublin: Lilliput Press, 1995.

Shanahan, Dennis M. "The Eucharistic Aesthetics of the Passion: The Testament of Blood in *Ulysses*." *JJQ* 27 (Winter 1990): 373–86.

Sheehy, Eugene. [Untitled Memoir]. In *The Joyce We Knew*, edited by Ulick O'Connor, 15–35. Cork: Mercier, 1967.

Smith, Warren S., ed. *Bernard Shaw's Plays*. New York: Norton, 1970.

Smith, William. *A Dictionary of Greek and Roman Antiquities*. London: John Murray, 1875.

Spoo, Robert. "Joyce's Attitudes Toward History: Rome 1906–07." *Journal of Modern Literature* 14 (Spring 1988): 481–97.

———. *James Joyce and the Language of History*. Oxford: Oxford University Press, 1994.

Stach, W., and H. Walther, eds. *Studien zur lateinischen Dichtung des Mittelalters: Ehrengabe für Karl Strecker*. Dresden: Wilhelm und Bertha von Baensch Stiftung. 1931.

Staley, Thomas F., and Bernard Benstock, eds. *Approaches to "Ulysses."* Pittsburgh: University of Pittsburgh Press, 1970.

Steppe, Wolfhard. "The Merry Greeks (With a Farewell to *epicleti*)." *JJQ* 32 (Spring–Summer 1995): 597–617.

Strecker, Karl, ed. *Monumenta Germaniae Historica: Poetae Latini Medii Aevi*. IV.2.1. Berlin: Weidmann, 1914.

Sullivan, Kevin. *Joyce among the Jesuits*. New York: Columbia University Press, 1958.

Taylor, A. B. "The Fellies, Spokes, and Nave of Fortune's Wheel: A Debt to Arthur Golding in *Hamlet*." *English Language Notes* 25 (September 1987): 18–20.

Tennyson, Alfred, Lord. *Poems and Plays*. London: Oxford University Press, 1965.

Theoharis, Theoharis C. *Joyce's "Ulysses": An Anatomy of the Soul*. Chapel Hill: University of North Carolina Press, 1988.

Treip, Andrew. "Recycled Historians: Michelet on Vico in VI.B.12." *AFWC* 4 (Summer 1989): 61–72.

———, ed. *"Finnegans Wake": "teems of times."* Amsterdam and Atlanta: Rodopi, 1994 (*EJS* 4).

———. "Histories of Sexuality: Vico and Roman Marriage Law in *Finnegans Wake*." *La Revue des lettres modernes*, 1173–82 (1994) (*James Joyce 3: Joyce et l'Italie*): 179–99.

Van Caspel, Paul. *Bloomers on the Liffey: Eisegetical Readings of Joyce's "Ulysses."* Baltimore: Johns Hopkins University Press, 1986.

———. "Annotations of 'Annotations'." *JJLS* 5.2 (Fall 1991): 18–19.

Van Mierlo, Wim. "Traffic in Transit: Some Spatio-Temporal Elements in *Finnegans Wake*." *EJS* 4 (1994): 107–17.

———. "St. Martin of Tours." *AFWC* 7 (1991–1992 [1995]): 29–44.

Verene, Donald P., ed. *Vico and Joyce*. Albany: State University of New York Press, 1987.

Vickery, John B. "*Finnegans Wake* and the Rituals of Mortality." In *The Literary Impact of "The Golden Bough,"* edited by John B. Vickery, 408–23. Princeton: Princeton University Press, 1973.

———. ed. *The Literary Impact of "The Golden Bough."* Princeton: Princeton University Press, 1973.

Viereck, Peter. *New and Selected Poems.* Indianapolis: Bobbs-Merrill, 1967.

TABLES

The Tables that follow provide easy cross reference to my discussion of both the Latin texts cited and Joyce's use of them in his fiction, letters, and notebooks. A very few other Joycean sources are also included. The three columns of Table I list Latin works, Joyce's citations of them, and pages in this book in which the item is discussed. In Table II, the first column lists the Joycean citation, the second the Latin work, and the third the pages on which the items are discussed.

Table I

AUSONIUS

Mosella	*FW* 207.23	213–14

CAESAR

opera	VI.C.5.59	40
Gallic War		
1.16.5	*FW* 48.7	48
5.11–22	*FW* 77.3	48
7.1–90	*FW* 54.3–4, 66.12, 88.22, 281.F1, 346.19, 518.25, 617.12	48
8.preface	*P* 43; *FW* 4.30–36, 467.16, 518.33–34, 552.19–20; VI.B.8.106	48–49, 259

CATULLUS

5.1, 7–10	*FW* 122.21–34	188–89
7.1–2	*FW* 122.21–34	189
17.8–9, 15–17	*FW* 97.18–23	190
21.7–8	*FW* 167.6–7, 240.27; VI.B.31.33	202–3, 271
37.18	*FW* 78.25	190–91
39.17	*FW* 78.25	190–91
63.26–27	*U* 15.2770, 15.4012–13	192
63.76	*U* 18.1377–78	193, 270

LUCAN
Pharsalia   FW 353.24; VI.B.19.56   125, 213

LUCRETIUS
1.12–20   FW 112.9–14   80–81, 247, 262
2.600   U 18.1377–78   93–94, 212

MARTIAL
6.57   U 705–10, *UNBM* 298:57,
                     Scribbledehobble 117 [721]   33, 36–38, 258
12.18.10–11   FW 78.25   190–91, 270
12.57.21   FW 40.7–8, 309.9–10, 332.34   205
13.63   FW 209.27–212.19   205–6
14.12   FW 209.27–212.19   206–7
[pseudo-Martial]   U 14.928–30, 15.3815–16   208, 272

OVID
Metamorphoses
1.168–72   FW 426.25–26   161
1.253–415   FW 179.9–12, 197.3, 199.21, 35, 244.15–23,
                     367.20–21,538.29–33   178–79
1.383, 399   FW 134.4–6   160–61
1.468–565   FW 203.30, 244.34   179–80
2.1–339   FW 426.21–30   160–61
2.105–10   FW 214.24, 447.2–4   161–62
2.239–59   FW 196.18, 211.5, 208.2, 214.1, 235.9   162–63
2.340–66   U 14.76–79, 14.243, 14.380   164–65
3.316–38   FW 307.3–4, VIII.A.5.29   180–81, 269
3.420   FW 234.13–14   177–78
3.428–29   FW 423.17–18   175–76
3.501–2   FW 474.1–2, 475.9–10   178
3.509–10   U 5.239, 5.567–72   170–71
7.122   FW 134.4–6   179
8.119–82   U 14.992–96   156–57
8.188   P epigraph   154–55, 222
8.201   P 253; U 9.952   155
8.648, 662   P 179   155–56
9.739   U 15.3864–67   156
10.215–16   FW 118.28–30, 293.22   181

7	*U* 3.139–40, 15.1892–96	197–98
10.7, 38.3	*FW* 19.15–17, 52.9–10, 84.5, 311.33	198
35.1–5	*FW* 240.27, 167.6–7; VI.B.31.33	202–3
64	*FW* 240.27	202–3, 271
68.27–28	*U* 18.1530–31; VIII.A.5.10	195, 270
68.30	*FW* 287.26	233–34
68.33	*U* 18.148–50	195
77.8–9	*FW* 499.30–32	200–1

ST. COLUMBA
Altus Prosator

3–5	*FW* 140.4–5	224
522, 539	*FW* 185.14	223

SALLUST
Jugurtha

opus	*FW* 403.12–13	53
4.6–7	*UNBM* 407:227	257

SEVERUS SULPICIUS

Chronica	*FW* 254.7–9	215

SUETONIUS

opera	VI.C.5.59	40
Augustus		
5	*FW* 271.3–7	103–4
Caligula (Gaius)		
37	VI.B.6.36	261
31	*FW* 161.36–162.1–2	67, 260
46	*FW* 4.32–5.2; *Letters* I.243	69–70
54–55	*U* 15.1504–5	69
Domitian		
3	*FW* 306.L2, 22	72
4	*FW* 480.24–25	72
Julius Caesar		
37	*FW* 58.5–6, 512.8, 610.35–36	47–48
Tiberius		
42	VI.C.7.204	211
43	*FW* 115.15–16	211, 272
45	*FW* 115.11–12, 123.30–31	210–1

1.328–30	FW 185.27–28	137–38
1.486	FW 6.14–17	136
1.498	FW 6.4–5	136, 150
3.272–75	U 14.242–44	121
[Culex]	FW 418.23	123

Table II

PORTRAIT

epigraph	Ovid M 8.188	154–55, 222
43	Caesar Gallic War 8.preface	45–49, 250
168–69	Ovid Ars Amatoria 2.91–92	157–58
179	Ovid Amores	156
179	Ovid M 648, 662	155–56
210	Venatius Fortunatus	199, 272
241	Horace Ars Poetica 173–74	144
253	Ovid M 8.201	155
266	Hardian Animula	184–87

ULYSSES

3.1, 13	Vergil A 2.324	124–25
3.139–40	Priapea 7	197–98
5.239	Ovid M 2.509–10	170–71
5.567–72	Ovid M 2.509–10	170–71
6.285–95	Vergil A 6.243–49	128
6.459–61	Vergil A 6.313–14	129
6.476–78	Vergil A 6.430	129
6.487–89	Vergil A 6.443–44	129
6.487–89	Vergil A 6.451	129
6.877	Vergil A 6.441	129
6.957–59	Pliny the Elder N.H. 35.36.66	89–90
7.909–10	Vergil A 6.451	324–25
9.953–54	Ovid Ars Amatoria 2.91–92	157–58
9.939	Terence Autontimorumenos	208
10.1004–5	Cicero Catilinarians 1.22	114–15
10.1115	Justinian Digest 4.2.21.5	214
10.1249	Vergil A 1.52–56	126–27
11.122	Horace O 1.19.5	148

FINNEGANS WAKE

244.11–12	Horace *O* 1.9.5–6	147
244.15–23	Ovid *M* 1.253–415	178–79
244.23	*Priapea* 1.5–6	201–2
244.34	Ovid *M* 1.468–565	179–80
251.29	Cicero *Catilinarians* 1.2	113
253.27	Horace *O* 3.16.9–11	149
255.1–2	Vergil *E* 10.76–77	124
258.20–21	Vergil *A* 7.141–47	101
254.7–9	Severus Sulpicius *Chronica*	215
271.3–7	Suetonius *Augustus* 5	103–4
280.32	Horace *O* 3.13.1	147–48
281.F1	Caesar *Gallic War* 7.1–90	48
287.26	*Priapea* 68.30	233–34
290.19	Catullus 68.17	191
290.26–27	Vergil *A* 10.465, 505	142
291.1	Livy 5.48.9	45
291.23–24	Livy 5.41.9	45
293.7–8	Cicero *Sominum Scipionis*	119
293.22	Ovid *M* 11.157–93	167–68
305.27–28	Catullus 101.10	191
306.L2, 22	Suetonius *Domitian* 8	72
307.1–2	Horace *Epistles*	145
309.9–10	Martial 12.57.21	205
311.33	*Priapea* 10.7, 38.3	198
316.23	Horace *Ars Poetica* 15–16	145
318.2–9	Horace *Ars Poetica* 139	146
318.11	Horace *Epistles* 2.1.156	146
328.8	Horace *O* 1.30.5–6	148
328.28–29	Livy 1.9.10–12	43
332.34	Martial 12.57.21	205
335.11	Horace *O* 3.16.9–11	149
336.21	Horace *O* 2.10.5–6	147
337.9	Horace *O* 1.22.23–24	148
346.19	Caesar *Gallic War* 7.1–90	48
352.30–32	Petronius 61–61	204–5
353.22–29	Vergil *A* 9.54–42	138
353.24	Lucan *Pharsalia*	125, 213
357.15–16	Vergil *A* 4.68	140
367.20–21	Ovid *M* 1.253–415	178–79
375.23–24	Cicero *De Senectute* 17–18	117

480.26–28	Livy 1.16.1	44
482.2–4	Ovid *M* 11.157–93	167–68
487.30–31	Ovid *Heroides* 19–19	181–82
493.23–24	Horace *O* 1.5.5, 3.11.35	148
497.12	Horace *Epodes* 4.14	151
499.30–32	*Priapea* 77.8–9	200–201
512.8	Suetonius *Julius Caesar* 37	47–48
518.21–22	Tacitus *Agricola* 10.3	55
518.25	Caesar *Gallic War* 7.1–90	48
518.33–34	Caesar *Gallic War* 8.preface	48–49, 259
535.3	Horace *O* 133.2	149
538.1	Livy 5.47	46
538.29–33	Ovid *M* 1.253–415	178–79
545.28–29	Vergil *A* 6.851–53	130–31
545.32	Vergil *A* 1.260	138
545.32–33	Vergil *A* 3.577,632	138–39
551.13	Horace *O* 4.7.16	148
551.28–29	Ovid *Ars Amatoria*	158–59, 160
551.28–29	Ovid *Fasti*	158–59
552.19–20	Caesar *Gallic War* 8.preface	48–49, 259
553.2	Horace *Epistles* 2.6.80	147
570.5–8	Pliny the Younger *Letters* 6.16	93–94, 212
581.22–23	Tacitus *Agricola* 14.1	55–56
588.19–20	Pliny the Younger *Letters* 6.16	93–94, 212
599.12–13	Vergil *A* 7.141–47	101
600.7	Catullus 101.10	191
610.35–36	Suetonius *Julius Caesar* 37	47–48
617.12	Caesar *Gallic War* 7.1–90	48
628.6	Catullus 101.10	191

NOTEBOOKS
Scribbledehobble (=VI.A)

75 [251]	Plautus *Mercator* 272, 290–91, 574–75	209–10
117 [721]	Martial 6.57	33, 36–38, 258
117–18 [721]	Vergil *A* 2.201–2	267
VI.B.1.115	Livy 6.20.12	62–63, 260
VI.B.122	Vergil *A* 7.72–73	141
VI.B.2.148–49	Cicero *De Senectute* 1–25	115–18
VI.B.4.248, 298	Hadrian *Animula*	184–87
VI.B.4.141	Livy 5.41–49.3	44–46

INDEX

DATE DUE

APR 25 1997	